Theories of Counseling and Psychotherapy

Theories of Counseling and Psychotherapy

A *Basic-Issues Approach*

William A. Wallace

Marshall University

Allyn and Bacon, Inc.
Boston London Sydney Toronto

Series Editor: Jeffery Johnston
Production Coordinator: Susan Freese
Editorial/Production Services: Total Concept Associates
Text Designer: Judith Ashkenaz
Cover Coordinator: Linda K. Dickinson

Library of Congress Cataloging in Publication Data

Wallace, William A., 1929–
    Theories of counseling and psychotherapy.

    Includes index.
    1. Counseling. 2. Psychotherapy. I. Title.
BF637.C6W29   1986   158'.3   85-23021
ISBN 0-205-08668-3

PHOTO CREDITS:

p. 20, The Bettmann Archive
p. 48, Alfred Adler Institute, courtesy of Dr. Kurt A. Adler
p. 82, Courtesy of Dr. Carl Rogers, Center for
    Studies of the Person
p. 108, Courtesy of Saybrook Institute
p. 130, Esalen Institute
p. 162, Courtesy of Institute for Reality Therapy
p. 192, Courtesy of Institute for Rational-Emotive Therapy
p. 230, Courtesy of Stanford University, News and Publications,
    and Albert Bandura
p. 260, The Bettmann Archive

ART CREDITS:

Original ink drawings by Deb Hogshead.

Printed in the United States of America.

10 9 8 7 6 5 4 3 2 1   89 88 87 86 85

To Lois

Contents Overview

A Note about This Book

Unanswerable questions about the nature of being human have resulted in a number of basic, recurrent issues that are of primary concern to today's theorists, counselors, and psychotherapists. Such a basic-issues approach serves to give *Theories of Counseling and Psychotherapy* both distinction and an integrating organization and structure. Each theory and theorist is introduced, analyzed, and eventually compared around the eleven basic issues:

- conscious and/or unconscious determinants
- conditioning and/or freedom to choose behavior
- biological and/or social determinants
- uniqueness and/or commonality
- early and/or continuous development
- psychological and/or reality environment
- explanation of learning
- importance of role assigned to self-concept
- importance of group membership
- number and weight assigned to motivational concepts
- importance of reward

Special research was done to assemble each theorist's most recent thinking in regard to these eleven basic issues. Also, each theory is examined in relationship to its goals, process, and effectiveness.

Readers are encouraged to use this book to guide them as they seek to resolve each of the basic issues, establish their goals of counseling and psychotherapy, and determine their behaviors for achieving these goals.

Jeff Johnston,
Series Editor

Contents

Preface

Like their teachers before them, most of today's counselors and therapists are introduced to theories of counseling and psychotherapy by some variation on the survey approach. This approach acquaints student counselors and therapists with a wide range of the best theoretical thinking available so that they may identify with a particular theory or school or, if that is impossible, construct a personal theory by carefully evaluating the hypotheses, principles, and constructs consistent with their own values and beliefs. The first expectation implies that, in order to become effective therapists, new and inexperienced counselors must first align themselves with and then become committed to one of the major theories or systems. The second expectation implies that beginning and inexperienced counselors possess the readiness, the skills, and the self-knowledge required of the true eclectic.

Neither assumption is justified. Only a fortunate few are able to identify fully with an existing theory. Fewer still are ready, at this point in their preparation, to develop a personal theory of counseling and psychotherapy without first receiving some structure and organization.

Although this book was not written expressly for those counselor-candidates who find it impossible to identify with a particular theory, it was written with them in mind. Through my involvement in their search for personal meaning in the existing theories, I became interested in the process of developing and formulating personal theories of counseling and psychotherapy—a process that *all* counselors and therapists enter sooner or later.

This book blends the basic-issues approach with the survey approach, offering the advantages of both without neglecting the unique features of either. The basic-issues approach gives this book the structure that so many survey books lack. In addition to instructing the reader in the basic-issues approach to theoretical construction and providing a single format that may be used to analyze, compare, and evaluate existing theories, this book offers readers an in-depth, clear, and consistent presentation of nine major theories of counseling and psychotherapy. It may be used as a survey of contemporary psychotherapies; when survey is the purpose, it may be studied chapter by chapter (in any order), each reader concentrating on a single theory until fully satisfied with his or her level of understanding. Further, this book may be used to analyze, compare, and evaluate the theories selected for presentation or, for that matter, theories not included in this book. Because the same set of basic issues is used throughout, it is possible to study this book across chapters, issue by issue, analyzing the commonalities and differences in the various theories or comparing one theorist's resolutions of the basic issues with those of another. Indeed, a table entitled "Issue Resolution across Chapters" is provided for this purpose.

Still, the primary purpose of this book is to assist those counselors who wish to develop personal theories of psychotherapy. By seeing how each of the nine major theorists has resolved the eleven basic issues and how each resolution contains clear implications for specific therapeutic goals and for specific counselor behaviors to achieve those goals, students—whether new or experienced in the field—may use the book to guide them as they resolve the issues, establish their goals of therapy, and determine the most effective methods and techniques for achieving these goals. In a very real sense, these students are becoming theorists as well as counselors.

Of the eleven basic issues selected to provide a structure for the theories presented in this volume, six contain the characteristics of polar opposites. The remaining five concern the theorists' positions on more specific questions. In a basic-issues approach, values are not forced on the student-counselor, but students are forced to confront those values they hold and serve. Moreover, they are forced to examine their values for clarity, consistency, and comprehensiveness. Through the discovery of clear meaning in what they are doing, they can commit themselves to firm professional identities and, because they are applying a theory that is right for them, become more effective counselors.

When I first set out to test the basic-issues approach in the classroom, I doubted that it would work. I knew from experience that developing a personal theory of counseling and psychotherapy is a difficult exercise in proactive self-development, and I was not at all convinced that my students were ready for this. As is often the case, they proved me wrong. They demonstrated that it is not only reasonable, but essential, to assume that they possess and are willing to invest effort and enthusiasm, idealism and insight, frustration and philosophy into their own self-development and professional advancement. Not only did they produce surprisingly sound psychotherapeutic theories with clear behaviorally defined goals and techniques, but they also eagerly applied their theories in a prepracticum setting. Follow-up revealed that they evaluated their experience in theory construction as one of the most valuable in their preparation for the counseling profession.

Acknowledgments

No one writes a book alone and unassisted. Thus it is more a pleasure than a duty to acknowledge the many debts I accumulated during the three years I worked on this book.

There would probably be no book without the sustained encouragement and unwavering enthusiasm and support of my wife. Through what must have seemed an endless task, Lois persevered. She was always available to read, proof, comment, or discuss, whether presented with a single paragraph, page, or an entire chapter. She was there, too, to listen when I became blocked or discouraged or to celebrate a completed chapter or the arrival of a set of favorable reviews. I am deeply grateful.

I am especially indebted to two of my former students, E. Nick Maddox and Deborah Hogshead, both of whom read and criticized every chapter of this book. Involved from the beginning as friend and colleague, Nick devoted countless hours to reviewing my work. His insightful ideas and suggestions contributed significantly to both the structure and the scope of the book. I learned to rely on Nick for honest and constructive criticism. Though Deb arrived on the scene much later, her careful reading and detailed comments were invaluable. Her unique and thoughtful illustrations appear throughout the book, and she assisted with the construction of many of the charts and graphs.

I am grateful, also, to friends and colleagues who read and evaluated selected chapters in their areas of expertise. While the persons listed here often read more than one chapter, I am particularly indebted to Dr. Violet Eash and Dr. Donald Hall for their review of the chapter on Freud. Dr. Lawrence Barker and Dr. John Smith gave me their knowledgeable views of the Adler chapter. Howard and Michele Young were especially helpful with the early draft of the Ellis chapter. Dr. Steven Cody reviewed and criticized the chapter on Bandura. Finally, Dr. William J. Wyatt offered insightful suggestions after reading an early draft of the Skinner chapter. Special thanks are extended to my chapter reviewers for their encouraging and instructive comments, many of which I incorporated in the final revision of the book.

I am thankful, too, for the enlightening feedback of my students who participated in the field-testing of the basic-issues approach to personal theory construction. It was their efforts that first convinced me of the merit of this approach and stimulated me to write this book.

Finally, although I assume full responsibility for its content, including all its shortcomings, this book could not have been written were it not for the inspiration and challenge of the theorists whose ideas and theoretical constructs were selected for presentation.

Issue Resolution
Across Chapters

Issue Resolution Across Chapters

	Freud	Adler	Rogers	May	Perls	Glasser	Ellis	Bandura	Skinner
					Page				
Conscious versus Unconscious	32	63	93	115	139	171	198	238	273
Conditioning versus Freedom to Choose	35	65	94	117	139	172	203	242	270
Biological versus Social	26	54	88	114	136	166	196	235	266
Uniqueness versus Commonality	37	64	95	120	144	169	207	246	275
Early versus Continuous Development	29	57	90	118	140	173	206	239	271
Psychological versus Reality Environment	33	63	89	116	138	168	205	246	274
Explanation of Learning	34	64	95	121	142	169	204	236	269
Importance of Role Assigned to Self-Concept	35	66	91	119	142	173	201	241	274
Importance of Group Membership	37	59	96	121	143	172	208	245	270
Number and Weight Assigned Motivational Concepts	34	54	89	120	137	170	208	244	272
Importance of Reward	36	67	96	122	145	175	209	243	266
Goals of Therapy	38	68	97	122	145	176	210	247	275
Therapeutic Relationship	39	69	98	123	147	178	213	249	280

Theories of Counseling and Psychotherapy

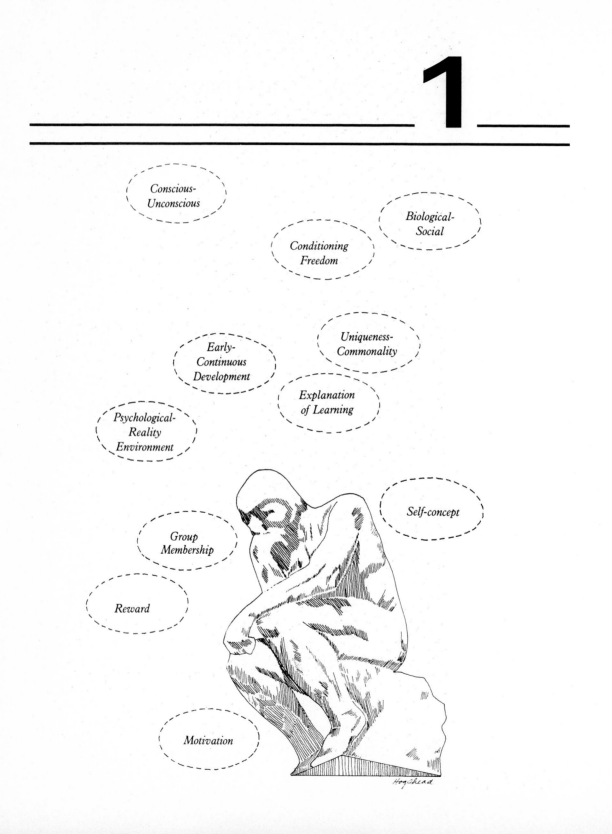

Basic Issues as an Integrating Structure to Theory

FROM THE TIME we humans were first able to form questions, our favorite and most difficult subject has been the human situation. However, even the most contemporary theories of counseling and psychotherapy are pioneering ventures, producing more questions than answers and uncovering more issues than resolutions. Our unanswerable questions about the nature of being human have given rise to the primary issues of concern to today's theorists and therapists. Those fundamental, constant, recurring issues appear to have a number of intrinsic characteristics that make them especially relevant to the counselor or therapist in the process of developing a personal theory or of analyzing and comparing existing theories.

A basic issue is one that cannot be avoided. Theorists or therapists may sidestep a basic issue, but only temporarily. Sooner or later, a basic issue will surface and force the theorist or therapist to take a stand. Existing theories of counseling and psychotherapy are conscious or unconscious attempts by theorists to resolve basic issues. Fortunately, potential theorists and counselors in preparation who choose to employ the basic-issues approach in their study have a variety of resolutions of each basic issue readily available to them.

Once identified, basic issues may be employed by the theorist or the therapist to evaluate existing theories as well as personal theories under development. The comprehensiveness of a theory may be determined and evaluated by the number of basic issues resolved and the degree of depth of each resolution.

If an issue is basic, it is value-laden: leaving it unresolved activates the potential for producing tension. Working toward a personal resolution of a value-laden issue offers the theorist and therapist some distinct advantages. Because basic issues have specifiable values, work with these issues will be personally relevant and significant. This effort will nearly always lead to an increased understanding of both self and others. Because basic issues are value-laden, they may be arranged in hierarchical order of significance; this hierarchical order can be used as an integrating structure for one's personal theory of counseling and psychotherapy as well as for understanding the theory of others.

Although basic issues are fairly easy to separate and to arrange in hierarchical order, they are composed of interrelated questions. Any attempt to resolve one issue will converge with or overlap with the resolutions of other basic issues. This overlapping gives the theorist or therapist the opportunity to check for inconsistencies within the theory and to look for gaps in resolutions of other issues. In addition, issue resolution provides an opportunity to expand the comprehensiveness and clarity of one's theoretical thinking, since overlapping can complement the resolutions of other issues and can provide experiential recall of events supportive of a particular direction of resolution.

Often a basic issue involves polar opposites. In this case, either extreme serves to define the other, although neither extreme is simply the absence of the other. For example, life requires death, its polar opposite, to give it meaning. Unlike *either-or* opposites, such as *good* versus *evil*, polar opposites can be viewed as integrative, internal differences within a single structure, system, or organism or different parts of a single process. When good and evil are viewed as polar opposites, good that blocks a greater good can be evil, and evil that motivates good can be good. Good is not entirely good unless there could be nothing better; evil cannot be totally evil until there is nothing worse. Polar opposites exist together as a dimension of the unified organism, the whole human being. They make up the being's uniqueness. Wertheimer (1972) asserts the advantage of the phenomenon of working with an issue composed of two polar opposites when he writes that these issues "have the intriguing property that if their opposites were combined, a new, higher level and more productive structure emerges" (p. 9). Shostrom, Knapp, and Knapp (1976) refer to this new, higher level of understanding as the "*tertium quid.*" Every value has an equal opposite or countervalue; neither can be fully understood without the other. In fact, neither would exist without the other.

When student-counselors and therapists are able to resolve a basic issue in some depth, they discover that their resolution holds clear implications for specific therapeutic goals and equally clear directions (specific counselor or therapist behaviors) for achieving those goals. The process of resolving the basic issues, then, helps the student make the leap from theory to application.

The cognitive exercise of issue consideration and resolution encourages counselors and therapists in preparation to work beyond present knowledge. To resolve a basic issue, it is necessary to reach beyond certainty. This effort, and the realization that they are exploring the unknown, teaches student-counselors and therapists that a resolution of a basic issue is no more than a theoretical construct, justified by need, expediency, and the tentativeness of time. Student-counselors and therapists who realize fully that they are going beyond the known are more likely to consider and to value their theoretical constructs through perceptual-cognitive frames open to new experiences. Their theories motivate them to commitment and action rather than to closed thinking and rigid behavior. Further, the criticality of their thinking will allow for examination, refinement, and revision of theory as new data accumulate. As they experiment with this issue-resolution approach, even those who adhere closely to some existing, popular theory of counseling and psychotherapy are less likely to become mere followers or, worse, disciples who distrust their own experience and force themselves into a mold of another's making.

The basic-issues approach also may provide the student-counselor and therapist with awareness of and insight into current controversies that exist within their profession, thereby stimulating new thought, discussion, and creativity among professionals.

Resolving the basic issues requires close self-examination. Personal values must be stated explicitly and arranged carefully in hierarchical order. Once accomplished, these personal resolutions to the basic issues give student-counselors and therapists personal bases for valuation. Whatever they are most certain about in themselves, they can also be most certain of in others.

In addition to assisting the counselor's growth toward a personal theory, the basic-issues approach offers the counselor or therapist a framework for analyzing and evaluating existing theories. This same framework may be used to view major differences and commonalities between theories or major strengths and weaknesses within a single theory.

A personal theory of counseling and psychotherapy, constructed from the individual's resolutions of the basic issues, provides a framework or valuational base for positive mental health. It offers criteria for the good life, the facilitative interpersonal relationship, the productive learning process, and the healthy environment.

Perhaps more than any other approach to the teaching and learning of theories of counseling and psychotherapy, the basic-issues approach is less likely to become quickly dated. Basic issues are by definition significant, relevant, and timeless. They have always been with us and seem likely to remain.

Like all other approaches, the basic-issues approach has distinct disadvantages. First, basic issues abound with judgmental controversy. If various theorists or therapists were asked to identify the basic issues in our discipline, it is unlikely that any two lists would be identical, and even less probable that these listings would rank the issues in the same order. Those who have worked in this area state emphatically that it is necessary to be subjective, arbitrary, and more than a little presumptuous to define a list or set of basic issues (Ford & Urban, 1963; Wertheimer, 1972). Few wish to be tagged with those adjectives; consequently, few books on theories of counseling and psychotherapy have been written wherein the basic-issues approach is employed to analyze each theory presented. Second, as stated earlier, examination of a basic issue introduces value consideration. Since no value classification system has been devised on which the majority of the professionals in our discipline can agree, this too must be included among the disadvantages of the basic-issues approach. Third, it often appears that data support both polarities of a given basic issue. Nevertheless, if a theory is to be comprehensive and consistent, each theorist and therapist must take a stand, even if that stand is firmly in the middle of the road. Failure to take a stand can result in a theory that is less comprehensive than it might otherwise be.

THE APPROACH, USE, AND PURPOSE OF THIS BOOK

A combination of the survey approach and the basic-issues approach offers the advantages and disadvantages of both methods without the loss of the unique features of either. Further, combining the two approaches can produce a book that can be used for a number of different purposes. Each of the theories selected for this book is analyzed in depth, with an arbitrarily defined but carefully selected set of recurring basic issues.

This book may be used as a survey of contemporary theories; it provides an overview of the wide variety of thinking currently available. Those who prefer a survey approach to theories can study the book chapter by chapter, each reader concentrating on a single theory until fully satisfied with his or her level of understanding. Additional readings are recommended for the student-counselors or therapists who wish to work beyond the coverage level of the chapter.

This book also may be used to analyze, compare, and (if the reader wishes) evaluate the theories presented or, for that matter, theories that are not included. Because the same set of basic issues is used throughout, it is possible to study this book across chapters, issue by issue, analyzing the commonalities and differences of the various theories or comparing one theorist's resolutions of the basic issues with another's.

The primary purpose of this book, however, is to assist those counselors and therapists who wish to develop their personal theories of counseling and psychotherapy. By seeing how each of the theorists has resolved the basic issues, how each resolution contains clear implications for specific counselor or therapist goals and equally clear implications for the specific counselor or therapist behaviors for achieving these goals, student-counselors and therapists may use the book to guide them as they resolve each of the basic issues, establish their goals of counseling and psychotherapy, and determine their behaviors for achieving these goals.

These readers are thus becoming theorists as well as counselors and therapists. This seems an essential developmental step toward becoming a counselor or therapist if they accept an observation made by Brammer and Shostrom (1968) over a decade ago: "Freud was not a Freudian, Jung not a Jungian, and Rogers not a Rogerian. Each was himself most fully and completely, while building upon the wisdom of the past" (p. 32). Counselors and therapists gain confidence from the feeling that they have studied the best and, from their study, have developed theories and practices that accurately reflect their individual personalities and experiences—their uniqueness.

Concentrating on basic, recurring issues—as opposed to the charisma, zealousness, and single-mindedness of various theorists—lessens the coercive nature of all other theoretical argument. This concentration lends balance and evaluative acuity to the mind of the therapist who is open to persuasion but has no wish to be coerced.

Although many theorists tend to agree that there are basic, recurring issues in counseling and psychotherapy, few seem to agree on what these issues are or, for that matter, on a process or a set of criteria for identifying and separating these issues. Some of the heated discussions in this discipline relate to the weight and significance assigned to a particular issue, or even to the nomenclature applied to various issues. Certainly some of the most exciting and memorable professional meetings are those that bring together two brilliant major theorists with opposing views on basic issues for a no-holds-barred, one-to-one confrontation.

Given that basic issues in counseling and psychotherapy are controversial, arbitrary, idiosyncratic, and elusive, why employ this approach? The unique advantages already cited are reasons enough, but Wertheimer (1972), who uses a basic-issues approach in an introduction to general psychology, adds this bit of interesting logic:

> No one needs to agree with the particular set of issues included, nor with the characteristics of particular ideas, men, or movements on these issues, but the exercise of thinking in terms of these issues or another comparable set of issues may well provide a framework that can help organize the fascinating diversity that is psychology today. [p. vii]

In addition, he notes that this approach can "fit with a wide range of prejudices, a broad diversity of different orientations, and a great variety of special interests" (p. vii). Certainly a book written with this approach may prove controversial, but there seems at least an equal chance that it might prove compatible with the many diverse theories of counseling and psychotherapy available today.

In the basic-issues approach, values are not forced on the student-counselor and therapist. Instead, they are encouraged only to confront what they already claim to believe and to value. Excessive concentration on existing theories of counseling and psychotherapy may diminish the motivation to develop a personal theory. By following a basic-issues approach, however, student-counselors and therapists become aware of the values they serve, and they can examine their values for clarity, consistency, and comprehensiveness. Through the discovery of clear meaning in what they are doing, student-counselors and therapists can commit themselves to firm professional identities and effectiveness.

ELEVEN BASIC ISSUES

Eleven basic issues make up the structure of the theories presented in this book. Six contain the characteristics of polar opposites discussed previously; five concern the theorists' positions on more specific questions. Many of these issues have been discussed by other writers in the field (Hall & Lindzey, 1957, 1970; Ford & Urban, 1963; Wertheimer, 1972; Schultz, 1976). Examples of the variety of questions student-counselors and therapists may ask themselves about each issue are included in the next sections.

Conscious and/or Unconscious Determinants

Do we have an unconscious, an inherited, inaccessible entity, outside our sphere of control, or are we conscious beings with the power to choose among alternatives, capable of self-awareness thinking, and decision making and, therefore, responsible for our existence and destiny? Is our behavior genetically predetermined and unconsciously conditioned by our environment, or can we consciously select potentials and aspirations? Are we the unconscious results of our unique combination of personal experiences, circumstance, chance, and life scripts, or do we consciously create ourselves through our choices and the lessons we learn? Is our behavior predictable and controllable because of its mechanistic and unconscious origin in genetics and the environment, or are we unknowable and unpredictable because of our ability to transcend genetic endowment and environmental circumstance? Are we capable of full awareness moment to moment, or must we seek self-knowledge through unconscious recall, dream analysis, defense mechanisms, free associations, projective techniques, and hypnosis? Is consciousness a myth we have created to justify our existence? Do some areas of our minds lie beyond the realm of our knowledge [ESP (extrasensory perception), other dimensions, other worlds]? Are the conscious and unconscious compartments of our personalities part of our total awareness, or are these concepts we have invented to describe the regions of an awareness continuum within us? Does our conscious awareness extend beyond the present, beyond the moment, beyond what seems apparent? Is it justifiable to reject any concept of conscious/unconscious because of the unobservability of either? Does consciousness imply self-awareness? Can we enhance self-awareness, thereby increasing choice?

As one of the oldest issues in philosophy and psychology, the debate over the conscious and unconscious aspects of being human continues. Perhaps there is no single correct resolution to the issue. You yourself must decide how you operate and what directly influences your behaviors and choices of thought, feeling, and behavior. You must reconcile your stance from questions similar to those asked here. You must personalize them and, thus, ponder your inner nature.

Conditioning and/or Freedom of Choice Behaviors

Are we free to choose our behavior in any set of circumstances, or is this freedom a contingency we hold because it has been well reinforced in the past? Are our decisions based on innate needs and antecedent causes, or can we transcend our biological dimensions and past learning to reach a level of personal objectivity? Are we passive victims of fate, circumstance, and conditioning, unable to assert responsibility for our existence and choice of behavior, or do we initiate our own goals, methodologies, and achievements? Do we learn merely to accept and adjust to our environments and our life circumstances, or do we choose our attitudes toward all we encounter: past, present, and future? Do we differ from other animals only in our degree of complexity, and is this degree of complexity something self-defined or part of a determined environment in which we exist? Is our ability to choose an attitude the ultimate human freedom, giving us the resources to view ourselves and reality from an especially personal and relevant inner locale? Are we enmeshed in the web of reinforced behaviors we experience from the moment of birth? Is change possible by reordering our cognitive and attitudinal perspectives? Do we, if victims of fate, relinquish responsibility for our approach to life? Are our behaviors justified because we cannot exercise a freedom of choice? Is personal insight an integral factor in our life changes? Are we reactive beings, simply responsive to stimuli introduced through the environment or proactive beings, able to encounter the environment on a personal level and able to make choices designed to minimize difficulty and maximize effectiveness? Can we reach beyond the conditioning of government, education, and conventionality to make of ourselves what we wish to become, or are we pawns in a macrocosmic chess game?

These are but a few of the many considerations to be confronted in pondering the issue of conditioning and/or freedom of choice. You must evaluate and critically decide for yourself who and/or what governs you. Are you in control or are you moving in a flow that surrounds everyone?

Biological and/or Social Determinants

Will future discoveries and interpretations of DNA-RNA research lead to a belief in a genetically prescribed limitation to our endeavors, or will this research lead to an even stronger affirmation of our ability to choose our own destinies from the available alternatives? Is our growth and development a dynamic, ongoing set of processes subject to innumerable experiential and/or environmental factors? Is our love of our children rooted in the fact that our children will reproduce our genes, or do we establish this loving relationship on a higher level of social awareness and innovative emotion? Are our most pressing problems to be resolved by genetic manipulation, cloning, psychosurgery, molecular biology, the manufacture of humanoids/androids, the surgical/biochemical intervention in the embryonic and neonatal life phases? Can therapy, education, and improved interpersonal communications/relationships lead to the answers we are seeking? Are we biologically fixed without fluctuation, or do we have experiential elasticity? Should we focus our investigations of human nature on the interaction of inherited or environmental factors, or should we work toward an understanding of the significance of both elements in our growth and development processes? Are we complex primates to be studied with mammalian biology, or must we also seek out a novel methodology for the study of our subjective experiences? Is human intelligence an attribute or an entity? Does the selfish-gene theory explain our powerful emotions regarding abortion, child abuse, divorce, suicide, and euthanasia, or is there a humanistic explanation for these feelings? Are we ultimately and innately pushed, pulled, and driven by impulses, basic needs, and urges that override the influences of environment?

You must consider your feelings about this issue. What element has played the greater part in your development, the society of which you are members or those attributes received from parents and ancestors? Resolution of this issue has definite implications for helping you to resolve the other issues. All issues are interrelated and to provide consistency in your own theory, you must provide consistent resolutions of the individual issues.

Uniqueness and/or Commonality

Is our shared experience of humanness a prerequisite to mental and emotional fitness, or does emotional and mental fitness arise from our interactions with those around us in the everyday setting of our environment? What are the specific constituent parts of our uniqueness, and how do these parts interact to form our entirety? What factors, characteristics, and experiences do we share with all other individuals, regardless of race, color, or societal configuration? Does uniqueness, for individuals and nations, lead to an unhealthy egocentrism and ethnocentrism? Is a personal feeling and appreciation of our uniqueness beneficial or detrimental to our interactions with others? Can we feel that we are unique without feeling that all other persons are also unique? If we share a human ancestral and hereditary commonality, why do we impose war, famine, and interpersonal hardship on ourselves? Does commonality imply a herd mentality we cannot transcend, or does this commonality imply a social instinct that is beneficial to us and our society? Is uniqueness a biological nuance, or is uniqueness something we can foster and utilize for our personal growth and development? How much do we incorporate from the environment and transform into something we consider unique to ourselves? Is human commonality a part of the *zeitgeist* of the present and the legacy of the past, or is it something that reaches deeper into each person throughout the history of humankind? Does a concept like Jung's *collective unconsciousness* imply that we are all linked by a chain of being that exists in the twilight regions of our understanding and being? Is uniqueness (or commonality) the cause or the result of our various behaviors?

This particular issue encourages you to view how you perceive yourself in a personal and social context. As mentioned before, this issue links with the other issues to form a whole conception of self, others, and the world. Your personal theory and issue resolution are unique, and you should enjoy and assert your uniqueness when resolving this and the other issues. The key is that you realize how you feel about yourself. From this feeling will grow the resolution of these basic issues.

Early and/or Continuous Development

Are there stages or critical periods we must traverse to develop normally and healthfully? Are there developmental tasks within such stages or periods that we must accomplish so we can grow and approach or acquire self-awareness? Can we transcend early trauma and grow continually in the present, or are we linked with inescapable misery and stagnation because of familial or environmental deprivation we experienced as children? Are early experiences permanently imprinted on us, or is personal development amendable by choice and advancement throughout life? Is the past indispensable in the understanding of development, or if we have full understanding of the present, is there any reason to consider or understand the past? Are convenient life milestones—for example, the ages 18, 30, 40, 65, 100—and the characteristics of these ages something we are taught and encouraged to accept as real and inescapable? What factors contribute to a stagnation of personal growth? Are some regions of our being undeveloped or underdeveloped because we are educated to question and to doubt their existence? Are there more than two seemingly natural developmental events—birth and death? Are theories of early development amendable by the pursuit of self-awareness during adulthood? Is there a natural developmental process that fosters self-realization if uninhibited, or is development the result of chance circumstance and interactions? Does our educational system instruct us to seek self-development and personal growth actively, or does this system encourage us to accept things as they are with little opportunity for change and improvement? Can deprivation in some critical stage of development stifle and possibly destroy our attempts to express and activate our potentials? Is mental health something we acquire at a certain time in life, or is it something we develop, perpetuate, and prosper by throughout our lives?

You must develop your own questions based on consideration of the ideas and concepts that are relevant—thus, meaningful—to you. While others may provide you with a framework for resolution of the issue, you only reach resolution after much self-searching. The developmental issue is especially important because it is a statement of where you believe you are at the moment and an expression of where you will be in the future.

Psychological and/or Reality Environment

Do we live in an objective world, a reliable, rational, measurable entity, or do we live in a private world of subjective perception, valuing, and emotion? If objective reality is a fact, if a constant and ordered environment exists, how can we know this reality when we have only our unique experiences in it and our personal perceptions and interpretations of it? Although dreams and visions appear to exist in an inner, psychological realm, how are we to know where this inner reality is? If our experiences and perceptions are personally and psychologically unique, how can we ever enter into the world of another person? Is understanding of ourselves and others best approached through analysis or synthesis, or is a dual approach the better choice? Do we exist as objective realities unto ourselves, motivated or pushed by universal natural laws, or are we potentialities moving toward actualization and discovery of realities beyond those we now consider? How far does our inner reality extend to influence what we encounter outside ourselves? If robbed of our sense of perception, would awareness and sense of being continue to exist? Does truth exist on a universal level, or are we tied to a prejudiced view of our existence because of our attachment to an inner, psychological reality? Can our perceptions and, thus, our understanding of reality ever approach completeness given the fact that our senses are imperfect and subject to deterioration and disease? Are all persons given the same potential for understanding their inner psychological being, or is there an inequity of potential that belies concepts such as survival of the fittest and natural selection? Is consideration of and belief in this psychological being something that has occurred in the societal development of humans in civilization, or is it something that lies innately within us and provides us with identity?

Many of the great thinkers of the world have long pondered the question of reality. Since no one has resolved the question, you should not expect to do it yourself. How do these interactions affect your behavior? Also, consider your interactions with what is outside yourself. How do you perceive that around you? You must consider the interactions between these two realms and how you mediate your life in both.

Explanation of Learning

What are our biochemical bases of learning? Is our learning a completely biochemical exercise, or is it influenced by factors and considerations we can initiate for ourselves? Is learning a natural, continual process, or is it something we must discipline ourselves to undertake? How do we store and recall the information that is presented to us? Is there a difference between how we learn about ourselves and how we learn about the environment? Does the significance or relevance of information affect our ability to remember and associate it? Can we be certain that what we learn is valid, or at least beyond the probability of revision? What is the process that allows us to know this? Is knowledge acquired because we desire to acquire it or because we cannot stop ourselves from acquiring it? Is the learning process purposive, determined, or teleological? How do others affect or influence our learning? When others attempt to influence us, why do some succeed and others fail? Is there a facilitative relationship, or is teaching simply the arrangement of the contingencies of reinforcement? Do we teach others in the same manner we were taught? How do learning processes such as recall and association operate? Can learning occur as a result of personal insight into knowledge? Can the learning process be reduced to naturalistic or mechanistic determinants? How many different types of learning are there? What variables—for example, motivation, maturation, attending power, relevance, and reinforcement—facilitate learning in others, and which of these are particularly significant in the therapeutic setting? Do we learn through personal experiences and validate this learning through interpersonal relationships?

You are learning all the time, but do you understand how this learning occurs? You must look at numerous considerations as you determine how you personally go about collecting, organizing, and utilizing the information you gather. It is up to you to decide how you learn. The answer or resolution may have many dimensions, and your task is to sort through these dimensions and arrive at your personal conception of the learning process.

Importance of Role Assigned to Self-Concept

What is self-concept? How do we develop this form of self-perception? Is self-concept established within us, beyond us, or somewhere in between, in a middle zone of interaction between our inner, psychological state and what we perceive as reality? Is self-concept simply a personally relevant perception of ourselves, or does it affect the way we work, play, and relate to others? Should self-concept be assigned a central position in our theory development since it may significantly influence our behavior, or should we discard the concept because it is an abstract, unobservable concept that has little meaning beyond our own personal experience?

Is the denial of self pathogenic? Are self-awareness, authentic behavior, and candid self-honesty prerequisites for personal growth and development? Is self-acceptance purely tautological and readily available to anyone whose definitions are in good order? Under what conditions might significant others influence our self-concept? Does the modeling process lead us to improvement of our self-concept or to dependence on role models for definition of ourselves? Can significant others come to some point of understanding of how we feel about ourselves? Is there a biological predisposition toward the development of a self-concept? Are self-awareness and self-concept the same thing? Without the existence of self-concept, is there a personal identity above the animal level? Is the self-concept a flexible concept that changes according to our age, life circumstance, and emotional stability, or is it established at an early or critical period in our lives without the possibility of revision or improvement? Do we possess many different constituent selves? Is our conception of self a continuous process? Is it possible to expand and improve our self-concept? What conditions or relationships contribute to the creation of a healthy self-concept? Conversely, what conditions or relationships contribute to formation and maintenance of a negative self-concept? Can our self-concept be communicated to others? Do our behaviors serve as an extension of our self-concept into the world? Is it possible to create and maintain a neutral self-concept? For our concepts of self to be favorable, must our concepts of others be less favorable? Will or must our self-concept influence our conception of others? Can we rate ourselves as competent without rating others as less or more competent? Is there a difference between how we act with others and how we act with ourselves? Is self-acceptance more important to self-actualization than self-concept? Are feelings of personal value and significance related to our self-concept? Can a negative self-concept be altered if enough positive and authentic reinforcement is received? Does the positivity or negativity of our self-concept tend to attract positive and negative people to us?

As can be seen by the number of questions for consideration, self-concept is an important factor to consider in theory development. You will be looking at yourself and your experiences to see if your self-concept is important to your development. The issue of self-concept will put you in touch with your innermost personal feelings and how these feelings help or hinder your personal operation and therapeutic effectiveness.

Importance of Group Membership

Are we really social animals with an innate and powerful instinct toward social interest? If we are members of a group, regardless of the constituency, do we assume a group identity at the sacrifice of personal identity, or can we discover ourselves as we move toward commitment and concern within the group environment? If we accept a self-as-group-member concept of ourselves, how do we maintain and balance this concept with our self-as-individual concept? Is group affiliation necessary for mental well-being? In opposition to group affiliation, are there any advantages to a life of solitude and retreat? Can we come to valid self-awareness in solitude? Does group affiliation facilitate learning? Does group affiliation provide us with a testing ground for our self-concept and for any changes we may want to make in our lives? Are we attracted to groups that mirror our nuances of character, our weaknesses, our strengths? Are we predisposed toward group affiliation since birth, or does our societal environment inculcate a belief in group affiliation?

You, as a counselor, therapist, or theorist, must decide whether to focus on group membership, past, present, and future, to develop your own theory and whether to apply this theory in the facilitative relationship. You must review your personal history to decide how significant group membership has been for you. By drawing from personal experience, you learn about yourself and how your experience influences the resolution of this issue.

Number and Weight Assigned to Motivational Concepts

What motivates us to behave as we do? Where and when does motivation begin? How can we best recognize, investigate, and measure our motivation? Are we motivated solely by innate, genetically established instincts laid down by the cloudy laws of human nature? Are we motivated in the present by childhood experiences, appetites, hopes, and aspirations? Do our motivations change as our life experiences or circumstances change? Is there an innate motivating power, essence, or principle in human life, and what conditions provide for its discovery and enhancement? Is love a legitimate motivational force? Are there motivational concepts that are common to all of us—for example, will to live, to power, to procreate? Are we motivated by a complex array of habit patterns that were intentionally or inadvertently reinforced in our past? Can we be selective and exercise choice over those things that motivate us? Can we come to awareness and appreciation of new things and add them to our motivational inventory? Are we motivated by the principle of pleasure more than by pain, avoidance, tension reduction, conflict/anxiety elimination, equilibrium, system unity and harmony, or an internal belief or value system? Are our motivations stimulated, conditioned, reinforced, sublimated, or elaborated by innate and unconscious drives? How much do parents and significant others influence our development of motivational patterns? Are we motivated only by objects associated with primary drives and then only to the degree our responses were rewarded or gratified in the past? Why can some of us delay gratification in pursuit of a goal, while others seem unable to exist without constant gratification? Is self-actualization a legitimate motivational goal? Does the value we place on life increase our motivation in a general sense? What nuances of constitution make one individual motivated by spirtual or ethical concerns and another by prurient or material concerns? Does our educational system encourage us to develop our potentials or to compete with others for rewards such as money, fame, and ego gratification? Are we sometimes motivated by fear and insecurity, and is this type of motivation important to movement and personal growth?

What motivates you as a counselor, therapist, theorist? What is important: people? wealth? freedom? Your resolution of the issue depends on what you hold dearest and for what you are willing to work and to fight the hardest. You can gain some insight into your personal motivations through resolution of this issue, and such insight will no doubt help you with resolution of some of the other issues. You must find what things keep them going and that help you to establish your reason to be.

Importance of Reward

Do we operate on a pleasure-pain continuum, or is life innately rewarding to us most of the time? What makes life rewarding to some and deprivating to others? How much of our behavior is guided by rewards? Are we reacting beings directed by sociocultural reinforcements, or is internal and personal reward possible? Do we exist from day to day on the premise that there is some long-term reward to life, or do we go from one transient reward to another just to maintain some degree of comfort? Is it realistic to believe that life is its own reward? If we were to lose everything, what is the one thing we would retain if we could do so? Is all civilization and society based on a reward system, and if so, does this mean that we cannot advance beyond the system? Can cultures be purposefully designed through the shaping of humans? Should concern about reward and reinforcement be central to theory development, or do other considerations account for the rightful place of reward as a constituent part of our existence? How are our hierarchies of reward built?

You are dealing with concepts that perpetuate your growth or stagnation as a human being. You must look at what concept is important to you and its degree of importance. The things that motivate and reward you have grown out of your value system and, as such, provide a window from which to view yourself, whether you are a counselor, a therapist, a theorist, or a client.

FINAL COMMENTARY

Not only are these eleven issues relevant to an understanding and an appreciation of the theories in this book, they also will provide you, as student-counselors or therapists, with a foundation from which to consider your personal and professional orientation in your career. Consideration of these issues reveals the essence of each theory in a concise and understandable manner. In addition, such consideration offers you the exceptional opportunity to begin developing and consolidating your own theory of counseling and psychotherapy.

Each theorist discussed in this book began the quest for theoretical expression with a first, and most likely tentative, step. It is hoped that this book will provide you with the impetus to take your own first step into the theoretical arena.

REFERENCES AND SUGGESTED READINGS

Brammer, L.M. and Shostrom, E.L. 1968. *Therapeutic psychology* 2nd ed. Englewood Cliffs, N.J.: Prentice-Hall.

Burks, H.M., Jr., and Stefflre, B., eds. 1979. *Theories of counseling*, 3rd ed. New York: McGraw-Hill.

Burton, A., ed. 1974. *Operational theories of personality*. New York: Brunner/Mazel.

Corey, G. 1982. *Theory and practice of counseling and psychotherapy*, 2nd ed. Monterey, Calif.: Brooks/Cole.

Corsini, R.J., ed. 1982. *Current psychotherapies*, 3rd ed. Itasca, Ill.: F.E. Peacock.

Corsini, R.J., ed. 1973. *Current personality theories*. Itasca, Ill.: F.E. Peacock.

Corsini, R.J., ed. 1979. *Current psychotherapies*, 2nd ed. Itasca, Ill.: F.E. Peacock.

Cunningham, L.M. and Peters, H.J. 1973. *Counseling theories: a selective examination for school counselors*. Columbus, Ohio: Charles E. Merrill.

DiCaprio, N.S. 1974. *Personality theories: guides to living*. Philadelphia: W.B. Saunders.

Ford, D.H., and Urban, H.R. 1963. *Systems of psychotherapy, a comparative study*. New York: John Wiley & Sons.

Hall, C.S., and Lindzey, G. 1957. *Theories of personality*. New York: John Wiley & Sons.

Hall, C.S., and Lindzey, G. 1970. *Theories of personality*, 2nd ed. New York: John Wiley & Sons.

Hansen, J.C., Stevic, R.R., and Warner, R., Jr. 1977. *Counseling theory and process*, 2nd ed. Boston: Allyn and Bacon.

Harper, R.A. 1975. *The new psychotherapies*. Englewood Cliffs, N.J.: Prentice-Hall.

Patterson, C.H. 1980. *Theories of counseling and psychotherapy*, 4th ed. New York: Harper & Row.

Prochaska, J.O. 1979. *Systems of psychotherapy: a trans-theoretical analysis*. Homewood, Ill.: Dorsey Press.

Sahakian, W.S., ed. 1976. *Psychotherapy and counseling: techniques in intervention*. Chicago: Rand McNally.

Schultz, D. 1976. *Theories of personality*. Belmont, Calif.: Brooks/Cole.

Shostrom, E.L., with Knapp, L., and Knapp, R. 1976. *Actualizing therapy, foundations for a scientific ethic*. San Diego: Edits.

Wertheimer, M. 1972. *Fundamental issues in psychology*. New York: Holt, Rinehart & Winston.

2

The Psychoanalytic Theory of Sigmund Freud

IN THE PLANNING STAGES for this book, Freud's psychoanalytic theory was not to be included. Purpose, depth of coverage desired, and limitations imposed by time and space dictated that only a representative few of the most currently accepted and widely practiced theories of counseling and psychotherapy could be considered. It became evident, however, that omitting Freud would be a serious mistake.

Every theorist presented in this book made specific references to Freud's concepts and methods. Indeed, nearly half (Adler, Ellis, May, and Perls) began their careers as psychoanalysts. Motivation for a few (particularly, Adler and Perls and, to a lesser degree, Rogers, Ellis, and Glasser) seemed to emerge from their direct opposition to the orthodox psychoanalytic approach to psychotherapy. Perls, for example, admitted that a life-long love-hate relationship with Freud served as the prime motivating force for much of his theoretical effort (see Chapter 6). The theories of others evolved largely from attempts to modify, expand, or integrate Freud's therapeutic concepts and techniques. Though Freud's impact varies considerably among the theorists presented here, it can be neither ignored nor denied. Moreover, because of his influence, an overview of Freud's resolutions of the eleven basic issues may facilitate a greater understanding of the following theories.

There are sound reasons for beginning this book with Freud's theory other than the fact that it has served as a direct or indirect stimulus for the development of many of the current psychotherapies. The significance of Freud's work extends far beyond this. By providing the first truly comprehensive and scientific theory of human nature and behavior, as well as the first systematic method of inquiry and approach to psychotherapy, Freud filled a void in human thinking. His influence, however controversial, has been traced to a multitude of varied disciplines including medicine, psychology, philosophy, literature, the social sciences, drama, art, education, parenting, and criminal justice. In fact, Freud's name is often linked with historical giants such as Copernicus, Darwin, Marx, and Einstein, individuals who, among others, have been credited with revolutionizing modern thought.

BIOGRAPHICAL SKETCH

Although the reasons for it are still being questioned, Freud has become a legend. The life and achievements of few individuals have been investigated more thoroughly, or for that matter more controversially, by so many. While Ernest Jones's (1953–1957) three-volume biography is accepted as the major presentation of Freud's history and theoretical development, numerous authors have attempted over the years to discredit or at least question both the objectivity and the value of Jones's work. Sulloway (1983) and Masson (1984) are just two of the more recent authors of such efforts. While the research quality of some of these works is high, legends, once given birth, have a remarkable resilience, as well as the capacity for distorting objective appraisal.

Early Years

Sigmund Freud was born May 6, 1856, in the village of Freiburg, a province of Moravia, Austria, now a part of Czechoslovakia. Freud was the eldest son of his father's second marriage. His mother, Amalia (Nethansohn) Freud, was 21 years old at Freud's birth, half her husband's age. During the next ten years Jacob Freud's family grew. In addition to the two sons from his first marriage, who were by this time married with children of their own, Sigmund was followed by five daughters, Anna, Rosa, Marie, Adolfine, and Paula, and two other sons, Julius, who died at 8 months, and Alexander. Since Alexander was ten years Freud's junior, Freud's nephew, John, only a year older than he, was Freud's closest boyhood companion and major rival.

Initial movement toward industrialization and mass production made competition for the small business owner difficult. In 1859, when Freud was 4 years old, his father, an independent merchant dealing principally in wool, moved his family to Vienna where he thought business opportunities might improve. Vienna was to remain Freud's home for nearly eighty years.

Education

Adored and protected by his mother who was convinced her precocious firstborn was destined for greatness, Freud held a privileged position in the family. Their apartment was overcrowded, but Freud had a room of his own. Moreover, while all the other rooms had to be lighted by candles, Freud's room, a combination bedroom and study, was lighted by an oil lamp. When Freud complained that his sister's piano practicing interfered with his study, her lessons were stopped and the piano removed.

Encouraged by an indulging mother and his dreams of becoming a famous Austrian general or minister of state, Freud became a serious young student. Gifted in language, he mastered Hebrew, Latin, Greek, French, and

English and taught himself Italian and Spanish. He was especially interested in English and enjoyed reading Shakespeare at the age of 8. When 9 years of age, he passed the entrance examination to the Speri Gymnasium where he stood at the head of his class the last 6 of his 8 years. At 17, Freud was graduated summa cum laude.

Professional career choice for an impoverished young Jew in Vienna was limited to industry, business law, or medicine, none of which Freud found especially appealing. Attracted to natural science, particularly after reading the theories posited by Darwin, Freud decided to become a medical student shortly before finishing his final year of high school.

Freud entered the University of Vienna to study medicine in 1873. With Brucke as his model of the disciplined scientist, Freud became involved in research, and in 1876, he was accepted to work under Brucke's patriarchal direction in the Institution of Physiology. It was here that Freud, immersed in the study of the histology of nerve cells, was introduced to the standard of scientific method and intellectual honesty that was to be with him for life. It was here, too, that he became acquainted with Joseph Breuer, who, though 40 years Freud's senior, became a close friend and colleague and assisted Freud financially in later years with substantial loans.

Freud was called for a year's military service in the Austrian Army in 1879. He passed his final medical examinations in March 1881. Brucke, who was aware of Freud's poor financial position and who knew of his limited prospects for promotion within the institute, urged Freud to leave research and begin private practice as a physician.

Freud resigned his position at Brucke's institute in 1882 to begin his residency at General Hospital. After 2 months in surgery, Freud applied for and gained the position of aspirant in internal medicine. In 1883, Freud transferred to the Psychiatric Clinic where he began a specialty in neurology the following year and for 5 months undertook a course of psychiatric studies.

In 1885, Freud was appointed lecturer in neuropathology. Also in 1885, Freud visited Charcot in France and volunteered his services as a German translator for Charcot's lectures. He published *Lessons*, a three volume set, the following year. In 1886, Freud accepted the post of director for a new neurological department at the Institution for Children's Diseases. In addition to his clinical duties, Freud, with referrals from Breuer and Nothnagel, opened his private practice and gave his first paid consultations. He married Martha Bernays that year, after a 4-year engagement. Their marriage, often described as ideal, lasted 53 years and produced six children: Mathilde, Jean Martin, Oliver, Ernst, Sophie, and Anna.

Emergence of Psychoanalysis

Finding prevalent methods of psychiatric treatment ineffective, Freud turned to hypnosis, not only to trace the origin of a symptom but also, through hypnotic suggestion, to arrest the symptom. However, while he sometimes appeared to cure miraculously cases of hysteria and some forms of neuroses, he discovered that changes produced through hypnosis seemed to depend on the relationship between the doctor and patient. The benefits of therapy were often lost on termination of that relationship; that is, the patient overcame his or her symptoms to please the doctor. This phenomenon and the inability to hypnotize some recalcitrant patients as deeply as he thought necessary to effect a cure, motivated Freud to search for other more effective and lasting therapeutic methods.

In 1889, Freud returned to Breuer's cathartic method. The cathartic method necessitated hypnosis, but Freud discovered that all forms of suggestion, whether by hypnosis, touching the patient's forehead, or asking questions, interrupted or covered client transference and resistance. He reduced his use of hypnosis and developed the so-called "concentration technique." While lying down with eyes closed, the client was asked to concentrate on the symptom and, without censoring, recall all memories of the symptom. At the sign of initial resistance, Freud urged, pressed his hand on the client's forehead, and questioned, methods used to assure the client that the memories were there and could be recalled.

When some of his clients complained that his interventions interfered with their efforts to recall early or painful memories, Freud gradually withdrew to the background. Free association as a therapeutic method had evolved. Though this procedure lengthened the therapeutic process considerably, his patients eventually became able to recall the early childhood events responsible for their traumatic hysterias.

From this point, Freud moved rather rapidly toward his theory of psychoanalysis, far too rapidly for his friend, Breuer, his colleagues in the medical community, and the lay public, all of whom reacted with incredulity when he presented his ideas. Through his client's free associations and the wealth of symbolism in their dreams, Freud ascertained the significance of the unconscious and began to map its structure and topography. More important, he assigned early sexuality and aggressive impulses new and greater importance in the etiology of later emotional disturbances. Thus, he had intuitively constructed the foundation upon which his theory of psychoanalysis would rest. Since Freud needed data to confirm his ideas, in 1897, he decided to undertake in-depth autoanalysis to obtain answers to many of his questions.

Freud's engrossing self-analysis, accompanied at times by serious neurotic disturbances, continued for nearly 4 years, but he emerged from it a different person (Jones, 1955). The turmoil in his life had largely subsided; personal relationships were less intense and upsetting, and his life was more ordered and harmonious. As a result, his thinking seemed clearer and his judgments more critical. He gained greater confidence, both in himself and his discoveries, and he channeled his energy into the development, application, and advancement of his ideas. In reference to this period of Freud's life, Ellenberger (1970) presents a convincing argument for creative illness, "a polymorphous condition that can take the shape of depression, neurosis, psychosomatic ailments, or even psychosis" (p. 447). He describes a creative illness as one that "succeeds a period of intense preoccupation with an idea and a search for a certain truth," the termination of which may be spontaneous, rapid, and marked by a permanent transformation in personality along with the conviction of the discovery of a great truth and a feeling of elation (p. 447).

Whether neurosis or creative illness, this period of Freud's life was followed by one of high productivity and increasing recognition. He was appointed to the position of extraordinary professor.

In 1902, the Wednesday Psychological Society was formed by a small group of interested friends who met weekly at Freud's home to discuss problems of psychoanalysis. By 1908, this group became the Viennese Psychoanalytic Society. In 1907, after returning to Zurich from a visit with Freud, C. G. Jung and Ludwig Binswagner founded a similar group. The first International Congress of Psychoanalysis met in Salzburg in 1908. Freud's psychoanalytic movement had acquired an international character.

The following year Freud, with Jung and Ferenczi, was invited to the United States to present lectures on psychoanalysis at Clark University, Worcester, Massachusetts, an event which, for Freud, marked the beginning of world recognition and support. During the Second International Congress in Nuremberg, the International Psychoanalytic Association was created and, along with it, a second professional journal. Although not all went smoothly (for example, Freud's breaks with Adler in 1908; with Stekel in 1912; and with Jung in 1913 and the interruption of two world wars), the International Psychoanalytic Association continues to serve as the parent organization for psychoanalytic societies and institutes all over the world, as well as the organization behind the World Congress, which meets every 2 years.

Accomplishments and Awards

Freud's accomplishments and awards are too extensive to be documented fully in a brief biographical sketch. He was, as indicated, the author of the first comprehensive theory of personality development. This achievement alone should have assured him a place in history. However, in addition to his original and dynamic theoretical constructs, Freud developed a new approach to psychotherapy, a new method of dealing with the unconscious. Further, Freud was the founder and prime mover of the worldwide psychoanalytic association with its own publishing house. More than creating a psychotherapeutic theory, method, or organization, Freud created a world movement and lived to see his name become synonymous with it.

RESOLUTIONS OF THE ELEVEN BASIC ISSUES

Most presentations of Freud's theory are historical, covering more than 4 decades of his work. While this approach may be necessary for a full understanding of theoretical development, such a presentation risks the introduction of confusion. By including all early conceptions, many of which Freud later discarded, modified, or supplemented, clearly specified hypotheses are not evident. Further, such a presentation lacks integration or synthesis.

Resolutions of the eleven basic issues are largely based on, though not limited to, Freud's third and final theory, often referred to as the tripartite model, or the structural conception to distinguish it from the earlier topographic formulations. Freud first presented this model in *The Ego and the Id* (1962) and elaborated more fully on it a decade later in the "New Introduction Lectures" (in *Ego and the Id*, 1962).

Biological and/or Social Determinants

While Freud does not deny the influence of social determinants, he relegates extraorganic reality to a secondary role in personality development. Human nature, according to Freud, is essentially biological. As with all living creatures, we are viewed as closed, complicated, and dynamic energy systems. Our energy, derived from the food we eat, takes mechanical, thermal, electrical, and chemical forms. Moreover, this energy may, when necessary, swiftly convert from one form to another to serve better our various physical and psychic processes, functions, mechanisms, and dynamisms. Physical energy may be used for bodily processes such as circulation, respiration, digestion, and motor activities, while psychic energy may be used for mental functions such as perceiving, thinking, emoting, and remembering.

Psychic energy originates in the id, the innate component of our personality, from excitations or tension caused by some tissue or organ of our body that is experiencing a deficit. These excitations create mental representations or wishes. Freud refers to a collection of wishes as instincts whose aim is to reduce the tension. Hence, all instincts have a *source*, the state of excitation within the body; an *aim*, the removal of that excitation; and an *object*, that which can be found in either our body or our environment to satisfy the aim.

Freud (1960, 1962) identified two essential instincts, Eros and Thanatos, or life and death instincts. Positive and constructive aspects of our behavior such as hunger, sexual desire, and thirst, as well as creative aspects of our culture, including art, music, literature, cooperation, and love, represent the life instincts. He refers to the energy behind the life instincts as the *libido*. Death instincts are responsible for the negative, aggressive aspects of our nature and account for all destructive behavior, violence and cruelty, murder and suicide. The death instinct, the energy of which is not named, is defined simply as the unconscious desire to return to an inanimate or tensionless state that is the ultimate aim of all instincts. Although in conflict, all normal mental activity involves both life and death instincts.

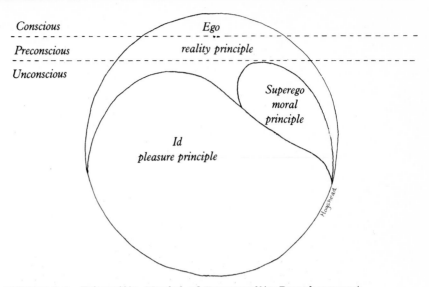

FIGURE 2.1 Tripartite Model of Personality Development

In the tripartite model of personality development, Freud (1962) constructed a structural hypothesis of three levels: id, ego, and superego. While these terms have neither meaning nor significance in and of themselves, they do serve to explain the different processes, functions, mechanisms, and dynamisms within the total personality.

The Id. The id is the original system of our personality structure. It is the product of our evolution—hence, the deepest and most inaccessible dimension of our personality, representing the raw, animalistic component of our psyche. It is the unintegrated repository for all that is inherited, permanent, and shared in the human species. The id is present at birth and remains basic to us throughout life. As explained earlier, all instincts and psychic energy originate in the id, and as with the instincts, the id cannot tolerate tension. It operates on the pleasure principle, demanding immediate and unhampered gratification of all wishes. It is impulsive, irrational, unsocialized, and devoid of values, ethics, reason, or logic. The id serves no survival functions and takes no precautions in expressing its wishes. Left on its own, the id would soon destroy the personality that houses it.

The id is directly linked with the somatic processes; it has no contact with the external world, no connection with reality. With only two processes at its command—reflex action (blinking, sneezing, coughing) and primary process (fantasizing, dreaming, hallucinating)—the id alone is unable to reduce the intolerable sensory excitations of the instincts. The id either discharges the tension through reflex action or wish fulfillment or yields its energy to the influence of the ego.

The Ego.   With the realization that there is a world of reality separate from ourselves, the ego begins to form. Because ego evolves from the id, both its structure and function are acquired from this original psychic system. Ego evolves to serve id, to seek both within the body and the external world those instinctual object choices, whether people or things, that will satisfy, postpone, or repress id's needs. Of the three systems of personality, only ego has contact with extraorganic reality and the capacity to reduce the instinctual excitations and resultant tension so intolerable to the id.

Ego operates on a reality principle and concern for the survival of the organism. With its secondary process, the cognitive capacities to perceive, think, reason, memorize, imagine, decide, and learn, ego is able to distinguish between what is only in the mind and what actually exists in the world; it differentiates between fact and fantasy. While the secondary processes of the ego are identical to the activities of consciousness and the ego seeks to bring the influence of reality to bear on the id, ego is not entirely conscious. Censorship and repression are also ego functions; hence, some parts of the ego are preconscious and some are unconscious.

Operating on a higher dynamic level than the id, ego is able to tolerate moderate amounts of tension and, considering the consequences of its actions, to repress, redirect, or gradually discharge the psychic energy of the id within the restrictive bounds set by society and the conscience of superego. The dynamics of ego require the cooperation of id and superego. To capture and bind the energy required to operate effectively while also avoiding the pain of guilt, ego must on a conscious level meet some of the id's needs and superego's demands. Ego is more than simply a buffer between blind instinct and reality; it is a mediator of psychic energy and societal dictate.

The Superego.   The final major personality system to develop is the superego. An internalized reflection or introjection of society's rules, norms, values, ethics, and attitudes, superego evolves as we differentiate right from wrong, good from bad, and moral from immoral. While relevant introjections of parental values occur early in childhood and evolve into conscience and ego-ideal (see "Early and/or Continuous Development"), superego is not fully developed, according to Freud (1962), until we have replaced parental control with self-control.

Although superego evolves from ego, it is exclusively the product of the social world and shares many characteristics of the id. It is, for example, unconscious, irrational, and demanding. Superego is unconcerned with the survival of the personality. Indeed, the demands of superego would destroy ego. Recognizing its destructive potentialities, Freud (1962) sometimes referred to the superego as the agent of the death instincts.

In summary, while Freud recognizes the role of the social milieu, he believes we are primarily biological beings motivated by instincts that constitute the total psychic energy available to operate all mental processes and functions. The dynamics of personality, an interaction and blending of urging (cathexis) and checking (anticathexis) forces, is determined by the distribution of psychic energy. Our behavior is an expression of the dominant system or principle controlling the bulk of psychic energy at any particular time. When the id retains its energy, we behave impulsively, irrationally, sensually, and indiscriminately. When psychic energy is bound by the ego, we act realistically, rationally, and in a goal-directed fashion. And, when superego controls the psychic energy, we behave rigidly, moralistically, compulsively, and fearfully. While our instinctual drives derive from our biological nature, their expression is always influenced by the people and objects available and the restrictions imposed by society and superego.

Early or Continuous Development: Critical or Significant Life Stages

According to psychoanalytic theory, personality development occurs largely as a consequence of two pervasive inseparable phenomena: (1) maturation or natural growth processes, and (2) learning associated with the avoidance of pain, the conquest of frustrations, the resolution of conflicts, and the reduction of anxiety. For Freud (1949, 1963), early life stages, particularly those in the first 5 years of life, are both *essential* and *decisive*—that is, critical to personality formation. During infancy and early childhood we first encounter conflicts and frustrations that force the learning of numerous and varied forms of adaptation, compromise, defense, displacement, and sublimation and that can influence our personalities in subsequent years. Moreover, Freud (1949) identified these early critical life stages with the erogenous zones of the body.

Oral Stage. We enter this world as small, helpless, but demanding blobs of id, totally dependent on others, particularly our mother, for our survival. Limited at this stage of our development to reflex action and wish fulfillment and unable to tolerate the tension created by hunger, our mouths become the first of the erogenous zones to produce both irritating excitations and experiences of pleasure. The tactile oral pleasure we receive from nursing becomes associated with love and approval; conversely, the withholding of this pleasure becomes associated with rejection and disapproval. Our perceptions of others and the world as good or bad and safe or dangerous are reflections of our perceptions of our mother's responses.

Hall (1954) notes that the mouth has at least five main modes of functioning: "taking in, holding on, biting, spitting out, and closing" (p. 104). Moreover, each of these modes is a *prototype* for certain personality traits that can, if we experience an inordinate amount of frustration and anxiety in connection with its expression, serve as a model for later adaptations. "Taking in through the mouth is the prototype for acquisitivenes, holding on for tenacity and determination, biting for destructiveness, spitting out for rejection and contemptuousness, and closing for refusal and negativism" (Hall, 1954, p. 104). Were we, for example, to be weaned too soon, holding on to things might become a personality trait we adopt. In fact, through various displacements and sublimations, fixation on any one of the prototypic oral modes might result in a constellation of functional and dysfunctional interests, attitudes, and behaviors that become incorporated into the personality.

Fixation at the incorporative, or taking in, stage of oral development may result in strong feelings of dependence, although we may express this dependence in a variety of ways. We can, for example, project our fixation and experience a strong need to assist others, working in one of the helping professions. We might compensate and work toward total independence, refusing any form of help or favor from others. Through displacement, we might disguise our need and become hungry for knowledge or power. We might become proficient in foreign languages or take great pride in a collection of pipes.

Defense of a fixation at the aggressive, or biting, stage may also result in many different forms of personality traits and behaviors. We may find criticism, sarcasm, or cynicism gratifying ways of responding to others and the world, or we may become interested in professions that emphasize and reward oral and verbal skills. We may project our oral aggression on others or the world in general, viewing ourselves as victims and the world and the people in it as dangerous. We might conversely employ the defense of reaction formation and make only kind and favorable comments about others.

The spitting out and closing prototypes can also result in a variety of character transformations, depending on the defenses we employ. Disdainfulness, haughtiness, and contempt are characteristics of the spitting out stage while the closing prototype is guarded and defensive. Introjection, or the swallowing whole of ideas, attitudes, and values, may be a reaction formation of the closing prototype. Projection of this mode can result in viewing ourselves as untouchables rejected by others and society.

The personality character manifestations cited here are only a few of the many possibilities that may occur as the result of oral fixation during this critical stage of early development. Moreover, these manifestations may arise in any aspect of our lives, including areas such as sexuality; career choice and decision making; interpersonal relationships; aesthetic, cultural, and recreational interest, as well as social, political, racial, and religious attitudes and values.

Anal Stage.   The anal cavity is the second of the erogenous zones of our bodies on which we are likely to focus during infancy. Elimination of fecal material relieves the tension on the sphincter muscles created by the accumulation of waste products within the digestive system. Defecation is experienced as instinctual gratification, and we find it pleasurable. Conflict arises around the second year of life when we are expected to learn voluntary control of our elimination process. Our instinctual need to defecate conflicts with the external prohibitions imposed by parental toilet training, an instinctual cathexis to be replaced with a learned set of hygienic, socially acceptable behaviors, and we resist.

Distress and frustration may occur at this stage as a result of inordinately harsh or demanding training methods. Defiance may manifest itself in intentional soiling or withholding feces. Adults with fixations resulting from punitive interference during toilet training may defy authority figures in their lives by appearing dirty, disorderly, irresponsible, undisciplined, and extravagant. In contrast, a reaction formation employed as a defense against the instinctual impulse to defecate during this period may be expressed in later years as compulsive cleanliness and neatness, an inordinately strong sense of responsibility and orderliness, a rigid adherence to the principles of self-discipline and thrift, even to the point of miserliness.

When pleading and praise precede and follow each bowel movement during toilet training, the 2-year-old may perceive the product of his or her effort as something of great value and, in later years, be motivated to produce or create other pleasing objects for him- or herself and others. Excessive valuing of the feces by the parent during toilet training, however, may result in a child's perceiving defecation as the loss of something valuable. Response to loss is anxiety, and defense to loss is retention. Fixation may manifest itself later in personality traits such as thriftiness and an interest in collecting and possessing. Reaction formation in this instance may result in careless investments; indiscriminate donations of money, gifts, and possessions; or impulsive gambling.

Phallic Stage. The third and possibly most important of the psychosexual stages of development is the phallic stage. At this stage, children, as early as the age of 3, discover the sensual pleasure of genital stimulation and become conscious of sexual differences. This is also the period in which children experience an intensification of sexual longing for their parents. The difference in the genitals of male and female led Freud to view this period differently for the two sexes.

MALE PHALLIC STAGE—With the emergence of the phallic stage, the male child moves from loving his mother and identifying with his father to incestuous feelings for his mother and feelings of jealousy for his father. Borrowing from Greek mythology, Freud (1949, 1963) referred to this as the *Oedipus complex*.

The incestuous desire for exclusive sexual possession of his mother places the male child in a dangerous, antagonistic position with his father. He fears physical punishment in the form of castration and suffers a castration anxiety. His defense against castration anxiety is the repression of his incestuous feelings for his mother and the hostility he feels toward his father. Successful repression ends the Oedipus complex.

With the resolution of the Oedipus complex, the boy, who is constitutionally bisexual, may identify with either the mother or the father. If the feminine tendencies of the boy predominate, he will identify with the mother. Conversely, if the masculine tendencies of the boy are stronger, his identification with his father will intensify. The identifications that occur at this stage give rise to the repression of erotic wishes and the formation of the child's superego, which replaces the Oedipus complex.

FEMALE PHALLIC STAGE—As with the male, a female child's first cathexis is the mother. Unlike the male, however, she has not identified strongly with the father prior to the Oedipus complex. The discovery that she lacks a penis (castration complex) weakens the cathexis with the mother, whom she partially blames for bringing her into the world without a penis, and strengthens her preference for her father. At this time, her feelings of love for her father are mixed with feelings of envy because he possesses a penis.

The female Oedipus complex weakens with maturation and the realization that sexually possessing the father is impossible. Identification occurs with one of the parents, depending on the dominant sexual component, and gives rise to the formation of superego. The success and strength of her identifications affect the direction of sexuality in later years, as well as the nature of interpersonal relationships. If the Oedipus complex is resolved successfully, the cathexis for the mother is preserved.

LATENCY STAGE—Usually between the ages of 5 and 12, sexual and aggressive impulses are in a relatively repressed or sublimated state. Libidinal energy is sublimated in school activities of learning, participating in sports and hobbies, and making friends. Freud referred to this period as the latency stage of psychosexual development and focused little attention on it.

GENITAL STAGE—The genital stage emerges with the advent of puberty when the energy of the sexual instincts is again heightened and the aims of sexual instincts are no longer autoerotic. This stage, along with the physiological changes of the reproductive systems characteristic of the adolescent years, brings an awareness of sexuality and creates stress and conflict that require new adaptations and adjustments—displacements and sublimations. If there are no libidinal fixations, the genital stage culminates in the stablilizing of the personality. Freud believed the first 5 years of life are the critical years. Less attention was focused on the latent and genital stages of development because much of what we are is determined during the very early years of childhood.

Conscious and/or Unconscious Determinants

The unconscious was the central concept in Freud's early theory. However, about 1920, much of what he had assigned to the unconscious, Freud then attributed to the id. The distinction between levels of consciousness was replaced by the tripartite model of the id, ego, and superego.

While Freud continued to refer to the three levels of consciousness, he no longer considered conscious as a synonym for mental or psychic life. Rather, consciousness or unconsciousness became only a quality of mental phenomena, and the division between them was neither absolute nor permanent.

Freud defined the conscious stratum of the psychic processes as all feelings, thoughts, wishes, and sensory perceptions of which we are aware at any given moment. Because a great deal of psychic energy is required to keep perceptions, wishes, ideas, and experiences conscious, and since energy may shift rapidly in its focus, the conscious is highly transitory and only a small part of our mental life is represented in the realm of consciousness at any particular time.

The preconscious, that quality of mental processes between conscious and unconscious, consists of all readily available memories. It includes all experiences and wishes associated with language that can be recalled, either spontaneously or with a minimum of psychic energy.

The unconscious, by far the deepest and major stratum of the three levels of consciousness, has a life of its own. Indeed, mental processes are essentially unconscious, with the potential for proceding farther into the conscious system. The unconscious is comprised, among other things, of basic psychobiological motives that often conflict with our conscious motives and create most of the major problems we experience. We can, for example, have unconscious thoughts, wishes, and desires that may be expressed by slips of the tongue or pen; selective, hence intentional, forgetting; and accidents. The unconscious quality of our mental processes ranges from memory that, because it has no association with language, can never become conscious, to preconscious memory that rests on the tip of our tongue.

Psychological and/or Reality Environments

While our survival depends on our ability to adapt to experiences in reality, the world in which we live is privately constructed from individual perceptions and interpretations. Considering the dynamics of Freud's personality structure, our personal reality is both a function and a product of the distribution of psychic energy among the three major personality systems. Reality testing requires the secondary processes and is, therefore, an ego function. Only when ego controls the bulk of psychic energy are our perceptions and interpretations of reality likely to be congruent with actual reality, but even then perceptual reproductions are corruptible.

Even with ego in control and our perceptions closely linked to the sensory stimuli from the outer world, our personal, emotionally toned realities often differ significantly from the realities of others. Reality is a subjective creation, a product of imagination and memory. We naturally endeavor to fill the gaps of our sensory perceptions with plausible inferences and, then, to translate our inferences into conscious material. We are phenomenological beings. Ego learns to scan the stimuli of the outer world and to select only those features of the environment relevant to the problem it is attempting to solve or the defense it is constructing. Further, ego will summon memories and ideas from the preconscious to assist in decision making or to adjust to the confronting situation.

Our perceptions and interpretations of reality will be influenced unconsciously by the defense mechanisms of ego. Inner feelings, for example, can be projected outward to other people or things, even the world in general. Repression can keep us from becoming aware of important stimuli in the outer world. Displacement can cause us to focus on or attend to something other than what requires our attention. Reaction formation can cause us to act exactly opposite the way we feel.

Number and Weight Assigned to Motivational Concepts

According to Freud (1940/1964, 1923/1925), all behavior is motivated. We are impelled to act when psychic energy, aroused by bodily needs or impulses seeking expression and tension release, is reflected in the form of an instinctual object choice or wish. Freud believed that motivational strength is determined by the impetus of the life instincts and the id's desire to remove immediately the excitation they create. In addition, Freud (1960, 1962) believed we are motivated by death instincts, a compulsion to re-establish the inanimate state out of which we were formed.

Since both life and death instincts reside in the id, we are motivated to act by instinctual urges and drives that are persistent, irrational, conflictual, nearly uncontrollable, and most important, largely outside our consciousness. The aim of every instinct is the cessation of tension and the resultant sense of gratification. All behavior aims at maximizing instinct gratification while minimizing punishment and guilt.

We are motivated, also, to identify with the ethical choices of the ego-ideal and the mandates of the conscience. Superego confers pride on the ego for following its decrees and being virtuous. Conversely, it uses its energy to punish ego for behavior that runs counter to its demands.

Explanation of Learning

Learning is an ego function situated in the defensive postures we assume as we encounter the internal conflicts and external frustrations of living. Ego is an achievement of living, an organization of experience with reality. In our efforts to avoid pain and experience pleasure, we form identifications, displacements, rationalizations, sublimations, compromises, and compensations that involve new object-cathexes for instinctual object choices, hence, learning. In short, pleasure and pain are the necessary and sufficient conditions for learning, and cathexis is the equivalent of learning. We learn what is positively cathected and avoid what is negatively cathected.

When efficient in gratifying the instinctual needs of id and adhering to the constrictions of superego, ego attracts and binds surplus psychic energy that it then can divert to the secondary or cognitive processes required for learning. Examples of the secondary processes of ego are perceiving, attending, discriminating, remembering, reasoning, imagining, judging, and deciding. As we mature, develop language and memory systems, and repeatedly invest surplus psychic energy in the secondary processes of ego, our perceptions become more acute, our discriminations more precise, our defense mechanisms more elaborate and complex, and our judgments and decisions more astute.

With ever-increasing knowledge of our world, we are better able to manipulate and control the environment to suit our purposes. Our ego is able to gratify instinctual needs with greater economy. Thus, as we mature and learn, we develop greater skill in resolving conflict and coping with frustration and anxiety.

Conditioning and/or Freedom to Choose Behavior

Freud's stance on the conditioning issue is clear. While he recognized that we experience a strong illusion of freedom, Freud remained a strict biological determinist. We are, according to Freud, governed by the natural laws that apply to all living organisms. There is no place in psychoanalytic theory for concepts such as free will, choice, spontaneity, self-determination, or self-actualization.

For Freud and his followers, all impulses, thoughts, feelings, aspirations, dreams, and actions are events in a chain of causally related phenomena determined largely by unconscious instinctual forces. Anything considered uncaused is, according to Freud, simply ignorance of cause. Our experience of freedom is a deception. Even our highest motives are disguised forms of libido. We are biologically incapable of choosing between alternative courses of action. Id, not reason, is ultimately in control. Our cognitive capacities operate only to serve our primal desires. Our primary aim is the fulfillment of perpetual life and death instincts and the resultant homeostatic balance, thus precluding either choice or self-actualization.

Importance of Role Assigned to Self-Concept

While self-concept is implicit in the functional interactions of ego and the ego-ideal of superego, Freud did not grant much importance to the self as a dynamic psychic system or theoretical concept. By stressing the necessity of successfully repressing and redirecting the instinctual impulses of the id, particularly sexual desire and aggression, far greater importance is conferred on ego functions and social adapatations than on any notion of being or becoming one's self. The maneuvers of ego are defensive rather than self-actualizing.

As pointed out earlier (see "Early and/or Continuous Development" and "Psychological and/or Reality Environment"), we begin in infancy to differentiate various aspects of our body imagery from objects (persons and things) in the outer world of reality. These perceptual differentiations, along with the accumulation of identifications in the ego and the developmental changes in superego, gradually integrate to form a relatively stable concept of self. Consciousness entails self-perception. Both ego and superego functions serve, however indirectly, to give us a sense of personal identity, a sense of being an individual separate and distinct from all others.

The self in Freud's theory, then, is not synonymous with the total personality that, as an entity, remains somewhat vague and hence difficult to define. Self also does not play a highly significant role in personality development as, for example, do the dynamic systems of id, ego, and superego. Rather, our sense of identity or self-perception is a complex, pregenital, developmental concept emerging from multiple self-presentations and identifications and gradually achieving constancy.

Importance of Reward

While Freud did not focus directly on the importance or role of external reward as a behavioral determinant or grant it great significance in personality development, internal reward is implicit in his concept of the pleasure principle as well as in the reciprocal relationship of the three major systems of the psyche. Gratification of id's instinctual wishes or, perhaps more accurately, the relief of tension (pleasure) that accompanies instinctual gratification is inherently rewarding. An efficient ego is free from the pressure to spend its limited energy on serving id, and an effective ego is rewarded by being in a position to bind surplus energy for its own purposes. Ego efficiency is also rewarded by feelings of competence and being in control. Conversely, fear and anxiety are the constant companions of an inefficient ego. Id will not long tolerate ego inefficiency and retain the psychic energy ego needs to operate.

Superego is also in a position to reward or punish ego. On the one hand, ego is rewarded with feelings of self-satisfaction and virtuousness when it manages to locate instinctual object choices in a manner that complements the ego ideal of superego. On the other hand, thoughts and behaviors that run counter to ego-ideal are negatively reinforced by superego with painful feelings of guilt, shame, and remorse.

Uniqueness and/or Commonality

As biological beings, we have much in common with others of our species. For example, we are all closed energy systems, unconsciously motivated by the same irrational id forces or impulses. We must experience the same psychosexual stages of early development. Our ego and superego functions are the same, and we are all defensive creatures. However, despite our many commonalities, Freud asserts that we are truly unique beings.

While instinctual id impulses derive from our biological nature, their expression must await life experiences. Experience, according to Freud, is always modified by the social milieu. We pass through the same psychosexual stages of early development, but our experiences during each stage vary significantly from family to family. Indeed, because we are each influenced by a unique set of family interactions and relationships, experiences will differ even among siblings in the same family. No two of us will perceive our experiences precisely the same. While ego and superego perform the same functions for all of us, their content or nature produce numerous variations; hence, ego and superego differ from one person to another.

Usually by the age of 5 we have developed a personal set of character attributes, a unique and consistent *schema of apperception* and behavior that defines us as individuals. We are, then, according to psychoanalytic theory, unique beings.

Importance of Group Membership

Although we are biological beings driven by the force of our id's needs, the social milieu, the people and objects we encounter in living, and the limits and restrictions imposed by authority and society have a significant impact on the expression of our instinctual drives. An important part of our social milieu, particularly during the critical formative years, is the primary group. Few theorists assign greater importance than Freud to the family (see "Early and/ or Continuous Development"), and he assigns special importance to the parents or parent surrogates.

Group affiliations provide us with a sense of security, but always at a cost—namely, the inhibition or sublimation of our instinctual discharges. We must gratify our desires in a sublimated manner if we are to remain members of the group. There is an independent autonomy with laws, customs, conventions, along with rewards and punishments. Restrictions and renunciations are the dues paid for security of the group. We are expected to introject a collective psyche, a common ego-ideal created by the group.

The impact of the group as a behavioral determinant can be great, especially when the individual members have become bound to or identified with a strong group leader, giving up their individuality by sharing certain superego elements. The leader's commands and precepts then become the moral laws of the group. Moreover, remorse or guilt is less acute when following the leader's conscience. Even the most inhuman acts can be carried out with little self-incrimination when they can be attributed to a leader-dominated conscience. In contrast, this same principle can lift the individual beyond him- or herself to acts of bravery, dedication, justice, and altruism. We become, in essence, comrades in arms, children of God, fellow advocates for justice, friends united for peace.

GOALS OF THE PSYCHOANALYST

While at first glance the goals of psychoanalysis may appear incautious, even grandiose, closer inspection reveals that they reflect the spirit rather than the letter of the psychoanalytic approach. They are goals for which one strives, realizing simultaneously that they will never be fully realized. It is undesirable—indeed, impossible—to uncover all repressed material. Nevertheless, bringing repressed material into consciousness is a therapeutic goal. Working through is a life-long process—hence, not achievable within the therapeutic tenure of the client. However, this is a goal. Insight, integration, and psychic reorganization are accepted as both means and ends, processes and products of psychotherapy. Still, while emphasis is on means and processes, they remain no less ends and products.

Freud made rather modest claims for his therapy. He never presented it as a panacea for all psychic ills or offered it as a modality to perfection. Further, he never guaranteed that the benefits gained were permanent or beyond reversal. For a carefully selected group of patients (see "Initiating Therapy"), psychoanalysis offers only the promise of helping those who are willing and able to endure a lengthy, arduous, and often painful process to achieve a resolution of some intrapsychic conflicts so they might encounter the normal conflicts of life's tasks in a mature—hence, responsible and pleasant—way. As expressed earlier, promises made and goals attempted can differ significantly.

The ultimate goal of psychoanalysis is *reorganization*, a form of ego development that promotes the integration of dissociated psychic material and results in a basically changed, firmly established new structure of personality. Subgoals of psychoanalysis include:

> Establishing a therapeutic relationship that will facilitate the psychoanalytic approach to therapy (see the next section);
> Teaching the process of free association;
> Extending the unconscious into consciousness, thereby elevating repressed material, abolishing symptom formation, and exchanging pathogenic conflict for normal conflict;
> Strengthening ego so behavior is more reality based;

Helping the client gain insight into and work through the transference process, becoming more responsible and independent than before in relation to life tasks.

THERAPEUTIC PROCESS: METHODS AND TECHNIQUES

The Therapeutic Relationship

In the psychoanalytic approach to therapy, the client-therapist relationship is conceptualized in conjunction with the induced transference neurosis. The nature of the transference process calls for a therapist-client relationship in which the client can resurrect and relive the highly emotional conflicts initially encountered with significant others in early childhood and then transfer these emotions to the therapist. Because the client's early conflicts originated from difficulties during the psychosexual stages of development— particularly the oedipal stage—the feelings directed toward the therapist during transference, while displacements, are nevertheless often intense and of a sexual or hostile nature. The therapeutic alliance must be not only strong enough to withstand this level of emotional intensity but also sound enough to ensure that the client's emotions are only expressed verbally.

Freud consistently asserted that a compassionate neutrality was the proper attitude for the analyst to convey in the psychoanalytic session. While attentive, accepting, and nonjudgmental, the analyst is a neutral observer of the free association and transference processes, intervening only occasionally to offer interpretations of the significance of the client's past experiences and distorted displacements. Objectivity demands that the analyst protect the relationship from becoming contaminated with the subjective feelings normally associated with interpersonal relationships. In fact, should the analyst begin to experience transference, collegial consultation is sought so the countertransference can be worked through and resolved. The therapist neither offers advice nor extends sympathy. Interpretations and explorations that are empathic—hence, emotionally significant and personally meaningful to the client—enhance the psychoanalytic relationship by providing support, understanding, and stability.

Initial Procedures and Strategies

Initiating Therapy. The analytic situation is launched with the first contact between the prospective client and the analyst. Literally everything clients say and do in their initial approach has potential signficance, not only for the analyst's assessment of the client's emotional, circumstantial, and physical readiness for therapy but also for therapy proper should the analyst agree to accept the client for treatment. Data for the acceptance decision include the manner and style of the client's self-presentation, the nature and onset of the problem or crisis, all client reactions and responses to the early structuring of the analytic contact (see "Structuring and Client Expectations"), and any disclosures of the client's current life situation, family background, developmental history, interpersonal relationships, and accomplishments.

Structuring and Client Expectations. Freud believed it essential that every person desiring to undergo psychoanalysis understand fully the structure of the analytic process. Certain rules, therefore, were carefully explained and agreed to at the outset. Indeed, the patient's willingness and capacity to follow these rules were often put to the test of a trial period, with acceptance for treatment resting on the outcome.

The fundamental rule of psychoanalysis is free association. The patient develops the ability to free associate (discussed in the next section)—no small accomplishment for the average client but crucial to the analytic process. Freud's second rule of psychoanalysis was the rule of abstention. Freud's patients were expected to suspend all major life decisions for the term of therapy. This included decisions such as marriage or divorce, new business ventures or sizable investments, career choice or change. To avoid outside interference that might hinder the analytic process, Freud never accepted patients who were not independent in all life relations. Further, because psychoanalysis requires lengthy, intensive, and exhaustive self-study, Freud accepted only patients who expressed a willingness to commit themselves to fixed appointment hours and an agreed upon fee and payment schedule. Freud usually scheduled his clients for 1-hour sessions, 3 to 5 days a week, and analysis was seldom completed in less than 2 years and often required as many as 5 years.

In addition to these rules, Freud restricted treatment to those individuals he subjectively thought would benefit from the psychoanalytic process. His clients were expected to be of at least normal intelligence, to possess a certain degree of ethical development, and to be under the age of 50, the point of life at which Freud believed the ability to undo psychic processes begins to diminish.

Thus, an agreement to undergo psychoanalysis is not to be entered into lightly by either the client or therapist. Indeed, it is an agreement that calls for sacrifice in time, effort, and money and that requires both commitment and patience. It is also evident that Freud's criteria preclude the use of psychoanalysis with many client groups.

Structuring, if conducted properly, may help to avoid many potential misunderstandings and problems that can evolve in the long and arduous psychoanalytic situation. Moreover, at this point, the therapist and client share an opportunity for goal alignment, a working agreement between the client and therapist that enhances the cooperative, responsible effort that is necessary in psychoanalysis.

Course of Therapy

While there have been modifications, elaborations, and additions to the early methods and techniques of psychoanalysis, the five basic techniques established by Freud remain the modus operandi of the psychoanalytic approach to therapy. In his attempt to uncover the contents of the unconscious, Freud's major tools were (1) free association, (2) interpretation, (3) dream analysis, (4) analysis of resistances, and (5) analysis of transference.

Free Association. Often referred to as the *rule* of psychoanalysis and based on the hypothesis that repressed material constantly seeks discharge, free association is an analytic technique designed to facilitate emotional regression and recall of early childhood memories. Reclining on the analyst's couch with the analyst seated behind them and out of view, clients are encouraged consciously to abandon their normal censoring activities, to flow freely with their feelings and thoughts, verbalizing immediately and spontaneously everything that comes to mind, regardless of how ludicrous, nonsensical, preposterous, irrational, irrelevant, or painful these might seem. During this process unconscious material is permitted to enter consciousness; however, it enters disguised or in symbolic form and must be interpreted by the analyst.

Initial resistance to free association is usually met with assurance from the analyst that every thought and feeling is significant and relevant to the client's improvement. Further, clients are assured that thoughts and feelings will emerge in their minds and that the past, whether pleasant or unpleasant, will return to be re-experienced once they manage to relax and flow with the process. Later resistances, signaled by blocking or disrupting behaviors, serve as cues for analysts that their clients are avoiding anxiety-arousing material. Unconscious wishes, dreams, fantasies, conflicts, and motivations emerge as regression progresses, and analysts then attempt to reconstruct the original conflict to uncover and interpret the developmental sources or fixations that are the roots of their clients' present difficulties.

Interpretation. Interpretation is an important psychoanalytic technique that requires a great deal of skill and experience on the part of the analyst. It is a major goal of the analytic process. Further, it is an integral part of each of the other four basic techniques and as such is employed complementarily with the analysis of free associations, dream symbols, psychosomatic symptoms, defensive postures, and resistance and transference behaviors.

Client readiness and involvement are crucial to successful analytic interpretation. Correct timing is essential, and therapist insights may be withheld until the climate is right. The manner in which an interpretation is expressed may alone determine whether or not client insight occurs. Interpretations are effectively communicated only when clients are prepared to recognize and accept them. Expressed too soon, interpretations evoke resistance or further repression and can, if anxiety becomes too great, result in premature termination of analysis.

Dream Analysis.   Freud (1965) considered dreams to be symbolic gratifications of id's instinctual demands, designed to promote and realize wish fulfillment. Unlike simple, direct dreams that Freud granted little psychological importance, heavily disguised dreams (those that on the surface appear senseless, ridiculous, or terrifying) could, when skillfully analyzed and interpreted, reveal much about the client's unconscious and irrational desires, beliefs, attitudes, defenses, interpersonal relationships, and problem-solving methods.

Freud differentiated between a dream's manifest content (apparent meaning) and latent content (true meaning). He was convinced that, while universal dream symbols exist that might facilitate dream analysis, individual dream symbols are understandable and interpretable only as they relate to the individual dreamer's life experiences. By motivating his clients to provide associations about various elements in the dream, Freud was often able to synthesize their associations into a coherent interpretation.

Freud did not consider it necessary to analyze everything that appeared in his clients' dreams. He did, however, look for things such as the emotional tone, the sequence of events, and the outcome of the dream. Recurring dreams were also considered significant because they often revealed unresolved conflicts, whether in the client's life outside therapy or in the therapeutic process. He discovered, too, that his clients' dreams were often fruitful sources for information about their transferences.

Analysis of Resistances.   In psychoanalysis, client behaviors that interfere with or hinder the analytical process are considered a form of resistance. All forms of client resistance are significant, and they are viewed by the analyst as opportunities to gain insight into their clients' unconscious motivations, intentions, desires, attitudes, and avoidance or defensive styles. Furthermore, client resistances can be used by the analyst, through interpretation or confrontation, to facilitate clients' insights into the hidden or disguised purposes for their feelings and actions.

Some of the common client resistances of the analytic process are not attending sessions, arriving either early or late, or constantly attempting to change the agreed time for appointments; complaining about, supposedly forgetting, or refusing to meet fee payments; blocking, censoring, or disrupting the free association process; and either not recalling dreams or developing a fascination for them and dwelling almost exclusively on dreams for entire sessions. Transference (dealt with here as a separate psychoanalytic technique) is also a form of client resistance, and unless treated as unreal and interpreted, it will impede therapy.

Analysis of Transference. While transference is a resistance to therapy, analysis of the transference neurosis is considered a major technique of the analyst. As mentioned earlier, free association facilitates emotional regression. As childhood remembrances and feelings surface during the free association process, clients re-experience their early conflicts and identify the analyst as a substitute for their parents, an object of their infantile libidinal cathexes and aggressive tendencies. The love and hate they feel for their analyst can become intense, thwarting all efforts by the analyst to continue therapy.

Transference can be neither satisfied nor ignored by the analyst; it must be treated as distorted displacements of significant relationships in the client's past, hence unreal and inappropriate. As clients gain insight of the true nature of their transferences with their analysts, they begin to understand their characteristic ways of perceiving, feeling, and acting or reacting to significant others in their lives, as well as how these psychic habits impede their growth or development as adults.

The posture of analysts during transference is the same as it has been throughout therapy. They recognize their client's feelings, whether positive or negative, as unreal and use the transferences to interpret, calmly and objectively, clients' buried feelings, traumatic conflicts, and unconscious fixations of early childhood.

ASSESSING PROGRESS

In the psychoanalytic assessment strategy, the case study, derived from clinical observations, is the primary method of research. Freud trusted this method fully. He never doubted that his clinical observations were the necessary and sufficient data of assessment, whether determining the progress of a single client, testing the process of psychoanalysis, or verifying his theoretical constructs.

Freud had many critics on this issue. Many argued that clinical observations were subject to observer bias. Others called for sound empirical verification and adequate sampling. Freud used a simple form of statistical reasoning: assuring his reader that he had repeatedly observed the phenomenon presented. He dismissed the arguments of most critics by stating that psychoanalysis could be properly understood, hence assessed, only by those who had themselves been psychoanalyzed, trained as analysts, and conducted successfully the analyses of others. Thus, he treated his critics' arguments as he treated his clients' resistances, by analyzing their conscious and unconscious motivations.

While difficult to measure, some characteristics of successful psychoanalysis might be used in an assessment of client progress. Many of these have already been discussed but are worth repeating here. For example:

> Extending the unconscious into consciousness, evidenced by insight into repressions and defensive behaviors and increased understanding of self;
>
> Giving ego a greater grasp of reality, evidenced by improvements in reality testing and finer discriminations in perceptions of self, others, and the world.
>
> Renouncing infantile demands, evidenced by more rational behavior;
>
> Exchanging pathogenic conflict for normal conflict, evidenced by the obviation of symptom formation;
>
> Increasing effort to function autonomously, evidenced by giving up the need for parental figures and transferences, especially in the final stages of therapy;
>
> Achieving life tasks, evidenced by an increasing ability to love and work.

FINAL COMMENTARY

Much of the controversy Freud created when alive remains with us today, nearly 5 decades after his death. Any attempt to assess objectively either the nature or extent of his contributions must overcome the distortions of the Freud legend, a herculean task according to Sulloway (1983). In addition, there are, as Ellenberger (1970) points out, many extensions, adjunctions, interpretations, distortions, and vulgarizations of the theory, factors that must be considered in any comprehensive evaluation of Freud's influence (p. 547).

Putting legend and controversy aside, most theorists, even his critics, would agree with the following influences:

1. While many of Freud's ideas can be traced to others, he was the first to synthesize these ideas, express them in dynamic and functional terms, and organize them into a comprehensive theory of personality development that included both a theory and method of therapy. By providing us with the first comprehensive theory, Freud offered those who followed him to a solid ideological theory and methodology of treatment upon which to build. This feat alone ensures him a place in the history of counseling and psychotherapy.

2. Though based on the recollections of adult patients rather than the direct observations of infants and infant behavior, Freud's theory awakened interest in early childhood development and the origins of adolescent and adult experiences and difficulties.
3. Freud demonstrated that consciousness and rationality play a

FIGURE 2.2   A Schematic Analysis of Freud's Stand on the Basic Issues

Biological Determinants	▬▬	Social Determinants
Unconscious Determinants	▬▬	Conscious Determinants
Early Development	▬▬	Continuous Development
Psychological Environment	▬▬	Reality Environment
Conditioning	▬▬	Freedom
Commonality	▬▬	Uniqueness

Importance of Group Membership	The primary group and parents or parent surrogates are particularly important in the formative years. The group provides security, but only in exchange for inhibition and sublimation of instinctual drives. We are expected to introject the group's collective ego ideal.
Explanation of Learning	Learning is an ego function, a defensive posture assumed as internal conflicts and external frustrations are encountered. Pleasure and pain are necessary and sufficient conditions for learning and cathexis (instinctual object choice) is equivalent to learning. As the id is gratified, the ego uses surplus energy for secondary or cognitive processes.
Number and Weight Assigned to Motivational Concepts	Psychic energy motivates. Instinctual drives (particularly sex and aggression) residing in the id impel instinctual object choice or wish—goal of every instinct is relief from tension and subsequent gratification. We are also motivated to identify with ego ideal and conscious mandates to minimize punishment and guilt.
Importance of Reward	Internal reward is implicit and comes with relief of tension accompanying instinctual gratification (pleasure). This reward is also experienced as feelings of competence by the efficient ego utilizing surplus energy for itself and as self-gratification and virtuousness by the ego making instinctual object choices congruent with superego.
Importance or Role of Self-Concept	A concept of self is implicit in the interactions of the ego and the superego's ego ideal; however, maneuvers of the ego and the superego are defensive rather than self-actualizing. Perceptual differentiations, ego identification, and superego developmental changes integrate to form a sense of personal identity.

relatively minor role in determining human behavior; the instinctual demands of the unconscious were major determinants for Freud.

4. Freud's psychoanalytic method—free association and the analysis of resistances and transference—is an original method of treatment and is the major therapeutic approach in psychoanalysis today.

5. Perhaps his greatest achievement was the creation of the psychoanalytic movement with an international organization and publishing house.

While today's theorists may accept or reject Freud's originality, theory, and method, few can dismiss him entirely or deny that he made an impact on the field of psychoanalysis.

REFERENCES AND SUGGESTED READINGS

Brenner, C. 1955. *An elementary textbook of psychoanalysis.* New York: Doubleday.

Eidelberg, L., ed. 1968. *Encyclopedia of psychoanalysis.* New York: The Free Press.

Ellenberger, H.F. 1970. *The discovery of the unconscious.* New York: Basic Books.

Freud, S. 1949. *An outline of psycho-analysis*, J. Starchey, trans. and ed. New York: W.W. Norton.

Freud, S. 1952. *An autobiographical study*, J. Starchey, trans. New York: W.W. Norton.

Freud, S. 1954. *The origins of psychoanalysis, letters to Wilhelm Fliess*, E. Musbacher and J. Starchey, trans. New York: Basic Books.

Freud, S. 1960. *Psychopathology of everyday life*, A.A. Brill, trans. New York: The American Library.

Freud, S. 1961. *The future of an illusion*, J. Starchey, trans. and ed. New York: Anchor Books.

Freud, S. 1962. *The ego and the id*, J. Riviere, trans. and J. Starchey, ed. New York: W.W. Norton.

Freud, S. 1963. *The sexual enlightenment of children.* New York: Collier Books.

Freud, S. 1965. *The interpretation of dreams*, J. Starchey, trans. and ed. New York: Avon Books.

Freud, S. 1966. *On the history of the psycho-analytic movement*, J. Riviere, trans. and J. Starchey, ed. New York: W.W. Norton.

Freud, S. 1977. *Five lectures on psychoanalysis*, J. Starchey, trans. and ed. New York: W.W. Norton.

Gelman, D. November 30, 1984. Finding the hidden Freud. *Newsweek*, pp. 64–70.

Hall, C. 1954. *A primer of Freudian psychology.* New York: The American Library.

Jones, E. 1953. *The life and work of Sigmund Freud*, vol. 1. New York: Basic Books.

Jones, E. 1955. *The life and work of Sigmund Freud*, vol. 2. New York: Basic Books.

Jones, E. 1957. *The life and work of Sigmund Freud*, vol. 3. New York: Basic Books.

Lauzun, G. 1962. *Sigmund Freud, the man and his theories*, P. Evans, trans. Greenwich, Conn.: Fawcett.

Masson, J.M. February 1984. Freud and the seduction theory. *The Atlantic Monthly*, pp. 33–53, 56, 59–60.

Munroe, R.L. 1955. *Schools of psychoanalytic thought*. New York: Holt, Rinehart & Winston.

Nuttin, J. 1962. *Psychoanalysis and personality. A dynamic theory of normal personality*, G. Lamb, trans. New York: Mentor-Omega.

Rycroft, C. 1968. *A critical dictionary of psychoanalysis*. New York: Basic Books.

Sulloway, F. 1983. *Freud, biologist of the mind*. New York: Basic Books.

Wyss, D. 1966. *Depth psychology, a critical history*, G. Onn, trans. New York: W.W. Norton.

3

The Individual Psychotherapy of Alfred Adler

TO STUDENTS of personality and psychotherapeutic theories, the Adlerian phenomenon is a puzzle. Although his ideas permeate current psychotherapies, parenting, and educational practices, Adler is rarely acknowledged as their author. When Adler first presented his theory in 1912, many mistakenly assumed that, because he had been closely associated with Freud, individual psychotherapy was only a minor deflection from Freud's theory of psychoanalysis. This group simply ignored Adler's theory. Others, blaming Adler for the breach in the Freudian school of psychoanalysis, joined Freud in attacking both Adler and his ideas. In addition to the erroneous assumptions and the open resistance that Adler encountered, World War I interrupted further dissemination of his theory.

After the war, Adler was forced to reach the majority of his followers through his lectures, presented by invitation at universities and academic and medical societies in Belgium, Czechoslovakia, Germany, France, the United Kingdom, and the United States (Orgler, 1963, p. 182). Although Adler never gained the recognition his ideas seemed to merit, he proved a gifted and persuasive speaker, and the theory of individual psychotherapy became known throughout Central Europe and the United States. In fact, many of Adler's conceptions were so widely accepted as common sense that they were treated as public domain during his lifetime. How often, for example, have you heard or read the terms, *inferiority complex, life-style, striving for superiority, compensation, social interest, or empathy* without reference to Adler?

Even limited knowledge and understanding of the current theories of counseling and psychotherapy must be accompanied by the acknowledgment that Adler's influence on other theorists over the years has been both minimized and undervalued. His ideas and concepts have been assimilated into numerous theories with surprisingly little mention of their origin. Fortunately, theorists' tendency to overlook the contributions of Adler is being reversed, at least since the 1970s. Mozak and Dreikurs (1973) cite acknowledgments of Adler's work by many of today's theorists, including the existentialists, May and Frankl; the rational-emotive theorist, Ellis; the humanistic theorist, Maslow; and the founder of transactional analysis, Berne. Adler's concepts can be found also in a number of social theories including the theories of Horney, Fromm, and Sullivan. Many of his ideas are repeated in Glasser's reality therapy, and there are certainly similarities in the psychotherapeutic theories of Rogers and Perls.

In addition to contributing to current psychotherapies, Adler increased our awareness of parenting and educational practices that facilitate the healthy growth of children. Further, he heightened our awareness of the need for social justice and institutional change. His insights into and concern for the plight of women in our biased society preceded the feminist movement in the United States by several decades. Adler was one of the first to defend the practice of group and family therapy in front of large audiences made up of physicians, teachers, and parents. We can see that Adler had many ideas that were in advance of their time.

Adler's individual psychology is social, teleological, phenomenological, holistic, and humanistic. A separatist from the Freudian camp, Adler neither portrayed us as victims of our instincts nor viewed us as cursed forever by our biology and early childhood experiences. Throughout his theory we are depicted as social, consistent, responsible, creative, purposive, and active beings. He believed we are motivated and guided by unique perceptions, values, beliefs, and a life goal of which we are largely unaware.

Individual psychology stresses consciousness and cognition, encouragement, social responsibility, choice, and action. Therapy is an endeavor in which equals cooperatively work through an educative or re-educative process. It is not only for the discouraged who have lost courage but also for normal people experiencing normal problems with life tasks. We might elect to enter individual psychotherapy to improve our understanding of ourselves and to actualize ourselves.

BIOGRAPHICAL SKETCH

It is not surprising that the genesis of many of the ideas and concepts that make up a theory of counseling and psychotherapy can be unveiled in the theorist's biography. It is surprising, however, to discover that a significantly large number of those that make up individual psychotherapy can be traced directly to Adler's perceptions of his early childhood experiences.

Early Years

Born February 7, 1870, in Penzig, Austria, a suburb of Vienna, Alfred Adler was the second of six children in a middle-class Jewish family. His close relationship with his mother abated drastically when a third child arrived on the scene, and a sickly and pampered Adler, feeling dethroned, turned to his father for encouragement and support. Adler's earliest memories were of jealousy and illness and marked the beginning awareness of an intense sense of powerlessness whenever confronted with death. This feeling was with him throughout life.

As a child, Adler felt that he had to overcome a strong sense of inferiority. Not only did he see his older and stronger brother as a rival, but also he had a deficiency of vitamin D that led to rickets, which made him feel ugly and awkward. At the age of 3, spasms of the glottis were accompanied by the fear of suffocation when he cried. That same year, Adler witnessed the death of his younger brother in the bed adjacent to his. When 5 years old, Adler developed pneumonia and overheard his physician tell his father, "Your boy is lost." Fortunately, a second physician recommended a treatment that resulted in a rapid recovery. Nevertheless, this experience led Adler to the unwavering decision to become a doctor.

As Adler grew older, his health improved, and because sun, fresh air, and exercise had been ordered as treatment for rickets, he spent a great deal of time outdoors playing with neighborhood children. To compensate for his physical disabilities, he intentionally cultivated the qualities of leadership and formed friendships with a large number of playmates.

Education

Although Adler loved music and had, by the age of 4, memorized many operettas, Adler's elementary school years left him with few pleasant memories. At the secondary level, Adler performed so poorly in mathematics that his teacher failed him and recommended that his father remove him from school and apprentice him to a shoemaker. Determined to overcome his deficiency in mathematics, Adler studied diligently at home until he not only managed to repeat his form successfully but also became one of the best disciplined students of mathematics in his class.

After passing his examinations, Adler began the study of medicine at the University of Vienna; he was graduated in 1895. In 1897, Adler married Raissa Timefejewna, who had come from Russia to study at the university. He entered private practice as an ophthalmologist in 1898. Adler later became a general practitioner, but as diabetes took the lives of his younger patients, the fear of death and the sense of utter helplessness became more than he could tolerate, and he turned to neurology. Convinced of the need to understand the total personality of his patients, Adler worked to gain knowledge of their psychic and physical processes and social situations. His practice flourished, and he established an excellent reputation as a highly skilled psychiatrist.

Emergence of Individual Psychotherapy

At Freud's invitation, Adler, then a young practicing physician, joined the psychoanalytic circle in 1902. Often referred to by Freud as *Der Adler*, German for "The Eagle," he soon became a valued member of the circle and, in 1910, was named Freud's successor as president of the Vienna Psychoanalytic Society. Along with Freud and Stekel, he edited *Zentralblatt fur Psychoanalyse*, the society's journal.

Adler began his theoretical formulation in 1908, with the concept of organ inferiority. In 1910, he introduced the concept of masculine protest, establishing a distinct shift from biological drives to subjective feelings as the primary motivating force. It was immediately obvious that the differences between Adler and Freud were acute. So they could discuss these differences at length, the society asked Adler, then president, for a comprehensive presentation of his theories. Adler complied and read three position papers under the title, "Critique of Freud's Sexual Theory of Psychic Life." A heated discussion continued for three meetings following his presentations. When the society determined that Adler's position was in direct opposition to Freud's, Adler voluntarily resigned from the presidency and the editorial board and, along with nine of the thirty-five members, withdrew to form the society for Free Psychoanalytic Research. The following year Adler and his followers renamed this affiliation the Society of Individual Psychology, and in 1914, Adler founded the journal, *Zeitschrift fur Individualpsychologie*.

As mentioned earlier, the momentum generated by Adler for his theory was slowed significantly during World War I, in which Alder served as a physician in the Austrian army near the Russian front at Cracow and Brunn. After the war Adler worked for school reform and established the first child guidance clinics in the Viennese school system. He worked also to re-establish his theory of individual psychology and managed to make great gains until the rise of Hitler and World War II.

Beginning in 1925, Adler visited the United States regularly. He lectured at Columbia University in 1927. In 1932, he was appointed to the first chair of medical psychology in the United States at the Long Island College of Medicine. In 1935, Adler fled Europe and settled in the United States. He continued his private practice and his clinics were very popular. On May 28, 1937, Adler died of a heart attack while on a lecture tour in Aberdeen, Scotland. He was survived by his wife, son, and two daughters. His daughter, Alexandra, and son, Kurt, were practicing Adlerian psychiatrists in New York City.

Accomplishments and Awards

Beginning with his first paper, "The Physician as Educator," published in 1904, Adler published some 300 books and articles and founded a professional journal. A renowned speaker, Adler was invited to lecture in numerous countries in Europe and in the United States.

In 1923, Adler delivered a paper to the International Congress of Psychology, and the president of the Oxford University Psychological Society later invited him to lecture before that distinguished body in 1926 and in 1936. In 1932, the Long Island College of Medicine created the chair of medical psychology especially for Adler. The Psychogogic Society in Geneva and the Psychological Society in Leningrad awarded Adler honorary memberships. The Institute for Scientific Treatment of Delinquency in London elected Adler vice-president. Wittenberg College of Springfield, Ohio, awarded Adler the title, Doctor Honoric Causa. In recognition of his scientific achievements, Vienna bestowed on Alder the highest honor that can be accorded one of its sons, the Freedom of the City.

Perhaps the greatest recognition of Adler's theory is the fact that, years after his death, individual psychology is still the theory of choice for many counselors, psychotherapists, and teachers. The International Association of Individual Psychology meets every 3 years. The American Society of Adlerian Psychology meets annually, publishes the *Journal of Individual Psychology*, and reports a growing membership. Adlerian training institutes, offering certification programs in individual psychotherapy, are located in New York, Chicago, Minneapolis, Berkeley, and Toronto. Special courses, workshops, and programs are offered at many universities and colleges in the United States, including Arizona University, DePaul, Governor's State, Oregon, Rhode Island College, San Fernando State College, Southern Illinois, Vermont, and West Virginia University.

RESOLUTIONS OF THE ELEVEN BASIC ISSUES

In the attempt to uncover Adler's resolutions of the eleven basic issues, three major difficulties were encountered. The first, and initially most obvious, was the lack of systematization in Adler's writings. Because of this, it was often necessary to search through numerous sources for his response to an issue. The second, and the greatest difficulty experienced, was the major modifications in Adler's resolutions from his early to later writings. When viewed from a basic-issues framework, Adler's resolutions underwent considerable evolution during the 3 decades that he developed his theory. Some changes are so drastic that his final stance appears to be in direct opposition to his initial position. Therefore, Adler's resolutions of the eleven basic issues are those that appear in his final theory.

Although Adler's earlier works are not ignored, they are discussed only when they are considered necessary to a fuller understanding of a particular resolution. Fortunately, Heinz and Rowena Ansbacher (1964) have not only organized Adler's writings but also have explained the major changes in his thinking over the years. Many books and articles were reviewed in preparation for writing this chapter, but their book proved most helpful.

Finally, separating and weighting Adler's resolutions of the eleven basic issues so they could be presented in hierarchical order proved especially difficult. Adler used only a few global constructs to explain all human behavior in all its complexity. Although this might be considered a testimony to the parsimony and holism of Adler's theory, it does make some repetition in this presentation impossible to avoid.

Biological and/or Social Determinants

According to Adler, we have evolved as a species to the point where we have subdued most of the basic animal instincts. Drives and urges, once instinctual and characterized by fixed or predetermined directives and objectives, have been supplanted by or subordinated to innate possibilities that, although inevitable and ubiquitous, need not always be followed and, in some instances (social interest, for example), may require conscious development. We are not, then, if we accept Adler's thinking, victims of our biology.

We also are not victims of our past environments. When Adler introduced the concept of the creative self (see "Conditioning and/or Freedom to Choose"), he granted us autonomy with our environments. We inherit cerebral potential that permits us to hope, dream, aspire, plan, form attitudes, draw conclusions, and set goals—that is, to be creative and self-directing. We are interpreters of life. All our behavior is purposive. With our unique creative powers, our ability and predisposition to form opinions and attitudes, we can direct the impact of our environments on our attitudes and our lives.

Adler's position on this issue is clear: our heredity and our environments merely provide us with the raw materials we use to form our unique and creative life-styles (see "Early or Continuous Development"). It is not so much what we have that determines our behavior but what we do with what we have. Adler does not look for cause but seeks purpose, a teleological stance.

Adler identifies and develops three important, innate, primary human potentials: (1) striving for superiority and perfection, (2) social interest, and (3) degree of activity. Each of these global concepts is an integral part of one or more of the remaining ten resolutions. Since each is discussed in some depth, any description here would constitute repetition. It is enough at this point to stress again that our unique creative powers can, when fully and healthfully developed, enable us to overcome or transcend both biological and social determinants. The relationship of innate potentials and environmental forces to our strivings is, in Adler's mature theory, one of subordination.

Number and Weight Assigned to Motivational Concepts

Underlying nearly every psychotherapeutic theory that attempts to substantiate the unity and self-consistency of our unique personalities is an innate, paramount, dynamic motivating force that drives or at least predisposes us to move in a particular direction. The individual psychology of Alfred Adler is no exception. However, as Adler developed his theory, first to explain the behavior he observed in his neurotic patients and, later, to account for the motivation of the normal or healthy personality, his motivational concepts changed.

In line with his early acceptance of a biologically oriented drive psychology and his experiences with neurotic patients, Adler believed that a constellation of instinctual drives relinquishes autonomy to form a higher principle of motivation, a superordinated aggression drive, that directs the drive constellation. At this point, Alder theorized that we strive to be aggressive, to dominate others and the world. We are viewed as hedonistic and concerned with our self-esteem and personal aggrandizement. Later, Adler referred to this superordinated principle as the *masculine protest*, a striving to become a real man. Aggression, domination, and power still play major roles in our strivings. However, although the superordinated drive principle seemed to explain the motivation of Adler's neurotic patients, he found it inadequate for the normal or healthy personality and continued to seek answers.

Strongly influenced by Vaihinger's concept of fictionalism, the philosophy of "as if," Adler moved from a drive psychology to a socially oriented, subjectivistic psychology of attitudes as the governing force of healthy behavior. In 1912, Adler posited the fictional goal as the ideal of perfection and completion developed in infancy (see "Early or Continuous Development") as the primary reason for the unity and self-consistency of our personalities, and he posited the striving toward that goal as our primary motivating force.

Adler was convinced that striving for superiority or for perfection and totality is the force behind every psychological act. For Adler, this everpresent and necessary great upward drive, this impetus to move from below to above, from minus to plus, is life itself. Everything we do is an expression of this innate motivating principle, guided by a personally constructed life goal and influenced by compensations for perceived inferiorities.

The difference between normal and healthy striving and abnormal and unhealthy striving is, according to Adler, our degree of social interest. While the purpose of abnormal or unhealthy striving may be self-preservation, superiority over others, power, self-esteem, or perfection, normal or healthy striving is concerned with perfection of skills and competencies necessary to overcome difficulties and to complete life tasks. Furthermore, healthy striving is concerned with the welfare of others and contributes, directly or indirectly, to society. When social interest is present, striving becomes a higher and healthier form of motivation. In brief, a deficiency in social interest is pathogenic: abnormal development begins where social interest ends.

Adler neither relinquished nor contradicted his earlier concepts of motivation (the aggression drive and the masculine protest); rather, he subordinated them to the higher principle of striving for perfection and completion reserved for the healthy personality. In a sense, Adler was the first to suggest a

Striving for completion and perfection:
Life goals develop in infancy and life-styles
emerge as strategy for reaching those goals.

hierarchical conceptualization of motivation. However, unlike Maslow's hierarchy in which we *strive to become* by actualizing our innate potentials, Adler's hierarchy is based on feelings of inferiority that we *strive to overcome* by compensating for real or imagined weaknesses. For Maslow the actualizing tendency is innate. Adler, in contrast, followed a psychology of attitudes and employed the concept of fictional finalism to explain the tendency toward perfection and completion. Rather than striving to express inherited potentialities, we are, he believed, striving toward unique, ideal, fictional goals created during our first years of life (see "Early or Continuous Development").

Adler used the term *perfection* because he believed it to be the most abstract and general ideal or fiction characteristic of our striving tendency.

Perfection is never fully achieved because as soon as we attain one goal the next goal beckons. Whatever our present position, it is always inferior to what might be reached with greater striving.

Early or Continuous Development: Critical or Significant Life Stages

If we concentrate on the last decade of Adler's work, we see that he presents a holistic theory of counseling and psychotherapy that does not hold with any arbitrarily defined critical or divisible life stages. He firmly believed that our development, including the rapid development that occurs during our early years, is a unified, continuous process of unique, gradual, holistic emergence. Furthermore, because Adler believed that we possess a free creative power (see "Conditioning and/or Freedom to Choose"), even our earliest experiences function only as possibilities, opportunities, and limitations. Experiences, regardless of chronology, are teleological, not causal; significant, not critical, Even as infants we are not simply passive receptors of early family influences. In fact, Mozak and Dreikurs (1973) tell us that the infant is "actively and creatively busy modifying his environment, training his siblings, and 'raising' his parents" (p. 46).

We do not, then, just become; we actively create our own distinctive personalities. It is not the events in our lives that shape our personalities, our goals and strivings, but our unique perceptions and interpretations of those events. When attempting to understand behavior, seek purpose rather than cause, advises Adler. At the same time he warns us to hold our answers loosely since there is always the possibility that everything could be different.

Although Adler refutes the idea that our early childhood experiences are critical, in the sense that they function as permanent determinants of our future behavior, he certainly considers the first 4 or 5 years as extremely significant. During these years, he informs us, we first experience the natural human phenomenon of feeling inferior, formulate ultimate life goals, and design our distinctive styles of living.

Feelings of Inferiority.   We are totally dependent on others for our survival when we enter this world and remain dependent long after we become aware of our helplessness. It is only natural that we become aware of strong general feelings of inferiority very early in our lives, particularly in regard to our interactions with the larger, stronger, and more competent members of our families. However, for Adler, feeling inferior is far more than an inescapable sense of inadequacy. It is the necessary, constant, and vital motivating force behind all our growth and development. All our strivings, whether healthy or unhealthy, are manifestations of our attempts to overcome or compensate for our feelings of inferiority. Adler believed that our innate sense of inferiority may well account for our survival in the evolutionary process while numerous other species, seemingly far better equipped, became extinct.

Constructing a Life Goal.   Generated by our early feelings of inferiority, we subjectively and creatively construct ultimate life goals and then act as if the achievement of that personal construction will give us our place in the world, provide us with the security we believe we lack, and guarantee us the self-esteem we believe we need. Thus, our life goals are expressions of our ultimate desire for a perfect and complete life, the final meaning of our existence, our personally constructed Utopia. Our actions can only be understood fully when we become aware of this ultimate guiding fiction, since it is the underlying purpose of all our behavior and we are perpetually responding to the necessity of moving in the direction of completion.

Unfortunately, this process takes place during our earliest years of childhood. Not only are our perceptions limited, but also our interpretations of them are often faulty. Furthermore, we construct our life goals before we have the language to symbolize them. Thus, our life goals, our portentous promises of superiority and perfection, are constructed from partial truths and fictions. Because they have not been symbolized, these guiding fictions remain subjectively within us, hidden from our immediate awareness.

Developing a Style of Life.   Once our life goals are formulated, thoughts, emotions, and actions are directed toward their achievement. We set about developing unifying, unique sets of convictions, individual strategies for reaching our goals that, in turn, govern our beliefs about ourselves, others, and the world and become our personal styles of living.

According to Adler, our unique life-styles are fairly well concerted and crystallized by our fifth year, only to become more complex and fixed as we mature. Our individual conceptions about ourselves, others, and the universe combine to form a resolute schema of apperception through which we filter our perceptions of all future experiences. For Adler, our life-styles are synonymous with our personalities, our selves, our whole attitude to and movement in life. We are truly unique beings, self-created, self-defining, self-expressive.

Cultivating Social Interest.   To Adlerians the definitive characteristic of healthy life-styles is social interest. Life-styles that do not exhibit an interest in and concern for the welfare of others are deficient and pathogenic. Social interest remains the most important quality necessary to health. Pathogenic life-styles are characterized by strivings that are self-centered, exploitive, demanding, uncaring, and often hostile and aggressive. Furthermore, in nearly every case of a pathogenic life-style there is a victim or, when families are involved, victims.

Although Adler believed social interest to be innate, he was quick to point out that we inherit only the possibility of social interest, that it must be consciously developed, particularly during the first years of our lives as we construct our life goals and our life-styles. It begins with the mutual cooperation between infant and mother and extends to interactions with other family members and eventually with society. The aggressive aspect of superiority becomes socialized only with continuous, conscious effort.

Importance of Group Membership

We are, according to Adler, social beings. Our experience of social embeddedness begins at birth when we enter this world as totally dependent members of a family group. Early feelings of inferiority and a strong need to belong lead to the development of a private logic or life plan that results in special ways and means, individual styles of living, to establish our place in the family. Our views of ourselves and the world are but extensions of our particular *schema of apperception* that we develop from our personal and subjective interpretations of early childhood experiences in our family groups.

While our relationships with both parents are crucial for encouraging the development of healthy life-styles, our first, and to Adler, most important, social interaction is with our mothers. The infant-mother relationship holds the greatest potential for the enhancement of our innate possibility for social interest, the singular path to a healthy life-style. Adler believes that it is our mothers who first interpret society to us, and it is, therefore, the mother's function to develop a warm, loving relationship based on affirmation, encouragement, and cooperation and, then, to help us to extend this attitude, first, to other family members; later, to individuals and groups outside the family; and finally, to all other beings. When our mothers perform their function well, we learn early that interpersonal relationships require a reciprocity based on mutual respect, trust, and cooperation.

Adler believes that our relationships with our parents, our interactions with other family members, and the particular feelings of inferiority we experience are influenced somewhat by our ordinal positions in the family group. Our birth order may present us with special problems and encourage us to form complex rivalries and alliances—all grist for the milling of our unique styles of living. Five ordinal positions in the family constellation are emphasized in the literature: the firstborn, the secondborn, the middle child, the youngest child, and the only child, (Dinkmeyer, Pew, & Dinkmeyer, Jr., 1979; Dreikurs, 1950, 1957, 1964; Sweeney, 1975, 1981).

The Firstborn. Because it is natural that inexperienced parents tend to lavish a great deal of time and attention on their first child, the firstborn often holds a unique, enviable, and secure position in the family group. In his writing, Adler refers to the firstborn as a "reigning monarch" who receives full and undivided attention. This unique position changes suddenly and drastically, however, with the arrival of a second child; the monarch is dethroned.

Parental time and attention must be shared with an intruder. The former monarch suffers the indignity of waiting to be served. Resentment builds, and the battle is on to regain the once privileged position.

According to Adler, all firstborns experience the loss of their singular positions, but those who were excessively pampered by their parents feel most discouraged and manifest greater resentment, even hatred, toward the interloper. The degree of the firstborn's discouragement is affected by numerous factors (the age when displaced or the amount of parental preparation for the new arrival, for example), but the firstborn's place in the family will never be the same, regardless of the effort to make it so. Suddenly, the only child is the elder child. Furthermore, inherent with the new position is the expectation of responsibility, cooperation, and accommodation.

Adler claims that the firstborn understands best both the significance and exercise of power. Moreover, the elder child is most likely to become conservative in attitudes, nostalgically oriented to the past, and inordinately interested in organization and the maintenance of the status quo. As an adult, the firstborn is also most likely to support, refer, and defer to authority. Adler found that firstborns may become highly organized, responsible, and conscientious; excellent with order and detail; or when deficient in social interest, extremely insecure, suspicious, and hostile toward others and society.

The Secondborn. The secondborn never knows the experience of being an only child, of being the focus of full and undivided attention. However, by virtue of being second in the birth order, the younger child will never be forced to suffer the loss of the firstborn's favored position and will never experience as devastatingly as the elder child the sudden shock of being dethroned. The secondborn has always had to share parental time and attention, has always had the model or threat of an older sibling. Unconcerned with the loss of power and authority, many second children are optimistic, competitive, and ambitious. They are likely to view their older siblings as pacesetters to be overtaken and, if possible, surpassed.

If the older child is supportive, encouraging the secondborn's efforts to catch up and attempts to excel, growth is more likely to be in a healthy direction or, from an Adlerian viewpoint, "toward the useful side of life." Conversely, should the secondborn continually experience only strong resentment and malicious treatment by the older sibling or should the firstborn excel in almost every area, the second child may mistakenly set irrationally high goals that ultimately lead to failure and discouragement or decide that it is impossible to compete successfully and give up.

Typically, however, secondborn children strive in directions opposite those of the firstborn. All depends on the child's interpretations of the family situation, and children in the same family perceive the situation differently.

The Middle Child. As the position implies, middle children often believe that they are in an extremely unfair and difficult position. They are denied many of the advantages they once received as the baby of the family. This evaluation is confirmed if, as is often the case, the firstborn helps to care for and becomes an ally of the youngest child.

So-called squeezed children may be defeated by their older and younger siblings or surpass them. In either case, they develop a keen awareness of family politics and learn the skills of manipulation and negotiation. Not only will their personalities be different from their older siblings, but also they will usually strive in directions opposite those of the firstborn, directions in which the firstborn child shows little interest or is unable to master. This is especially likely to occur when the siblings are near in age and of the same sex.

The Youngest Child.   Youngest children often receive the attention of most members of their families. In addition to their parents, they have older siblings to look after them and serve their needs. Further, they usually have an older ally in the sibling group to protect them when they get into difficulty. They may become the family pet and be considered cute, a charmer, the baby. With so many role models, they may be encouraged to excel over all others to establish their place in the family.

On the one hand, youngest children with a competitive orientation often develop at a surprisingly rapid pace and become high achievers at the tasks they undertake. On the other hand, youngest children who are spoiled and pampered may learn to expect others to tend to their needs. They may become helpless and dependent or reliant on their charm to have their needs met. They may also find life tasks difficult to cope with as adults.

The Only Child.   As with all the ordinal positions, the position of the only child has both advantages and disadvantages. Only children are firstborns who are never dethroned, although they may experience both surprise and disappointment when they discover they are not the center of attention or universally admired outside the family setting.

Because only children spend most of their early years with adults, they mature early and introject adult manners, behaviors, and attitudes. Because they spend more time alone than children with brothers and sisters, they may develop rich imaginations and learn to be highly creative. However, without models or rivals only children seldom learn to share or to compete for attention and, if, as adults, their efforts receive little acclaim or recognition, they may become easily discouraged. Adler found that only children were likely to be pampered children and be deficient in social interest.

Influence of the Family Constellation.   The ordinal positions described here are not to be taken as explanations for the development of particular life-styles or as means of understanding individuals. Birth order alone is meaningless, except to point out that no two children ever experience the same family situation. Our creative and subjective interpretations of our place in the

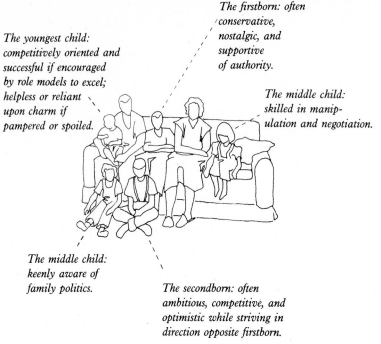

The firstborn: often conservative, nostalgic, and supportive of authority.

The youngest child: competitively oriented and successful if encouraged by role models to excel; helpless or reliant upon charm if pampered or spoiled.

The middle child: skilled in manip-ulation and negotiation.

The middle child: keenly aware of family politics.

The secondborn: often ambitious, competitive, and optimistic while striving in direction opposite firstborn.

The only child: mature early, quickly introjecting adult attitudes and behaviors; generally pampered and deficient in social interest.

FIGURE 3.1   Family Constellation

family influence our unique styles of living, our personalities. These descrip-tions are only possible interpretations. A myriad of factors must be considered for any dynamic understanding of the family constellation; the order of birth is but one. We can make some inferences about an individual's personality when we know his or her ordinal position—for example, "Firstborn children are . . ." or "second children tend to . . . ." However, we do so knowing that the actual case may be entirely different, depending on the individual's per-ceptions, interpretations, feelings, and actions.

Psychological and/or Reality Environments

We live in unique worlds privately created by our personal perceptions, individual worlds that we can never know fully since parts were created before we mastered language. A reality, then, cannot exist; rather, there are individual realities, and no two are identical. One of the early phenomenologists, Adler (in Ansbacher & Ansbacher, 1964) tells us that to understand another individual it is necessary "to see with his eyes and listen with his ears" (p. 14).

Adler believes that, from the moment of birth, we think, feel, and act in accordance with our subjective perceptions and interpretations of our experiences, including all inherited possibilities, bodily sensations, and environmental influences. Further, he believes that, even as infants, our unique creative power enables us to mold and shape all situational influences and, thus, our realities. What we are does not determine our behavior but what we think we are. No event determines our behavior, but what we think about that event influences what we feel and do in given circumstances. Moreover, as we form life goals and life-styles, our perceptions and interpretations are shaded by our strivings. We view our worlds through the prejudice of our interests and, in a very short period of time, through a relatively firm and constant schema of apperception. We develop expectations that tend to become self-fulfilling prophesies. Our future, after all, is only our present perceptions of what we believe to be ahead of us. Our past, likewise, is a matter of present attitudes. Our style of living, that unique, unifying set of convictions developed during our first years of life, provides the reference point from which we work, play, celebrate, and cooperate with all persons and events.

Conscious and/or Unconscious Determinants

Although we may perceive the polarities of consciousness and unconsciousness and act as if conscious and unconscious determinants were responsible for moving us in different, even opposing, directions, Adler reminds us that this is only subjective experience, that conscious and unconscious are not separate and antagonistic entities with discrete functions and qualities. Our unconscious is only what we are unable or unwilling to formulate clearly, what we either do not understand or withhold from understanding, like our life goals.

Once we form a style of life, the function of our memories, according to Adler, is to fit our perceptions, thoughts, feelings, and actions into our striving. Those that fit, we understand and remember; those that are determined unfit, we reject and forget. The issue of consciousness is settled by our individual style of living. The unconscious is not some deep, guarded recess of our psyche. It is not actuality. Adler's concept of the unconscious is simply that it is a convenient term used to cover what we fail or refuse to understand.

According to Adler (in Ansbacher & Ansbacher, 1964), "as soon as we understand an unconscious tendency it has already become conscious" (p.232).

Adlerians believe all human behavior is purposive. Rather than being driven by unconscious forces over which we have no control, we consciously create our goals and decide our futures. Consciousness is at the center, or core, of our personalities and in service to our goals. We are, then, far more active than reactive, consciously determining ourselves by the unique meanings we give to our experience and moving toward goals of our own creation and according to our individual attitudes.

Uniqueness and Commonality

Although we share the common biological needs of our species (air, water, food, shelter, and warmth) and the same basic physiology and body structure, our innate potentials differ from those of every other person. Though we share a vast number of similar experiences, what and how we perceive are open to an infinite variety of interpretations. We share our distinctive and unifying source of direction and movement with no other person. Our world views are extensions of our life-styles. We project our unique styles of living on all we encounter. We are neither predictable nor typical. We pursue our own goals and choose our own actions.

As the name, individual psychology, clearly implies, our singular styles of living define each of us as unique, and we define our uniqueness through the indivudual choices we make. In all our encounters with others, we must remain conscious of individual nuances and variations because, as humans, we are each unparalleled with potentials, perceptions, attitudes, characteristics, and values.

Explanation of Learning

While Adler affirms the value of learning in our growth and development, particularly in the formation of our life-styles, his explanation of how we learn is both general and limited. Apparently, he was more interested in what and where we learn than in any explanation of the exact learning paradigm. He focused on the early acquisition of social interest, the necessity of the democratic process, and the desirability of permitting natural and social consequences to prove their value in the learning process. He stressed the importance of understanding, patience, praise, cheerfulness, cooperation, and optimism. In brief, since Adler was convinced that we learn only what we believe is useful to us, the primary goal of the parent, teacher, or therapist is to encourage.

As indicated earlier, we are unique, active, creative beings, striving toward personally formulated fictions or life goals that we believe will lead us to our idea of perfection and completion, our concept of Utopia. We subjectively and creatively form associations, discriminations, generalizations, and definitions that fit our life-styles. We elect to learn only from those experiences that promise us success in our strivings, that assist us in overcoming or compensating for our perceived inferiorities, that help us to gain control of our lives. Conversely, we elect not to learn from those experiences that do not offer the promise of success. In summation, we choose to learn whatever serves our purposes, our meaning of life, and then act as if this were the only relevant and useful learning for our striving.

Adlerians (Dreikurs, 1950, 1964; Dinkmeyer, Pew & Dinkmeyer, Jr., 1979; Sweeney, 1975, 1981) believe reality is our most effective teacher. Specifically, we learn best from the natural and social consequences of our actions. Very early in life we learn that nature has its own recourse for those who choose either to ignore or to violate its laws. The natural consequences of our behavior can teach lasting, and sometimes painful, lessons. When we consume more calories than we burn, we gain weight. In a natural consequence the intervention of others is not required.

Social consequences of our actions prove equally effective in our education. Here, too, we learn in our early years that every group has expectations, rules, and regulations regarding the behavior of its members and that when our actions exceed the limits or break the rules, we risk and must accept the consequences. If the family agrees that only the clothes in the hamper are washed on washday, then the only consequence of not placing dirty clothes in the hamper is that they will not be washed until the next washday. Warnings, admonishments, and punishments are not involved; in fact, the question of power and the issue of punishment does not arise if the social consequence of an action is to be effective. The goals of learning are encouragement and cooperation, to teach the logic of social living.

Conditioning and Freedom to Choose

It should be remembered that the resolution of this issue emerged from Adler's final theory. As pointed out earlier (see "Biological and/or Social Determinants" and "Psychological and/or Reality Environment"), his theory underwent considerable development and elaboration over the years, especially in response to the issue of freedom. Adler moved from an absolute causality, or hard determinism, to a limited freedom to choose, or soft determinism, when he expanded his theory of counseling and psychotherapy to include the normal or healthy personality. In his mature theory, Adler subordinated causal determinants of behavior to a creative self, that "free creative power" that resides in each of us and enables us to choose the opinions and attitudes we hold toward our heredity and environments and, thus, to transcend nearly any situation or circumstance.

We apply our creative freedom by choosing to accept those experiences that fit our schema of apperception. We view what we experience through the unique doorways of our styles of living. Because it matters to us that the perceptions we accept affirm our life-goals and life-styles, we are actively and creatively determining how much and in what ways others and our environments influence us. Even as infants we develop skills and strategies to manipulate those around us to gain our own ends. We are the animated extension of our individual styles of life.

By choosing our life-styles, we are constructing a unique base that guides our singular law of movement. Our behavior is purposive and, therefore, predictable only in terms of probabilities. It is best, according to Ansbacher (in Burton, 1974) to "regard man *as if* nothing in his life were causally determined and *as if* every phenomenon could have been different" (p. 112, emphasis in original). Reality is an individual comprehension. Psychological phenomena are not simply reactions but individual creative responses carefully tailored to fit our styles of living. By interpreting and giving personal meaning to our experiences, we are self-determined. Our choice to act or not to act is based on the purpose and the function our action or inaction serves.

Importance of Role Assigned to Self-Concept

For Adler, the concepts of self, ego, personality, and life-style were synonymous. The self is the life-style; the life-style is a unifying set of convictions or beliefs about the self, the personality conceived as an integrated whole, the ego. Our life-style defines us as unique individuals both to ourselves and to others. It is responsible for our unity and self-consistency. The self gives us our creative power, freedom to choose, and self-determination, because not only are we each a representation of a unified personality (a self), but also we actively and creatively shape that unity (a creative self). We manage this by the meaning we choose to give our encounters with others and the world.

> All inherited possibilities and all influences of the body, all environmental influences, including educational applications, are perceived, assimilated, digested, and answered by a living, striving being, striving for a successful achievement in his view. [Adler, in Ansbacher and Ansbacher, 1964, p. 178]

The self, with its creative power, is the prime mover, the significant intervening variable in the structure of our personalities. The self keeps us from becoming the products of our biology and environments. We are interpreters of our circumstances.

Adler also introduces the concept of a guiding self-ideal that he uses interchangeably with the fictional goal (see "Number and Weight Assigned to

Motivational Concept"). From our private construction of perfection and completion emerges a guiding self-ideal, a personal and unifying concept of our forward movement. With our self-ideal, our personal view of future success, we are able to differentiate between useful and meaningless strivings. We feel a sense of security and support even as we are compensating for our previously perceived inferiorities. Thus, we create and build a model or an image of the self we want to become, and we move toward making that image a reality. The fact that our goal is fiction makes no difference; we act as if our subjective image were objective and strive for its successful completion.

Of the three terms, *self*, *creative self*, and *self-ideal*, Adler's concept of the creative self is the least specific. Though it appears to be synonymous with the life-style, it implies a freedom of choice. Adler usually defines the creative self as our way of affecting our perceptions, cognitions, emotions, and behaviors; however, he does, on occasion, seem to endow the creative self with a mystical quality similar to that proposed by Rogers (see Chapter 4).

Importance of Reward

Except to point to the fallacy of using an extrinsic reward system as an incentive in child training, the term, *reward*, seldom appears in the literature of individual psychology. According to Dreikurs (1964, 1972), reward, like punishment, emphasizes superiority and power, teaches favorable behavior only under coercion, restricts the healthy development of social interest, denies the sense of intrinsic satisfaction that comes from cooperation and participation, and stifles free and creative movement or striving. Encouragement, in contrast, is strongly emphasized in the literature (Adler, 1965, 1969, 1973; Dreikurs, 1957; Dreikurs et al., 1959; Dreikurs and Soltz, 1964).

Dreikurs et al. (1959) tell us that "the child needs encouragement as a plant needs water" (p. 23). If this statement seems strong, we need only recall that, from an Adlerian viewpoint, all forms of abnormal behavior are rooted in discouragement, the loss of courage that can occur when we are confronted with a life task for which we feel unprepared. Deliberate encouragement, according to the Adlerians, is the only antidote for discouragement and is, as such, an essential element in every phase of the therapeutic process. Dinkmeyer, Pew, and Dinkmeyer, Jr., (1979) refer to encouragement as "the prime factor in stimulating change" (p. 64), and according to Sweeney (1981), all people start life with a desire to discover, develop mastery of, and enjoy life. Through encouragement, we feed these inclinations and bring them to consciousness to be enjoyed all the more (p. 57). Any genuine affirmation of our inherent abilities, our physical and mental strengths, or our positive attitudes and expectations has the intrinsic capacity to renew our self-confidence and self-esteem, to motivate us to risk change and attempt novel life tasks. In brief, we regain our courage. We are encouraged by the understanding and caring of others, for their understanding and caring are an indication of their faith in us, in our abilities and competencies. Success of any kind encourages us: completing tasks, approaching problems as challenges rather than threats, setting and achieving goals, establishing attitudes, and developing skills that lead to mastery and independence.

To summarize, encouragement for the therapist is both goal and strategy and, for the therapeutic process, both means and end. Encouragement is fundamental to the development of a healthy life-style and primary to therapeutic intervention in a mistaken or unhealthy life-style.

GOALS OF ADLERIAN THERAPISTS

Although it would be relatively easy to compile a lengthy list of goals for Adlerian therapists, writers and practitioners in this field (Ansbacher & Ansbacher, 1956; Corey, 1982; Dinkmeyer, Pew, & Dinkmeyer, Jr., 1979) specify four major therapeutic goals for most Adlerians:

> To establish collaborative relationships with clients, based on genuine interest, respect, acceptance, empathic understanding, equality, and encouragement;
>
> To gain a comprehensive understanding of clients' life-styles, which includes (1) earliest memories or recollections, (2) the dynamics of their family constellations, (3) childhood disorders, (4) day and night dreams, (5) the exogenous factor (the tasks, occasions, or situations present at the onset of their symptoms, problems, or difficulties), and (6) the basic mistakes included in their styles of living;
>
> To interpret or explain clients' life-styles in a manner acceptable to clients so they will recognize, question, and alter the motivations and goals that are the purposes of their mistaken and, therefore, dysfunctional behaviors;
>
> To assist and support clients as the clients consider available options or alternatives (beliefs, feelings, goals, and behaviors) and experience new or different courses of action.

As discussed in later sections of this chapter, when these goals are accomplished satisfactorily, clients' feelings of inferiority are decreased, discouragement is replaced with courage, perceptions and goals are positively modified, and social interest becomes increasingly evident. Psychological distress may be decreased or cease to exist; however, this is not the primary purpose of therapy. Adlerian therapists are working with their clients to change goals, concepts, and attitudes, to unmask their life-plans. Purpose, not cause, is the primary goal of therapy.

THERAPEUTIC PROCESS: METHODS AND TECHNIQUES

Adler intended his theory to be a practical, common-sense approach for solving and preventing psychological and social problems. He expended much time and energy presenting his ideas to individuals and groups outside the medical profession, particularly to parents, teachers, and the clergy. Yesterday's intent is today's tradition. Adlerian institutes, workshops, and seminars are often open to and designed specifically for individuals and groups from a myriad of mental health professions including counseling, therapy, psychology, social work, education, and clergy from a broad variety of institutions. In addition, presentations, demonstrations, and workshops for the general public focus on topics such as marriage, the family, and parenthood.

To knowledgeable and experienced practitioners, the fact that Adler's ideas are widely applied by no means indicates that Adler's theory of counseling and psychotherapy is simplistic or that Adlerian therapy requires little training or experience. Quite the contrary, institutes offering professional certification training are usually at the graduate or postgraduate level, and there is no substitute for supervised experience in formally organized practicums and internships. Reading and study are essential for a full understanding of any therapeutic theory. The theory of individual psychology and therapy is no exception. Building therapeutic skills to a professional level in the practice of Adlerian therapy is equally essential and requires many hours of experience.

To be effective in the therapeutic process, Adlerian therapists must be highly skilled at establishing and maintaining a proper therapeutic relationship, at understanding and explaining the dynamics of the family constellation, and at analyzing and interpreting their clients' earliest recollections, dreams, and nonverbal communications. Their observational and analytical skills must be developed and polished to the greatest extent possible. Their timing must be exceptional, and their techniques and methods must remain flexible and creative.

Therapeutic Relationship

Convinced that all human behavior is purposive, that all human purpose is a personal creation, and that humans strive only for what serves their purposes, Adlerians regard the therapeutic process as a collaborative effort of equal and active participants and the therapeutic relationship as a partnership based on respect, parity, trust, and cooperation. All therapeutic endeavors are, of necessity, mutual endeavors, including the alignment of therapeutic goals and the assessment of therapeutic progress. Without cooperation, therapy cannot occur. The first postulate of Adlerian therapy, then, is to establish and maintain an accepting, caring, cooperative, interpersonal relationship with the client.

Convinced, too, that clients are discouraged when they enter therapy, Adlerian therapists work to develop and maintain a supportive relationship. Support, a synonym in Adlerian therapy for encouragement, can be expressed in a variety of ways. Accepting clients as persons of equal worth is supportive. Accurately reflecting their clients' feelings, or, to Adlerians an even higher form of empathy, communicating a deep understanding of their clients' life-styles, is supportive. It is therapeutic for clients to learn that their life-styles are logical in light of the goals they pursue, and the therapist's ability to understand and explain clients' styles of living in a genuinely accepting and caring manner results in more meaningful, cooperative, and therefore, supportive relationships.

Accurate understanding and interpretation of their clients' life-styles are expressions of the therapists' faith in their clients, their belief in their clients' creative power to choose and ability to change. Furthermore, expressions of faith by therapists encourage clients to consider options available to them and, then, to risk change.

Just as the infant-mother relationship facilitates the awakening, development, and expansion of the infant's innate possibility for social interest, it is the function of therapists to establish a therapeutic relationship that encourages clients to develop an active concern for the well-being of others. The therapeutic relationship forms a realistic model of social interest, an experience in cooperation. By relating to therapists who genuinely care and who, through their actions, demonstrate an interest in others, clients are encouraged to form similar relationships outside therapy.

Initial Procedures and Strategies

Although a number of different therapeutic stages, skills, and strategies are discussed in this chapter, the practice of therapy overlaps and integrates these elements. The client-therapist relationship, for example, does not end with the initial establishment of rapport or become less important to the therapeutic process when framing goals or interpreting the client's life-style. And certainly assessment occurs throughout the process of therapy; it is not something the therapist waits to do after therapy is terminated. Likewise, goal alignment is not a one-time, permanent operation; it is not unusual for client goals or expectations to be modified as therapy progresses.

Chapter divisions appear in this format because each area appears to play a significant part in the therapeutic process of Adlerian therapy, but Adlerians are committed to the idea that the unique life-styles of both therapist and client must determine the approach to therapy. Various therapeutic skills, strategies, and techniques will ultimately be integrated into the therapist's own life-style along with those essential qualities of genuineness and spontaneity that already exist.

Initiating Therapy. For Adlerian therapists, the importance of the initial phase of therapy cannot be overemphasized. A keen observer, Adler began the work of therapy even as his clients entered his office and, in many instances, formed tentative hypotheses or educated guesses about his clients' life-styles in the first few minutes of the initial interview. During the early phase of therapy, he relied primarily on unobtrusive observation, empathic listening, intuition, guessing, and patience.

Adler found nonverbal behavior especially insightful, and as his clients entered the room, he concentrated on their slightest actions, including their manner of dress, posture, gait, approach, facial expressions, tone and pitch of voice, eye contact, handclasp, and the distance they maintained. He intentionally did not indicate which of the three or four chairs, purposefully arranged at various distances and angles from his own, that his clients were to take because their selections helped reveal their life-styles.

Adler believed all clients introduce themselves according to their specific law of movement. Because behavior is purposive, each movement, each action or reaction, is indicative of the clients' life-styles. Because everything has some degree of significance, Adlerians work diligently to develop their observation and listening skills.

Subjective and Objective Conditions. Adler learned of his clients' subjective conditions by letting them talk about the situations, symptoms, problems, feelings, thoughts, and behaviors they believed brought them to therapy. He learned about their objective conditions by inducing them to discuss their life tasks, involving their work and interpersonal relationships.

The Question. At the appropriate time, usually before ending the first session, Adler asked The Question: What would be different if you were well? Not only would his clients' responses indicate whether or not their symptoms or conditions had psychological (as opposed to physiological) significance, they also would reveal the purpose of their symptoms or conditions, what they were attempting to avoid; that is, "I would be a better husband," "I would quit this job and start a new career," "I would be successful," "I would be able to accept the promotion that was offered to me." If, however, they responded, "Nothing, I just wouldn't have this headache," referral for a physical examination would seem justified.

Structuring. Without structuring, or goal alignment, a proper therapeutic relationship is impossible. Clients should leave the initial interview with a clear understanding that therapy is a collaborative effort, that they are expected to be active participants in the therapeutic process, and that, although there certainly is reason to hope, there is no promise of success.

Like the therapeutic relationship, structuring is not limited to the initial phase of therapy but is returned to many times throughout therapy. Resistance in Adlerian therapy is a sign of incongruence in the goals of the therapist and those of the client and signals a need for further structuring.

Discouraged when entering therapy, clients are prone to represent themselves as inferior and dependent. They often attempt to place the therapist in a position of leadership or authority. These displacement attempts must be consistently thwarted. The therapeutic alliance formed in Adlerian therapy is one of equality. Clients are encouraged to recognize their strengths because this recognition marks the beginning of success.

Course of Therapy

Very early in the course of therapy, usually after an initial rapport is established, Adlerlian therapists begin work toward a comprehensive understanding of their clients' unique styles of living by assessing their clients' family constellations and earliest memories. In recent years, both the formulation and assessment processes for these two important areas have been standardized. Many Adlerian therapists today employ *The Family Constellation Questionnaire* to gather pertinent information about their clients' perceptions of early family experiences (Sweeney, 1981) and follow formalized interview and assessment procedures for the interpretation of earliest memories (Dinkmeyer, Pew, & Dinkmeyer, Jr., 1979).

The Family Constellation Questionnaire. The Adlerian therapists, especially those with limited experience, should find this questionnaire helpful when investigating the life-styles of their clients. Both experienced and inexperienced therapists may wish to use the questionnaire as a time-saving device when exploring their clients' perceptions of the pertinent conditions prevailing when their clients were forming their life-style convictions.

The initial section of the questionnaire focuses on the client's parents and includes both factual data (names, ages, vocations, etc.) and subjective data (major personality traits, favorites, ambitions for the children, siblings most similar and dissimilar, etc.). The second section of the questionnaire deals almost entirely with subjective information. For instance: Which of the children was most like and unlike the client? Who fought and argued the most? Who played together? Who among the siblings took care of whom? The emphasis of the questionnaire then shifts back to the client: Indicate outstanding or unusual traits, ambitions, accomplishments, perceptions of physical development, strengths, and weaknesses. In the final section, clients are asked to rate themselves and their siblings on 24 characteristics or attributes, indicating who least exemplified and who most exemplified each characteristic—that is, greatest sense of humor and least sense of humor, most intelligent and least intelligent, most responsible and least responsible, and so on.

Because an infinite variety of life-styles does seem possible from even a single family, skilled analysis of the client's responses to *The Family Constellation Questionnaire* requires both knowledge and intuitive abilities. The Adlerian therapist acknowledges and understands fully the many factors considered influential in the development of personality, as well as the common styles of living identified by the theory. In addition, the therapist can recognize and understand patterns and trends to discern their similarities and differences, to see relationships, and to uncover implications, however subtly or illusively presented, as their clients describe their perceptions of the family atmosphere and their psychological positions in relation to other family members.

Similarities signal alliances, and differences may indicate rivalries or competition. Basic mistakes are implied in the clients' perceptions and strivings. Integration and summarization are important parts of the analytic task of the therapist. And, since encouragement is essential in therapy, the clients' strengths are a significant part of any summary.

Earliest Memories.   Adlerians are confident that when asked to relate their earliest memories, their clients will remember only those incidents that are consistent with their present perceptions of self, others, and the world. Furthermore, Adlerians are convinced that it is unnecessary to determine the validity of their clients' earliest memories because whether actual or imagined, genuine or manufactured, Adlerians believe that their clients' selections can never run in opposition to their life-styles. Moreover, because their clients think of their earliest memories as facts and are unaware of their meanings, they freely and openly reveal their self-defeating perceptions, attitudes, and goals—their overriding law of movement. Adlerian therapists view their clients' earliest memories as projections, consistent with the intent of their present strivings and their anticipations regarding the outcomes of their strivings. And while memory content is given first consideration, consistent themes and unifying patterns offer more coherent understanding of their clients' styles of living. Earliest memories also contain hints as to the degree of social interest, optimism, and courage present in their life-styles.

Again, as with the family constellation, the analysis and interpretation of earliest memories require the ability to elucidate implications, relationships, patterns, and consistencies and to integrate these discoveries into the client's present circumstances.

Day and Night Dreams.   Like human behavior, dreaming is purposive. Adlerians believe dreams train or prepare dreamers to solve present problems or to overcome present circumstances by rehearsing them for possible future actions. The dream mode, then, is present and future, and the dream function is to connect present problems or conflicts to future goal attainment.

Adler warned against therapists becoming too involved in uncovering common symbols when working with dream material since the symbols of one client's dream may represent something entirely different when present in the dream of another client. Nevertheless, he did refer to a few common dream symbols such as flying (moving or striving from below to above), falling (moving or striving from above to below), being chased (an expression of inferiority or weakness in relation to others), and being unclothed in public (fear of disclosure or being found out). The emotional tone of the dream may be more significant and revealing than the symbols involved.

Adlerians insist that the only valid dream interpretations are those that can be documented and integrated with the client's present problems, the family constellation, and earliest memories. Caution is thus the key because everything could be different.

Interpretation.   The third phase of therapy, the insight phase, involves interpretation of the client's beliefs and purposes. Not only is interpretation a major goal of Adlerian therapy, it is also a major therapeutic method or technique that requires both skill and experience. Interpretation in Adlerian therapy is holistic and teleological. It is concerned with the total movement of the client and calls attention to the direction, expectation, and consequences of that movement, enabling the client to understand both the movement and its meaning. When an interpretation is accurate, well timed, and communicated in a manner the client can understand and accept, it provides the client with insight into the purpose of a particular feeling, belief, symptom, or behavior.

To help make the interpretation palatable and avoid an authoritarian stance, the therapist usually presents it only as a possibility to be considered: "Is it possible . . . ?" "Do you think it might be . . . ?" An accurate interpretation encourages the client to view behavior from a fresh perspective; the client is free to recognize its validity, deny it outright, or offer an alternative explanation. Although presented tentatively, usually in the form of a question, the interpretative statement should be direct, clear, and specific.

The client who accepts and learns from the interpretation usually responds, if not verbally, then by some recognition reflex such as a quick smile, glance, or nod of the head. Adlerian therapists are alert for this signal, particularly from the shy, reluctant, or resistant client. In the early stages of therapy, it tells the therapist her guesses are on the right track. Client involvement is crucial during interpretation. Since every reaction to an interpretative statement has purpose, it is the function of the therapist to read the client's meaning.

Additional Methods and Techniques

Although Adler believed interpretation and encouragement to be the major methods of therapy, he did mention a number of specific techniques in conjunction with interpretation and encouragement in his attempts to facilitate his clients' awareness and understanding of their mistaken perceptions, beliefs, attitudes, and dysfunctional behaviors. Some of these techniques will be described.

The Surprise Tactic.   When Adler determined that a session was no longer moving and he wanted to jar the client into listening or being more receptive, he occasionally employed the element of surprise by doing the unexpected. He might, for example, suddenly side with or express appreciation of his client's defensive stance. When effective, the client would stop to consider the reason for the therapist's sudden shift in attitude or, better still, change roles and view the situation from a different perspective. Caution is advisable when using the surprise tactic since the client may feel ridiculed and become defensive.

Antisuggestion or Paradoxical Intention.   This technique appears most effective in functional behaviors such as stuttering or facial tics; however, it may be employed successfully in other instances. In antisuggestion or paradoxical intention, therapists encourage their clients to exaggerate, practice, or perform on a schedule the symptoms or behaviors they are attempting to avoid or overcome. Constant nail biters, for example, may be instructed to stop once every 2 hours during the day and intentionally bite their nails, right hands in the morning and left in the afternoon. Each evening they are to spend at least 3 minutes biting their nails in front of a mirror. Clients who complain of being unable to sleep may be instructed to stop trying; the next time they have difficulty sleeping they are to try not to sleep, to concentrate fully on remaining awake. Antisuggestion, like telling someone that they are not, under any circumstances, to think of an elephant in the next hour, often works in reverse. Moreover, by practicing a behavior, clients become overtly aware of the behavior and may gain some insight into the purposes it serves or the gains they derive from it. Fighting a behavior often only acts to strengthen it.

Avoiding the Client's Hidden Agenda.   This technique amounts to avoiding traps set by the client so the therapist will confirm a faulty assumption or mistaken attitude. As explained earlier, clients often form opinions and attitudes and then behave in a manner that invites confirmation; they fullfill their own prophesies. Examples of this are playing stupid to trap the therapist into being more explicit or taking the responsibility of therapy, thus confirming clients' beliefs in their helplessness or that others should serve them; seductive behavior from clients who believe all members of the opposite sex want them only for their bodies; working to fail at therapy because they are convinced they are failures or because they want to convince themselves and others that they have tried everything to get well and just cannot. Not only is it important that these clients' mistaken assumptions and private logic be challenged, but also it is important that counselors break their clients' self-fulfilling prophesies by not becoming entrapped in their snares.

Confrontation.   Confrontation is closely related to interpretation. However, it forces clients to face their private logic and to stimulate an immediate response. While interpretation is presented in a tentative manner, confrontation is much more intense, direct, and evocative. Confrontation may be descriptive of the clients' feelings, beliefs, and behaviors, the purposes of which clients are unaware, and may be in the form of a question—What were you telling yourself just before you became afraid?—or a statement—Although you are talking about how afraid you are, you are smiling.

Spitting in the Client's Soup, or Besmirching a Clean Conscience.   Adler borrowed this first phrase from a practice he witnessed in a private school dining hall. By spitting in their neighbors' soup, boys often obtained second helpings. The intent of this therapeutic technique is similar. By revealing awareness of the hidden purpose of a symptom or behavior, therapists deprive their clients of the personal satisfaction they receive from the secondary gains their symptoms or behaviors bring them. Private arena perceptions and thoughts are brought into the public arena of therapy and are de-energized as sources of client resistance or displacement. Like the boys in the dining hall, clients may continue to eat the soup, but it will never taste the same and they can never enjoy it as much.

Encouraging Clients to Act As If.   Clients who claim they would do thus and so *if only* they had this quality or that trait are encouraged to act for a short period of time *as if* they possessed the quality or trait they believed they lacked and to do the thing they wished to do. This technique is based on the assumption that when clients change their behavior they elicit different responses from others and learn that change is not only less risky than they thought but also rewarding. For example, the college freshman who would ask a woman for a date if only he had more self-confidence might be instructed to act as if he possessed self-confidence and for the next week to approach at least three women he liked and invite them to dinner and a movie. At the very least he would learn that he could ask a woman for a date, that it was not nearly as terrible as he thought it would be, and that he must possess at least some degree of self-confidence or he would not have accomplished the task agreed to in therapy.

Final Phase.   As clients gain insight into their mistaken perceptions and beliefs, they often begin to experience dissatisfaction and discomfort with their life-styles. At this point they usually discover that insight alone is not enough, that insight, however clear, must be translated into actions consistent with their newly formed and more rational perceptions and beliefs. Only when clients are thoroughly convinced that change is in their best interest is it possible to initiate the reorientation phase of therapy. Only when clients are committed and willing to face the risk of change is it possible to enter the final phase, the real purpose of the therapeutic process. Everything to this point has been preparation.

Dinkmeyer, Pew, and Dinkmeyer, Jr. (1979) believe that the first step in reorientation is the clear establishment of the client's goals and the determination of their realism because unrealistic goals serve only to discourage. Once clients decide on the kind of person they want to be and the kinds of relationships they want to establish, they can begin the serious investigation of alternatives that promise success in the achievement of their goals.

In the reorientation phase of therapy, therapists help their clients not only in the search for new and more appropriate meanings, purposes, and behaviors but also to understand how their beliefs and goals are related to their feelings and actions, as well as to assist their clients to determine and evaluate the possible consequences of any changes being considered.

Action is encouraged in the final phase of therapy. Clients are instructed to act as if they were already the persons they wanted to become and to act as if they possessed the courage to live differently. Realistic alternatives are selected and acted upon.

ASSESSING PROGRESS

Although Adler did not clearly specify methods for asssessing progress, he did, on occasion, address the question of success in therapy. Moreover, he advised therapists to keep a constant watch for their clients' movement. Any movement toward "the useful side of life" is an indication of progress within the life-style choices of the client.

From the holistic viewpoint, even the smallest change affects the whole. When clients recognize, understand, and alter a single mistaken premise, they are no longer the same as they were before that change. Their life-styles are different, and the difference is progress. Success, however, depends on whether or not that difference is sufficient for more effective living. Time, then, becomes the ultimate test of therapeutic success. The greatest improvement may come after therapy when the client must endeavor to establish and maintain a more socially interested and self-supporting orientation to life.

Adler often looked to his clients' earliest memories and dreams when attempting to assess therapeutic progress. Earliest memories change as mistaken beliefs and attitudes change. They reflect corrections of a faulty life-style.

Dreams are also expressions of the dreamer's life-style. Furthermore, because dreams are forward looking and rehearsals for future action, they can be especially helpful in progress assessment. For example, short dreams with little or no action may indicate little change; inability to recall dreams may in-

FIGURE 3.2 A Schematic Analysis of Adler's Stand on the Basic Issues

Biological Determinants	Social Determinants
Commonality	Uniqueness
Conditioning	Freedom
Early Development	Continuous Development
Psychological Environment	Reality Environment
Unconscious Determinants	Conscious Determinants

Importance of Group Membership	We are social beings; born dependent on our family group. Feelings of inferiority and a need to belong facilitate formulation of a life-plan and subsequently a life-style. Our schemas of apperception may be significantly influenced by our ordinal position within the family (family constellation). The quality of the infant-mother relationship is particularly crucial to the development of our social interest.
Explanation of Learning	We learn only that which serves our purposes, creatively and subjectively forming associations, definitions, discriminations, and generalizations that fit our life-styles. The natural and social consequences of our behaviors shape our learning; and the primary goal of the parent, teacher, or therapist is encouragement.
Number and Weight Assigned to Motivational Concepts	Adler presents a hierarchical conceptualization of motivation based on feelings of inferiority: we strive to overcome, to compensate for weaknesses. A fictional goal represents our desire for completion and perfection, and striving for that goal represents the primary motivating force behind every action. Healthy striving reflects social interest.
Importance of Reward	Extrinsic reward inhibits free, creative, and courageous striving. Intrinsic reward, however, facilitates a healthy life-style. Inner satisfaction comes with the courage to risk change and attempt new tasks, the experience of success, and through cooperative participation with others. Genuine affirmation and encouragement from others bolster our efforts to develop healthy, intrinsically satisfying life-styles.
Importance or Role of Self-Concept	Our self is our life-style, a unifying set of convictions, and with its creative power (freedom of choice), our self guides our striving. Our guiding self-ideal (fictional goal) represents the personal and unifying concept of our forward movement, allowing us to differentiate useful and nonuseful strivings and propelling us toward completion and perfection.

dicate the desire to postpone action; and frightening dreams or nightmares may indicate the wish to avoid action.

FINAL COMMENTARY

Adler's ideas have resurfaced in a number of current psychotherapies. Certainly, Adler should be credited as the forerunner of the present existential movement in the United States and for exerting a strong influence on the theories of Berne, Ellis, Glasser, Maslow, and Rogers. However, although there seems some promise of future research with the move of Adlerian therapy into academic institutions, Adlerian therapy has attracted few researchers, the result of which is a scarcity of empirical studies of either the theory or its effectiveness.

One possible explanation for the limited research is that when there are so few constructs to explain behavior as complex as that of humans, the application of those constructs, of necessity, is both general and vague. Imprecise applications of general theoretical constructs not only lack satisfactory guidelines for therapists who wish to practice the theory but also discourage scientific investigation.

Perhaps the vaguest and, therefore, most difficult Adlerian construct to understand is that of the creative self or the creative power. Although at times it appears to add freedom of choice to the style of life, on other occasions it seems to take on the mystical quality of free will that is totally independent of any prior experiences or development. The source of this power is unclear. Is it a part of the striving for perfection and completion and, therefore, innate, or is it similar to Rogers's explanation, a phenomenological expression of the healthy life-style, a feeling of freeom? In brief, although Adler's position on the individual's freedom to choose is clear, his explanation of the individual's creative power that permits this freedom is not.

Adler, like all theorists of counseling and psychotherapy, is not without his critics. In defining social interest as the only path to health, Adler implies that the development of social interest involves only cooperation and equality. Porchaska (1979), for example, questions this single approach to health: "It is ironic that Adler called his approach *individual* psychology when in fact he ultimately values social interests over the interests of the individual" (p. 196).

The application of Adler's theory in one-to-one therapy has declined somewhat over the years, but there has been a marked increase during the last 2 decades in the application of Adler's theory in the classroom, marriage and family counseling, and child-rearing practices. Some of the leaders responsible for the renewed interest in individual psychology and psychotherapy are

Ansbacher, Dinkmeyer, Dreikurs, Mozak, and Sweeney. As with all the theories included in this book, the chapter on Adler is not closed. Adlerian therapy has survived the test of time and holds promise for the future.

REFERENCES AND SUGGESTED READINGS

Adler, A. 1965. *Understanding human nature*, W.B. Wolfe, trans. Greenwich, Conn.: Fawcett.

Adler, A. 1969. *The science of living*, H.L. Ansbacher, ed. New York: Anchor Books.

Adler, A. 1973. *Individual psychology*, P. Radin, trans. Totowa, N.J.: Littlefield Adams.

Adler, A. 1974. *Social interest, a challenge to mankind*, J. Linton and R. Vaughan, trans. New York: Capricorn Books.

Ansbacher, H.L., & Ansbacher, R.R., eds. 1964. *The individual psychology of Alfred Adler, a systematic presentation in selections from his writings*. New York: Harper & Row.

Burton, A., ed. 1974. *Operational theories of personality*. New York: Brunner/Mazel.

Dinkmeyer, D.C., Pew, W.L., and Dinkmeyer, D.C. Jr. 1979. *Adlerian counseling and psychotherapy*. Monterey, Calif.: Brooks/Cole.

Dreikurs, R. 1950. *Fundamentals of Adlerian psychology*. Chicago: Alfred Adler Institute.

Dreikurs, R. 1957. *Psychology in the classroom*, 2nd ed. New York: Harper & Row.

Dreikurs, R. 1972. *The challenge of child training, a parents' guide*. New York: Hawthorne Books.

Dreikurs, R., with Soltz, V. 1964. *Children: the challenge*. New York: Hawthorne Books.

Dreikurs, R., Grunwald, B., & Papper, F. 1971. *Maintaining sanity in the classroom: illustrated teaching techniques*. New York: Harper & Row.

Dreikurs, R., et al., eds. 1959. *Adlerian family counseling, a manual for counseling centers*. Oregon: The University Press.

Herman, I. 1971. *Adlerian psychology, a review of therapy and counseling methods of Rudolph Dreikurs and Manford Sonstegard*. Chicago: Alfred Adler Institute.

Mozak, H.H., & Dreikurs, R. 1973. Adlerian psychotherapy. In R. Corsini, ed. *Current psychotherapies*. Itasca, Ill.: F.E. Peacock.

Orgler, H. 1963. *Alfred Adler, the man and his work: Triumph over the inferiority complex*. New York: The American Library.

Prochaska, J.O. 1979. *Systems of psychotherapy: A transtheoretical analysis*. Homewood, Ill.: Dorsey Press.

Sweeney, T.J. 1975. *Adlerian counseling*. Series 8, Guidance Monograph Series. Boston: Houghton Mifflin.

Sweeney, T.J. 1981. *Adlerian counseling, proven concepts and strategies*, 2nd ed. Muncie, In.: Accelerated Development.

4

The Person-Centered Therapy of Carl R. Rogers

CREATED FROM AND NURTURED IN the personal experience of therapeutic relationships, Rogers's theory of person-centered therapy has been in process for 4 decades. Both theorist and theory have undergone marked changes that, particularly early in Rogers's career, sometimes took surprising directions (Rogers, 1961, 1980).

Person-centered therapy is an established system of psychotherapy, supported by numerous loyal practitioners and backed by sound research, but this has not always been the case. Nondirective therapy, as Rogers's theory first became known, began in the early 1940s with the publication of *Counseling and Psychotherapy* and spawned great controversy in the therapeutic community. Not only were his ideas new, he also introduced therapeutic techniques that departed radically from then accepted approaches. Although a few members of the therapeutic profession welcomed his ideas, many considered them revolutionary and attempted to discredit both Rogers and his ideas by labeling his work naive and superficial. Heated debates were often conducted in the journals. It is important to note that Rogers was the first therapist to take an electronic recorder into therapy sessions and to analyze and study the exchange between clients and therapists. Furthermore, he used both recordings and transcripts in his teaching and research, practices welcomed by therapists in training and by researchers investigating the therapeutic process.

A decade later, and only slightly less controversial, nondirective therapy became client-centered therapy when Rogers (1951) changed his focus from the techniques of the therapist to the perceptions of the client. As the name implies, this approach centered on the inner-subjective world of the client.

In 1974, after extensive scrutiny of the therapeutic value of the close interpersonal relationship—the I-Thou relationship affirming both participants—Rogers and his colleagues again changed the name of their system of psychotherapy to the more descriptive *person-centered therapy*. Rogers has been committed consistently to the belief that theory should be viewed as process and, as process, be open continually to the data provided by experience and research. Holdstock and Rogers (1977) cite five stages that characterize the development of the current person-centered approach:

Precursor stage,
Nondirective stage,
Client-centered stage,
Experiential stage,
Person-centered stage.

It appears, then, that the future can only hold the promise of innovation for Rogerian theory and practice.

Although there have been evident changes in the implementation of Rogers's approach to psychotherapy, the basic constructs or principles that make it distinctive have remained relatively constant over the years. Rogers brings us an optimistic and humanistic theory based on a deep underlying faith in our inherent actualizing tendency. He credits us with an innate, organismic wisdom, as well as the freedom, for positive self-direction within the actualizing process. He continues to address our need to give and to receive unconditional positive regard. He challenges us to be aware, to be open to new experiences, and to take risks. In brief, he encourages us to live our lives fully in the present, trusting ourselves in the process.

Today, the person-centered approach of Carl Rogers receives enthusiastic response from large numbers of adherents in a wide variety of professions: counseling and psychotherapy, education, medicine, social work, rehabilitation, religion, business, industry, group work, and community relations. Perhaps no other American has had greater influence or impact on psychotherapy than Rogers. Although person-centered theory is considered strictly an American phenomenon, Rogers's books and articles are printed in numerous languages, and his theory is taught in universities around the world. According to Rogers (1980), "I had expressed an idea whose time had come" (p. 49).

BIOGRAPHICAL SKETCH

Seldom do we have the opportunity to witness a single theory of psychotherapy evolve and grow over a 40-year period or find theorists willing to share fully their personal life experiences with us. Carl Rogers offers both. Rogers's theory of counseling and psychotherapy is especially shaped by autobiography since he trusts personal experience as his ultimate guide, and because he remains open to new experiences, he is willing to change his views and to modify his theory.

Students who wish to study Rogers's life in greater depth are referred to his books, *On Becoming a Person* (1961) and *A Way of Being* (1980). Both are largely autobiographical. For the most part, each is a collection of previously published papers, talks, and articles written in first person singular; prepared for a wide variety of groups, occasions, and journals; and organized into a gestalt. Readers are often left with the impression that Rogers is speaking directly to them.

Early Years

Born January 8, 1902, the fourth of six children in what Rogers (1980) later describes as "a narrowly fundamentalist religious home" (p. 27), he introjected the righteously tolerant, aloof attitudes of his parents toward people outside the immediate family and led a solitary childhood with "no close friend and only superficial personal contact" (p. 29).

As a child, Rogers (1980) was certain that his parents loved him but just as certain that he would be "judged and found wanting" (p. 28) should he share any of his personal thoughts, feelings, plans, or dreams with them. Although he was close to his younger brother, the five years that separated them made sharing of any depth difficult.

As an adolescent, Rogers (1961) was painfully aware that he was socially inept. He was a loner throughout his high school years. Still, Rogers learned to appreciate the independence of solitude. He developed a voracious appetite for reading, devouring every book he could find, including encyclopedias and dictionaries. Further, he actively pursued an intense scientific interest in agriculture and a fascination with a species of the night-flying moths found in the woods near his home.

Education

At 17, Rogers enrolled in the School of Agriculture at the University of Wisconsin, the school attended by his parents, his two older brothers, and his sister. College marked a turning point in his social development. He met regularly with a self-directed group of young men at the YMCA and, for the first time, experienced the meaning and value of good friends. He began dating that year, also, and met Helen Elliot, the first person with whom he could be fully open and trusting.

Rogers was one of ten American students selected in 1922 to attend the World Student Christian Federation that met in Peking, China. During the 6 months he traveled with this group, Rogers accepted more liberal religious views and broke with his parents' fundamentalist religion. About this time he decided to prepare for the ministry, changed his major to history, and transferred to the College of Arts and Letters. In 1924, he received his A.B. degree and married Helen Elliot. They moved to New York where he entered Union Theological Seminary for formal study of the ministry.

Discouraged with academic religious courses after 2 years, Rogers transferred to Teachers College, Columbia University, concentrating on clinical and educational psychology. Here, Rogers was introduced to the teachings of John Dewey. He received his M.A. degree in psychology in 1928 and began his intership at the Institute for Child Guidance. Rogers completed his dissertation on personality adjustment in children and was awarded the Ph.D. in clinical psychology in 1931.

Emergence of Person-Centered Therapy

The seeds for person-centered therapy may have been sown in childhood experiences, but germination occurred during the 12 years Rogers worked at the Society for the Prevention of Cruelty to Children in Rochester, New York. During this period Rogers held the positions of psychologist (1928 to 1930), director of the Child Study Department (1930 to 1938), and in 1939, when the agency was reorganized and renamed the Rochester Guidance Center, Rogers was appointed director. Rogers's personal priorities changed from an analytic interest in diagnosis to the process of counseling and psychotherapy. He became convinced, particularly after careful study of many recorded counseling sessions, that the techniques of counseling should focus on the development of a free and permissive counselor-client relationship and of the client's self-understanding.

Rogers moved from an agency to an academic setting in 1940, when he accepted a professorship at Ohio State University. Here, his ideas about the techniques of counseling were put to the test of the searching and discriminating questions of his graduate students who, in the process of becoming counselors and therapists, wanted reasons for the techniques they were learning. *Counseling and Psychotherapy*, Rogers's second book, was published in 1942.

In addition to teaching, doing research, and writing, Rogers was active during the 1940s and 1950s in a number of professional organizations. He was chairman of the Clinical Section from 1942 to 1944 and president of the American Association for Applied Psychology from 1944 to 1945. He served as vice-president of the American Psychological Association (APA) and of the Division of Clinical and Abnormal Psychology from 1949 to 1950.

After 5 productive years in Ohio, Rogers joined the faculty of the University of Chicago and, with the assistance of his graduate students and colleagues, continued to research the counseling process and to develop his theory. It was here that he wrote *Client-Centered Therapy* (1951), the title applied to his theory for many years.

Rogers returned to his home state in 1957, accepting joint appointments in the departments of psychology and psychiatry at the University of Wisconsin. Rogers and his colleagues organized the Psychotherapy Research Group, which designed and conducted a lengthy, complex study of psychotherapy with hospitalized patients diagnosed as schizophrenics. The results of this extensive research program were published in a 1967 book, *The Therapeutic Relationship and Its Impact: A Study of Psychotherapy with Schizophrenics*. While at the University of Wisconsin, Rogers published one of his most popular works, *On Becoming a Person* (1961), a book widely accepted by the general public as well as by professionals in the field.

In 1964, Rogers moved to California as resident fellow of the Western Behavioral Sciences Institute. Joining with others in 1968, Rogers contributed to the formation of the Center for Studies of the Person at La Jolla. An increasing dissatisfaction with traditional educational practices in the United States, coupled with the conviction that the therapeutic relationship is but a single instance of all interpersonal relationships and communications, led Rogers to write *Freedom to Learn* (1969). He proposed a student-centered, experiential approach to learning that called for radical change in the educational system of the 1960s. *Freedom to Learn* drew heavy criticism from the traditionalists, and Rogers, once again, was immersed in controversy. The major impact of *Freedom to Learn*, it seems, was on the thousands of teachers across the country who were individually seeking new and innovative ways to facilitate learning in their classrooms.

In addition to working for greater freedom in the U.S. educational system, Rogers was involved in the encounter group movement from the beginning and still considers the intensive group experience one of the most exciting and potentially significant social forces in facilitating individual and institutional change. Rogers (1970, 1980) is especially interested in the process of the encounter group. He shares with his readers some of the personal group experiences that helped him to become more open, revealing, transparent, and spontaneous. Essentially, he learned to risk being himself in the interpersonal relationship of the therapeutic process, whether with an individual or with a group. Perhaps one of the greatest changes in Rogers's theory over the years is his concept of the facilitative therapist, a way of being with self and others.

Looking to the future, Rogers (1980) believes current developments and trends will "profoundly transform our concept of the person and the world that he or she perceives" (p. 347), will "constitute a 'critical mass' that will produce drastic social change" (p. 347), and "will be in the direction of more humanness" (p. 356).

Accomplishments and Awards

Rogers's list of publications is impressive. His first article appeared in 1930, and with the exception of 3 years in the 1930s, he has published each year since. He is the author of 14 books, hundreds of articles and papers, and chapters in numerous edited textbooks. Rogers's works have been translated into more than a dozen languages, including Japanese, Spanish, Portuguese, Italian, and German. In addition to his writing, he has prepared an extensive library of tapes, films, and video cassettes that are used in counselor education programs around the world.

Ten years after serving as vice-president of the APA, Rogers received that organization's most prestigious award, the Distinguished Scientific Contribution Award. In 1972, Rogers was honored by the APA once more, this time with the highly prized Distinguished Professional Contribution Award. He was recognized a third time, in 1977, when three presentations of special papers were scheduled at the APA convention in San Francisco as a tribute to his seventy-fifth year.

Rogers was elected to the highest offices of the American Association of Applied Psychology and the APA. He has been appointed or elected chairman of many important committees and divisions within these and other professional organizations.

Rogers has been awarded honorary degrees from Lawrence College and from Leiden University, Holland. Columbia University presented him with the Nicholas Murray Butler Silver Medal in 1955, and in 1957, he was appointed to the honorary Knapp Professorship at the University of Wisconsin. He is a diplomat in clinical psychology of the American Board of Professional Psychology. Few people have been honored more by their colleagues than Carl Rogers.

RESOLUTIONS OF THE ELEVEN BASIC ISSUES

Whether or not Rogers is in full accord with the eleven basic issues that structure the theories presented in this book, he has, in the course of developing a comprehensive theory, addressed them in his writing. The position of the issues in the hierarchical arrangement presented here was assigned by the present author and, therefore, may be open to debate. However, as pointed out in the first chapter, the advantages of the issues approach far outweigh any risk of disagreement.

Biological and/or Social Determinants

Rogers (1951, 1961, 1980) has constructed a person-centered theory of personality development around a strong biological core. He is convinced that all living things enter this world with an inherent actualizing tendency, a biological drive to actualize, maintain, and enhance the self, an inner motivation, or will, to become. Furthermore, Rogers (1951) explains that our biological actualizing tendency provides us with a naturalistic value system, or bodily wisdom, to differentiate between actualizing and nonactualizing experiences and to select behavioral options that facilitate the growth and development of our innate potentials. We are, then, according to Rogers, inner-directed, forward-moving, positive beings, innately good.

Since we possess a natural predisposition to actualize our innate potentials, it would seem that self-actualization should be both simple and easy. In reality, such is not the case. Our actualizing tendency, Rogers reminds us, requires external stimulation that can be provided only by the physical, social, and cultural environments in which we live. Environmental conditions are not always conducive to healthy growth and development. In fact, we often encounter stimuli that are hostile to the actualization of our potentials. We are thrown into a world in which we are driven to become what we potentially are. How much we realize our potentials depends to a large extent on how favorable the conditions of our world are to human development.

Rogers's response to those who claim his is a deterministic stance is that the inborn, forward movement of the actualizing tendency is away from external control toward an experiential freedom, a sense that we are free to live our lives in the manner we choose. Because we are rational, choosing beings, we can, to the degree we experience a sense of freedom, transcend our biological and environmental influences. By recognizing our creative ability, Rogers stands with the existentialists and moderates on the issue of biological and/or social determinants of behavior. Our sense of being free is an inextricable part of our inherent actualizing tendency that, in turn, can only be initiated by stimuli from our environments.

Number and Weight Assigned to Motivational Concepts

As Rogers's resolution of the previous issue indicates, there is but one all-encompassing, master motivational construct: the actualizing tendency—an inherent, sovereign drive to actualize our potentials. The actualizing tendency is rooted in the physiological processes of our bodies and encompasses all our needs from the most basic maintenance needs such as air, water, food, and shelter to the most complex and sophisticated enhancement needs such as autonomy, self-reliance, freedom, and creativity. Rogers sees this forward-moving life force, this tenacity to become, in all living things. Our behavior is guided and energized by this unitary active force of energy that aims to the future and strives for the fulfillment of self-directed goals and purposes to facilitate our growth and development.

Two special, learned needs emerge from the actualizing tendency and require our understanding: the need for positive regard and the need for self-regard. These two important needs are considered later in this chapter. However, it is noted here that these two needs can work at cross purposes with the actualizing tendency by influencing us to distort or deny our perceptions of our experiences.

Psychological and/or Reality Environment

Rogers's position on this issue is radically phenomenological. Rogers (1980) views holding to a belief in a reality or in a real world as "a luxury we *cannot* afford, [and] a myth we dare not maintain" (p. 104, emphasis in original). For Rogers, there is no absolute world but a world of multiple realities, "millions of separate, challenging, exciting, informative, *individual* perceptions of reality" (p. 106). We live in separate worlds, worlds we create with our subjective interpretations of our experiences. At the very center of each of our perceptual systems, Rogers sees the self-concept.

In Rogers's view, we respond to our worlds as we experience and perceive ourselves, others, and events. Because our worlds are private, our responses cannot be predicted by another person with any degree of certainty. Moreover, because some of our experiences are subceived (stimuli not symbolized and, therefore, not part of our awareness), we are somewhat unpredictable even to ourselves—a condition that can create a great deal of confusion, even consternation.

The implications of separate, private, subjective realities are apparent. If we wish others to know and understand us, we must share our perceptions of our worlds with them. Likewise, if we desire to know and understand others, we must relate to them in a manner that makes it possible for them to open their worlds to us. We need not agree with another's views of reality to accept and affirm them as subjectively valid.

Early and/or Continuous Development: Critical or Significant Life Stages

Over the years, Rogers apportioned little space in his writing to development per se. He has not proposed a schedule of specific developmental stages through which we must pass during our lifetimes. However, work by Holdstock and Rogers (1977) recognizes a number of important developmental periods in our lives, periods of genetically determined biological changes and culturally determined social growth. Here again, however, no timetable of specific life stages was identified.

Rogers has consistently directed our initial attention to the period of early childhood because it is during this period, he claims, that we begin the construction of our self-concepts and learn the needs of positive regard and of self-regard. We enter this world with a number of inherent, functioning attributes (see "Biological and/or Social Determinants"). We become a part of an undifferentiated phenomenal field, and we perceive our experiences as reality. However, even as newborns, the bodily wisdom of the actualizing tendency enables us to differentiate between those experiences that facilitate the actualization of our potentials and those that do not. Moreover, as infants, we trust fully this inner way of knowing, this innate will to health.

The same tendency toward differentiation that serves us in choosing actualizing over nonactualizing experiences serves us also as we begin to develop our self-concepts, to discern and own those experiences that are part of our functioning while designating ownership of other experiences to people and objects in our environments. As these perceived self-experiences accumulate, we begin to form our self-concepts.

Whether because of our totally dependent condition as infants or because the self-concept contributes to our maintenance and enhancement, we learn during this early period the need for positive regard. Rogers (1951) describes this universal need as the desire to experience warmth, acceptance, respect, admiration, and love from our significant others. In addition to defining it as a learned need, Rogers tells us that the need for positive regard is so pervasive and persistent that it can inhibit the actualizing tendency. Should our need for the positive regard of others become inordinately strong, we may choose to become other-directed as a way to meet it. Unfortunately, other-directed behavior is often antithetical to the self-direction of the actualizing tendency.

A second learned need that arises during this period is the need for self-regard. We discover rather early in our lives that, while it is important to be accepted and loved by others, it is important also to like and respect ourselves. When we feel positively about ourselves or experience self-worth, our self-concepts are not limited to the assessments of others, even significant others. We can then evaluate our experiences in terms of our actualizing tendency.

These three theoretical constructs are included here because the self-concept and the needs of positive regard and self-regard emerge during early childhood. It is important not to lose sight of the fact that, although Rogers considers this a highly significant period of our lives, he does not list it as critical in the sense of being impossible to overcome or to change. A theory based on an inherent actualizing tendency naturally leads to an acceptance of and a commitment to continuous growth and development.

In summary, we actualize ourselves according to our hereditary directives, particularly the forward-moving actualizing tendency. We have the potential and the motivation to become more differentiated, complex, self-directed, socialized, and fully functioning as our experiential world broadens and as our choices remain clearly perceived and accurately symbolized.

Importance of Role Assigned to Self-Concept

Early in his practice, Rogers considered the term, *self*, vague and abstract, best left to philosophers and poets. However, daily contact with clients who continually related their situations, feelings, and attitudes in terms of their selves and who had entered and remained in therapy with the hope that they might become more their real selves, led Rogers to view the self as a distinct and important theoretical construct for understanding human experience. Over the years, Roger's descriptions of the self-concept became more explicit and organized, particularly regarding attributes and function. Today, it is one of the most operational and researched theoretical constructs in the field of counseling and psychotherapy.

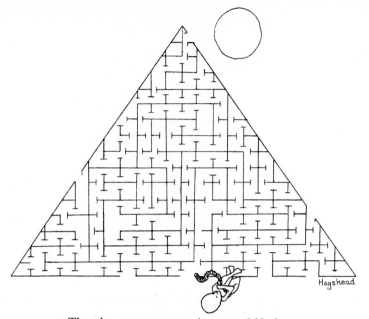

Though we encounter environmental blocks,
hereditary directives move us on to actualize.

The discussion of the importance of the role assigned to the self-concept appears at this point, not because it is considered less important than the issues preceding it but because the resolutions presented earlier contain concepts and ideas judged important for the understanding of this most significant theoretical contribution.

From our total phenomenal field we differentiate certain of our experiences as self-experiences. We perceive and symbolize the physical experiences of our bodies. We interpret and categorize our interactions with other people and with objects in our environments. We become aware of a feeling of separateness, a subjective feeling of being, or having, a self. As we mature, our symbolizations become more complex, and our self-perceptions form into an organized, conceptual gestalt, which each of us perceives as the I, me, and my. Our self-concepts are fluid; they grow and change as we do. At any instant, however, we can perceive our self-concepts as entities with specific characteristics, traits, values, and attributes. These self-perceptions, although not always in our awareness, are admissible to our awareness. Though differentiated from our other-perceptions, we often assume and act on within ourselves those views we assume about our worlds. Rogers views the self as both an entity and a process, both an actuality and a potentiality. Still, Meador and Rogers (1979) remind us that our selves do not do anything;

rather, our selves serve to symbolize our present, conscious self-experiences and are reflections of our actualizing tendency.

As pointed out in the discussion of the previous issue, with self awareness we develop the need for positive regard. This need remains persistent and pervasive and has the potential to exert even greater force than the actualizing tendency. Meeting our need for positive regard depends on whether or not we experience positive interactions with others, especially with those persons we perceive as significant in our lives. Unconditional positive regard—a feeling of acceptance, approval, and love—facilitates the actualizing tendency and enhances our selves. As we develop self-regard, we come to believe that we have sufficient inner strength to achieve autonomy.

Conditional regard (I love you when . . . or I love you if . . .) hinders the actualizing tendency because we feel valued in some respects and devalued in others. With conditional regard we experience conditional self-regard. Our feelings of worth are dependent on others, and we strive to define our selves in terms of the values set by the conditional regard of others. We become closed to the bodily wisdom of our actualizing tendency, and because we need positive regard, we become closed to those experiences inconsistent with the conditions set by significant others in our lives. We become outer-directed rather than inner-directed, dependent rather than autonomous, closed rather than open to our experiences, rigid rather than flexible in our self-concepts, and experience self-estrangement rather than self-fulfillment.

When the gap between our self-concepts and our experiences becomes too great, we experience incongruence, which in turn elicits some degree of anxiety, defensiveness, and disorganized behavior. Incongruence need not be perceived at a conscious level to occur. It may be subceived, not symbolized, and therefore not in our awareness. Anxiety in this instance is often described as free-floating anxiety.

In summary, positive regard from others leads to self-regard and results in a fully functioning individual who is accepting of self and others and open to nearly all experiences. Conditional regard leads to conditional self-regard and results in an individual who is distrusting of self and others and who selects, distorts, or denies experiences.

Conscious and/or Unconscious Determinants of Behavior

Determining Roger's position on this issue proved difficult. Although his existential stance in the 1960s clearly favors conscious determinants of behavior, since the late 1970s it appears that Rogers (1977, 1980) is tempering the importance of the role of consciousness in the functioning of healthy people. Where once he hypothesized that our actualizing tendency could operate only when our choices were "clearly perceived" and "adequately symbolized"

(Rogers, 1951), he now seems to think that when we are healthy and functioning well, our actualizing tendency may elicit actualizing behaviors even though our needs are not symbolized (Rogers, 1980). The unconscious processes may serve as dependable, intuitive directives from the actualizing of healthy persons, enabling them to be wiser than their intellects if they trust and act on their intuitions (Rogers, 1980).

Rogers (1980) is reluctant to predict any timetable, but he believes that our evolutionary flow may bring us other sources of self-knowledge, including sources that transcend reason. In *A Way of Being*, he writes of the possibilities of paranormal or uncommon perceptions and experiences and of the possibility of separate and different realities or levels of reality.

Although Rogers may be revising his view of consciousness, his concept of the unconscious differs considerably from that of the psychoanalytics. Certainly it is not the animalistic, demonic, impulsive unconscious posited by Freud; Rogers's unconscious represents another doorway to self-knowledge. It epitomizes a part of the organismic tendency toward fulfillment, a trustworthy tendency toward fulfillment, a trustworthy tendency that expresses itself "in the widest range of behaviors in response to a wide variety of needs" (Rogers, 1980, p. 123).

Conditioning and/or Freedom to Choose Behavior

As indicated in the discussion of previous issues, Rogers is well aware of the influences of our biology, environments, and past experiences on our behavior. Nevertheless, his experiences with the therapeutic process convince him that the unitary, motivating force of the actualizing tendency is away from external control and conditioning and toward an experiental freedom, an inner sense or subjective feeling that we can think independently, live authentically, determine our own values and directions, and accept the consequences of our choices and actions. Since freedom is an integral part of the actualizing tendency, the more we conquer our inner fears, the more we increase our self-regard by overcoming the conditions of worth introjected during our early childhood years. Further, the more open we are to our experiences in the present, the greater is our realization of the freedom to will and choose and the more likely we are to choose wisely.

Because Rogers believes we are inherently unpredictable (see "Psychological and/or Reality Environment"), it follows that we have some degree of freedom to choose our destinies. It also follows that the more we facilitate or enhance our actualizing tendency, the greater the degree of freedom we experience. A healthy self-regard gives us the power to choose our attitude toward nearly any situation and to mediate consciously the influence that situation will have on us. With the freedom to choose our attitudes, we can change the influence of past experiences and our expectations of the future; we have the potential to create our own lives.

Explanation of Learning

Roger's consideration of the learning process focuses on significant, meaningful, experiential learning that includes both thinking and feeling. The person-centered learning described by Rogers (1969) is self-initiated, self-directed, self-appropriated, self-evaluated, and self-rewarding. Only this special kind of learning gives us a sense of self-discovery and makes a difference in our attitudes, behavior, and personalities.

Rogers believes that certain conditions must exist for person-centered learning to occur. We must experience a sense of freedom—freedom to think, to feel, to believe, to express, to act, and to follow our own paths and purposes—governed largely by curiosity and interest. We are able to do this when we feel trusted and respected, when we perceive and symbolize that our counselor or teacher genuinely believes in us and in our capacity to learn, when we do not feel that we are being judged and evaluated, and when external threats are at a minimum and we can trust our actualizing tendency. Rogers (1969) cautions us, however, that even when these conditions exist, learning may not be easy. In fact, when learning involves a threat to our self-concepts, it can be painful, and our natural tendency is to resist. Learning the process of learning, "a continuous openness to experience and incorporation into oneself of the process of change," is "the most socially useful learning in the modern world" (Rogers, 1969, p. 163).

Uniqueness and/or Commonality

We share with others of our species the common biological needs, processes, and predispositions of our inherent and formative actualizing tendency, as well as innumerable common stimuli from our physical, social, and cultural environments. Each of us can recall occasions when our perceptions, thoughts, and emotions were shared by others.

Person-centered theory encourages us to recognize and accept our commonalities. However, it places even greater emphasis on the importance of recognizing and accepting our uniqueness. Holdstock and Rogers (1977) encourage us to "accept that your eyes and ears and brain select, perceive, and process information differently from anyone else" (p. 143). We do not perceive our physical, social, and cultural environments the same (see "Psychological and/or Reality Environments"). We are forced to accept the idea that we live in separate realities. Although we share an inherent tendency to fulfill our potentials, in no two of us are these potentials identical. Even when potentials are similar, given the infinite possibilities of living in this world, their actualization will almost certainly occur to a greater or lesser extent.

Rogers's position on this issue might best be summarized by the following statement: "Person-centered theory recognizes the unique individuality of each person as well as the relatedness of each person to the other—the necessity of community" (Holdstock and Rogers, 1977, p. 147).

Importance of Group Membership

The position of this issue in the hierarchical order of presentation is not a true indication of its importance within person-centered theory. It appears here because the writer decided that the resolutions presented earlier contribute to a fuller understanding of the importance of group membership.

As disclosed earlier, Rogers believes that we are naturally gregarious. He informs us that we need and strive for positive regard from others. Only when that positive regard is unconditional do we develop healthy self-regard. Our sources of unconditional positive regard are limited or, in some cases, nonexistent. Therefore, many of us settle for conditional self-regard, thinking of ourselves as worthwhile only when we meet the expectations of others.

Formal groups, associations, and organizations normally offer conditional positive regard to the membership. There are specific conditions, whether explicitly stated or subtly implied, for belonging. Because the needs for positive regard and self-regard are expressions of our actualizing tendency, it is important for us to find at least one group that facilitates the fulfillment of these needs. Rogers (1970) thinks the encounter group—a planned, intensive group experience—may be one way to provide us this opportunity. He believes the encounter group offers "psychological growth promoting effects" (p. 129), especially to those of us experiencing difficulty in adapting to change, clarifying values, overcoming feelings of depersonalization or alienation, improving interpersonal relationships, or becoming more self-reliant (pp. 172–182).

Importance of Reward

A review of the literature of person-centered therapy reveals that Rogers is interested in but one kind of reward, self-reward. All experiences that facilitate the inherent actualizing tendency are sought and prized. With self-rewarding activities, we are aware of an inner subjective sense of satisfaction, as well as an increased sense of self-regard. Experiences we perceive as harmful or dysfunctional to our maintenance or enhancement are not valued and are avoided. Person-centered therapists, because of their strong commitment to self-reward, do not intentionally employ reinforcement to guide or manipulate their clients; they endeavor to provide an atmostphere in which the actualizing tendency of their clients will naturally unfold and express itself.

Examples of facilitating and rewarding experiences appear throughout this chapter, but a few seem worth repeating here: sharing close interpersonal relationships in which each person experiences affirmation by the other (see "Therapeutic Relationship"); experiencing the freedom and the courage to choose and actively pursue our goals, directions, and purposes; expanding our feelings of self-worth or self-regard; and having creative experiences.

GOALS OF THE PERSON-CENTERED THERAPIST

Rogers (1951, 1960, 1961, 1980) believes the primary goal of the therapist is to provide a climate that facilitates the innate actualizing tendency of the client. Essentially, a relationship is created in which the client is encouraged to grow, to become fully functioning. The counselor-client relationship is the essence of the Rogerian therapeutic process. Everything that happens in therapy occurs within this special person-to-person, I-Thou relationship. To the uninitiated or to the therapist accustomed to working in a system where clear behavioral objectives and outcomes are known in advance, this goal may appear vague, unsystematic, and unscientific. However, those familiar with the basic principles of Rogers's theory realize that person-to-person therapy is an open system of psychotherapy. It deals with the inner subjective lives of people, their perceptions, feelings, attitudes, beliefs, values, hopes, fears, and aspirations.

Person-centered therapy is a process of personal exploration and discovery. Specific, individualized, client objectives or outcomes emerge from the process. The direction of exploration and the specific nature of the client's discoveries are not known by either the client or therapist at the start of the process. Since the client is in the best position to know which directions best fit his or her needs, the therapist chooses to be a facilitator rather than a director.

The therapist's goals are directly related to the therapist's attitudes. To facilitate the client's awareness of and trust in his or her inner direction, the person-centered therapist expresses an attitude of uncompromising trust or faith in the actualizing tendency of the client. The therapist believes that the client's innate predisposition to become is a constant therapeutic ally, that the client's will to health is ever present, positive, and predictable. Therapy, then, promotes conditions that facilitate natural growth and development. The therapist's attitudes and intent become the criteria for judging method and technique.

THERAPEUTIC PROCESS: METHODS AND TECHNIQUES

Patterson (1959) observes that, "when [therapists'] techniques are subordinated to attitudes, they in effect cease to be techniques in the strict sense of the word" (p. 185). This observation is in agreement with Rogers (1951), who views the counselor as totally engaged in and focused on an empathic understanding of the client; thus, "it is no longer a technique in operation, but the implementation of an absorbing personal purpose" (p. 112). The difference between the utilization of a technique and the implementation of an attitude seems to be the amount of personal meaning or value that attitude holds for the counselor or therapist and the degree of concentration given to its implementation. The genuinesness of the therapist's belief and intent is the key variable. The therapist's self is the instrument of therapy.

Therapeutic Relationship

Even a brief review of Rogers's resolutions of the eleven basic issues reveals that he is convinced that an intensely personal and subjective person-to-person relationship is the heart of the therapeutic process. Further, it is evident that Rogers believes that three conditions are directly related to the therapist's attitudes and intent, and all must be present and communicated in the relationship if the therapist is to create an atmosphere for the client that is growth promoting. Since these three conditions are considered both necessary and sufficient for an effective psychotherapeutic relationship, they merit special attention.

Genuineness.   The first of the necessary and sufficient conditions of psychotherapy Rogers calls genuineness, realness, or congruence. In *A Way of Being* he writes, "The term 'transparent' catches the flavor of this condition" (Rogers, 1980, p. 115). For the therapist it is the risk of letting the self go, of giving up roles and facades, so the interaction with the client becomes an encounter with a significant other whose intention it is to be helpful. It is a matter of being genuinely and immediately present and accessible in the relationship so the therapist is

> [W]ithout any conscious thought about it, without any apprehension or concern as to where this will lead, without any type of diagnostic or analytic thinking, without any cognitive or emotional barriers to a complete "letting go" in understanding. [Rogers, 1978, p. 65]

The person-centered therapist literally launches him- or herself into the process, trusting fully the outcome.

The implication of the therapist's self as the instrument of therapy is rather awesome. There is an undeniable obligation of the person-centered therapist to examine his or her attitudes and intent to know, refine, and improve the self as an instrument. The method and techniques of the person-centered therapist is to be without method and techniques, to be therapeutically present and to remain congruent in the relationship.

Acceptance.   The second major condition that Rogers includes is acceptance. Again, acceptance is not communicated by any method or technique in a strict sense or by what the therapists do to or for their clients. Rather, acceptance is communicated only when clients perceive that their therapists genuinely and consistently hold accepting attitudes toward them. Rogers

(1961, 1960, 1980) defines acceptance as a deep and genuine caring for the client as a person; a positive regard or prizing without reservations, conditions, judgments, or evaluations; a respect for the client's individuality, complexity, freedom, and potential; and a firm belief or faith in the client's innate goodness as a human being, regardless of his or her present situation, values, feelings or behaviors.

Rogers is convinced that, in the person-to-person relationship, the attitudes held by the therapist will be communicated to and eventually perceived by the client, whether genuine or phony, positive or negative, constructive or destructive. Thus, for therapists to communicate caring, they must genuinely care, and to communicate acceptance, they must genuinely accept. Conversely, clients will not feel accepted until they believe someone genuinely accepts them just as they are and will not feel worthwhile until they believe someone treats them with dignity and respect.

If the person-centered therapist should experience negative feelings or attitudes toward a client, making it impossible to offer that client unconditional positive regard, immediate self-examination is required. If, after an honest and thorough search of self, these negative feelings persist, authenticity requires that the therapist own and disclose them, or refer the client to a therapist capable of offering the necessary conditions of therapy. For the person-centered therapist to play a role, or to act as if the proper attitudes were present when they are not, is not only unethical but also destructive to both the therapist and the client.

Empathy. Empathic understanding is the third condition of person-centered therapy. Empathy exists in the counseling relationship when therapists sense accurately, and moment by moment, the feelings and personal meanings their clients are experiencing and, subsequently, communicate this understanding to their clients.

Empathy requires person-centered therapists selflessly to lay aside personal values, needs, meanings, and expectations so they can immerse themselves in their clients' inner subjective worlds. When empathy is present, there is both cognitive and emotional congruence between the therapist and the client. The client's internal frame of reference is assimilated by the therapist, and this assimilation is then communicated to the client. Rogers tells us that it is as if the person-centered therapist were the client but quickly warns that the therapist should never lose sight of the *as if* quality of the relationship. The self-as-instrument is as important in the communcation of empathy as it is in the communication of genuineness and acceptance. The therapist's self, therefore, remains the therapist's referent throughout the therapeutic relationship.

It is often possible to define empathy through therapist responses that attend to and reflect client feelings. Further, accuracy can be checked by listening for client confirmation. In their attempts to be fully with their clients, person-centered therapists learn to suspend personal evaluations and judgments. As a result, explanations, questions, and advice are avoided. The following dialogue is fairly typical person-centered opening with a client experiencing free-floating anxiety.

Client: My doctor recommended counseling, and when I told my friend this, he suggested I see you. I guess they both think my problems are psychological (nervous laughter, hands clenched tightly).

Therapist: That bothers you a little—to think your doctor and your friend believe your problems are psychological.

Client: Yes it does . . . a little. I went to the doctor because I thought I might be having a heart attack. Everything was fine until about three or four weeks ago. Then, while I was driving to work, my hands and feet suddenly became cold—almost as though they were immersed in icewater. My heart began to pound and I had this cold, tight feeling in my chest. I felt lightheaded, and I thought I was going to pass out. It was really scary. I didn't know what to do. I pulled to the side of the road hoping someone would see me and stop to help. No one did. It went away after awhile, and I drove home.

  I was relieved at first when the doctor told me there was nothing physically wrong—at least it wasn't my heart. But it's still scary, especially not knowing what's wrong with me. I think I could handle it if I knew what makes me feel like this. All I can do when it happens now is think, Oh my God, here it comes again.

Therapist: Knowing would help. It's not knowing what causes these feelings that makes you anxious. Telling you there's nothing physically wrong doesn't help. You need to know what to do to stop them.

Client: Right. It's as though I'm losing control. It just happens to me, and I can't seem to do anything about it.

Therapist: As it is now, you're helpless. No matter how hard you try to fight it when it starts to happen, it happens. You don't know what to do.

Client: Yeah. And I feel embarrassed too. I think . . . well, if it isn't physical, then I should be able to do something about it. I should be strong enough to fight it.

Therapist: It's as though these feelings are part of some foreign, outside force that is stronger than you are. It's as though you're being invaded by some invisible force over which you have no control.

Client: Ordinarily, I'm a pretty strong person. I mean, I don't usually let things get to me like this. It isn't like me to feel like this.

Therapist: You've always been in control—on top of things. Now, suddenly, you're experiencing feelings that just aren't like you. It's scary to feel out of control and helpless. It's scary to think you might not be the strong person you've always believed yourself to be.

Client: Right. But how do you fight something when you don't know what it is? I can't fight something that isn't there.

Therapist: It sounds a little silly as I say it, but it would be easier for you to accept something physically wrong.

Client: At least I'd have something to fight. I'd know what was wrong and what I'd have to do.

Therapist: You could still see yourself as a strong person. You wouldn't have to see yourself as scared and helpless.

Client: I don't like what this is doing to me. I like to be independent. I'm afraid to drive alone now because I worry about what might happen if these feelings hit me and I black out when I'm driving or when I'm alone somewhere.

When therapists experience empathy, they manage to stay with their clients, and their clients feel understood. They feel that they have at last found someone who truly understands. Empathy also communicates acceptance and caring. Clients feel their therapists accept them, without judging and evaluating.

Rogers cautions person-centered therapists that they are not immune to the power of the relationships they establish with their clients. When genuineness, acceptance, and empathy are present, the climate of the therapeutic relationship is growth promoting for both participants. The more involvement person-centered therapists offer in the relationship, the more they benefit from it. Conversely, becoming an ineffective or poor counselor or therapist may indeed be detrimental.

Initial Procedures and Therapist Strategies

There is only one procedure in person-centered therapy: the establishment of a facilitative relationship, a climate that promotes change and growth in its participants. The therapist's strategy throughout therapy is the communication of the therapist's attitudes and intent, particularly those considered essential to effective therapy: genuineness or congruence, acceptance or unconditional positive regard, and a deep empathic understanding. Prerequisites have been discussed in some detail in the preceding sections of this chapter. Before moving to a discussion of the course of therapy, however, it is worthwhile to review how the person-centered therapist opens the initial counseling session.

Initiating Therapy. In the person-to-person approach to therapy, the therapist might open the first session by saying, "This is our first session together; I hope we can use this hour to get to know each other better, to understand one another in some meaningful way." Not only does the therapist hope to establish a here-now presence with this statement, he or she also wants to introduce the idea that the relationship is the process of therapy. Further, by expressing an interest in the client as a person, the therapist avoids focusing on the client as a person with a problem or of giving the client the impression that the therapist's intent is to solve the client's problems. This is the therapist's first attempt to communicate the attitudes of genuine interest and caring. Thereafter, the direction of therapy is decided by the client.

Client Expectations and Structuring.   Person-centered therapists are well aware that their clients' initial perceptions of them and of therapy are influenced significantly by the expectations they bring to the first counseling session. However, rather than attempting to describe the therapeutic relationship or process, person-centered therapists count on the client's direct sensory experiences of the process to structure the person-centered approach. Many practitioners believe that any attempt to describe intellectually the character and purpose of the person-to-person relationship or the process of the person-centered approach is needless and may impede the process of therapy.

Most person-centered therapists agree that therapy is possible only when the client decides personally to enter therapy or, if referred, to remain in therapy. Little can be achieved if the client is forced into therapy, or if the client is there only to please someone else.

Course of Therapy

When therapists are able to provide the necessary conditions of the intensive therapeutic relationship, and when clients can permit themselves to experience those conditions, a natural, observable process of client change or movement begins. The literature of the past 30 years is replete with reports of the course and effectiveness of person-centered therapy; however, considering the space allotted to this topic, a summary of that research is impossible. Following is a brief outline of the numerous objective and subjective descriptions of client change or movement within the therapeutic process recounted throughout the writings of Rogers (1951, 1961, 1967, 1980).

In the security of relationship in which they experience genuine acceptance, deep personal understanding, and unconditional positive regard, clients in person-centered therapy become less defensive and more open to their perceptions. Experiences that were once subceived, inaccurately perceived, or denied because they threatened the clients' self-concepts are permitted accurate symbolization and are subsequently integrated. This integration results in a greater congruence between the self and experience for these clients, as well as an increasing openness to new experiences. Also, as clients become more integrated, they become more spontaneous and better able to live fully in the moment.

Experiencing acceptance and unconditional positive regard from their therapists, clients in person-centered therapy develop an increasing positive regard for themselves as persons of worth. They develop confidence in their ability to form standards and to be self-directing. They learn to trust their decisions, particularly as their perceptions become more differentiated and as their goals and ideals become more realistic and achievable. Finally, they become more objective, more rational, and less emotional.

Consistently accepted without conditionality, clients begin to experience unconditional positive regard for others and become more accepting of the world. Though less likely to conform, they become more tolerant of customs, traditions, and situations.

Client movement in person-centered therapy is away from facades, from the rigid and tyrannical shoulds or musts, toward openness and trust in inner direction, the bodily wisdom of the actualizing tendency. Client growth in the course of therapy is best summarized by Rogers (1961): "This openness of awareness to what exists at *this moment* in *oneself* and in *the situation* is, I believe, an important element in the description of the person who emerges from therapy" (p. 116, emphasis in orginal).

ASSESSING PROGRESS

As noted in the previous section, the process of client change in the course of effective therapy has been studied extensively by Rogers. From his data, Rogers (1961, pp. 132–156) developed a process scale comprised of seven behavior stages:

> (1) Feelings and personal meanings, (2) manner of experiencing, (3) degree of incongruence, (4) communication of self, (5) manner in which experience is construed, (6) relationship to problems, and (7) manner of relating. [Meador and Rogers, 1979, p. 165]

Using this process scale, it is possible to determine the current behavior stage of a client by analyzing the content of a taped therapy session. Periodic analysis of tapes permits the therapist to assess both the amount and rate of client growth during therapy.

The Q-sort technique (sorting applicable self-concept statements from those not applicable) has also been used by person-centered therapists to assess client growth in therapy. Used in conjunction with the process scale, particularly with the behavior stages related to self-constructs, it is possible, for example, to assess change in congruence between the self and the self-ideal of a client.

FIGURE 4.1 A Schematic Analysis of Rogers's Stand on the Basic Issues

Biological Determinants		█		Social Determinants
Commonality			█	Uniqueness
Conditioning			█	Freedom
Early Development			█	Continuous Development
Psychological Environment	█			Reality Environment
Unconscious Determinants			█	Conscious Determinants

Importance of Group Membership	We are naturally gregarious, and we need and strive for positive regard from others. Our need for positive regard and self-regard are manifestations of our actualizing tendency, and only when we receive unconditional positive regard do we develop healthy self-regard. All too often we receive conditional regard and, perceiving ourselves as worthwhile only when we meet others' expectations, we develop an inhibiting, conditional self-regard.
Explanation of Learning	Person-centered learning focuses on self-discovery, the personal meaningful experiential learning occurring on both affective and cognitive levels. Nonthreatening environments and unconditional positive regard promote the sense of freedom requisite to self-discovery and, subsequently, to effective learning.
Number and Weight Assigned to Motivational Concepts	Rooted in our biology, the actualizing tendency is an innate, sovereign drive to actualize potential, encompassing both our most basic needs for survival and our needs for self-enhancement. All behavior is guided by this unitary force, which aims for the future and fulfillment of growth facilitating goals. Learned needs, however, may work at cross-purposes with this tendency by influencing perceptual distortions or denial of experience.
Importance of Reward	For Rogers, there is but one kind of reward: self-reward. We seek and prize experiences that facilitate our actualizing tendency and bring us a sense of inner satisfaction and increased self-regard.
Importance or Role of Self-Concept	From our total field we differentiate experience, formulating self-perceptions as organized, conceptual gestalts perceived as *I*, *me*, or *my*. Fluid and subject to change, at any given moment the self is perceived as distinct. Indeed, self is both an entity and a process, an actuality and a potentiality.

Person-centered therapists, like most therapists of other systems of psychotherapy, have neither the time nor the inclination to assess the progress of every client formally. Nevertheless, most use informal criteria to determine whether or not their clients are benefiting from therapy:

1. Is this client becoming less defensive, more open to his or her experiences?
2. Is this client more able to own and to take responsibility for his or her feelings and actions?
3. Is this client becoming less rigid, more tolerant or accepting of self, others, and the world?
4. Is this client becoming more independent, more self-directing?
5. Is this client becoming more objective, more rational?
6. Is this client more able to live in and enjoy the present?
7. Is this client less anxious, less fearful, less unhappy than when he or she entered therapy?

The questions will vary with the client and the therapist, but when they can be answered affirmatively, the therapist is satisfied that therapy is progressing well. Negative responses, conversely, should cause the therapist to look for ways to improve the conditions of therapy.

FINAL COMMENTARY

Although a theory of psychotherapy may be clear, comprehensive, parsimonious, philosophically sound, and persuasive, the crucial test of any theory is empirical validation. Rogers has never been defensive about his theory. He views his theory as he views the person, always in the process of evolving or becoming. Skeptical of dogma, Rogers believes in evidence, of being open to experience and research data. All theoretical formulations, by definition, are tentative and subject to investigation. Not only did Rogers submit his hypotheses for testing, but he and his followers, graduate students, and colleagues, also developed new research methods and instruments, while contributing heavily to the literature of research. This was particularly true when Rogers worked in academic settings that encouraged and rewarded high research productivity.

Certainly Rogers's theory is heuristic. His hypotheses regarding the controversial nature or role of the self and the self-concept, in both personality development and psychotherapy, created an explosion of empirical investigations during the 1950s. To investigate the process and outcome of psychotherapy, Rogers was the first to record and analyze the content of the therapeutic session. His theory has generated more research than any other system of psychotherapy, and his efforts have stimulated others to examine their personal theories and therapeutic styles. Even his severest critics acknowledge his contributions. Perhaps the greatest acknowledgment granted

Rogers is the fusion of many of his ideas and methods into other systems of counseling and psychotherapy.

For all the accolades, nevertheless, disproving critics remain vocal. Some note that much of the research on person-centered therapy is questionable because it is based primarily on the self-reports of the subjects under investigation. Others point to methodological errors: lack of control groups or the use of control subjects who are not candidates for therapy, failing to control for placebo effects, inappropriate statistics, heavy relaiance on correlational studies, limited instruments, and lack of follow-up studies for recidivism. Still other critics object to the number of subjective and abstract concepts that tend to defy operational definition and accurate measurement. Nevertheless, in spite of its critics, Rogers's person-centered approach to counseling and psychotherapy remains an extremely popular theory after more than 3 decades.

In comparison to other theories, when viewed from the vantage point of the eleven basic issues, Rogers's theory of person-centered therapy is clear, consistent, comprehensive, highly applicable, and heuristic. Rogers responds explicitly and fully to every issue selected for this book. His resolutions are reflective of his close alliance with the humanistic psychotherapies. The writer encountered only one major difficulty, which is discussed under the section, "Conditioning and/or Freedom to Choose." Although he assumes a phenomenological stance, which is deterministic, he grants the client both the will and the freedom to choose, to become self-directing. This appears inconsistent. However, when this issue is accepted as a polarity (see Chapter 1), neither freedom nor determinism could exist without the other: each concept receives meaning from the other. Further, from a phenomenological stance, when the freedom to choose is perceived and experienced by the client, it is, for that client, reality. This may be an example of the tertium quid referred to in Chapter 1; freedom to choose may be a reality only when perceived and experienced, and, when it is thus, that individual can, at least to a limited degree, transcend the determinism of conditioning.

There have been a few major changes in his basic theoretical assumptions for a number of years, and Rogers (1980) appears more confident in the validity of his theory and more conscious of its wide applicability. This is evident in his preface to *A Way of Being*, as he writes about the change from client-centered therapy to a person-centered approach: "I am no longer talking simply about psychotherapy, but about a point of view, a philosophy, an approach to life, a way of being, which fits any situation in which *growth*—of a person, a group, or a community—is part of the goal" (p. ix). Rogers's interests have moved beyond the one-to-one counseling relationship, the small personal growth groups, and human relations training sessions. He is now working to apply the person-centered approach to solve human problems in a much wider social context, including institutional change, labor-management disputes, and interracial and intercultural struggles on community, national, and even world levels.

REFERENCES AND SUGGESTED READINGS

Boy, A.V., & Pine, G. J. 1982. *Client-centered counseling: a renewal*. Boston: Allyn and Bacon.

Coulson, W.B., & Rogers, C.R., eds. 1968. *Man and the science of man*. Columbus, Ohio: Charles E. Merrill.

Frick, W.B. 1971. *Humanistic psychology: interviews with Maslow, Murphy, and Rogers*. Columbus, Ohio: Charles E. Merrill.

Holdstock, T.L., & Rogers, C.R. 1977. Person-centered theory. In R. Corsini, ed. *Current personality theories*. Itasca, Ill.: F.E. Peacock.

Meador, B.D., & Rogers, C.R. 1973. Client-centered therapy. In R. Corsini, ed. *Current psychotherapies*. Itasca, Ill.: F.E. Peacock.

Meador, B.D., & Rogers, C.R. 1979. Person-centered therapy. In R. Corsini, ed. *Current psychotherapies*, 2nd ed. Itasca, Ill.: F.E. Peacock.

Patterson, C.H. 1959. *Theories of counseling and psychotherapy: theory and practice*. New York: Harper & Row.

Patterson, C.H. 1980. *Theories of counseling and psychotherapy*, 3rd ed. New York: Harper & Row.

Rogers, C.R. 1939. *The clinical treatment of the problem child*. Boston: Houghton Mifflin.

Rogers, C.R. 1942 *Counseling and psychotherapy: newer concepts in practice*. Boston: Houghton Mifflin.

Rogers, C.R. 1951. *Client-centered therapy: its current practice, implications, and theory*. Boston: Houghton Mifflin.

Rogers, C.R. 1960. My philosophy of interpersonal relationships and how it grew. In H. Chaing and A.H. Maslow, eds. *The healthy personality, readings*, 2nd ed. New York: D. Van Nostrand.

Rogers, C.R. 1961. *On becoming a person*. Boston: Houghton Mifflin.

Rogers, C.R., ed. 1967. *The therapeutic relationship and its impact: a study of psychotherapy with schizophrenics*. Madison, Wis.: University of Wisconsin Press.

Rogers, C.R. 1969. *Freedom to learn: a view of what education might become*. Columbus, Ohio: Charles E. Merrill.

Rogers, C.R. 1970. *On encounter groups*. New York: Harper and Row.

Rogers, C.R. 1972. *Becoming partners: marriage and its alternatives*. New York: Delacorte.

Rogers, C.R. 1974. Remarks on the future of client-centered therapy. In D.A. Wexler and L.N. Rice, eds. *Innovations in client-centered therapy*. New York: John Wiley & Sons.

Rogers, C.R. 1977. *Carl Rogers on personal power*. New York: Delacorte Press.

Rogers, C.R. 1980. *A way of being*. Boston: Houghton Mifflin.

Rogers, C.R., & Dymond, R.F., eds. 1954. *Psychotherapy and personality change: coordinated studies in the client-centered approach*. Chicago: University of Chicago Press.

Rogers, C.R., & Stevens, B. 1967. *Person to person: the problem of being human*. Lafayette, Calif.: Real People Press.

5

Existential Approach to the Psychotherapy of Rollo May

THERE IS NO SINGLE THEORY of existential psychotherapy; it is a divergent theoretical arena. While some agreement exists among existential therapists, they have not achieved the unanimity of thought necessary for the establishment of a separate, clearly defined system of psychotherapy. Hence, rather than a special theory or method, existentialism can be considered an approach to therapeutic practice, as well as an attitude held, prized, and expressed by counselors and therapists. Rollo May (1977, 1983), whose works were selected as the primary source for this chapter, supports this perspective. Moreover, he contends that any attempt to establish a single theory of existential therapy at this time would be a serious mistake. Indeed, he believes that the nature of the existential attitude makes even the idea of a separate school or theory impossible.

In *Existence* (May, Angel, & Ellenberger, 1958), May traces the philosophic lineage of existentialism to nineteenth century Europe. He cites Edmund Husserl, the founder of modern phenomenology, and Soren Kierkegaard, the tormented Danish philosopher and theist whose rhetorical treatises criticized the prevalent reductionistic view of humans, as the two main precursors of existentialism. Ahead of their time, Husserl's and Kierkegaard's works were largely unnoticed until shortly after World War I, when their concerns were echoed in the writings of philosophers, such as Martin Buber, Fëdor Dostoevski, Martin Heidegger, Karl Jaspers, Gabriel Marcel, and Paul Tillich.

Rooted in the French resistance to German occupation during World War II, existentialism again moved through Europe and, in the 1950s, spread to the United States. Jean-Paul Sartre and Albert Camus were two outstanding spokesmen of this period. Both were awarded the Nobel Peace Prize in Literature.

Existentialism became a viable force in art, literature, and religion, and as often happens with popular movements, it attracted intellectuals, university students, as well as various groups of dissidents. A small group of independent psychoanalysts, disquieted with the reductive Freudian view of humans, felt that existential analysis added both breadth and depth to the therapeutic concepts and understandings presented by Freud and developed an existential approach to therapy. Two of the more influential persons to follow this path were the Swiss psychiatrists, Ludwig Binswanger and Medard Boss.

Among the advocates of an existential approach to psychotherapy in the United States are May, Abraham Maslow, Carl Rogers, James Bugental, Clarke Moustakas, Adrian Van Kaam, and Irvin Yalom. According to May (May, Angel, Ellenberger, 1958; May, 1977, 1983), one of the most ardent American exponents of existentialism, the existential approach to therapy provides a sound, flexible philosophy that lends meaning to, and can be integrated with, many of the current humanistic or third-force theories of counseling and psychotherapy, including, for example, three rather different therapies presented in this book (see Chapters 4, 6, and 8).

Although he rejects much of Freud's theory, May (May, Angel, & Ellenberger, 1958) asserts that many of the Freudian and existential positions are complementary and can be integrated. Both positions ask fundamental questions about human existence, focus on the rational and irrational sides of human nature, are concerned with the ways conflict and anxiety impede human growth and functioning, and concentrate on understanding human nature. Under the influence of Freud, Adler, Kierkegaard, and Tillich and an intense personal experience and interest in anxiety, May developed a theoretical approach that closely follows existential philosophy.

BIOGRAPHICAL SKETCH

Early Years

Rollo May was born April 21, 1909, in the small town of Ada, Ohio. He was the second of six children (three boys and three girls) and the eldest son of Earl and Matie May. As a child May detested the name, Rollo, which had been selected for him by his mother. She had named him after Little Rollo, a juvenile hero in a series of nineteenth century character-building books by the New England churchman, Jacob Abbott. Throughout his childhood, Little Rollo's exploits were presented to May as the model for proper conduct. May's intense dislike for his name remained with him until, as a young adult living in Europe, he learned of a medieval Norman leader, referred to as Rollo the Conqueror; the name, Rollo, suddenly became acceptable.

While May was very young, his father, a field secretary for the YMCA, moved the family from Ohio to Michigan. Through his father's association with the YMCA, May was subjected to a planned regimen of swimming and character building. He developed a closer relationship with his father than with his mother, who, he said, did not make him feel acceptable. Looking back on his early years, May *(Current Biography Yearbook 1973)* "pictured himself as a loner in childhood, unaware of being friendly and appealing" (p. 282).

Education

May entered Michigan State College, but his stay there was brief. He and a friend had founded a campus magazine, *The Student*, and, convinced that they had evidence, published an editorial charging the state legislature with using the college to conceal graft. Expecting dismissal, May set out for Oberlin College in Ohio to which, after an hour's conference with the dean, he was admitted without formal application. Majoring in English and minoring in Greek history and literature, May received his B.A. degree in 1930. On the basis of his credentials, in spite of the fact that he had no knowledge of the Greek language, May was offered and accepted a position teaching English at Anatolia College in Salonika, Greece. He held this position for 3 years, and during two summer vacations he visited Vienna where he enrolled in seminars conducted by Alfred Adler. To support his stay in Vienna, May worked as secretary for the International School of Art and in his free time studied painting. His work with Adler marked the beginning of May's interest in psychoanalysis.

May returned to the United States in 1933 and enrolled in the Union Theological Seminary in New York. Feeling responsible for his younger brothers and sisters after his parents' divorce, May withdrew from seminary at the completion of his first year and returned to Michigan. He was employed as a student adviser and counselor at Michigan State College from 1934 to 1936.

In 1936, May returned to New York and the Union Theological Seminary. Completing his studies under Paul Tillich, who, like Adler, strongly influenced May's thinking, he was graduated cum laude with a B.D. degree in 1938.

May began his ministry in a Congregational parish in Verona, New Jersey. His 2 years there were filled with disappointments, and he enrolled in Columbia University to major in clinical psychology. Again his studies were cut short; this time the crisis came in the form of tuberculosis. Faced with a fifty-fifty chance of surviving, May entered a sanatorium at Saranac Lake in upstate New York where he remained for 18 months. His struggle with death reinforced his existential leanings, and he was especially impressed with Kierkegaard's explanation that anxiety is the result of a threat to one's being. He learned from this experience that he alone had to decide whether he lived or died.

Though not fully recovered, May worked as a counselor at New York City College in Manhattan while he completed his work in clinical psychology at Columbia University. He received his Ph.D. in 1949. Shortly before completing his doctorate, May became a member of the faculty of the William Allanson White Institute of Psychiatry, Psychoanalysis and Psychology, and, in 1957, was appointed an adjunct professor of clinical psychology at New York University. May has also served as visiting professor or lecturer at other universities including Harvard, Yale, Princeton, and Cornell.

Two faces of anxiety: one that motivates and one that paralyzes.

Emergence of Existential Approach to Therapy

Recognized as a classic and prophetic work today, May's doctoral dissertation, *The Meaning of Anxiety*, was published in 1950. After comparing and synthesizing the existing theories of anxiety, May challenged the popular view that health was life without anxiety and argued that anxiety, at least the free-floating anxiety experienced by most people, is both normal and essential to the human condition. For May (1977), normal anxiety is the phenomenon of increased intelligence and characterizes human risk taking and creativity. An inordinate amount of anxiety can paralyze, but normal anxiety motivates positive change. May contends that in an age of anxiety, self-realization is the result of confronting and coping with the tension that emerges with every new possibility and from the threats to being that all persons encounter.

In *Man's Search for Himself*, May (1967), concerned with the human dilemma of living in a society marked by traumatic change, decimating values, and vanishing myths, offers his readers the opportunity to encounter their "problems of personal integration" (p. viii). Following an approach reminiscent of Karen Horney's *Self-Analysis* (1942) and the humanistic perspective of Eric Fromm, May guides us to a clear understanding of the causes of emptiness, loneliness, and boredom predicated by various forms of anxiety. Further he assures us that we have the capacity to achieve greater self-consciousness and, with it, the qualities of honesty, integrity, responsibility, courage, and love in our relationships with others.

Accomplishments and Awards

In 1955, the New York Society of Clinical Psychology presented May their award for Distinguished Contribution to the Profession and Science of Psychology. *Love and Will* (1969) brought him the Ralph Waldo Emerson Award from Phi Beta Kappa in 1970.

May was named visiting professor at Harvard (1965), Princeton (1967), and Yale (1972). He was appointed to the position of dean's scholar at New York University in 1971, and regent's professor at the University of California, at Santa Cruz, in 1973. May has received a number of honorary degrees, including the D.H.L. from the University of Oklahoma in 1970, the LL.D. from Regis College in 1971, and the L.H.D. from Vincent College, 1972; Michigan State University, 1978; Rockford College, 1977; and Cedar Crest College, 1978.

May is a fellow of Bradford College, Yale University, the APA, and the National Council on Religion in Higher Education. He is a member of the board of directors of the Manhattan Society for Mental Health and the Foundation for Arts, Religion and Culture. He serves as a trustee of the American Foundation of Mental Hygiene, and he is a member and past president of the New York State Psychological Association. At present Dr. May is a member of the adjunct faculty of Saybrook Institute Graduate School of Psychology, San Francisco.

RESOLUTIONS OF THE ELEVEN BASIC ISSUES

May intentionally makes no attempt to systematize his approach to psychotherapy. It was often necessary, therefore, to pursue his resolution of an issue through numerous sources. Moreover, while some of the eleven basic issues presented here are of concern to May and are resolved clearly and comprehensively, others are not. In one or two instances, the resolutions had to be inferred by the writer.

Terminology and nomenclature employed by existential writers are often elusive and imprecise, as well as difficult to grasp and apply in the therapeutic situation. May, though a stimulating and careful writer, is no exception. Terms such as *daimonic, being, potentiality,* and *ontological guilt,* are vague and difficult to define. Further, a psychoanalyst, May refers to the psychoanalytic dynamisms of his background but always in terms of their meaning for the existential situation in immediate experience. The result many times is a new meaning for a familiar term, requiring adjustment in both understanding and thinking.

Following a basic-issues approach imposes an arbitrary and rigid structure on May's unstructured approach. There is always the danger that May, as well as other existentialists who reject any attempt to systematize their approach, might find this structure objectionable.

Biological and/or Social Determinants

For May (1958, 1977, 1983), we are experiencing beings existing in a world. We and our world are a reciprocal totality, a unity, each dependent on the other for existence and neither understandable except in relation to the other. May (1982) describes this reciprocal relationship most succinctly in an open letter to Carl Rogers: "It takes culture to create self and self to create culture; they are the yin and yang of being human" (p. 12). Being and world are, therefore, intensely personal. We are viewed as subjects who can never be separated from the object we experience without loss of being. Our world exists as we relate to it and design it. Both our being and our world are in process and necessarily centered in coexistence. Isolation from self, others, and the world results in feelings of estrangement and alienation—in short, anxiety (in May, Angel, & Ellenberger, 1958).

As beings in the world, we are part of the nature of the world. We share our biology—thus, many of our biological needs, including the central need to become—with all living organisms. We inherit the need to actualize fully our being because it is only by fulfilling our potentials that we can live an authentic life. However, we are more than our biology. Among all the living organisms, we are distinct. Our innate need to become is never automatic. Even under the most ideal conditions, our actualization is never a gift of nature. Unlike other living organisms that have no choice but to follow a predetermined biological program, we are both blessed and cursed with the uniquely human capacity of self-consciousness. We have the distinct capacity to be aware of ourselves as beings in the world. We can see ourselves as both subject and object, both as the "I am" who is acting in the world and the "I am" on whom the world acts. Unlike other living organisms, we are aware of our past and can project ourselves into the future. We must, at least to some extent in our striving, choose and affirm our actualization (see "Conditioning and/or Freedom to Choose").

May (May, Angel, & Ellenberger, 1958) contends that we will fulfill our possibilities in the world only to the extent that we consciously choose and act on our goals. Moreover, our strivings and choices are often painful since they must be made in the face of doubt, loneliness, and anxiety. Biological and social influences can limit and inhibit but not determine our movement and growth. Becoming, then, is our self-conscious search for and expression of our singular identities and personal meanings, a projection of our *potentia* in action. We cannot deny our existence or the reality of the world into which we are thrown, but we can choose to deny our being and our innate need to become.

For the existentialist, there are three modes of being in the world. In addition to self in relation to self (the *eigenwelt*) and self in relation to the physical world (the *umwelt*), the unique human quality of self-consciousness includes self in relation to others (the *mitwelt*). We experience the need for contact and communication with other beings, for authentic encounter. We need involvement with our fellow beings deeply and vitally. In fact, much of our humanness, as well as our sense of significance and purpose, can only be actualized within the social context of significant others.

Being in relationship with significant others validates our existence, affirms our being, facilitates our becoming, and contributes to our sense of meaning and purpose. Moreover, such an interaction is reciprocal; being in the world together benefits related participants. In contrast, when our social needs are frustrated, we experience a sense of abandonment, loneliness, and loss of a sense of self. Without the courage to risk sharing our world with others or to accept the invitation to enter another's world, our social integration, and with it our development, falters and stops.

In summary, we are bundles of constructive and destructive potentials, and because we constitute a culture, our culture is partially good and partially evil. We must "actively confront the issues of evil and good in ourselves, our society, and our world" (May, 1982, p. 19).

Unconscious and/or Conscious Determinants

May (1966, 1983) rejects any hypothesis of unconscious as an internal state or entity. "One cannot say *the* unconscious, for it is never a place" (May, 1966, p. 125, emphasis in original). It is not to be thought of as a psychic repository for impulses, thoughts, and wishes. Things (in the sense of entities) also cannot be unconscious. We can and do, however, repress part of our potential and some of our experience. May (1983) contends that when repression is understood from the perspective of our relationship to our potentials, our concept of unconscious must be increased to include our unrealized or repressed potentials. Hence, May (1983) defines the unconscious as *"those potentialities for knowing and experiencing which the individual cannot or will not actualize"* (pp. 17–18, emphasis in original).

For existentialists, consciousness is the totality of awareness. We develop a distinct self-consciousness and, through this consciousness, a heightened sense of the nature of our possibilities of relating to the world and the responsibility and guilt that accompany this awareness. Consciousness is the source of human freedom, creativity, and change. The greater our awareness, the greater our intentionality, spontaneity, and creativity. May (1977) writes of rare moments of joy and insight, similar to Maslow's concept of peak experience. At these times, our capacity for creative consciousness of self enables us to transcend the usual limits of awareness. In these rare moments we see truth without distortion and experience fully our unity with the world. By transcending the usual limits of consciousness through imagination and symbolization, we not only perceive alternative possibilities but also enlarge our human dimensions and decrease determining influences by creating new possibilities of relating to the world. The more vigorous our expression of our psychological needs, the more the *umwelt* will include taste and subtlety; the *mitwelt*, intimacy and love; and the *eigenwelt*, complexity and individuality (Maddi, 1972).

Conversely, when we experience severe anxiety, we restrict our consciousness. We ignore our possibilities and avoid our responsibilities. We exchange spontaneity for conformity. Avoiding decision, we give up our margin of freedom and feel controlled. Biology, history, or present circumstances become our alibis. Rather than self-directed, we are other-directed. If our failure to learn the use of symbolization, imagination, and judgment is great, our behavior will resemble that of animals, at least as much as humans can resemble animals (Maddi, 1972).

We are individuals. We each have our own heredity and unique experiences. Moreover, since we are constantly in the process of becoming, it is impossible to define us at any particular moment. We are different at different times. Because we are individuals, we are alone. We must decide and accept responsibility for our decisions. Our self is like no other, and our mental health rests on our acceptance of our uniqueness. When we attempt to assume the self of another, we err. When we deny our unique being, we experience anxiety and guilt.

Psychological and/or Reality Environments

Though not a pure phenomenologist (in the sense that perception is considered the sole determinant of behavior), May (1975, 1983; May, Angel, & Ellenberger, 1958) advocates a phenomenological approach to understanding the world of the client. We live in personal and subjective worlds that we are constantly reconceptualizing and reshaping. Our worlds, experienced through our individual streams of consciousness, are both the process and product of our private interpretations. By expressing our need for form through our creative processes, we ingest sensory data, sift these data through our personal value systems, and then, with imagination and judgment, postulate bodies, lines, surfaces, cause and effect, motion and inertia, shape and content to evolve structure, relationships, meaning, and value. We are co-creators of our phenomenology.

We can only be known as beings in the world, and that can only occur when we permit another to be in our world with us, to experience our private, subjectively created world as we experience it, to experience our being. In *Existence* (May, Angel, and Ellenberger, 1958), May discusses the difference between knowing and knowing about another person. When we wish to know another person, we must put aside what we know about that person. Knowing is to experience the being of another, to see that person becoming. Knowing requires the personal encounter of the I-Thou relationship. Knowing about a person, on the other hand, lacks encounter; it is an I-It relationship. The person becomes an object of knowing. His or her being is not part of the knowing; his or her personhood is diminshed.

Conditioning and/or Freedom to Choose

May's stance on this issue is clear. For humans, freedom is a life sentence. We are confronted with a myriad of possibilities from the time we are thrown into the world to our inevitable exit from it; and for May (1966), "The healthy person is he who chooses wither the gap" (p. 21). In existentialism, living and choosing are synonymous; hence, freedom, a characteristic that separates us from animals, is one of the ultimate concerns of living and must be faced, courageously and responsibly.

This does not mean that our freedom to choose is arbitrary and unlimited. It also does not mean that we bear the sole weight of responsibility for our actions. We are not without constraints. As beings in the world, we are limited by the restrictions of that world, including the limits of body, intelligence, social controls, illness, and death. Nature imposes rigid rules for living in this world, and our continued existence depends on our learning to recognize and accept the ground of our existence. The existential concept of freedom does not mean that we cannot be conditioned. Indeed, much of our behavior is the result of conditioning, although May (1977) reminds us that this need not occur.

May (1966, 1969, 1975, 1983) views freedom as our capacity to play a self-conscious role in our development, to be aware of ourselves as the determined ones, "to pause between stimulus and response and, thus, throw our weight, however slight it might be, on the side of one particular response among several possible ones" (1966, p. 175). By intentionally maintaining our impulses in a state of unbalance, we can choose the impulse that best serves our purpose. May (1966) does not view freedom as opposite determinism; rather he sees freedom as our capacity to know that we are the determined ones and then to play a self-conscious role in our development. He would have us face the proportion of responsibility that is ours to carry in ordinary human existence.

May (1977) reminds us, too, that as humans we inherit a mind that gives us the cognitive capacity for integrative learning that is significantly different from the learning capacity of animals. We are, for example, able to bring so-called time determinants into the learning process; that is, we have the ability to recall how we, and others we have observed, acted in the past and, by learning from past actions, influence our present actions. Moreover, through imagery, we can project ourselves into the future and, through fantasy, consider possible alternatives, weigh future against immediate consequences, and choose that action we believe will be most responsible and beneficial.

Heredity and environment may establish conditions for living in the world, but as self-conscious beings, we are free to be proactive when developing within these conditions. We must decide what we want in life, become committed to a course of action, and choose from the alternatives available to us. We are self-defining beings. We can choose to live either authentically or inauthentically. There is no less freedom in one choice than in the other, however differenct the consequences and resulting sense of guilt. Moreover, freedom is cumulative. Although freedom can be gained only through choice and affirmation, each choice adds a greater element of freedom to the next choice. Conversely, denial of freedom reduces our existence.

Early and/or Continuous Development:
Significant or Critical Life Stages

Unlike Rogers (see Chapter 4), May (1966) does not assume that development (actualization) is simply maturational. He also does not prescribe critical life stages. He does, however, recognize the formative power of early childhood experiences and postulates transitional stages of consciousness that lead to widening experiences of growth and autonomy.

Consciousness and its fosterling, self-relatedness, are key concepts in May's existential approach to early development as he views consciousness moving through four stages in healthy development:

First, the innocence of the infant;

Second, rebellion—the emergence of self-relatedness and the move toward autonomy, usually fairly well developed by the age of 2 or 3. At this point, the values of love and care take on new meaning; "they are not something *received*, but are reacted to by the child with some degree of awareness. The child may now *accept* the mother's care, *defy* it, *use* it, for various forms of power demands or what not" (May, 1966, p. 74, emphasis in original).

Third, ordinary consciousness of self;

Fourth, creative consciousness of self or transcendental consciousness—the capacity to stand outside of self.

May (1966) emphasizes the importance of a supportive setting for the child's early years. Like Adler (see Chapter 3), May advocates that parents, or parent surrogates, exercise authentic care and support by encouraging independence, exploration, and self-accomplishment. They must value and model self-reliance. Parents who pamper or indulge their children deprive them of a sense of accomplishment. Again like Adler, May recommends the establishment of limits and the recognition of natural consequences so that children learn to understand that freedom is not absolute and that there are limits and restrictions beyond their control that they must learn to accept. Much of early development, according to May, is learning to break the binds of dependence on the parents. Because anxiety is present in every growth experience, parental support is necessary as children learn to cope with anxiety, give up their past values, and accept the risk of new and mature challenges.

Importance of Role of Self-Concept

For May (1977, 1983), the concept of self embodies all our capacities. Moreover, he includes freedom, choice, and autonomy as facets of the holistic self. Viewed from this perspective, self-consciousness becomes the highest level of human consciousness because it implies transcendence. Our capacity to be aware of ourselves as both subject and object enables us to transcend the immediate situation, to see ourselves as ends rather than means, and "to think in terms of 'the possible'" (May, 1983, p. 145). In transcendence we are no longer stimulus bound or limited to the here and now. We have the capacity to detach ourselves from a situation, view it in its entirety (including ourselves in its midst), and expand the possibilities of behaving and relating to ourselves, others, and the world.

May (1983), aware that the term, *transcendence*, can create misunderstanding, reminds his readers that self-transcendence, as he uses it, is a characteristic of any normal human being and is evident in all kinds of human behavior (p. 144–145). Any normal human being, for example, can transcend the boundaries of the present moment by bringing the distant past (via memory) and the long-term future (via imagination) into present existence. We have the capacity to use our imaginations to rehearse different ways of behaving in a given situation. The inability to transcend a specific self-world relationship is the mark of mental disorder, as exemplified by Kurt Goldstein's (1942) brain-injured patients; soldiers who had portions of their frontal lobes missing lost the capacity for abstract thinking—hence, consideration of their possibilities. Obsessed with a fixed-world relationship, they suffered an inordinately high level of anxiety if anyone as much as rearranged their closets. Transcendence, as it is interpreted by May, is a natural phenomenon, a normal human capacity that is a characteristic of self-awareness.

Self may also be lost through unconcern and retreat into nonbeing. When being becomes too painful, we take refuge in an existentially false self, a self disguised and constricted in social roles. Authentic selfhood, then, can be attained only through dynamic confrontation with nonbeing.

Uniqueness and/or Commonality

We all share the common experience of being and the ultimate threat of nonbeing. Nevertheless, we are each unique and irreplaceable. Our heredities are uniquely our own (see "Biological and/or Social Determinants"). We have unique personal histories (see "Psychological and/or Reality Environment"). Our self-identities are uniquely our own (see "Importance of Role of Self-Concept"). We have the capacity to generate personal values, preferences, attitudes, and viewpoints, and the more we exercise this capacity responsibly, the more likely these characteristics will be distinct and unusual.

If we are certain of anything, it is that we are exactly like no other person—that in the end, we are individuals and alone. Good mental health rests on acceptance of that knowledge. Any attempt to be someone else is pathogenic. Our vantage points are singular and private, only to be understood as we reveal them to others in genuine encounter. The focus, then, of existential psychotherapy is directed to the individual. We must each resolve the contradictions of our being by asserting our individuality in a manner that causes us to take a stand against those forces in nature and in society that would quell our individual natures. Individuality requires both courage and defiance.

Number and Weight Assigned to Motivational Concepts

While we are pushed by our central need to become and are influenced by past experiences, human motivation, according to May (1969), is neither an emergence of needs nor the result of conditioning. He asserts we are motivated by new possibilities, the goals or ideals of which pull us toward the future. Every act of consciousness is thus a tendency toward some action.

Our unique ability to detach ourselves from the actuality of time and place and to see ourselves as both subject and object as we imaginatively play with the feasibility of some act or occurrence allows us to identify, create, and evolve toward new possibilities. Wishing for a new possibility is the first step in the process of willing. A wish is inculcated with meaning and hence different from need or drive. A wish is imbued with direction and time; it introduces intentionality and transports us into the future. A wish motivates because once a wish materializes it calls for decision, a weighing of future implications and consequences. We initiate through wishing. Through choice, we will and enact.

May (1969) cautions us in *Love and Will* not to mistake *willing* for *willpower*. Although both contain commitment and resolve, willing is related to our potentialities and hooked to the future, while willpower is based on oughts or shoulds.

Importance of Group Membership

The implications of *mitwelt* are clear. The world in which we exist includes other persons and groups, and we need to reach out from our centeredness to fulfill our capacity for social interaction and integration. Through shared participation with our fellow beings, we gain both our sense of identity and consciousness. During periods of nonaffiliation, we experience deeply the painful feelings of loneliness and alienation. The implication of *mitwelt* is relationship with significant others, and it has been developed fully by Buber in his I-Thou philosophy. The essence of the I-Thou relationship is genuine encounter that offers mutual presence and affirmation to both participants, a replenishment of our sense of significance and worth, and a confirmation of our identity as an individual.

We suffer an ontological guilt against our fellows (May, Angel, & Ellenberger, 1958). Because it is only possible to see others through our own values and biases, we do them an injustice and, to some extent, fail to understand and meet their needs fully.

Moreover, there is always threat. Not only can identification with another or with a group drain our sense of existence, but also to be unaccepted by or rejected from a group threatens isolation and loneliness. The group can influence, but it is we who partly determine the meaning of the group and, thus, our relationship with it. The meaning of the group depends, at least in part, on how much of ourselves we put into it (May, Angel, & Ellenberger, 1958).

Explanation of Learning

For the existentialist, learning originates in and is an integral part of immediate, vivid, experiential sensing. To know fully the meaning of anything, we must participate fully in it. We perceive, organize, and analyze the sensory data of our worlds (including our bodies), then impart our experience with personal meaning. We recall, imagine, and reconstruct the data of meaningful experience and from this process cognitively create new concepts, ideas, attitudes, knowledge—our worldview. We review history and tradition and infer knowledge. We learn our mistakes through failure, and we can use our failures to re-evaluate our goals and reformulate our plans. By reorganizing and accepting the reality of our world, we gain a clearer sense of our possibilities in it. We become aware of our inevitable death and develop a vivid sense of life and the urgency to experience what we value while alive.

Anxiety, present in all efforts to become, can be our most motivating teacher. We learn well, also, from natural consequences. A significant aspect of self-discovery is an awareness of the realities of both ourselves and the world of which we are an essential part. Only when our learning is meaningful do we gain a sense of self-discovery and an intuitive awareness of our possibilities.

Importance of Reward

While May (1977, 1983) recognizes the potential power of external reinforcement, particularly on the neurotic, he is much more interested in the rewarding inner sense of joy we experience when we are successful in our attempts to actualize. For May, all experiences that facilitate our becoming are rewarding. Being fully in the world is rewarding and imparts a sense of excitement, a zest for life and living.

We are rewarded when our identities are affirmed in close interpersonal relationships and when we can risk genuine, spontaneous encounter. We are rewarded when we experience the freedom to choose in the face of anxiety. We are rewarded in those moments when we are creative. We are rewarded when we are able to call on our capacities and courage.

GOALS OF THE EXISTENTIAL THERAPIST

Antitheoretical in its approach to counseling and psychotherapy, existentialism focuses on the individual client rather than any a priori definitions of his or her condition. The specific goals of therapy, then, emerge from the therapeutic process. General goals, when they are discussed, are usually voiced in vague and obscure terms. For example, May (in May, Angel, & Ellenberger, 1958) asserts, "The aim of therapy is that the patient *experience his existence as real*" (p. 85, emphasis in orginal). Full awareness of existence includes awareness of possiblities and the ability to act on the basis of these possibilities. Further, May insists that therapy is concerned with something more fundamental than curing the client's symptoms. Any lasting cures of symptoms must be a by-product of the client's full sensing and experiencing of his or her existence and the confrontation of guilt and anxiety that leads to a redefinition of the individual's perceptions of self in the world.

Corlis and Rabe (1969) maintain that the therapist's goals are "to stimulate the patient's willingness to work through pain, to offer help without the jeopardy of undercutting the other's own effort, to offer him strength without dependence" (p. 13). Corey (1982) describes the goals of existential therapists as the expansion of their clients' self-awareness and helping them to become aware of the freedom they possess and the responsibility they have for the direction of their lives (p. 64). Frey and Heslett (1975), in contrast, tell us that "existential counselors agree with the general goals of most other approaches to counseling and psychotherapy, but seek to embellish these general goals with existential points of view" (p. 43).

THERAPEUTIC PROCESS: METHODS AND TECHNIQUES

For May (1983), the therapeutic process is a series of client-therapist encounters wherein the therapist seeks to free the client to develop in his or her individual way in response to the unique demands, challenges, and limits of existence. The existential encounter requires a recognition of the client as an individual—separate and totally centered. Moreover, the therapist sees the client as a striving existence with the capacity for self-consciousness and self-affirmation, with the ability to sense and face the possibilities of existence and to judge and choose responsibly and creatively, even to reorient his or her whole existence.

May is more concerned with the philosophical presuppositions of and overall approach to the therapeutic encounter than with the development of precise methodology. His is an ontological approach; the purpose is to help the client recognize and experience his or her existence and to develop a strong enough sense of being for responsible, autonomous participation in the world. The therapeutic process, then, is always related to existence, and the encounter is seen as the circumstance of that process.

Therapeutic Relationship

Existential therapy is grounded in the immediate, ongoing, subjective experience of both therapist and client as they encounter each other in the therapeutic situation. The therapist emphasizes a full, selfless, and sensitive presence. To meet the client in the dimension of encounter during the therapeutic session, the therapist must be able to put all personal needs aside, center fully on the client, communicate a deep caring for the client's welfare, and express a continued faith in the client's potential. The therapist invites the client to move from isolation into an I-Thou relationship since the process and content of therapy are discovered only in moments of genuine encounter.

For May (1961), "There is no such thing as truth or reality for a living human being except as he participates in it, is conscious of it, has some relationship to it" (p. 17). The real datum of the therapeutic situation, then, is the existing, becoming person who is attending the therapeutic session. Therapy is two persons existing in a world together, and the world, at least for the length of the therapy session, is the therapist's office. The communication that occurs in therapy is "one existence communicating with another" (May, Angel, and Ellenberger, 1958).

There is risk in encountering another being, even in the temporary relationship of the therapeutic situation. In genuine encounter both persons risk change, and "unless the therapist is open to change the patient will not be either" (May, 1983, p. 22). Self-transcendence, rising above one's need for centeredness to reach out to another, is required of the therapist. Concern for the welfare and growth of the client takes priority. Self-disclosure as a person is not only a necessary but also an integral part of therapy. The therapist cannot be authentic and remain detached, passive, or hidden. Methods and techniques must emerge from the experience of the encounter; otherwise, they create distance, block understanding of the client's inner experiences, and obstruct the therapist's presence in the relationship. Any method with the purpose of manipulation or of putting distance between the client and therapist demeans the end. There is no room in authentic encounter for a means-justifies-the-end concept. The therapist must rely on spontaneity and permit methods and techniques to emerge from the relationship.

Like Rogers (see Chapter 4), the existentialists believe that empathy is the door to understanding the inner experiences of the client. Unlike Rogers, however, existentialists reserve an expression of positive regard for honesty and authenticity.

Genuine encounter is the primary event in the psychotherapeutic situation. "Encounter is always a potentially creative experience; it normally should ensue in the expanding of consciousness, the enrichment of the self" (May, 1983, p. 22). Moreover, both client and therapist experience the effects of genuine encounter and are enriched by authentic interaction in the therapeutic relationship. It does not matter that the therapeutic relationship is temporary because "the experience of intimacy is permanent," according to Yalom (1980); "it exists in one's inner world as a permanent reference point: a reminder of one's potential for intimacy" (p. 404).

Initial Procedures and Strategies

Initiating Therapy.   The initial therapy session differs little from the later sessions. The therapist begins where the client is at the moment and proceeds from there. For the client who does not know what to expect from therapy and who has not learned how to work therapeutically, the initial session can be frightening. During the first session the therapist must communicate to the client that he or she not only understands the client's plight but also is both interested and willing to work with him or her toward a resolution. Client and therapist expectations, then, may require more concentration in the first session than in later sessions, but the therapist's presence is the first priority because, in this as in all sessions, the personal encounter is the process and content of therapy.

Structuring and Client Expectations. Structuring can be a valuable therapeutic method for dealing with irrational or unrealistic client expectations. Clients often enter therapy expecting a quick and painless cure, preferably one that requires little or, better still, no effort on their part. When this is the case, the therapist is obligated to define the limits of therapy and may begin by informing the client that there are no simple answers or magical cures to the inherently difficult facts and possibilities of existence. Instead, therapy involves participation and risk and requires the hard and often painful work of self-reflection, self-discipline, and the will to act.

While it is necessary for the client to accept the limitations of therapy, it is important, too, that structuring communicates the therapist's faith in the client's capabilities. The client's participation and courage in therapy can be facilitated by the therapist's acceptance and belief in his or her capacity for change and growth. While there is no promise of success, the client needs some reason to hope.

Course of Therapy

Methods and Techniques. More a therapeutic attitude than a precise theory of psychotherapy, the existential approach to therapy focuses on understanding the existence of a single client rather than on any a priori system of techniques designed for all clients. The tendency of many Western theories to view the client as an object to be manipulated, managed, analyzed, or controlled, and to emphasize methods and techniques over understanding is viewed with concern. May (1983) asserts that existential assumptions may provide the therapist with notions for therapeutic technique, but for the most part, specific techniques must be permitted to emerge from the process of therapy and can only be decided on the basis of what will best reveal the existence of a particular client at a particular moment in the therapeutic encounter. Emphasis on techniques prevents existential understanding by blocking genuine encounter.

Existential therapists who permit their techniques to emerge from the process of therapy display both flexibility and versatility. Not only is there a wide latitude in their methods from one client to another, but also they may draw on a diversity of techniques from one phase of therapy to another with the same client. Though never merely eclectic, since techniques are determined by the encounter and consistent with the existential attitude, existential therapists do not hesitate to borrow procedures from other therapies, including those as diverse as the psychoanalytic, gestalt, cognitive, and behavioral therapies.

Rooted in the therapeutic relationship, existential techniques are selected to support, nourish, and enhance the encounter of the client and therapist. Techniques can be validated by the understanding that comes from the encounter, and they can be altered to fit the individual client and the therapeutic moment. An existential requirement for the therapist, deep empathic listening, may be the only premeditated technique in existential therapy.

On the surface, it would appear that a diversity of techniques is intuitively employed. While spontaneity and intuition do play an important role in existential therapy, the therapist does not act on whims; rather, the therapist eclectically selects techniques from his or her experiential knowledge of the client's existence and draws on his or her clinical experience, skill, and judgment. Clinical skills include a high level of presence and the ability to respond empathically, interpretively, and confrontively in a nonintervening, nonpersuading manner. The methods and techniques of the existential approach to therapy cannot be learned or, for that matter, taught, except through the experience of the personal encounter.

ASSESSING PROGRESS

As with specific therapist procedures, the data of therapeutic assessment are found in the encounter. Assessment is always a two-person process. It involves continuous feedback and an openness to new information, as well as new or revised interpretation by both the client and therapist. Furthermore, the client's existence is being assessed; hence, the client's ground and circumstance are as valid or more valid than those of the therapist. Not only should the client be an active participant in the data generation of the assessment process and have full access to the results, but he or she should also be involved in any decisions, planning, or arrangements that ensue.

The client may use the relationship with the therapist to practice for change in his or her world, but for change to be meaningful, it must remain with the client outside the encounter. Evidence of positive movement in the client's becoming might be manifested by less ambiguous language, an increased ability to experience feelings, an escalation of energy and decision making, heightened spontaneity and creativity, and acceptance of uniqueness, independence, and responsibility—that is, any signs of movement from being a client to becoming a potent person.

FINAL COMMENTARY

The direction and future of May's existential approach to psychotherapy is unclear, although the quality and appeal of his works almost certainly assure

FIGURE 5.1 A Schematic Analysis of May's Stand on the Basic Issues

Biological Determinants
Social Determinants
Unconscious Determinants
Conscious Determinants
Early Development
Continuous Development
Psychological Environment
Reality Environment
Conditioning
Freedom
Commonality
Uniqueness

Importance of Group Membership	Group membership influences our sense of identity and consciousness, but we—through our own values and biases—determine the meaning of the group and our relationship to it.
Explanation of Learning	Learning entails reorganization and acceptance of that which is experientially sensed during our participation in life. Both anxiety and natural consequences of behaviors facilitate this learning.
Number and Weight Assigned to Motivational Concepts	We are motivated by new possibilities that pull us in the direction of the future.
Importance of Reward	Reward is experienced as an inner sense of joy derived from successful attempts to actualize our possiblities in this world. Affirmation of identity, courage, creativity, freedom in the face of anxiety, being fully in the world, and becoming are all experienced as rewarding.
Importance or Role of Self-Concept	The concept of self embodies all our capacities. The ability to be aware of self as both object and subject implies self-consciousness or transcendence, the highest level of human consciousness, and expands our possibilities. And only through dynamic confrontation with the threat of nonbeing is authentic selfhood attained.

his continued influence on the counseling profesison. While rich in appreciation of the human condition, there is no systematic presentation of procedure, methodology, or empirical validation. His concepts, which are interesting and often highly provocative, are imprecise and hence difficult to define, learn, teach, or research.

May presents a convincing argument for the necessity of genuine client-therapist encounter that would appear to have relevance for most current humanistic psychotherapies, but his rationale is based on unsystematic clinical observations rather than controlled research. For May, experiential knowing holds priority over technique. Practitioners must, therefore, rely on their genuineness and spontaneity in the therapeutic process of the encounter to create techniques. They are free to borrow techniques from other psychotherapies as long as their purpose is to enhance their understanding of their client and contribute to the personal encounter of the therapeutic relationship.

REFERENCES AND SUGGESTED READINGS

Corey, G. 1982. *Theory and practice of counseling and psychotherapy*, 2nd ed. Monterey, Calif.: Brooks/Cole.

Corlis, R.B., and Rabe, P. 1969. *Psychotherapy from the center: a humanistic view of change and of growth*. Scranton, Penn.: International Textbook.

Frey, D.H., and Heslet, F.E. 1975. *Existential theory for counselors*. Boston: Houghton Mifflin.

Goldstein, K. 1942. *After-effects of brain injuries in war*. New York: Grune & Stratton.

Horney, K. 1942. *Self-analysis*. New York: Norton.

Maddi, S.R. 1972. *Personality theories: a comparative analysis*, rev. ed. Homewood, Ill.: The Dorsey Press.

May, R., ed. 1961. *Existential psychology*. New York: Random House.

May, R. 1966. *Psychology and the human dilemma*. New York: Norton.

May, R. 1967a. *The art of counseling*. Nashville, Tenn.: Abington.

May, R. 1967b. *Man's search for himself*. New York.: The American Library. Originally published 1963.

May, R. 1969. *Love and will*. New York: Dell.

May, R. 1972. *Power and innocence*. New York: Dell.

May, R. 1975. *The courage to create*. New York: W.W. Norton.

May, R. 1977. *The meaning of anxiety*, rev. ed. New York: W.W. Norton.

May, R. 1982. The problem of evil: an open letter to Carl Rogers. *Journal of Humanistic Psychology* 22: 10–21.

May, R. 1983. *The discovery of being*. New York: W.W. Norton.

May, R., Angel, E., and Ellenberger, H., eds. 1958. *Existence*. New York: Simon & Shuster.

Moritz, C. 1973. *Current biography 1973*. New York: H.W. Wilson.

Reeves, C. 1977. *The psychology of Rollo May*. San Francisco: Jossey-Bass.

Van Kaam, A. 1966. *Existential foundations of psychology*. Pittsburgh: Duquesne University Press.

Yalom, I.D. 1980. *Existential psychotherapy*. New York: Basic Books.

6

The Gestalt Therapy of Fritz Perls

FRIEDERICH SALOMON PERLS (1893–1970), addressed affectionately as Fritz by friends and followers, is recognized as the primary founder and master practitioner of Gestalt therapy. Perls introduced his theory to the United States in 1947 with the publication of *Ego, Hunger and Aggression, The Beginning of Gestalt Therapy*. However, it was not until the 1960s, when Perls's therapeutic skill and personal charisma drew hundreds of counselors and therapists to his training workshops at the Esalen Institute, that Gestalt therapy gained prominence as a major psychotherapeutic theory in the United States.

Perls entered the theoretical arena as a psychoanalyst trained in the classical tradition. Even after departing radically from the Freudian camp, he held Freud and his own experience in analysis as a benchmark against which he could react, check, and compare the similarities and differences of his own thinking. In addition to Freud's psychoanalytic theory, Perls's theoretical formulations reflect the influence of a wide variety of thinking, including Reichian character analysis, Jung's analytic theory, Gestalt psychology, Zen Buddhism, Taoism, existential philosophy, psychodrama, and general semantics. He was influenced, too, by Friedlander, Hegel, Kant, Marx, Vaihinger, Goldstein, and Horney, and he particularly enjoyed reading Huxley, Hesse, and Twain.

Reich contributed biological muscular armor, affect, body involvement in neuroses, and confrontation as a therapeutic method. Jung impressed Perls with his view of individuation—the idea that we are living systems engaged in processes of differentiation and integration. In addition to the name for his theory, Gestalt psychology furnished Perls with figure-ground perceptual principles and the insight that natural functioning is a continuous process in which all parts organize into a spontaneous, irreducible whole with characteristics not found in any of the elements. Eastern religions taught Perls the immediacy of the obvious, the importance of the intuitive, or organismic, way of knowing, and the necessity of actualizing one's true nature. Perls accepted the existential primacy of existence; responsibility for thoughts, feelings, fantasy, and actions; as well as the affirmation of an I-thou relationship. From psychodrama, he borrowed techniques including use of the so-called hot seat. From Friedlander, Perls acquired the concept of differential thinking, the meaning of balance, the zero center of polar opposites. From semantics Perls learned the need for clear and explicit use of language in therapy.

Always prepared to experiment with new ideas and techniques, Perls incorporated the most recent theoretical hypotheses or philosophic postulates if he believed they might improve the effectiveness of his therapy. Although he appropriated many of his ideas from others, his creative integration of these perspectives and his use of innovative applications resulted in a unique theory.

When pressed by both critics and followers to formulate and present a developed personality theory and therapeutic method, Perls refused. To do so, he feared, would detract from or possibly end the innovativeness of Gestalt therapy. His disdain for imitators made him antitheoretical, and, on these occasions, he acrimoniously referred to all theorizing as "elephant shit," an intellectual way of knowing that he considered inferior, imperfect, and limiting.

Perls viewed his theoretical hypotheses as truths but held them as incomplete truths to be kept open to experiment, to be considered merely a way of talking about experience, not experience. Considering the diverse sources of his ideas, one might argue that Perls was more a synthesizer than a theorist or that his gift was more methodological than theoretical, but it can hardly be denied that Perls's legacy is intuitively appealing to a large group of counselors and therapists who identify with Gestalt therapy.

BIOGRAPHICAL SKETCH

Perls defies clear description, but that fits his concept of mental health, his way of remaining sane in an insane world. By his account, to be without character is a goal worth pursuing:

> Once you have *character*, you have developed a rigid system . . . . So it seems a paradox when I say that the richest person, the most productive person, is a person who has *no* character. [Perls, 1972, p. 7 emphasis in original]

The gestalt that is Fritz Perls is more than the sum of available, conflicting descriptions. He is profound and perplexing, inspiring and frustrating, caring and hostile, generous and selfish, demonstrative and lustful, leader and manipulator, prophet and bum, kind and ruthless, vital and lazy. Whether simply a character or healthfully devoid of any character, he is unique, and the theoretical constructs left by this complex, controversial, charismatic entrepreneur continues to attract and excite large numbers of advocates.

In and Out of the Garbage Pail (1972), Perls's free-floating, often playful autobiography, provides hundreds of kaleidoscopic glimpses of his personal life. Alternating between poetic verse and a Perlsian prose as the mood struck him, Perls shared his reflections and memories, humor and wisdom, experiences and fantasies. Whether writing of his pleasure with sex games in the hot baths at Big Sur, the excitement of flirting with death by cutting the engine of his biplane, or the depression and suicidal thinking he experienced in conjunction with his angina attacks, Perls is candid. Further, he laces these stories together with the theory of Gestalt therapy.

Like his theory, his autobiography is an incomplete gestalt that awaits organization and validation. However, it does offer some additional knowledge and integration of Fritz Perls that can be found nowhere else.

Early Years

Born in 1893 into a Jewish family that he later describes as "obscure lower middle class," Perls's (1972) earliest memory was of the family's move to a more fashionable neighborhood in the center of Berlin when he was 3 years old (p. 61). Although his parents fought often, bitterly, and at times physically, Perls looked on his childhood as a happy period of his life. He loved his mother but lost respect for his father, a traveling wine salesman who drank heavily and whose primary avocation, from Perls's viewpoint, was to become Grand Master of the Freemasons.

Perls was a middle child and only son. He and Grete, his younger sister, were always close, but his dislike for his older sister, Elsie, grew to be both intense and lasting. He experienced practically no emotion when he learned that she died in a concentration camp (Perls, 1972).

Perls discovered both joy and pride in learning to read at a very early age. His father kept the library locked, but his grandparents' library was always open to him.

Education

Perls liked his elementary school teacher and took for granted that he was at the top of his class. His admission to the Mommsen Gymnasium, a new, conservative high school whose teachers were dedicated to rigid discipline and anti-Semitism, marked the end of a carefree childhood and the beginning of a stormy and rebellious adolescence. Perls (1972) refers to his experiences there as a nightmare (p. 178). He failed his seventh year, repeated it, failed again, and was dismissed. Assuming the fault was with their son rather than the school, Perls's parents apprenticed him to a soft goods merchant, but this, too, led to failure. Perls's rebellious behavior and adolescent pranks soon led to his dismissal.

After his short-lived apprenticeship, Perls passed the entrance examination to Askanishe Gymnasium, a more liberal and humanistic high school that seemed to complement Perls's personality. He performed well, and his papers impressed the faculty enough for them to waive his oral examination.

Perls joined the German Army in 1916, serving as a medical corpsman. He completed his medical training in 1920 and received his M.D. degree from Frederich Wilhelm University. He began his training in psychoanalysis the following year, studying at both the Vienna and Berlin institutes of psychoanalysis. Wilhelm Reich served as his training analyst; his supervisors were Otto Fenichel and Karen Horney. Years later, looking back on this period of his life, Perls (1972) wrote, "From Fenichel I got confidence; from Reich, brazeness; from Horney, human involvement without terminology" (p. 38).

In 1926, Perls accepted a staff position at the Institute for Brain Injured Soldiers in Frankfurt, working as an assistant to Kurt Goldstein. Forced to flee Germany in 1933, Perls, his wife, Laura Posner Perls, also an analyst, and their 2-year-old daughter crossed the German-Dutch border with only the clothes they could carry and 100 marks (about $25) hidden in his cigarette case. Perls (1972) describes their days in a small attic apartment in Amsterdam as "utter misery." Karl Landanner became his traning analyst, and Perls was able to complete his training.

In 1934, Ernest Jones found Perls a position in Johannesburg. As the first psychoanalyst in South Africa, Perls soon built a highly successful practice and lived an affluent life-style with servants, a nursemaid for the children, tennis courts, a swimming pool, an ice-skating rink, cars, and a biplane. Perls founded the South Africa Institute of Psychoanalysis in 1935.

Emergence of Gestalt Therapy

Perls's trip to Czechoslovakia for the International Psychoanalytic Congress, in 1936, may mark the emergence of Gestalt therapy. Not only was Perls excited about presenting a paper he believed would be accepted as an innovative and significant contribution to psychoanalysis, but also he had arranged a meeting with Freud. Both meetings were humiliating defeats for Perls. His ideas were neither welcomed nor appreciated by the orthodox psychoanalysts. Even Reich, his former analyst, had little time for him. Worse, his long-awaited meeting with Freud totalled less than 4 minutes and took place entirely in the doorway to the sickly Freud's room. When Perls told Freud that he had come all the way from South Africa to meet him, Freud's response was, "Well, and when are you going back?"

Perls was devastated. His feelings of rejection and embarrassment soon turned to anger accompanied by a deep resolve to prove to Freud and the members of the Psychoanalytic Society that they were wrong. The sting of his meeting with Freud remained, however, and 3 decades later Perls (1972) still considered this meeting one of the unfinished situations of his life.

Perls returned from the congress convinced that he needed no one, either personally or professionally, to support him or his views. He renounced Freudian analysis and his present life-style. He created an emotional distance between himself and his family, and although they continued to live together, he and his wife led separate lives.

Perls's early theoretical work was primarily a reaction to and a revision and expansion of Freudian and Reichian theory. He referred to his early therapy as concentration therapy and later, despite Laura Perls's protests, changed the name to Gestalt therapy.

Perls immigrated to the United States in 1946. By 1950, the name and style of Gestalt therapy were established but not widely accepted. The first Gestalt institute in the United States, located in New York City, was founded by Perls, Laura Perls, and Paul Goodman. That same year, Perls, Hefferline, and Goodman published *Gestalt Therapy* (1951), the first major work in this therapy since *Ego, Hunger and Aggression* (1969). The Cleveland Institute for Gestalt therapy was established in 1954.

In 1955, Perls traveled the world, with an extended stop at a Buddhist temple in Kyota, Japan, to study Zen. Perls's next sojourn was to Miami, Florida, where he became involved with Marty, whom he later describes as "the most significant woman in my life" (Perls, 1972).

Perls, Simpkin, and Kempler conducted a summer-long workshop in Gestalt therapy at the Esalen Institute, Big Sur, California, in 1963, and in 1964, Perls joined the staff at the institute as resident associate psychiatrist. He held this position until 1969, when he moved to Cowichan, Vancouver Island, in British Columbia, to establish the first Gestalt community.

Perls died in March 1970, in a Chicago hospital. A large crowd of anxious followers massed outside the hospital during the 6 days preceding his death, and a police guard was called to keep them away from the building. He was survived by his wife, Laura, his daughter, Mrs. Renate Gold, his son, Dr. Stephen Perls, and four grandchildren.

Accomplishments and Awards

Although rarely recognized by academic psychology or the academic community, few theorists have had the popular impact of Perls. His contributions to the human growth and human potential movements in the United States cannot be denied. Thousands of people have participated in the workshops and seminars offered by more than 50 Gestalt training centers across the country.

It is worth noting, too, that although Perls died in 1970, his name is inseparably linked with Gestalt therapy. He is still "top dog," a position in which he seemed to revel while alive.

RESOLUTIONS OF THE ELEVEN BASIC ISSUES

Formulating comprehensive resolutions of the eleven basic issues in the absence of a complete and systematic presentation of the theory of Gestalt therapy was difficult. Presenting those resolutions in hierarchical order was even more difficult. However, as the work progressed, the chapter began to acquire both shape and meaning, in brief, a gestalt. Perls's theory, like most of the theories presented in this book, is more than the sum of the resolutions, regardless of how comprehensive those resolutions might be or of the order in which they might appear.

Biological and/or Social Determinants

Viewed through the theory of Gestalt therapy, we are unified, complex collections of thousands of differentiating and growing biological, social, and spiritual processes (needs, potentials, and functions) that, except for purposes of discussion, are indivisible. Our behavior, however, is not determined by internal and external factors. We function as complete entities; we choose always as total organisms. Kempler (1973) expresses this holistic view well when he writes, "To recognize man as a process is a beginning. To see him as a composite of processes in an endless universe of processes is to define him" (p. 255).

Certainly we are biological beings, but we cannot exist, much less grow and mature, apart from our environments. We are beings in and part of the world. Biological and social determinants are inseparable. "We have to consider always the segment of the world in which we live as part of ourselves. Wherever we go we take a kind of world with us" (Perls, 1969, p. 6). Our biological needs include air, food, water, shelter, expression of self, sex, and aggression. Our social needs, learned through interaction with our environments, include managing our encounters with other people, preserving our identities, and coping with environmental restrictions.

Our needs, whether biological or social, are part of an innate actualization need that, in the healthy organism, is governed by a homeostatic process, a tendency to strive for balance, and is, thus, self-regulating. There is no universal hierarchy of needs. The need that emerges at any particular moment is an individual determination based on that need's pertinence to the individual's need for self-preservation, to grow, or to actualize potentials. Our most pressing need will naturally emerge and, unless attended to satisfactorily, will create tension and disequilibrium.

Like Rogers (see Chapter 4), Perls trusts the inner wisdom of the organism. If we are left to be, to develop naturally, actualization will occur. Growth comes from self-awareness. We have within ourselves at birth everything we need for immediate interaction with our environments. We innately possess all the resources for living effective, healthy, satisfying, productive lives. The processes of change are ever present if we strive to be what we innately are in the moment. Unlike Rogers, whose concept of the actualizing tendency is *to become* by realizing our potentials, Perls believes that we need only *to be* in the immediacy of the moment what we innately are. Anything that blocks, hinders, detracts from, or interrupts our immediate being in and of the world interferes with the actualizing tendency and is unhealthy.

Part of our actualizing tendency is an indestructive need for wholeness, for gestalt. We need and, therefore, strive for a sense of order, completion, and fulfillment. We actively seek to form meaningful wholes from our perceptions (see "Psychological and/or Reality Environments"). Unfinished situations or incomplete gestalts, thus, create tensions.

Further, we have the innate predispositon to symbolize our experiences in our worlds. We can and do transform our physical worlds into conceptual worlds. We live in a physical world in addition to our idiographically constructed abstract worlds of ideas and meanings, a symbolized world that we can explore mentally and communicate to ourselves and to others. We live in a reality and a fantasy, simultaneously, interactionally, and transactionally. However, if we identify with our fantasy, with conditions or qualities that should be or might be, we are involved in the actualization of a self-image rather than in self-actualization.

Number and Weight Assigned to Motivational Concepts

As stated under the previous issue, all our needs, potentials, and functions are a part of our superordinate need for actualization. At any given moment, the most pressing of these emerges from ground to figure and creates tension. The motivating force behind all our behavior, then, springs from this single, inherent, self-actualizing goal. Passons (1975) emphasizes the primacy of our actualizing tendency when he writes, "It can be assumed that at any moment a person's behavior, regardless of how it appears to any observer, is his current chosen means toward actualization" (p. 15).

Although our actualizing tendency is made up of thousands of physiological (internal) and social (external) needs (see "Biological and/or Social Determinants"), when living in the immediacy of the present, we identify with, feel most intensely about, and strive hardest to fulfill those needs we define as essential to continued life and living. By being what we are in the moment, we are aware of our needs as they emerge. Simultaneously, we are able to direct our actions toward need satisfaction. Our awareness leads to excitement, and excitement transfers to sensory and motor actions that, in turn, move us toward contact. Smith (1976) describes the natural cycle of need satisfaction through gestalt formation as "deficit-tension-awareness-excitement-contact-experimentation-action-satisfaction" (p. 55).

When living in the present, we can trust our bodily wisdom and act on it.

It is the natural order of life for our needs to arise (become figure) and to recede (return to ground) as we attend to them. Individual choice is the ordering principle, for although we may not always be aware of choosing, we do choose the controlling figure-ground relationship of any situation (Van De Reit, Korb, Gorrell, 1980, p. 7). Our choosing, along with the fact that different needs may emerge in similar situations, makes accurate prediction of our behavior impossible. Perls trusts our inner wisdom for the solution to life's problems and tasks. Further, Perls is convinced that we possess the necessary and sufficient resources to cope with the perplexities of living if we attempt to meet our actualizing needs through natural and spontaneous being in the here and now.

Unfortunately, according to Perls, too few of us live in the present. We avoid contact with the now by living in the past, which can only be recalled, or in the future, which can only be anticipated—that is, we live in fantasy rather than reality. Out of touch with the present, we are either unaware of or deny our present needs. Our actualizing needs go unmet. Our growth stops. Our lives become stagnant. We are more robot than human, more dead than alive. Should this state become chronic, we function poorly, even abnormally. For Perls, life can be lived only in the here and now because motivations originating from the actualizing tendency enter awareness only in the present.

Psychological and/or Reality Environments

Perls's stance on this issue is radically phenomenological. Objectivity does not exist. Awareness is always our subjective experience in the now: "Now = experience = awareness = reality" (Fagan & Shepherd, 1973, p. 14). Now is always in flux, that fleeting moment between the past and the future, and our perceptions of it depend on our individual systems of needs in the immediacy of the movement.

The level and acuity of our awareness determines the accuracy of our perceptions—thus, our behavior. We approximate reality in moments of acute awareness and concentration, when there is unity of awareness, motor responses, and emotion. We are not passive reactors in our contacts with our environments; we choose the meanings we give to ourselves and to our worlds and behave accordingly. It is not a question of the existence of a reality, but of how much reality (awareness) exists in each of us. Our individual realities are constantly changing processes of which we are essential parts.

Our innate need for gestalt formation predisposes us to perceive our environments as a total unit of meaning. Further, this same predilection causes us to respond to our environments holistically. We perceive events in our environments and from our perceptions attempt to create order, structure, meaning, and relationships. Our worlds are constructs from all we consider important at the moment. A change in the perception of either our environments or ourselves destroys the gestalt formation. We live by the dialectical process of contacting and withdrawing from persons and objects in our environmental fields as we decide they are good or bad, right or wrong, positive or negative. If appropriated or assimilated when perceived as good, right, or positive, the gestalt is closed. Likewise, if rejected or avoided when perceived bad, wrong, or negative, the gestalt is closed.

Conscious and/or Unconscious Determinants

Coming to believe in the wholeness and unity of the individual personality, Perls (1969, 1972, 1976) chose to reject the psychoanalytic concept of the unconscious. There was no place in his theory for a reservoir of instinctual impulses or uncontrollable drives. Further, he rejected the idea of a hidden repository of repressions.

Dismissing the unconscious as a theoretical invention to account for a major portion of human behavior, Perls (in Stevens, 1977) found the existing explanations of consciousness inadequate and hypothesized a "universal awareness" (p. 70). He discarded the terms, *conscious* and *unconscious*, in favor of *awareness* or the lack of it. According to Perls (in Stevens, 1977), "With the hypothesis of universal awareness we are open to considering ourselves in a living way rather than in the aboutism of having a mind, ego, superego, and so forth" (p. 71). That is, rather than having awareness, we are awareness. Although our awareness is often inaccurate, with much being misplaced or displaced, "nothing ever dies or disappears altogether in the realm of awareness" (Ivey & Simek-Downing, 1980, p. 72). The so-called unconscious is, then, merely a shifting of the figure-ground.

The human experience of awareness, consciousness, and excitation are considered the same and are often used as synonyms in the literature of Gestalt therapy. To be human is to be aware. Awareness is not something we possess; we *are* awareness. Although awareness may be displaced or misplaced as a result of being out of contact with our environment or of being absorbed in our fantasies, we have the potential to be fully aware of all our experiences.

Conditioning and/or Freedom to Choose

Autonomy of choice is paramount in Gestalt therapy. When aware and knowing in the present, we are free-functioning, responsible beings. Life is our attempt to strike a comfortable balance between the authentic, immediate needs of the self and the introjected, tyrannical shoulds of the self-image. Whether our choices are authentic (self-actualizing) or inauthentic (self-image enhancing), there is no less freedom in the choosing and no less responsibility in the choice.

While we may not be responsible for all life's situations, we are responsible for our thoughts, feelings, impulses, and behaviors in the situations we encounter. We choose what we accept and reject, think and feel, trust and value, demand and expect, are aware of and attend to, and deny and avoid. Our views of self and world, then, are unique creations based on personal awareness and choice in the immediacy of the moment. The issue is not whether our choices are intrinsically good or bad but whether we realize our possibilities for self-actualization or deny them in favor of self-image. As free-functioning beings, we choose our responses in any circumstances. The responsibility for our growth or stagnation is ours alone.

Awareness is essential to responsible choice and action. Through self-awareness, we discover our choices by understanding the what and how of our present behavior. Likewise, we understand how we avoid responsibility— thus, our essential freedom—by permitting others or circumstances to make critical decisions for us.

Although we cannot avoid living in the existential now, we can avoid the responsibility of living in the present by maintaining a nostalgic grip on the past or by anticipating and planning for the future. Further, our intellect gives us the ability to blunt our awareness, diminish our excitement, and thus, avoid any genuine encounter with either ourselves or our environment. Rather than experiencing the moment fully, we explain it, rationalize it, repress it, semanticize it, or forget it. Rather than free, spontaneous choice and action in the cause of our present, intrinsic needs, we choose evasive, defensive behavior in the service of our self-image. We lack incentive, avoid risks, lose touch with possibilities and alternatives, and experience anxiety. Rather than confronting life and choosing to live it fully, we deaden ourselves.

Free functioning neither guarantees less frustration, risk, or effort nor ensures that we shall easily overcome life's tasks and obstacles when we encounter them. Healthful choice simply means that we choose and act with what we are in the moment. In health, we are in contact with all the possibilities of ourselves and the world, and we choose those that move us toward the actualization of the self. When self-image is the goal, our contact with ourselves and our environment is impaired; we aim for victory and blame others or the world for our defeats.

Early and/or Continuous Development: Critical or Significant Life Stages

For Perls, our births mark the beginning of a life-long, continuous process of growth and maturation. As infants we must depend on environmental support for the gratification of our immediate needs and wants and for the facilitation of our inherent potentials. However, as we grow we become stronger and more mobile, our senses become more discriminating and reliable, and our ability to symbolize makes communication and abstract thinking possible. In brief, our contacts with our environmental fields become more varied, vigorous, and complex. We face the challenge of maturity, of transcending environmental support, by developing inner support systems and by accepting responsibility for and responding to our perceptions, thoughts, feelings, expectations, and actions.

The path to independence and maturity is not smooth. It does not follow an identifiable or chronological time schedule. For growth to follow its natural course there must be adequate, aggressive, environmental contact and a viable balance of support and frustration. As infants we need environmental support to survive, but frustration forces us to mobilize and learn to use our resources, to realize our innate potentials. We discover our boundaries by repeated contact with our environments. From these contacts, we develop a sense of self and not self. We learn about separateness, differences, and relatedness. Before we develop self-support, we encounter situations in which there is no external support and experience confusion and helplessness. Our typical reactions are to manipulate those around us, usually our parents, to avoid coping with the realities of life. We play stupid, helpless, or compliant. Unfortunately, if we are successful with our manipulations, we block the natural growth process.

Normal growth is difficult. The natural process of growth is neither programmed nor forced; it is allowed. Change and adjustment occur as we reformulate existing gestalts, not in our attachment to old gestalts. Different, dangerous, difficult, or painful situations often lead to deliberateness rather than spontaneity, to rigidity rather than openness, to stagnation rather than growth.

The socialization process we experience as children may facilitate or block the developmental process. If we introject (swallow whole) the values and behaviors of our parents and teachers that are incongruent with our organismic needs, we develop splits. We attempt to follow an enforced morality, a system of tyrannical shoulds and musts rather than a morality based on what we are and how we encounter reality. Introjection can lead not only to disgust but also to guilt when we behave in opposition to our authentic needs. Moreover, if our guilt is strong enough, we ignore our organismic needs and respond to our introjected shoulds. Thus, our spontaneous personality is superseded by a deliberate personality. We become closed and rigid rather than open and spontaneous.

We are fortunate if, when we need their support most, we can identify with our parents, accepting their values and direction. We are even more fortunate if, as we grow, we have their permission and support to be different, to make choices, and to accept the consequences of our choices. Gradually we must come to accept that our thoughts, feelings, and actions are only our responsibility.

Mature responsibility is our being what we are and permitting others to live their lives without our interference. We cannot blame others or society if we refuse to take the risks that lead to growth. Our parents, in their efforts to give us all they never had, may overindulge us and create environments that are so pleasant and satisfying that we may want to maintain them. We are responsible for refusing to use our own resources.

Importance of Role Assigned to Self-Concept

According to Perls, there are three components or subsystems of personality that are in full operation by the time we reach mid-adolescence: being, self, and self-image. Being, our essential core, is present from birth, while self and self-image develop during our interactions (adaptation, acknowledgment, and approbation) with our environments. Both self and self-image have the potential for development and evolution at any given moment. As we make contact with our environment, either self or self-image may emerge as a coping force in our lives.

When self emerges, we evaluate our possibilities in the immediate situation and then integrate and carry them through to completion in the pursuit of our organismic need's realization. The self, then, is awareness, intuitive knowing, and choice. Further, the self contributes to our existence and growth, our integration, our actualization. Self-image, in contrast, blocks awareness, preventing our contact with actuality and leading to a denial or disavowal of some aspects of self while overidentifying with other aspects, usually in the cause of introjected shoulds. The self develops in our quest for authenticity. Self-image develops in our attempt to be something we are not. Self is based on trust in organismic needs, while self-image emerges when we distrust our inner needs and capacities. Our self is genuine and spontaneous. Our self-image is phony and deliberate.

Explanation of Learning

For Perls (1972), healthful learning is discovery, and a coordinated psychophysical awareness of present experience is the means of discovery. When we are fully aware of the immediacy of sensing and experiencing, there is an interaction and integration between ourselves and our environment. We are in contact with the realities of ourselves and our world. In addition, when in full psychophysical awareness, there is a flowing merger of our affective and cognitive functions. Our intellect and affect form a symbiotic relationship. Even our most abstract thoughts are accompanied by feelings that lend personal meaning or relevance to our learning. Further, in psychophysical awareness, we are in tune with our inner wisdom. We intuitively know what direction and action to take. Awareness and actualization evolve as we learn to exist in the present.

Perls's oft-quoted line, "Lose your mind and come to your senses," was his way of promoting a psychophysical or organic awareness of the immediate. He believes strongly that learning originates in our human experience. Further, he believes relevant learning is impossible without feelings that give that learning personal meaning. If we repress, dull, or ignore our emotions, for whatever reason, we deaden our awareness and impair our learning capacity. If, for example, we split our awareness by favoring our intellect to the exclusion of our emotion, we tend to explain the why and, in doing so, reshape our awareness of the experience. Explanation replaces understanding.

Intelligent awareness is a description of an experience rather than an active expression or present sensing of the experience. Kempler (1973) refers to intelligent awareness as an "almost phenomenon" (p. 259). Perls (1972) calls the intellect "the whore of intelligence" (p. 24). Thus, he seeks a balance between awareness and understanding, between affect and intellect.

The implications, at least for the healthy, would seem to be that reason and logic are less important than immediate, vivid, experiential sensing; that intellectual explanation is less valuable than intuitive understanding; and that rational thinking is less trustworthy than our inner or organismic wisdom. To be spontaneously and authentically present in the moment is to learn. Schultz (1977) adds the dimension of choice to our awareness of experience as the source of personal knowledge when he writes, "The self 'knows' as it creates meaning. Through awareness 'the point of contact where being and consciousness meet,' the individual experiences aliveness and creates his reality" (p. 29).

Importance of Group Membership

We are, as indicated in the previous resolutions, biological and social beings. Both physiological and social-psychological needs must be met through contact with objects, people, and groups in our environments. On the psychological level, we need contact with others as much as we need food and drink on the physiological level (Perls, 1976, p. 25). Furthermore we are self-regulating beings. We are born with a sense of social and psychological balance as acute as our sense of physical balance (p. 27). In fact, Perls tells us that our sense of relatedness to and identification with others may indeed be "our primary psychological survival impulse" (p. 25).

It is natural, then, for us to relate to and identify with people and groups we contact in our environmental fields. Without others, the odds against our survival are extremely high.

As infants (see "Early and/or Continuous Development"), our initial group contact is with our families. Our existence depends on the support we receive from the members of this crucial primary group. Rooted in this group, we become bound with all family members. Our ego boundaries can expand to include every person in the family. It is now us rather than I. Slight or injury to any member of the group affects all members, and feeling a sense of shared hurt or anger, we respond accordingly.

Most early identifications and learning occur as our responses to the interpersonal demands of family members, particularly our parents or guardians. If the family is impoverished, all members are affected. Healthy functioning requires environmental support, especially during our early years. As relating organisms, we need contact with a healthy social environment to experience acceptance and affirmation and to exchange friendship and love. Our encounters with people and groups and the relationships we establish distinguish us, as well as define our identities by setting the limits of our ego boundaries.

We learn to trust and identify with our friends, and we can feel alienated by those outside our ego boundaries. We maintain contact with those we include in our ego boundaries and withdraw from the outsiders. Inside our ego boundaries there is familiarity, collaboration, friendship, even love. Outside our ego boundaries there is strangeness, suspicion, distrust, even hate (Perls, 1971, p. 8).

Identification or alienation with people or groups can be either healthy or unhealthy. When our identification with a group is excessive, loss of membership can result in a sense of self-loss or loss of personal identity. Alienation from a group can lead to withdrawal from contact that might otherwise provide us with need fulfillment. Again, balance seems to be the key. We must learn, usually through trial and error, to regulate our contact and withdrawal in the service of our needs. Even the most intimate personal relationships and the most significant group memberships require this balance.

Uniqueness and/or Commonality

From the Gestalt viewpoint, we hold much in common with our fellow humans, including, paradoxically, our uniqueness. Uniqueness is a human norm. We share many of the same needs and inhabit the same world, but there are no duplicates in the human species. Personality, the self of Gestalt therapy, is a unique, personal construction, fashioned of private perceptions and interpretations and based on a fluctuating, subjective awareness and an ever-present freedom of choice.

We share a universal awareness, but awareness is an intrinsically subjective experience. We exist in the here and now of reality, but we live in the place and time that is important to us at the moment. Phenomenologically, only the figure, what we presently know and want, exists; all else is background and outside our experiential focus.

Certainly, we are physical beings and must obey the laws of nature if we are to survive. Just as certainly, we are embedded in and must interact with an environmental field if we are to live and grow. As physical beings, we need water, food, shelter, and warmth. As psychological beings, we need acceptance, love, and emotional and intellectual stimuli. As free-functioning beings, we choose that particular portion of the world with which we are in contact and in which we live and grow. Our awareness encourages us to perceive ourselves in a personal and social context. Our intellect encourages us to conceptualize and hypothesize about the nature of our world. What we are aware of and how we are aware are open to an infinite variety of individual, interpretive shadings and choices. Both awareness and uniqueness are human phenomena.

Importance of Reward

Convinced that we are free-functioning, responsible beings, Perls assigns little importance to external reinforcement or reward as a behavioral determinant. He concentrates instead on internal reward that comes from change initiated by present awareness and choice, not external controlling variables or stimuli. As we become aware of and experience ourselves and our environments, we choose our responses. Our choices are based on an internal awareness and a personally constructed set of values and beliefs. The more open we are to ourselves and our world, the greater our awareness and contact with our intrinsic needs and environmental surroundings—thus, the better choices we are able to make.

The Gestalt approach not only accepts but also trusts internal reward. Awareness is its own reward. Being fully in the present is exciting; we possess a sense of aliveness, an exuberance for life and living. Awareness and fulfillment of our organismic needs as they emerge from ground to figure result in immediate gratification. Closure of a gestalt is innately satisfying. Completion of unfinished situations brings an inner sense of relief and fulfillment. Being able to call on resources to solve a difficult problem or to meet life's tasks is rewarding. There is an inner sense of affirmation when we are accepted for what we are by another, particularly a significant other. A sudden intuitive insight is accompanied by excitement and enthusiasm. In moments of acute awareness and concentration, when cognitive, emotive, and motor processes are harmoniously focused on the environment, we experience an inner sense of oneness with nature and the world. Through awareness, we reinforce the facility of awareness.

External reinforcement or reward is suspect. External rewards may encourage us to ignore our inner wisdom and measure ourselves and our needs against some criterion outside ourselves. Intellectual insights and interpretations into the why of our behavior can lead us to accept the behavior rather than to change it—thus, to stagnate rather than to grow.

GOALS OF GESTALT THERAPISTS

Prochaska (1979) contends that the "ideal outcome" of Gestalt therapy is the clients' discovery "that they do not and never really did need a therapist" (p. 164). Fully centered and secure in the present moment of existence, clients are now aware that they possess both the inner strength and personal resources necessary to cope with the challenges of living. They unconditionally accept themselves for what they are: free-functioning, self-regulating, integrated, expressive beings, totally responsible for their potentials, choices, perceptions, feelings, and actions. Further, they accept the risk of transcending rather than adapting, of being genuine, spontaneous, uninhibited, and unpredictable.

In any discussion of ideal therapeutic outcome, there are implications for ultimate therapist goals, as well as numerous immediate and intermediate goals thought to lead to an ideal outcome. Through awareness, experimentation and encounter, Gestalt therapists:

Facilitate and increase their clients' present-oriented sensory awareness and experiencing of self and environment;

Concentrate on the what and how of their clients' present behavior;

Induce their clients' movement into and through the polarities of the impasse where typical adjustment behaviors and avoided aspects of self are available to awareness;

Implement skillful frustration to foster self-discovery by holding their clients in the here-and-now of their experience;

Present opportunities for resolution and closure of their clients' unfinished situations and/or incomplete gestalts;

Encourage their clients' movement from environmental support to self-support through discovery that they can do much more than they think is possible;

Develop the self-support systems of their clients through conscious and responsible choices;

Facilitate integration and the motivation process through self-discovery and recovery of lost functions.

Underlying all goals of the Gestalt approach to counseling and psychotherapy is Perls's concept of universal awareness. Without awareness there is no therapy. Latner (1973) maintains that "the point of therapy is not to make solutions, it is to make the problem-laden present more actual by increasing the patients' awareness" (p. 211). It is through the clients' awareness that healthy functioning can be re-established; that the resistance behaviors of introjection, retroflection, projection, and confluence can be terminated; that unfinished business becomes accessible; and that integration can be restored. Awareness alone can be curative. It is both content and process, goal and tool, and is the focus of the counselor throughout Gestalt therapy.

THERAPEUTIC PROCESS: METHODS AND TECHNIQUES

The primary source for the resolutions of the eleven basic issues is the Gestalt therapy of Fritz Perls. It should be noted, however, that while the majority of

Gestalt therapists holds comparable concepts, beliefs, and values, their strategies, techniques, and styles can, and often do, vary considerably. Perls's hot-seat approach, working individually with volunteers in a group setting, is the prevailing style among Gestalt therapists. It is not the only style or necessarily the best style, but Fritz Perls's style.

However, therapeutic style is an individual creation. It emerges from the immediacy of the authentic relationship and is limited only by the imagination, innovativeness, and spontaneity of the therapist. Zinker (1977), for example, views Gestalt therapy as a creative process and the therapist as an artist. Perls's (1969) greatest concern about the future of Gestalt therapy was that many who called themselves Gestalt therapists were merely technicians, hiding behind a limiting set of rules and regulations, playing games, or worse, avoiding themselves by trying to be another Fritz. Perls feared that, should this group expand, Gestalt therapy would become, at best, a poorly practiced craft rather than a reputable psychotherapy.

Therapeutic Relationship

The counselor-client relationship in Gestalt therapy is often described as an existential encounter of the I-and-thou, here-and-now. As in any genuine encounter, there is a confrontive immediacy to this relationship, an insistence that both therapist and client remain in, experience fully, and take responsibility for, the present. Moreover, the therapeutic relationship of Gestalt therapy is frequently frustrating.

Unlike Rogers, who offers his clients unconditional positive regard, Perls intentionally and skillfully frustrates his clients, forcing them in the "safe emergency" of the therapeutic session to discover the possibilities in their lives to become self-supporting. Whatever their clients expect from them in the relationship, the purpose of Gestalt therapists is to show their clients that they can do as well themselves.

Gestalt therapy is experiential, and both therapist and client are active participants in the process of the therapeutic relationship. Kempler (1973) compares the therapist to a "composing maestro" and the client to an "accomplished musician" who meet to combine their talent and skill (p. 266). Prochaska (1979) refers to the Gestalt therapist as a director, challenging the client/actor to be more spontaneous, more intense, as he or she acts out scenes between top dog and under dog, social self and natural self, intellect and intuition (p. 155). In "The Trickster-Healer," Kopp (in Smith, 1976) writes of Perls and his clients as "the sorcerer and his apprentices" (pp. 69–82). There is a motif that runs through the three analogies just cited, a motif that also appears as a recurrent theme in Zinker's (1977) book: in Gestalt therapy, the therapist and client enter the creative process of the therapeutic relationship together, each agreeing to a concerted blending of their efforts, talents, and skills.

Empathy.   Empathy is a vital force in the interaction between therapist and client. It is important that Gestalt therapists feel and respond to what their clients are experiencing. Realizing that their clients always act as total organisms, Gestalt therapists are open to their clients' movements, expressions, voice tones, eye focus, and body language. All client communications in Gestalt therapy are significant. Patterson (1980), stressing the therapists' need to experience their clients fully, writes, "The therapist must be sensitive, aware, and able to experience the patient's total communication, since 'verbal communication is usually a lie' " (p. 448).

Spontaneity.   Spontaneity also contributes to the effectiveness of the therapeutic relationship. When therapists can be what they are in the moment of the relationship, their responses to their clients are the natural outcome of an authentic relationship. Zinker (1977) encourages therapists to draw on their spontaneity in the therapeutic relationship, then allow the relationship to create technique. When therapists' relationships with their clients are genuine and spontaneous, the therapists are their technique. Rather than playing a role using a technique, they permit their method to emerge from process.

Authenticity.   Passons (1975) recognizes that "who the counselor is remains the primary factor in his functioning" and will "permeate everything he does in his many functions as a counselor," including the relationship he establishes with his clients (p. 5). Kempler (1973) echoes this point when he writes, "It is the force of the total person that is his contribution to the movement in therapy" (p. 219). Although Perls (1969) seemed to place the greatest emphasis on the gestalt experiment in his own work, he abhorred those who avoided the I-Thou encounter of Gestalt therapy by hiding behind technique. Perhaps Kempler (1973) expresses the importance of the therapeutic relationship to Gesalt therapy most succinctly when he points out that it is the only process that cannot be absent in therapy (p. 268).

Initial Procedures and Strategies

As will be seen later, the procedures and strategies of Gestalt therapy do focus on a set of rules and games (Fagan & Shepherd, 1971); however, even a cursory understanding of the theory of Gestalt therapy reveals that it is far more. "Gestalt therapy is really permission to be creative" (Zinker, 1977, p. 18). The theory of Gestalt therapy is a unique existential joining of behaviorism and phenomenology. The method of Gestalt therapy is an integration of relationship, capacity, abilities, and techniques. The major tool of Gestalt therapy is the experiment.

Initiating Therapy.   In his autobiography, Perls (1969) claims that to work successfully he needs only his skill, Kleenex, the hot seat, the empty chair, cigarettes, an ashtray, and a "tiny bit of goodwill" (pp. 227, 229). Although he sometimes conducted mass experiments, Perls exhibited little interest in either group dynamics or the group process. His usual method of therapy was with the individual in front of the group. When conducting seminars in Esalen, he admitted as many as 70 to 80 people to the group. Therapy was initiated simply by asking, "Now, who would like to work?" A volunteer then moved to the hot seat, and therapy began.

Perls was always the expert and always in control. He decided whether or not the client was working or whether the group situation was appropriate for a particular client. He retained the right to refuse to work with any volunteer. On those occasions when he decided the client took the hot seat just to duel, he ended the session abruptly or, as reported on more than one occasion, went to sleep. Likewise, if he believed the situation inappropriate, he ended the session, either by inviting the client to see him at another time or simply by saying he did not think this the appropriate time or place. He determined the length of each session, also. When he felt closure or a new Gestalt or if he believed that either he or the client had had enough, he excused the client and asked for another volunteer to take the hot seat.

Kempler (1973) is more concerned about group dynamics. He believes the make-up of the group to be important and recommends that the therapist personally screen each potential group member to assess his or her capability for effective therapeutic encounter. He believes, too, that the heterogeneous group has the greatest success and usually strives to include both male and female, young and old, and a wide variety of occupations.

Structuring and Client Expectations.   In Gestalt therapy, structuring entails much more than a presentation of therapy and fee structure, although neither of these should be overlooked. An essential part of structuring is the introduction of the therapeutic process, a brief but clear delineation of therapist and client responsibilities. Further, the client must be made aware of any limits of confidentiality. This is especially essential if the client is a referral who represents the vested interests of referring parties (i.e., parents or guardians, a referral agent or agency, institution, or one of the court systems).

The nature of the Gestalt experiment requires active exploration of the impasse, the very point at which clients are avoiding contact with self and environment. Realizing that therapy will place their clients in the anxiety-laden dilemma of wanting to change and grow at the same time they desire to remain in the painful comfort of present situations, Gestalt therapists communicate early that their clients are expected to be active participants in the therapeutic process. Although the character of the experiment depends on the type of impasse and the degree of client avoidance, client expressions requested by the therapist are nearly always behavioral rather than verbal. The Gestalt experiment transforms a passive talking-about-a-problem session into an active exploring and experiencing of the moment. Briefly reviewing the rules of therapy can facilitate this understanding. Most Gestalt therapists agree that therapy is possible only when their clients decide to enter and remain in therapy and, even more important, to accept the responsibility of outcome.

Course of Therapy

Kempler (1973) contends that the process of therapy is really a compilation (gestalt) of numerous processes serving a triumvirate of three major processes: (1) the psychotherapy, including the therapuetic relationship; (2) the process within the client that is signaled by the symptom; and (3) the process within the therapist that responds to the client's symptomatic processes (p. 268).

In the first, the psychotherapy, therapists work to balance support with frustration while maintaining the I-Thou relationship with their clients. The quality of the relationship determines to a great extent the outcome of the therapy session for both clients and therapists.

Therapy proper begins with the emergence of the second process when clients, seeking relief from the discomfort of their symptoms, present their reasons for coming to therapy. Usually at this point, clients believe that their relief will result from something their therapists will do to or for them rather than from the result of their own efforts.

In the third process, therapists use all their relevant knowledge and skills to recognize the polarities of the predominant impasse and to create a dialogue between these polarities. Gestalt therapists, assuming that their clients have the resources to live as fully integrated persons, serve as catalysts or guides for the phenomenological learning of their clients. They work to facilitate their clients' awareness by accentuating immediate experience. Encouraging full expression of their clients' feelings and focusing on the here and now, what and how of experience, they minimize their clients' cognitive function, the tendency to intellectualize or talk about their experiences.

The immediate objective of Gestalt therapists is to assist their clients to reach closure of the most crucial polarities of the present impasse, ending their capacity to create discordance and discomfort. Ultimatley, this leads the client to greater integration of the self, the final goal of therapy. Working in the immediacy of the moment and under the assumption that the most pressing need will emerge to figure, therapists work on the symptom present, regardless of the symptom initially presented by the client.

In the therapeutic process, Gestalt therapists move from the general to the specific and from the past or future to the present. They use nearly any method or technique to encourage their clients to confront their impasse and to become aware of and accept responsibility for their present avoidance behaviors. Rather than interpret, they attend to the obvious, particularly to their clients' nonverbal communications. The techniques available to Gestalt therapists are limited only by the therapist's imagination and creativity.

Seldom is the therapeutic process easy or pleasant, although initially many clients experience brief periods of exuberance, energy, or urgency. Confronting, owning, and dealing with avoidances and disowned parts of the self may lead to greater integration, but the process of integration is nearly always perceived as difficult and, at times, extremely painful.

Following the exuberance stage, the promise of therapy turns to reality, and Gestalt clients often enter a stage of resentment. During this period they are likely to be depressed and critical of both the therapist and therapy. When unable to own and express their resentment, clients slow or completely stop the therapeutic process. However, when they can accept and fully express their negative feelings toward their therapist and therapy, the therapeutic process continues, even accelerates. The work of therapy begins to acquire personal meaning, even though clients realize that therapy may be more difficult and require more time and effort than they had imagined. These clients persist. Here again, the quality of the therapeutic relationship may be the intervening variable in fostering the client's movement through the various stages of therapy.

As with the decision to continue, the decision to terminate therapy is the client's responsibility. This decision, at least when sound, is based solely on the client's need and comes from the client's discovery that therapeutic support is no longer necessary.

The techniques (rules and experiments) of Gestalt therapy are based on the principles of direct communication and are designed to enhance client awareness of the immediate situation. When successful, they lead to greater integration of both the client's self and environment. The action invited focuses on the awareness continuum between active, responsible, and committed participants and is rooted in the client's perspective. Laura Perls (in Smith, 1976) reminds us that "a Gestalt therapist does not use techniques; he applies *himself in* and *to* a situation with whatever professional skill and life experiences he has accumulated and integrated" (p. 223, emphasis in original).

While awareness may be curative, it may also be slow to evolve. The techniques of Gestalt therapy are created by the therapist in the present moment of the therapeutic process to accelerate the client's awareness. Respect for and sensitivity to the client and the client's needs increase the experiment's therapeutic potential. There is usually greater gain, too, when the client is prepared, the experiment is appropriate, and the timing is accurate.

Although all Gestalt experiments are confrontive by nature, they need not be insensitive or abrasive. An effective experiment is an invitation, not a demand, to awareness, a challenge to participate. When effective, the experiment ends detachment, leads to excitement, and results in contact. There are no predetermined or anticipated results for an experiment; it is but a suggestion to try for fit, an invitation to experience. The client may always choose to stop the exercise or to withdraw from contact with it.

Rules of Gestalt Therapy.   The first rule of Gestalt psychotherapy is the significance of immediate awareness and experience, the absolute priority of the now. Only the now exists. Life is in the present tense. Therefore, now is the situation of therapy. Gestalt therapists are uninterested in a case history and do not permit their clients to talk about their problems in the past tense. Gestalt clients are not in therapy to recall their problems; they are there to live their problems. If clients can manage to experience their present fully, whether physically, verbally, or in fantasy, they will learn not only what their problems are but also how they are producing their problems and what they can do now to solve them. "Now I am aware . . . " becomes the primary client response in therapy. What are you feeling at this moment? What do you want? expect? need? What are you doing with your hands? foot? eyes? the muscles in your neck? shoulders? These are the questions of therapy.

Gestalt therapists are interested in facilitating their clients' awareness of the what and how of their living, not the why. How are my clients preventing awareness? What are my clients doing to avoid contact with their environmental fields? How are my clients disowning aspects of their selves? The goal is not interpretation but self-discovery through experience and integration through completion.

The second rule of Gestalt therapy is to change questions to statements. By refusing to answer questions and by requiring their clients to change their questions to statements, Gestalt therapists boost their clients' awareness that most questions are only manipulations to gain support or to avoid responsibility. For example, "What good will this do me?" might become "I don't believe this is going to help me." At the very least, the client becomes aware of resistance.

Rule three is own your language. So-called it-language and you-language are changed to I-language. To promote the awareness that we are active beings who do things, as opposed to passive beings to whom things are done or to whom things happen, Gestalt therapists request that their clients change "it" or "you" to "I," particularly when they are referring to parts of their bodies or to their activities. For example, "This head is killing me" becomes "I am killing me." "You make me angry" becomes "I am angry with you because I . . . ." "It scares me" becomes "I am scared because I . . . ." As active beings we are responsible for our actions. It-language and you-language are used to avoid responsibility. Self-support and self-responsibility are goals of therapy.

No gossiping is the fourth rule of therapy. Clients who begin to talk about another person or group of persons are encouraged to engage the person or group, through fantasy, in direct dialogue. The therapist may make use of the empty chair (see the following section) to accomplish this. The purpose of the dialogue is to foster direct communication of feeling and to keep the client in the present moment of existence.

The fifth rule of therapy is the primacy of the I-Thou relationship. Reasons for this rule were discussed earlier (see "Therapeutic Relationship");

however, Gestalt therapists usually try to see that their clients direct their talk to someone (I-Thou) rather than at someone (I-It). If, for example, the client is constantly looking down or staring at the wall while talking to the therapist, the therapist may ask, "What are you doing with your eyes?" or "What do you see?" or "Where are you now?" The purpose of these questions is to bring the client's behavior into awareness, making discovery of avoidance behaviors possible. During I-Thou communications, both participants look at and listen to the person talking.

Empty Chair Technique.   The Gestalt therapist may employ this technique whenever splits or projections are discovered. The client is first asked to imagine that the person or object involved is seated in the empty chair, and then to carry on a dialogue with the chair's occupant. The most common dialogue in Gestalt therapy is between the top dog and the under dog, or between the client's aggressive shoulds and passive, resistant excuses. However, the dialogue can include any polarity—that is, conversations between cognitions and emotions, mind and body, cautious self and risk-taking self, good self and bad self, masculine behaviors and feminine behaviors, natural self and social self, biological desires and moral values, headache and self, and so forth. By creating both sides of the dialogue, the client is likely to become more aware, accepting, and understanding of that part of the self that is typically disowned, avoided, or unconfirmed in awareness.

Realizing the client is avoiding contact with his or her emotions, the therapist employs the empty chair technique to facilitate the client's awareness and to bring the client into contact with that part of the self he or she is avoiding. The polarity in the following dialogue is the client's thinking self and the client's feeling self.

Therapist: Are you aware that you just related a highly emotional event in your life and there was no affect evident in your voice whatsoever? It was almost as though you were talking about something you read in this morning's paper that didn't involve you. Imagine, if you will, that this empty chair contains your feeling self, the emotional part of you. Now, as your thinking self, carry on a dialogue between the two parts of you, your thinking self and your feeling self.

Client:

Thinking Self: I don't trust you, Feeling Self. You're soft. You're vulnerable. You let yourself open to get hurt. Other people quickly see how soft you are and take advantage of you. They use you, and when they get what they want, they dump you. You can bet that will never happen to me.

Feeling Self: I'd rather be soft and vulnerable than cold and unfeeling. Sure, I get hurt occasionally. But many times I feel joy and pleasure in my relationships. I know what it's like to have close and trusting friendships. I am able to love and to be loved. You can bet that will never happen to you either. You're too afraid of being hurt. You're too afraid to risk yourself.

Thinking Self: At least I don't waste a lot of time feeling hurt and upset when things go wrong. I much prefer looking at a situation rationally, setting priorities, and getting the job done.

Feeling Self: I must agree you do seem to accomplish a great deal without much worry or concern, but you never feel any excitement in your work. You never feel any real sense of accomplishment or pleasure. For you, it's just another checkmark on your list of priorities, another job out of the way. If you feel anything at all, it's boredom. One day is like another—no highs, no lows—just routine. I may get upset occasionally or feel hurt when people let me down, but my life isn't a bore. My world isn't flat.

Thinking Self: You could do a lot more if you took life a little more seriously and looked at things a little more rationally.

Feeling Self: You could enjoy life more if you took yourself a little less seriously, if you could relax a little and laugh at yourself and the world occasionally.

Therapist: Good. Let's break it here. I think you may have learned something from your dialogue.

The empty chair may be used also when unfinished business, usually a form of resentment, is identified. Again, the client is invited to fill the empty chair, via imagination, with the person involved and create a dialogue that includes things left unsaid, feelings left unexpressed, or promises gone unfulfilled. The purpose here is to help the client reach closure in a significant relationship. Because this is an exercise in fantasy, the imaginary person in the empty chair need not be a living person or even real. The dialogue can be with a loved one who died, an unborn child, a historical or fictional character, or a stereotypical personality. It can be a god, ghost, devil, or angel, just as long as an unfinished situation in the client's life can be addressed and completed in the dialogue.

Exaggeration.   Exaggeration of body language—whether gestures, tone of voice, posture, or facial expression—can promote awareness of incongruencies between verbal messages and nonverbal communications, acceptable and unacceptable or denied feelings, or the avoidance behaviors at the point of the impasse—for example, talking of fear while smiling, relating an exciting story with flat affect, speaking kindly of someone while clenching a fist, or laughing at an accident in which someone was seriously injured. The therapist may bring the behavior to the client's awareness by copying or mimicking the client's posture or tone of voice or by asking the client to repeat a gesture or statement, expanding it each time it is repeated. The therapist may ask the client to translate an emotion into motion, even to dance it.

Reversals.   Asking clients to play a role or take a stand opposite that expressed or demonstrated can stimulate awareness and understanding of another person, a point of view, or a disowned or latent aspect of the self. For example, passive clients may discover aggressive qualities; gentle clients may become aware that they can also be cruel; and clients experiencing an unexplained dislike for another or for a group may learn they possess the very qualities they find repulsive in the others. Awareness and acceptance can lead to integration, a more whole or complete self.

Shuttle Technique.   Awareness can sometimes be enhanced by repeatedly directing the clients' attention from one activity or experience to another. It is possible, for example, to discover similarities, differences, feelings, avoidance behaviors, or a natural rhythm of contact and withdrawal. It is possible to move the client back and forth between fantasy and reality, past and present, from talking to listening, and from excitement to boredom. Bored or tired clients can learn the location of energy impasses. Tense clients can discover how they relax. Talkative clients can learn how they avoid listening to others.

Rehearsals.   Through rehearsal, clients can gain awareness of how much time they spend preparing to play their social roles or of the effort required when they are trying to be something other than what they are. Rehearsal can also be used to cultivate awareness of options available in a current situation or to decrease tension due to anticipations of future events. For example, using fantasy, clients can rehearse performing either well or poorly on an important examination and explore their feelings in each instance. In fantasy they can rehearse asking their supervisors for an increase in salary or asking a recent arrival in the neighborhood to dinner and dancing. Through imagination, they can feel what it would be like to lead a group or to give a speech. Rehearsal allows for covert practice and modeling of desirable behaviors, especially in situations where avoidance anxiety exists.

I Have a Secret.   Clients attempting to hide some personal weakness, past experience, or frightening desire that they simply cannot tell anyone may be asked to close their eyes, think of their secret, then, without revealing it, imagine how others would react on learning it. Awareness is the anticipated outcome. Typically, however, clients discover that their secret is not as frightening or horrible as they perceive it to be, that really very few people would become upset on learning it, that most of the people who care for them would continue to care. They learn that they created the catastrophe in their fantasies and that their anticipations are not necessarily what will occur in reality.

May I Feed You a Sentence?   This technique involves invitations from therapists to their clients to repeat a sentence to see how it feels to say it. Clients who claim they can't do something may be asked to say, "I won't do it." Clients who believe something is impossible for them may be asked to repeat, "It will be difficult for me to accomplish this, not impossible." Feeding the client a sentence often occurs in therapy when the client, consciously or unconsciously, misuses language. There is a natural tendency to use *can't* when we do not wish to admit that we *won't*, or to say something is "impossible" when we fear failure or wish to avoid difficulty. Trying on a sentence may bring this tendency to awareness. Therapists, however, should be aware that this technique may be a cover for their wish to interpret.

Contact and Withdrawal.   Gestalt therapists are sensitive to and accepting of their clients' natural need to withdraw. They permit, even assist, their clients to experience temporary withdrawal from the therapy session, particularly after an especially stressful exercise. One of the more common procedures is to instruct their clients to close their eyes, imagine a special place where they once felt relaxed and secure, then to go to that place in their imagination and remain until these feelings return. Once relaxed and at peace, they are instructed to open their eyes and return to the present.

Dream Work.   For Perls, the dream contains everything relevant to an understanding of the dreamer's present way of life. Every element in the dream—whether person, thing, or mood—is a projection, therefore an alienation of the dreamer's self. By identifying with and acting out any dream element, the dreamer opens the possibility of uncovering and understanding the underlying existential message of the dream, thereby gaining greater self-insight. To listen to the therapist's interpretations is to hear the therapist's projections, which can only interfere with and mislead the dreamer's discovery and integration.

Lack of dream recall and resistance to playing the part of any element of the dream are indications that the dreamer refuses to acknowledge and contact the rejected parts of self. Since everything necessary for integration is present in every dream, the dream renders a complete, although condensed and cryptographic, reflection of the dreamer's present state of existence and points the way to integration.

Perls was at his best in dream work seminars. He often used the empty chair technique to facilitate the client's dialogue with parts of the dream and self.

ASSESSING PROGRESS

The most thoroughly researched of the current psychotherapies are those most widely accepted by academicians, who have a clearly vested interest in the professional publication of their work and the works of their students. As a case in point, see Chapter 4, "The Person-Centered Therapy of Carl Rogers." Neither Perls nor his theory enjoys this advantage. For the most part, the academic ranks are either unimpressed with or actively opposed to any anti-intellectual approach to psychotherapy, and they place Perls and his ideas in this category. Further, since most Gestalt practitioners appear to have neither the time nor the inclination to design and conduct carefully controlled studies of their therapy, searching the literature for a list of criteria to assess progress is futile. The few controlled studies available use normal subjects who, for the most part, were seeking personal growth experiences through group therapy.

Although Perls (1972) expressed a willingness to put his work to the test of any research, he did nothing to encourage this. Further, most of the clients in Perls's demonstrations were normal people, often professionals, who attended his workshops and seminars for personal growth or to observe the master at work in the hope of sharpening their therapeutic skills.

Because Gestalt therapy places full responsibility on the client, both for entering and terminating therapy, there is little screening or follow-up of clients. Moreover, any assessment of the effectiveness of therapy is also the responsibility of the client.

For Perls, intuitive, or organismic, knowing is superior to intellectual knowing and is the validating evidence of Gestalt therapy. Perls could see and feel his therapy work, and that was enough for him. In fact, there is some question in the minds of those who accept Perls's theory whether any empirical research can accurately or fully measure the human experience.

FINAL COMMENTARY

The direction and future of Gestalt therapy are unclear. It is certain, however, that Perls's therapy is a unique psychotherapeutic approach anchored in a philosophy that for many adherents fills a gap or void in the myriad of existing theories of psychotherapy. Perls has solidly set the cornerstone with a theory and philosophy of life and living that is unquestionably assured and optimistic. He affirms that we are aware, active, self-regulating, free-functioning, self-supporting, organismically wise beings, innately capable of living our lives fully and responsibly in the present. It is not surprising, then, that so many find his theory appealing.

Although Perls's theory is similar in many ways to existing theories, his application varies significantly. Rather than passively talking about their trials and strife with life, Perls's clients are asked to live their problems in the therapy session, to give up their detachment, and to contact and communicate directly with their feelings. Held to the now of existence, the disturbing as-

FIGURE 6.1 A Schematic Analysis of Perls's Stand on the Basic Issues

Left Pole		Right Pole
Biological Determinants	▮ (center)	Social Determinants
Unconscious Determinants	▮ (right of center)	Conscious Determinants
Early Development	▮ (right of center)	Continuous Development
Psychological Environment	▮ (left)	Reality Environment
Conditioning	▮ (right of center)	Freedom
Commonality	▮ (right of center)	Uniqueness

Importance of Group Membership	It is natural to relate to and identify with people we encounter. Dependent upon our families as infants, we become bound with family members. As we grow, our affiliations help us to define our identities by establishing ego boundaries. A social-psychological balance is the key to effective living as we regulate our contact with and withdrawal from the group in service of our needs.
Explanation of Learning	Healthful learning is discovery facilitated by psychological awareness representing the interaction and integration of self and environment as both are experienced in the here and now. Learning originates in our human experience and seeks a balance of affect and intellect.
Number and Weight Assigned to Motivational Concepts	Behind all our behavior is an inherent actualizing tendency which consists of thousands of psychological and social needs, each need arising (becoming figure) and receding (returning to ground) as we choose to experience and attend it. Effective living requires spontaneous being—experiencing and attending to our needs in the here and now.
Importance of Reward	Reward is internal and experienced as change initiated by present awareness and choice. Indeed, awareness is its own reward; awareness facilitates identification of organismic needs, choice, need-satisfaction, closure of gestalt, and—at its height—oneness with nature.
Importance or Role of Self-Concept	Perls identifies three subsystems of personality: being (our core existence present from birth) and self and self-image (developed as we interact with our environments). Self represents awareness, intuitive knowing and choice; authentic and spontaneous, our self moves us toward actualization. Inauthentic and deliberate, our self-image blocks awareness by introjecting "shoulds."

pects of past and future are encountered and dealt with in the present. Helplessness, no longer an excuse for inaction, is synonymous with manipulation. Directed fantasy is a therapeutic tool rather than an escape. All elements of the dream are acted out by the dreamer. Nonverbal communication is considered more honest than the clients' words. Intuitive knowing holds priority over reason and logic. Authenticity becomes the primary goal for change.

Certainly there is strength in Perls's theory, but there is weakness as well. He is accused of irrational anti-intellectualism, with some justification. The strong emphasis in Gestalt therapy on experiencing and feeling diminishes significantly the importance and role of cognitive functioning in psychological health. Many in the field believe Gestalt therapy could profit from a greater integration of intellect and intuition. They maintain that human functioning includes conceptualizing as well as emoting and behaving.

Other critics point to an inconsistency between theory and application. Although Perls writes extensively about the I-Thou relationship, the existential encounter between equals, and the responsibility of clients to direct their own lives, they point out that, in practice, Perls functions as the expert and rather forcefully directs his clients' attention, verbalizations, and actions.

Still other critics argue that Gestalt therapy is yet to be tested on a wide variety of clients, and, in fact, may be ineffective, perhaps even harmful, to some of the more dysfunctional clients. Until then, they believe it should be limited to overly socialized, restrained, constricted clients. Kempler (1973) disagrees and asserts, "There is nothing in Gestalt Therapy itself to block its applicability" (p. 274). The limitations, he believes, are in the individual therapists.

The lack of empirical validation, the crucial test of any theory, has been discussed. Still, considering that Gestalt therapy is well into its third decade, it is surprising that there has not been greater effort to research both the process and outcome of this approach. The concentration has been on technique (rules and experiments) rather than on process. The course of effective therapy is vague.

Following the rationale of the basic-issues approach presented in Chapter 1, Perls receives high marks for developing a comprehensive and consistent theory of counseling and psychotherapy. He responds in some depth to each of the eleven basic issues. Validation rests on testimonials and self-reports, however, neither of which has proven very reliable in the past.

The Perls stage of Gestalt therapy is over. However, it is an established theory, and many able practitioners are identified with it. New leadership is being developed each year in the Gestalt institutes. It will be most interesting to see where the next generation will take it. Again, Kempler (1973) may have expressed it best: "Identification with Perls and what he represented was clear if not simple. Identification with the movement called Gestalt Therapy is neither clear nor simple" (p. 254).

REFERENCES AND SUGGESTED READINGS

Brown, G.I. 1971. *Human teaching for human learning: an introduction to confluent education*. New York: Viking Press.

Burks, H.M., Jr., & Stefflre, B. 1979. *Theories of counseling*, 3rd ed. New York: McGraw-Hill.

Dye, A., & Hackney, H. 1975. *Gestalt approaches to counseling*, Guidance Monograph Series 8. Boston: Houghton Mifflin.

Fagen, J., & Shepherd, I. Lee, eds. 1971. *Gestalt therapy now*. New York: Harper Colophan Books (originally published 1970).

Fagen, J., & Shepherd, I. Lee, eds. 1973. *What is gestalt therapy?* New York: Harper & Row (orginally published 1970).

Hatcher, C., & Himelstein, P. eds. 1976. *The handbook of gestalt therapy*. New York: Jason Aronson.

Ivey, A.E., with Simek-Downing, L. 1980. *Counseling and psychotherapy: skills, theories, and practice*. Englewood Cliffs, N.J.: Prentice-Hall.

Kempler, W. 1973. Gestalt therapy. In R. Corsini, ed. *Current psychotherapies*. Itasca, Ill.: F.E. Peacock, pp. 251–286.

Latner, J. 1974. *The gestalt therapy book*. New York: Bantam Books (originally published 1973).

Passons, W.R. 1975. *Gestalt approaches in counseling*. New York: Holt, Rinehart & Winston.

Patterson, C.H. 1980. *Theories of counseling and psychotherapy*. New York: Harper & Row.

Perls, F.S. 1969. *Ego, hunger and aggression, the beginning of gestalt therapy*. New York: Vantage Books (originally published 1947).

Perls, F.S. 1971. *Gestalt therapy verbatim*. New York: Bantam Books (originally published 1969).

Perls, F.S. 1972. *In and out of the garbage pail*. New York: Bantam Books, (originally published 1969).

Perls, F.S. 1976. *The gestalt approach & eye witness to psychotherapy*. New York: Bantam Books, (originally published 1973).

Perls, F.S., Hefferline, R.F., & Goodman, P. 1951. *Gestalt therapy, excitement and growth in human personality*. New York: Dell.

Perls, L. 1976. Comments on the new dimension. In E. Smith, ed. *The growing edge of gestalt therapy*. New York: Brunner/Mazel, pp. 221–226.

Prochaska, J.O. 1979. *Systems of psychotherapy: a transtheoretical analysis*. Homewood, Ill.: Dorsey Press.

Schultz, D. 1977. *Growth psychology: models of the healthy personality*. New York: D. Van Nostrand.

Simkin, J.S. Gestalt therapy. In R. Corsini, ed. *Current psychotherapies*, 2nd ed. Itasca, Ill.: F.E. Peacock, pp. 273–301.

Smith, E.W.L., ed. 1976. *The growing edge of gestalt therapy*. New York: Brunner/Mazel.

Stevens, J.O., ed. 1977. *Gestalt is*. New York: Bantam Books, (originally published 1975).

Van De Riet, V., Korb, M.P., & Gorrell, J.J. 1980. *Gestalt therapy: an introduction*. New York: Pergamon Press.

Zinker, J. 1977. *Creative process in gestalt therapy*. New York: Brunner/Mazel.

7

The Reality Therapy of William Glasser

CONVINCED THAT MANY of the basic assumptions of traditional psychiatry were in error, including the prevailing concept of mental illness, William Glasser worked to develop a new therapeutic approach while he was a psychiatric resident in the 1950s. *Mental Health or Mental Illness* (1970) represents an early statement of his work; however, not until his second book, *Reality Therapy* (1965), was published did his theory gain recognition. While few in the medical profession accept his ideas, Glasser's theory appeals to numerous professionals in the mental health and related fields.

Unconventional and essentially different in structure from other therapeutic theories, reality therapy is not entirely original. It shares similar concepts with other theories, particularly the individual psychology of Alfred Adler and the common-sense approach presented by Paul DuBois. Functioning primarily as teachers and models, reality therapists emphasize the importance of warm human involvement, focus on their clients' present behavior, and stress responsibility. Adherents do not diagnose, interpret, or analyze. They do not use free association, concentrate on early trauma or their clients' history, or work for insight by uncovering their clients' unconscious motivations. Reality therapists reject the existence of nearly all forms of mental illness and all deterministic theories. Instead, they emphasize what their clients can do to alter their negative behavior patterns in ways that will promote realization of physiological and psychological needs.

Rather than viewing behavior through a reinforcement paradigm like the behaviorists or phenomenologically like the person-centered therapists, reality therapists encourage their clients to judge their present behavior against reality, whether that reality is practical, social, or moral. Reality therapy focuses on what clients are consciously able and willing to do in the present situation to change behavior they have judged ineffective or growth disrupting. The touchstone of reality therapy, then, is responsibility, both for self and others.

BIOGRAPHICAL SKETCH

Early Years

Holding to his belief that present behavior has priority over past experience, Glasser has written very little about his early years. This, of course, limits any speculation about how early childhood experiences may have influenced his adult theory of counseling and psychotherapy. He has, when pressed, mentioned a relatively uneventful and happy childhood that he attributes mostly to a loving and supporting family.

Born in Cleveland, Ohio, May 11, 1925, Glasser was the third and youngest child of Ben and Betty (Silverberg) Glasser. The members of his family were and remain closely involved. For example, his cousin, Robert Lloyd Glasser, who Glasser describes as "an aeronautical engineer by profession and a psychiatric critic by avocation," spends hours editing the early drafts of Glasser's books.

Education

Glasser attended Cleveland Heights High School, where he played cornet in the band and developed a lasting interest in sports. After being graduated, he entered Case Institute of Technology, majoring in chemical engineering. He married Naomi Judith Silver while an undergraduate in this program and, after graduation, began work toward the Ph.D. in clinical psychology, receiving his M.A. degree in 1948. When his advisers rejected his dissertation, Glasser gained admission to medical school and received his M.D. degree from Western Reserve University in 1953. He completed a psychiatric residency at UCLA in 1957, spending the last year of his residency at the West Los Angeles Veterans Administration Hospital, an affiliate of UCLA's psychiatric program. Here, Glasser became disillusioned with the efficacy of traditional psychoanalytic procedures and, with the encouragement of Dr. G.L. Harrington, a teacher and friend, began to consider and experiment with alternative treatment methods.

Emergence of Reality Therapy

Relying on referrals from the faculty at UCLA that, because of his open resistance to the psychoanalytic approach during his residency, were not forthcoming, Glasser gave up the idea of devoting full time to private practice to accept the position of head psychiatrist at the Ventura School for Girls, the California Youth Authority state facility for female juvenile delinquents. Employing techniques he had developed earlier, Glasser (1965) cut recidivism in this institution to an unheard of 20 percent. He also used this period to develop his theory.

Shortly after the publication of *Reality Therapy, A New Approach to Psychiatry* (1965), Glasser founded the Institute of Reality Therapy to train human service professionals in this new therapeutic approach. That same year, Glasser joined with educators in California to apply the reality therapy approach in Watts public schools and the schools of Palo Alto. This led to the 1969 publication of *Schools Without Failure* and, with the assistance of an initial grant from the Stone Foundation, to the establishment of the Educator Training Center. In addition to teaching the methods of reality therapy to teachers and school administrators, the Education Training Center is dedicated to research ideas and the development of methods for decreasing the failure rate in schools. In 1970, the William Glasser–LaVerne College Center was established at LaVerne College in Southern California to provide off-campus graduate and in-service credit opportunities for teachers while working in their school settings.

Accomplishments and Awards

Since the publication of *Reality Therapy*, Dr. Glasser has lectured and taught extensively throughout the United States and Canada, averaging about 75 major presentations annually. He has worked within communities and school districts to establish teacher-training centers; conducted numerous special interest workshops and seminars for mental health workers; served as consultant for courts and probation, police, and welfare departments; and produced feature films, television programs, and instructional cassettes. In addition to this work, he is the author of seven books and numerous articles. Glasser's books have been translated into Danish, French, German, Italian, Japanese, and Spanish.

Glasser's major goal, at this writing, is to correlate further the ideas of reality therapy with the basic organizational concepts of control theory. Glasser (1976, 1981) believes the two theories can be expanded successfully into a combined approach that will make a significant impact on the helping professions.

RESOLUTIONS OF THE ELEVEN BASIC ISSUES

Repetition and overlap are two major characteristics of issue resolution with theorists who employ but a few global constructs to explain all the complexities of human motivation and behavior. Glasser's theory of reality therapy, based primarily on the inherent psychological need for a success identity, is no exception. While reliance on a limited number of theoretical constructs contributes to the parsimony and holism of the theory, arranging the eleven resolutions in a hierarchical order proved difficult.

Stations of the Mind (1981) and *Take Effective Control of Your Life* (1984) fill some of the earlier theoretical gaps evident in *Reality Therapy* (1965). However, reality therapy remains, as it was intended, a theory of counseling and psychotherapy, a practical treatment approach used successfully by Glasser and his followers with those who encounter difficulties in life and living. Reality therapy is not a comprehensive theory of personality development. The following resolutions, therefore, should not be judged or criticized on that basis.

Biological and/or Social Determinants of Behavior

According to Glasser (1965, 1969, 1981, 1984), we enter this world with two distinct but interrelated sets of general needs. The first set is comprised of our physiological needs. These needs relate to our survival and maintenance functions and include the necessities of life: air, water, food, shelter or warmth, and sex. The second set is the basic, socially derived psychological need for identity. Our general need for identity—to be different, separate, and unique persons—includes the need to love and to be loved, the need to feel worthwhile both to ourselves and to others, and the need to experience fun and freedom of thought and actions.

Reality therapists view our need for identity as the sovereign psychological need and the primary, intrinsic driving force for all our behavior. Although we are biologically and socially predisposed to seek a success identity, deficiencies in our need to love and be loved or to feel worthwhile to ourselves and others can lead us to develop an identity image of failure. It is not enough to perceive ourselves as distinct, separate entities; we must, according to Glasser (1981), associate meaning with our identities. Based on our involvement with others, particularly significant others, we begin as early as the age of 4 or 5 to associate either success or failure with our identities.

We develop an identity image of success when we possess a coherent sense of self, when we know what is right or wrong for us, when we believe we have the ability to choose our behavior, and when we think we can make a difference in the scheme of things. Only when we have developed a success identity will we feel any sense of responsibility and, since responsibility is equated with mental health, any sense of emotional well-being.

A deficiency in our inherent general needs leads to an identity image of failure. Our sense of self is unclear, or, if clear, includes the conviction that what we are matters very little. With the loss of a sense of significance, of feeling worthwhile, we relinquish a sense of personal responsibility, whether for ourselves, others, or society, and engage in behavior characterized by withdrawal from or denial of reality.

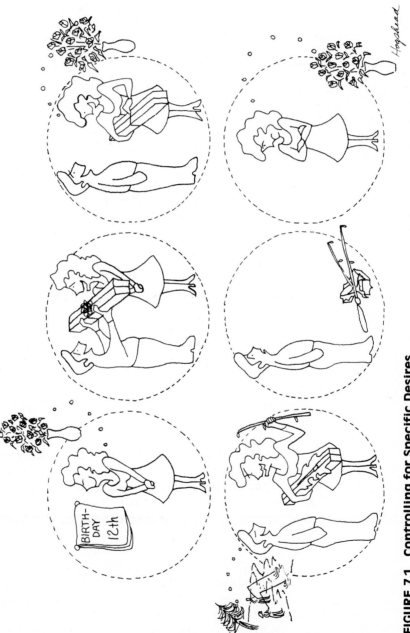

FIGURE 7.1 Controlling for Specific Desires

Were Glasser to have left us with only the concept of general needs to explain complex human behavior, he would have left us with a concept so global that it would be meaningless. However, in *Stations of the Mind* (1981, 1984), he informs us that from our inherent, general needs to love and to be loved, to feel worthwhile to ourselves and to others, and to experience fun and freedom, we develop an almost infinite number and variety of individual and specific learned desires (see Figure 7.1). These personalized and controlled needs, although important to us, may or may not be shared by others. Further, while we are usually aware of our inherent needs, we spend most of our daily time and effort controlling for or attending to our specific desires.

Even as infants we develop specific, learned, needs. Striving to fulfill our inherent need for love, we learn that love "may be a dry diaper, a soft nipple, or a toss in the air followed by a hug or kiss" (Glasser, 1981, p. 41). We quickly learn what we want, what we believe we need, and add these needs to a constantly growing, changing constellation of specific needs. According to Glasser (1981), we use these learned needs to build our internal worlds (p. 44; see also "Psychological and/or Reality Environments"). Some of the difficulties we encounter result from conflicting needs in our inner worlds or from differences between a need in our inner world and the demands of reality. Our identities of success or failure are based on our perceptions of how well we fulfill our specific (learned) needs and, ultimately, how well we are meeting our general (innate) needs.

To feel worthwhile we must establish and maintain a set of values or personal standards. We must be able to think rationally and to solve problems. Above all, we must be aware of our present behavior. When we can give and receive love and feel worthwhile to ourselves and others with some consistency, we develop a success identity and remain in touch with reality.

Psychological and/or Reality Environments

Glasser's stance on this issue is phenomenological. He often refers to the constraints of the real world or outer world of reality, but in *Stations of the Mind* (1981), he asserts that we are incapable of perceiving the world as it actually is (p. 89). Further, he tells us, "It is only our world, or the world in our head, that counts for us" (p. 90). We perceive reality in terms of our needs, those specific needs we learn as we attempt to fulfill our general needs for love and self-worth. Our feelings and reactions to any situation are based on our perceptions of reality rather than reality. There are, then, individual realities, and since we are unique, no two realities coincide.

Unless we become conscious of our two-world existence—the environment as it exists and our inner world—we attempt to shape or change the world to fit our inner world. Attempting to change reality is futile, but that seldom hinders our attempts to do so. According to Glasser (1970), "We constantly gripe, complain, and struggle with reality, living in hope and fantasy that we, or some miracle, will change our surroundings so that we can better satisfy our needs" (p. 8). We not only make the mistake of living in our own world but also compound our error by believing our world is the world of all others. However, all we ever know of the world is the energy that comes from the world that strikes the sensory receptors of our perceptual systems. "Everything else that we claim is the real world is in fact our own perceptions of that world, perceptions which we constantly try to change so that they coincide with the world in our head" (Glasser, 1981, p. 90). We are fortunate when our privately constructed inner world accurately reflects our reality environment since our needs must be met within the boundaries set by reality.

Uniqueness and/or Commonality

Following the premises of reality therapy, we are truly unique beings. We hold much in common with all other humans; we share, for example, the same general physiological and psychological needs, and we must conform, to some extent, to the physical, economic, and psychosocial realities of this world. However, an important part of our need for a success identity is the need to know that in some way we are unique.

We exist in an outer world, a world of reality, but we live our day-to-day existence in our internal worlds, individual worlds personally constructed from countless variations of specific learned desires. "It is as if the general needs . . . serve as a large background. They activate the system, but they themselves need to be satisfied or controlled for in many specific ways" (Glasser, 1981, p. 41). We all possess the same general needs; however, we vary, at times considerably, in our abilities to fulfill them. Our general needs are innate; our abilities to satisfy them are not. We must learn to fulfill our needs; hence, learning is an integral part of reality therapy.

In reality therapy, we are what we do, or even more accurate, we are what we learn to do, and our learning varies. As we strive for love and self-worth through our involvements with others and the challenges and problems we encounter in life, we develop countless specific needs or desires. In no two of us are these learned desires the same, and since we control for our specific desires, no two of us will behave the same. Moreover, since learning is a continuous process that begins at birth, our specific needs and desires are ever growing and changing. As we learn, we become more complex and even more separate and distinct from our fellow beings.

Explanation of Learning

Learning and the learning process are essential tenets both to the theory and the therapeutic procedures of reality therapy. The abilities and skills necessary to fulfill our general need for a success identity must be learned. We enter this world with our general needs intact, but we must learn those behaviors that will serve our needs with just a few innate behaviors such as breathing, blinking, sucking, swallowing, eliminating, kicking, grasping, grimacing, sleeping, crying, and random vocalizing. However difficult, we must learn to understand reality, decide what is right for us, and then, think, feel, and act responsibly.

Although Glasser discusses significant life stages (see "Early and/or Continuous Development"), he believes opportunities for learning are ever present and continuous. Perhaps the most important learning period for most of us occurs at age 4 or 5, about the time we enter the formal educational system and begin to develop social, verbal, and intellectual skills. With these particular skills we begin to distinguish between success and failure experiences and to form an identity image of success or failure.

We are fortunate if, as children, we have loving, responsible parents or guardians and teachers. According to Glasser, responsibility, a most critical element of a success identity, can be learned only from our interpersonal involvements with responsible people. It is important also that we be permitted the freedom to test our sense of responsibility as soon as we acquire it. We learn responsibility when we can accept ourselves as worthwhile enough to evaluate and judge our behavior critically, then choose behavior we believe will be most helpful to ourselves and others.

Glasser (1969) maintains that in the proper familial and school atmosphere, we learn early that attitude change follows behavioral change. For Glasser, learning focuses on behavior rather than on feelings or attitudes. Successful behavior results in a feeling of worth and a sense of responsibility and freedom.

Glasser (1969) believes that we can be taught in the proper educational atmosphere to think and to accept responsibility for our thinking at a very early age. As with his therapy, Glasser stresses increased personal involvement, relevance, thinking, and discipline in the schools, as opposed to memory, repetition, and punishment. An identity image of uncertainty and failure is improved by successful participation and involvement in a group, whether that group is the family or the classroom.

Number and Weight Assigned to Motivational Concepts

According to Glasser, we are inner-directed beings. We are motivated by our never-ending basic physiological and psychological needs. Once our physiological needs are met, our psychological need for a success identity becomes the motivating life-force behind our striving to achieve need satisfaction. We have a natural predisposition to strive for a success identity but no natural endowment of the necessary skills and abilities to do so.

Human motivations appear to take numerous forms, but all are related to the many specific desires we learn as we strive toward a success identity. We are motivated to strive for the four basic needs, even when this means temporary discomfort or privation.

On the one hand, unmet needs result in tension or anxiety, painful incentives at best. Successful achievement of needs, on the other hand, is accompanied by a variety of pleasant, positive feelings (see "Importance of Reward"). According to Glasser (1970), "All that is mature, artistic, creative, philosophical, intellectual arises from the achievement or the anticipation of positive emotions" and accompany successful achievement of our basic goals (p. 21). The memory or anticipation of pleasant feelings can serve as effective motivation for worthwhile achievement. Anticipation of pleasant feeling can lead us to endure tension for a surprisingly long period to achieve self-worth.

Recognition for a job well done motivates us to continue to do well and contributes to a sense of worthiness—hence, our success identity. Punishment or the threat of it decreases our sense of worthiness and motivates us only as long as we are intimidated by external threat—hence, reinforcement of failure identity.

Conscious and/or Unconscious Determinants

We are, according to Glasser, potentially autonomous, conscious beings capable of responsible, planned behavior. Although reality therapists recognize that we are not always aware of the reasons for our behavior, they reject any concept that holds we are driven by the instinctual urges of an unconscious dimension or that views us simply as the products of our environments or past experiences. Such a view would eliminate all possibility of personal responsibility for our feelings, thoughts, and actions and would be antithetical to the premise of reality therapy. Glasser (1965) contends that materials and motives considered inaccessible and attributed to the unconscious by other theorists, particularly the psychoanalytics, can more accurately be ascribed to our preconscious, the level of our awareness that lies just beneath consciousness and that can be recalled easily.

Regardless of how ineffective, dysfunctional, unrealistic, and irresponsible our behavior, it is not the result of unconscious motivation; rather, it is our conscious or preconscious attempts to attain our four basic needs of being loved and loving, our sense of worth to self and others, fun, and freedom of thought. Unlike many theories of counseling and psychotherapy, insight is not a therapeutic goal of reality therapy. Glasser believes that insight can, at least for some clients, become the excuse they seek for their irresponsibility. Equating self-responsibility with mental health, reality therapy concentrates on conscious, present behavior and involves careful, realistic examination, judgment, planning, commitment, and action with no excuses or blame accepted, regardless of how reasonable these excuses may seem.

Conditioning and/or Freedom to Choose

Although we must act within the boundaries of reality imposed by our heredity and environment, we are not victims of either. We are active participants in our quest for a successful identity. Our thoughts, feelings, and actions do not simply happen. We choose our behavior from the range of possibilities available to us. Moreover, we are always free to change the course of action we are presently taking. Our destiny, then, is a matter of choice rather than of either our conditions or conditioning. Our meaning and significance emerge from our responsibility for and commitment to the goals we choose because these goals reflect our movement toward basic need realization.

When we create a success identity, our consciousness tells us we are free. Our thoughts, feelings, and actions are our own. Conversely, when we have a failure identity, we react to life rather than act, and we feel little or no sense of involvement, commitment, or responsibility for our behavior. Alternative thoughts, feelings, and actions are not part of our consciousness because we are unaware of choice. Freedom or the lack of it, then, depends on the identity we develop.

Importance of Group Membership

Glasser regards us as complex social-competitive animals. Historically, as with all primates and many subprimates, our socialization needs have predominated over our need to compete. Belonging to a group offers the protection and assistance of the group, significantly increasing the probability of survival. Further, Glasser believes that it was from this ancient socialization-for-survival need that we developed the need to belong and, even more recently in our history, the need to love and to be loved. Conflict arose with the emergence of the need for dominance and, with it, the need to compete. As social-competitive beings, we possess a natural desire to compete and keep.

It is impossible to achieve a success identity alone. We need involvement with responsible people who are in touch with reality if we are to learn to grow, to develop a success identity. We need groups and institutions that facilitate rather than suppress our need for involvement.

Loneliness is a natural outcome of a failure identity. When attempts to meet our basic needs are thwarted, we tend to withdraw from any meaningful involvement with others, to become introspective, to focus only on our problems and symptoms. We blame others, conditions, God, or fate for our difficulties and misery. We fail to realize that we can overcome most of our problems through more socially responsible involvement and behavior.

For reality therapists, our quest for identity is a search for personal meaning and significance through the fulfillment of our basic needs. Since feelings of love and worthiness can only be affirmed by others, particularly the significant others in our lives, we need to develop and maintain meaningful involvement with others. Inherent in any meaningful involvement is the understanding that there is much more to life and living than self-concern and focusing on personal problems and symptoms.

Early and/or Continuous Development

Glasser (1965, 1969, 1981) asserts that human development is a life-long process, but he repeatedly denotes the significant influence of our early childhood years. During our first 10 years of life we encounter the learning experiences essential to the fulfillment of our needs for love and self-worth and our sense of fun and freedom of thought. As we utilize skills we learn to meet our needs; we differentiate between our successful and unsuccessful attempts to succeed and, from these interpretations, create meaningful feelings of who and what we are. Consequently, by the age of 10 we develop a rather firm identity with either success or failure as the dominant characteristic. While a failure identity can be corrected at any age through more responsible thinking, feeling, and acting, it can be prevented or, if formed, most easily reversed during the first decade of life.

Learning to think, feel, and act responsibly is difficult. We are fortunate, indeed, if, when we are beginning to forge our identities, we have parents and teachers who are fully involved with us as persons, who are genuinely interested in our activities, ideas, and concerns, and who respect us and affirm our worth. As children, we learn responsibility best from responsible adult role models. We need parents and teachers who care enough about our growth and development to refuse to condone irresponsibility, who teach commitment and encourage involvement, who believe in freedom enough to permit us to live with the natural consequences of our decisions and actions, and who are more concerned with helping us to improve our present behavior than with punishing us for our past actions.

As children, most of us have only two major courses to involvement and a success identity: our families and the schools we attend. Certainly no institution in our society has the involvement potential of our nuclear family. When our parents responsibly expose us to people of various ages, interests, and backgrounds, they give us the opportunities of social interaction we need to gain confidence in our worth and our ability to be actively involved with others. We need love, support, and warm human involvement, and as children especially, we are dependent on our families for our early socialization.

Importance of Role Assigned to Self-Concept

Self-concept is a term not often found in Glasser's works. However, he writes extensively about the primacy and dynamics of our inherent need for identity

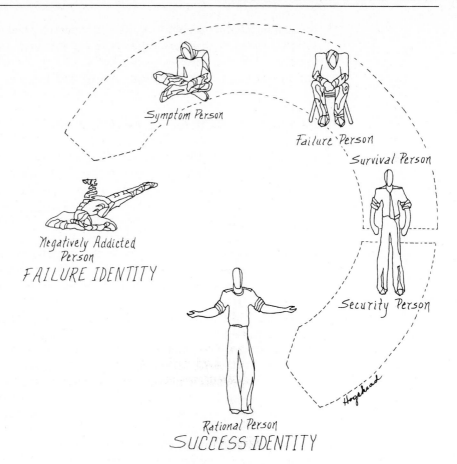

FIGURE 7.2   Glasser's Identity Images

and the "wonderfully unique strands of identity" that form the images of our individual "I"s, those experiences we order, synthesize, integrate, and focus into our unique concepts of who and what we are. It is not enough that we form a distinct identity image, an essential part of our quest for identity. According to Glasser (1965, 1969, 1981), we come to associate meaning with that image. We must, therefore, identify ourselves with either success or failure. Ultimately, the function of our behavior is to do those things that maximize the fulfillment of a success identity.

The identities we achieve are unique, multiple systems of interrelated ideas, attitudes, beliefs, values, experiences, and feelings seeking expression. We convey our identities in everything we do. They are persistent facts of our life and living through which we sift our perceptions. Further, we must see threads of consistency between our behavior and our identity. Our unity grows out of our need to be consistent with our identity image. Our perceptions, thoughts, feelings, and actions have greater consistency when they relate closely to our identity image and we have no need to control for error. Successful experiences will create discomfort if we have a failure identity, regardless of how positive these experiences are or of how helpful they may appear to others. We control for our perceptions. We reject or distort evidence contradictory to our identity image because even a failure identity, with all its pain, is preferable to no identity.

Once formed, our identity is stable and highly resistant to alteration. It defines us in relation to others and the world. The primary reason for Glasser's concern with the evolving identity of the child is his conviction that a failure identity is easier to prevent than to change (see "Early and/or Continuous Development").

Certainly our identity image is influenced by others and the particular circumstances of our lives, and just as certainly our identity, once formed, is persistent and pervasive—hence, difficult to change. Still, our identity is not impervious to change if we are willing to accept the realities of life and living, to examine our behavior, to judge its effectiveness for us, and to commit ourselves to more responsible goals and actions. Our behavior is not random; we do have opportunities to decide what we want and to work more responsibly toward that end.

Importance of Reward

According to Glasser (1965, 1981), the most significant human reward is the inner sense of joy and deep-seated satisfaction we experience as we are loved and loving and as we are positively regarded by both ourselves and others. Involvement and responsible behavior are intrinsically rewarding. When we are actively involved with others and responsible for our perceptions, thoughts, feelings, and actions, we feel needed, wanted, valuable, independent, and successful. We express a zest for life and find living rewarding. Moreover, we endeavor to help those around us to experience the same feeling. As we feel significant, we emerge as significant others to those individuals we encounter.

External reward is nearly always suspect. When an external reward is less than that to which we think we are entitled, we feel resentment. If, in contrast, we consider a reward greater than we deserve, we experience feelings of inadequacy and guilt. Even when we believe the reward we receive to be appropriate (a specific learned need for which we control) and just (in line with the value we place on our knowledge, skill, and effort), we may feel wronged. Our need for freedom is innate, and we naturally resent being controlled or manipulated by anyone in position to grant what we want in return for that freedom, regardless of how fair their system of reward.

GOALS OF REALITY THERAPISTS

For reality therapists, maladaptive functioning is viewed as the consequence of isolated self-involvement and irresponsibility. Therapy, then, is considered a rational, educative process directed toward promoting meaningful involvement with others and more responsible behavior. In brief, reality therapists work toward assisting their clients to fulfill their general physiological and psychological needs in ways that do not interfere with or hinder others in their attempts to do the same.

Glasser does not list specific therapist goals and techniques, but Glasser and Zunin (1979) discuss eight general procedures that therapists can flexibly apply as they help their clients become more autonomous, responsible beings (pp. 316–323). The following therapeutic goals are inferred in these principles:

1. *To establish a warm, personal, therapeutic involvement with their clients.* Essential to therapy proper, since little behavioral change is considered likely without involvement, are the reality therapists' abilities to convey genuine personal concern, empathic understanding, and a willingness to become personally involved in the lives of their clients (see "Therapeutic Relationship"). In addition to care and understanding, it is important that reality therapists communicate their faith in their clients' capacities to fulfill their needs and to live happier lives. Personal involvement includes also the therapists' willingness to self-disclose when doing so is in their clients' interest.

2. *To focus on behavior rather than feelings.* Reality therapists are convinced that the human cognitive, emotive, and behavioral functions are interactional and transactional, thus cyclical and mutually reinforcing. Of these functions, however, behavior is the most overt and observable, as well as the easiest to examine, appraise, control, and change. Because reality therapists believe their clients have more control over their behavior than over their perceptions, thoughts, and emotions, they attempt to influence the function cycle by concentrating on their clients' behavior. The message to be conveyed is, "I care about what you do, because I know that once you do better you will feel better." When behavior is examined closely and evaluated realistically, it often becomes apparent to clients that behavior is the root of their problems

and feelings. At this point, they are likely to agree with their therapist's observation that, given their present behavior, it is surprising they are not feeling even worse than they do.

Client feelings are neither denied nor denigrated; rather, they are accepted fully by the therapist. The focus, however, is on what they are doing that makes them feel as they do and on what they might do to feel better.

3. *To focus on the present and future rather than on the past.* Behavorial change can occur only in the present; therefore, reality therapy focuses on the present. When clients bring their past into the therapy session, it is quickly related to their current behavior and present attempts to succeed. Attention to the present is not only designed to make clients aware of their dysfunctional behaviors but also to articulate effective behaviors that show some promise of contributing to more successful living.

4. *To encourage clients to appraise and judge present behavior.* After closely examining clients' behavior, reality therapists ask their clients to make a critical value judgment: "Is what I am presently doing good or bad, right or wrong for me as I attempt to achieve what I want in this life?" The responsibility for this judgment rests with their clients; their clients must recognize their need for change. Moreover, all current behavior is to be judged, not only in relation to themselves but also in relation to its effect on others, particularly on those with whom they are or hope to be meaningfully involved.

5. *To assist clients in developing realistic, specific plans to change failure behavior to success behavior.* Once clients judge their current behavior dysfunctional and goal disrupting, reality therapists assist them in developing a carefully planned strategy that will help them attain success. The plan first involves setting goals, then determining the specific behaviors necessary to achieve them. When formulating a plan of action, therapists promote the discovery of alternative behaviors and discuss possible behavioral outcomes. However, here again, the final decision remains with the client. Teaching responsibility, then, is a major goal of therapy.

Although most clients know what they must do to attain what they want, their planning is not always realistic or functional. Further, since clients have self-identified with failure, a low failure risk is preferable. The plan must be achievable. Perhaps most important, no single plan is absolute. When one plan is unworkable, client behavior is again examined and another plan developed.

6. *To insist on client commitment to carry out the plan.* Commitment from clients identified with failure may be difficult because, as a group, they seem to have a strong reluctance to commit themselves seriously to any project or person. Still, reality therapists know that their clients can gain a sense of responsibility and self-worth by successfully completing a plan they helped to develop. Further, therapists know that their clients' chances of success increase significantly when they commit themselves to their therapists within

the therapeutic milieu. Making sensible commitments to others and following through with those commitments are crucial steps toward changing a failure identity.

7. *To accept no excuses for irresponsible behavior.* Not all clients will follow through with their commitments, and not all plans will lead to the successful completion of the goals they were intended to accomplish. Nevertheless, excuses for failure are unacceptable in reality therapy. Whether a plan fails for a valid reason or through some fault of the client is of no concern to the therapist. The benefit of reality therapy comes from recommitment to an existing plan or through creation of a new plan, not from seeking fault or rationales for failure. "To belabor the why's of a plan's failure is to reinforce failure identity" (Glasser and Zunin, 1979, p. 323). Reality therapists assume commitment is always possible, even with extenuating setbacks.

8. *To eliminate punishment.* For reality therapists, punishment for failure only reaffirms a failure identity. It certainly does nothing to enhance client-counselor involvement. When a client does not follow through with a commitment to a plan to attain a desired goal, the result is nonattainment of the goal and the pain of renewed failure. To add punishment to a logical consequence is to add insult to injury. At best, clients who feel depreciated or demeaned by their therapists take a defensive stance. They may become hostile, withdraw, or seek excuses for the failure. Such compensatory behaviors do not lead to the development of new plans or to recommitment to the existing plans that might facilitate a success identity.

THERAPEUTIC PROCESS: METHODS AND TECHNIQUES

Reality therapy is a special here-now, teaching-learning process based on a meaningful therapeutic involvement and directed toward behavioral change that emphasizes a rational, often confrontive, Socratic dialogue between therapist and client. The core of the therapeutic process is involvement, responsibility, reality, and right. The approach is verbally active, rational, and confrontive. Techniques vary, but the therapist typically utilizes a Socratic dialogue, questioning the client's current life situation to facilitate awareness of present behavior, force personal value judgments, formulate plans for change, make commitments, and successfully carry through the agreed plan of action.

Therapeutic Relationship

The therapeutic relationship is considered means rather than end, but a meaningful therapeutic involvement is, nevertheless, paramount to effective reality theapy. Therapy cannot be initiated unless and until there is at least minimal involvement between therapist and client. Rational therapists must genuinely present themselves as persons concerned with their clients' needs, plans, aspirations, and successes. They must become involved with their clients' lives and at the same time avoid entanglement and promotion of dependence. They must convey respect, caring, acceptance, and understanding but be strong enough to refuse excuses or to condone irresponsible, irrational, hostile, or bizarre behavior. Therapists must be open and willing to discuss their struggles and life circumstances and to have their values questioned or criticized. They must be able to communicate a genuine faith in their clients' abilities to behave more responsibly and to live happier, need-satisfying lives. They must be able to demonstrate through their demeanor and actions that there is more to life and living than self-involvement, than focusing on symptoms, misery, and ineffective, irresponsible behavior.

Glasser (1965) believes the ability of therapists to be involved with their clients is the major skill of reality therapy but the most difficult skill to achieve or to describe (p. 22). Further, he asserts, when there is true involvement in therapy, the client, continually confronted with reality, must become more responsible or leave therapy (p. 25). Only when there is true involvement and commitment do clients try new behavioral patterns and question their value systems.

For clients identified with failure, acceptance by their therapist as persons of equal worth is both supportive and encouraging. It becomes therapeutic for these clients to realize that their painful feelings and physical symptoms are logical in light of their present behavior. It is comforting to know their therapist will see them on a regular schedule and that there is at least one responsible person who does not think their problems are insoluble. These clients feel reassured when they are able to discuss their aspirations and values with an attentive, sensitive person. It is rewarding to work with a person more interested in their present strengths and successes than in blaming or punishing them for their past records of weaknesses and failures. Not only is it impossible to initiate therapy without involvement, it is also necessary to maintain involvement throughout the process of therapy. Glasser (1965, 1969) insists that involvement with at least one successful person is a prerequisite to any client change.

Initial Procedures and Strategies

Initially, Glasser's theory of reality therapy appears deceptively simple. It is a common-sense, action-oriented, pragmatic approach to therapy that is relatively uncomplicated and easy to understand. Moreover, because the theory of reality therapy can be translated into a number of clearly stated operational procedures and strategies, the therapeutic process appears to occur in a fairly consistent, thus predictable, progression or sequence. Proponents of reality therapy would remind us, however, that *simple* should not be mistaken for *simplistic*. It is crucial to understand that timing and sequence in the application of the methods and techniques are essential to the continuity and effectiveness of therapy. Thus, although knowledge and understanding of the theory are necessary, effective application of reality therapy requires skill and experience that is developed only through extensive training and practice. Further, many of the techniques employed by reality therapists (i.e., confrontation, humor, verbal shock) must be integrated into the personality of the therapist if he or she is to relate, with genuineness and spontaneity, to the client as a person.

Initiating Therapy.   In reality therapy the therapuetic process is essentially the same, whether working with a client who is hallucinating or with an adolescent who is experiencing test anxiety. What needs to be determined is whether the clients' difficulties are the result of organic illness or irresponsible behavior. During the initial, and for Glasser (1965, p. 21) the most difficult, phase of therapy, reality therapists are concerned with building a meaningful therapeutic relationship with their clients, realizing that until their clients can experience a close personal involvement with their therapist, there will be no therapy. Fortunately, clients with a failure identity are seeking involvement (Glasser, 1965). They need someone who cares for them and for whom they can care. They come to therapy to find someone who is concerned for their well-being and who will remain with them through their difficulties.

Therapeutic involvement may occur quickly or it may require months to develop; much depends on the skill of the therapist and the degree of client resistance encountered. Still, regardless of the time required, it is a necessary requisite to therapy. There is in reality therapy a direct link between motivation and involvement.

Structuring.   Reality therapists want their clients to leave the first session with some understanding of the nature, limits, and goals of therapy. This is especially true for those clients whose expectations of therapy are unreasonable or inappropriate or who believe they are being coerced into therapy by a third party. At the very least, clients must leave the first therapy session believing the decision to try counseling was the right decision. They must feel that therapy offers some hope for them, or there is little likelihood they will return. It helps if, along with this belief, they think their therapists are professionally competent, interested in them as persons, and genuinely concerned with their well-being. Skillful structuring can contribute to early involvement between the client and the therapist.

Fees and payment plans should be discussed openly during the initial phase, as should time and duration of therapy. Glasser (1965) sometimes limits the duration of therapy when he thinks a set number of sessions will motivate his clients to work more positively and intensely. He finds limited duration especially helpful when counseling with married couples and families attempting to improve interpersonal relationships.

Depending on the therapist's assessment of the client's needs, early structuring may consist of a simple explanation or description of the nature and purpose of the counseling process. Much of the structuring throughout therapy proper, however, is expressed through the therapist's specific responses and general modeling behavior. Most reality therapists agree that therapy is possible only when their clients commit themselves to it by accepting the responsibility for their behavior, including their decision to enter and remain in therapy.

Course of Therapy

Once reality therapists have begun to establish a meaningful involvement with their clients, they shift their focus to the reality of their clients' present behavior. From this point in counseling, therapists neither permit their clients to deny what they are doing nor grant them any opportunity to evade responsibility for their actions. Reasons and excuses for irresponsibility are neither accepted nor condoned. Therapists confront their clients with their behavior, require them to assess it, and ask them whether it is right or wrong, enhancing or inhibiting in light of what they want from life. Although clients may indicate what they want, goals may have to be articulated clearly and concisely. The therapeutic stance of reality therapists is linear. Until concerns are expressed and clarified, establishing goals is impossible. Without goals, it is impossible to evaluate either present or alternative behavior.

An example of the shift from the client's feelings to the reality of the client's present behaviors is demonstrated in the following excerpt from a taped counseling session.

Therapist: You've told me how disgusted you feel with yourself and your life—that you feel as though you're just marking time, going nowhere, accomplishing nothing. I'm sure that feeling like this day after day must be depressing for you, even frightening at times.

Client: It is frightening. What's worse, I feel helpless. I see no way out.

Therapist: What does getting out mean to you? What do you really want to do?

Client: I'm not sure exactly. . . . I guess I really want to feel that I'm doing something with my life—not just existing.

Therapist: What are you doing now to achieve that feeling? Describe a typical day in your life right now.

Client: Well, typically, I wake up when my alarm goes off, get dressed, and go to work. After work, I come home, fix something to eat, then, because I'm tired, I watch television until it's time to go to bed. To be honest, I'm usually not watching TV at all; I'm sitting there thinking about how terrible things are and feeling miserable or I fall asleep. You see, I'm not doing anything with my life.

Therapist: Oh, but you are doing something. You just told me: you wake up, go to work, come home, and watch televsion or sit there worrying about how terrible things are until you fall asleep. The question, then, isn't are you doing anything but rather is what you're doing helping you to feel a sense of accomplishment, helping you to feel that you're doing something with your life?

Client: Obviously not. It makes me feel miserable. But how can I accomplish anything as long as I feel so tired and depressed all the time?

Therapist: You've just struck at the heart of reality therapy: Once you do better you will feel better. We could spend this entire session talking about how tired and miserable you feel and all we would accomplish is to make you feel even more miserable and more helpless. You said yourself that when you sit in front of the television and dwell on how terrible things are you feel miserable. You've also just said that what you're doing now isn't helping you to feel that you're doing something with your life. Since what you're doing now isn't working for you, perhaps we should work toward setting some goals and planning what you can do to realize those goals. I have no magic to make you feel better, but I do know that if you do better you will usually feel better.

Insight is not a primary goal of reality therapy; however, when confronted with their behavior, clients often begin to realize that they are creating much of their misery. Further, they begin to see the need for changing their irresponsible, goal-disruptive behavior once they have judged it ineffective or dysfunctional.

Planning is the next phase of therapy. Now attention is centered on consciously planned behavior. The therapist insists on pinning the client down to specifics with a series of what, where, when, and how questions: What will you do if . . . ? When will you do . . . ? How will you do . . . ? Planning requires the abilities of both therapists and clients to think systematically to develop more constructive and responsible strategies and activities to attain client goals. When reviewing alternative behaviors, therapists ask their clients to evaluate each possible course of action in terms of the likelihood of success and to focus on the consequences of their decisions, not only as they relate to themselves but also to others.

Suppose we return to the session and see how the therapist assists the client in defining a realistic goal and devising a plan for achieving it.

Therapist: Wanting to do something with your life is a worthy goal, but it isn't very clear. Can you be more specific? Can you name one thing you really want to do?

Client: Well, I've always wanted to finish my degree. I had to quit after 2 years of college and find work. I've always intended to go back and finish, but something always came up and I just never got around to it.

Therapist: O.K., let's consider this. First, is it something you really want to do? Is it really important to you?

Client: Oh yeah. Like I said, I've always intended to go back. I really do want to get into accounting or management, and I need a degree for that.

Therapist: Is there any reason you can't do this now?

Client: Well, I still need to work. I can't just quit my job and go back to college.

Therapist: Is it necessary to quit work? Can't you register for one or two evening courses a week and keep your job?

Client: I suppose so. It would take quite awhile that way, but I suppose I could take one or two night classes. At least I'd be doing something with my life.

Therapist: O.K. You have your goal. Now, what are you going to do to achieve it? What immediate steps can you take toward returning to school and working toward your degree?

Client: Well, I suppose I could call and find out what I have to do to register for night classes next semester. I could ask for a schedule and see what's offered at night—you know, see if they are offering anything in accounting or management.

Therapist: Are you really serious about this?

Client: I'm serious.

Therapist: Will you do it? Will you make the call?

Client: I'll do it.

Therapist: When? When will you make the call?

Client: I'll call tomorrow morning from work.

Therapist: O.K., John, here's your plan. You're going to call the registrar tomorrow morning—first to inquire about what it is you must do to register for evening classes next semester, and second, to ask for a schedule of classes and a registration form. Are there any other questions you might ask when you call?

Client: I'm not sure of the cost. I think I can manage tuition and books for one or two classes a semester, but I'll ask about the cost tomorrow just to be sure.

Therapist: Good! You're going to ask what you have to do, how soon you can do it, and what you can expect it to cost you. You're also going to ask them to send you a schedule of classes. And, you're going to do this tomorrow morning. I shall be really interested, when I see you next week, to hear what you learned. We can begin making a plan about the next steps then also.

When a realistic, achievable plan has been formulated, reality therapists work for client commitment. Many therapists write the plan in contractual form and insist their clients sign it as a binding indication of their intent to fulfill it. Therapists and clients together monitor the early stages of the plan and are not hesitant to review and refine it or to formulate a new one.

Should clients fail to follow through with their plans, there are no excuses. Even valid reasons are unacceptable as a topic for discussion. Reality therapists concentrate on their clients' current behavior. When clients are unsuccessful, they and their therapists begin an immediate search for alternative behaviors that hold greater promise of success. If this means re-examination of present behavior or reassessment of goals, then that becomes their agenda. Reality therapists are convinced that there is no single way to attain success but a myriad of responsible paths awaiting discovery. When involvement between therapist and client is genuine, resignation to failure is not a consideration.

Confrontation.   The here-now, no-excuse stance of the therapist makes therapuetic confrontation inevitable throughout the entire process of reality therapy. Reality clients are first confronted with their present behavior. Once aware of what they are doing to create their present difficulties, they are confronted with a value decision: Is what I am doing now good or bad, right or wrong for me? If they decide that their behavior is indeed wrong, they are challenged to look for alternative behaviors that will better help them to attain their goals. They are next challenged to formulate a plan of action, listing and scheduling the sequence of new behaviors chosen specifically to meet their goals. When both the client and therapist agree the plans are complete, realistic, and achievable, clients are asked to make a commitment either to themselves or to their therapist to translate their plans into action. They may, at this point, be confronted with a contract requiring their signature as evidence of their commitment. They may be confronted yet again as the therapist requests they monitor their progress. It should be noted that most therapist confrontations in reality therapy represent questions that require client action and place responsibility for the action directly on the client.

Contracts. Reality therapists often make use of written contracts in therapy. A signed contract serves not only as evidence of the client's intent to change behavior but also as a reminder of the specific sequence and schedule of behavioral changes specified in the client's plan. Completion of a contract, like need fulfillment, facilitates the client's feelings of self-worth. Here is concrete evidence that the client is capable of working responsibly toward a goal and, more important, succeeding. Therapists' faith in their clients' abilities to change current dysfunctional, need-depriving behavior, which is often doubted by clients with failure identities, is reinforced for their clients.

Clients with failure identities hesitate to risk more failure by attempting any new course of action, regardless of how carefully that course has been plotted. Change, even when highly desired, is feared; therefore, commitment is necessary if they are to act on their plans. While verbal agreements closed with a handshake may suffice for some clients, the written contract, signed by both the client and therapist, reinforces the client's commitment to act on the plan.

Reality therapists do not hesitate to use their involvement with their clients to impose an obligation to change irresponsible behavior. If their clients are unwilling to try to change their behavior for themselves, therapists may ask their clients to make their commitments to them: If you won't do it for yourself, will you do it for me? If the involvement is sound, the client may try new behavior for the therapist and take the first step toward more responsibility. Later, the therapeutic focus will evolve toward encouraging self-commitment.

Instruction. When clients decide specific skill development is needed to implement a newly formulated course of action, instruction may be the most direct and effective method for attaining them. Whether this instruction becomes a part of the therapy session, however, depends on the therapist's competence to teach the desired skills. When the therapist cannot teach these skills, he or she may refer the client to skill instruction elsewhere. Reality therapists do not hesitate to teach specific behaviors or skills as long as their clients are convinced of their necessity to their plan and are willing to assume mutual responsibility in the instruction/learning process.

Information. Here again, should their clients express the need for specific information, whether to formulate or implement a new plan of action, reality therapists will readily provide it. Should they not have the information their clients require, they assist their clients' search for the information by suggesting the most probable and reliable sources. In either case, therapists encourage responsible client action.

Role Playing. Reality therapists may turn to role playing when their clients are experiencing difficulties in interpersonal relationships or feel the need to practice new behaviors or recently acquired skills. Role playing may help to bring their clients' pasts or futures into the present, to rehearse for feared events, or to prepare for consequences thought likely to occur once their clients begin to behave differently. When role playing is employed, it is frequently followed with a feedback session—a fairly thorough discussion of what the client and therapist experienced while playing the roles of others. The feedback session is often a valuable opportunity for therapists to encourage their clients by emphasizing what they did well.

Support.   Support is utilized by reality therapists to maximize their clients' awareness, anticipation, and expectation of positive outcome. Clients with a failure identity require much support, particularly as they initiate their plans into action. They have learned to expect failure and do not relish the idea of risking more of it. Encouragement and support are essential if clients are to commit themselves seriously to new behavioral patterns since client commitment is often only as strong as the client-therapist involvement.

Accepting their clients as persons of worth, seeking their clients' opinions and asking for their evaluations of their present behavior, expressing faith in their clients' abilities to change, and providing praise for successfully completing a plan of action are supportive. Encouragement and support not only increase client motivation but also serve to communicate feelings of worth to the client.

Feeling more worthwhile, clients need not exert as much energy controlling for perceptual errors in this particular station of their minds (Glasser, 1981), and the energy they once directed toward controlling for error may now be focused on living more effectively and responsibly.

Constructive Debate.   When held to a responsible and intellectual level, reality therapists are aware that constructive debate can be an effective technique to enhance their clients' self-concepts. Active participation in constructive debate demonstrates to clients that they have something worthwhile to say and that they have values to defend. They learn, too, that they can contribute meaningfully to the therapeutic process. Reality therapists are convinced that when values are at issue, the therapeutic session is being used advantageously (Glasser, 1965).

Humor.   Although it must be employed both sparingly and sensitively, humor can be a valuable therapeutic technique in reality therapy. It can, for example, be used to shock clients into the reality of their circumstances, to confront them with the irrationality of their behavior, or to make them aware of their tendency to evade responsibility for their actions. Perhaps most important, humor can be used to help their clients regain the healthy ability to laugh at themselves and to become less introspective and self-involved.

Appropriateness and timing of humor in therapy are essential. Therapists should avoid using humor in a punitive or demeaning manner because it can quickly undermine the therapeutic involvement they worked so long to achieve. Humor should never be mistaken for sarcasm. Inappropriate or poorly timed humorous remarks do little to inspire and solidify feelings of caring, trust, confidence, and credibility.

Self-Disclosure. Meaningful interpersonal involvement cannot occur without at least limited self-disclosure by the therapist. The collaborative, therapeutic effort of reality therapy calls for equal and active participation of both client and therapist. There will be occasions when interested clients ask their therapists how they deal with the problems they encounter in living or what they would do in similar circumstances. When the clients' questions have direct relevance to therapeutic concerns and goals, reality therapists often share their personal experiences and life struggles. They must be willing to reveal themselves as persons, to have their values questioned and their frailties uncovered.

ASSESSING PROGRESS

Reality therapists have not agreed on any fixed set of criteria for assessing progress or for terminating therapy. However, the goals of therapy can serve as a guide. Early in the therapeutic process, reality therapists will be concerned with the quality of involvement they are able to establish with their clients. They will be concerned also with their clients' awareness that the focus of therapy is centered on behavior and the present. As therapy progresses, therapists' criteria for progress will depend largely on the goals formulated in therapy by their clients. Progress is indicated when their clients are able to meet their goals by completing their plans of action effectively and independently. Termination is indicated, according to Glasser and Zunin (1979), "If the patient can act in increasingly responsible ways, resolve crises and adjustment problems through accepting that he is responsible for himself and his behavior and that he can fulfill his needs without hurting himself or other people . . . " (p. 327).

It would seem, then, that reality therapists can accept almost any constructive, responsible changes in their clients' behavior as evidence of therapeutic progress. Moreover, their clients' willingness to do something in a meaningful and involved way for others can be viewed as a strong inference of the degree and depth of change in their clients (Glasser and Zunin, 1973). The general criterion is client responsibility; specific secondary criteria are the clients' goals.

There is undoubtedly a close relationship between Glasser's responsibility for self and others and Adler's social interest, particularly as they relate to overt client behavior employed to assess progress in therapy. In both instances, insight alone is insufficient. Clients must be thoroughly convinced that change is both relevant and necessary. Further, they must be committed and willing to face the risks of behaving differently. Finally, and this seems the key to therapeutic progress, they must act, not only in their own best interests but also in a way that benefits others. Healthy life and living includes a responsible involvement with and concern for the well-being of others.

FINAL COMMENTARY

The direction of reality therapy is clear. Glasser (1981) has linked his ideas of reality therapy with the concepts of control theory, and he is working to develop a combined approach that he is convinced better explains human

FIGURE 7.3   A Schematic Analysis of Glasser's Stand on the Basic Issues

Biological Determinants	███ Social Determinants
Unconscious Determinants	███ Conscious Determinants
Early Development	███ Continuous Development
Psychological Environment ███	Reality Environment
Conditioning	███ Freedom
Commonality	███ Uniqueness
Importance of Group Membership	Meaningful involvement with responsible others, particularly signficant others, facilitates fulfillment of basic needs (love, self-worth, fun, and freedom) and achievement of a success identity.
Explanation of Learning	We learn behaviors that serve our needs to find identity. Success identity comes from responsibility and responsibility is learned through interpersonal involvement. Learning focuses on behavior rather than attitudes.
Number and Weight Assigned to Motivational Concepts	We are motivated by basic physiological and psychological needs. When physiological needs have been met, the need for a success identity (a psychological need) becomes a motivating life force.
Importance of Reward	Reward is experienced as an inner sense of joy, a deep-seated satisfaction from being loved and loving and from involvement and repsonsible behavior.
Importance or Role of Self-Concept	In our search for identity we form distinct identity images to which we associate meaning: failure or success. Once formed, identity is highly stable and resistant to change. It is the function of behavior to achieve success identity.

development and behavior. *Stations of the Mind* (1981) and *Take Effective Control of Your Life* (1984) have added considerable dimension to the rather limited and oversimplified global constructs presented in *Reality Therapy* (1965), pariculary in the area of human perception. Viewing the brain as a control system adds greater comprehensiveness to Glasser's resolutions of nearly all the eleven basic issues.

Although reality therapy has been employed successfully with clients experiencing a wide variety of behavioral and emotional problems (Glasser & Zunin, 1979), its greatest potential resides in its applicability as a preventive therapy. Working from the vantage point of the client's strengths and focusing on what the client can do now to improve his or her plight makes reality therapy an attractive choice of approach for mental health workers interested in prevention. Since the publication of *Schools Without Failure* (1969) and the establishment of the Education Training Center, the principles of reality therapy have increasingly been applied in the public schools of this country, particularly those in the Western states. Glasser is convinced that the public schools, especially the elementary grades, are uniquely suited for mental health efforts since this is the period in a child's life that success identities can be most easily developed and failure identities most easily changed.

Reality therapy does have limitations (Glasser & Zunin, 1973, 1979). Because its approach is highly verbal and highly rational, it has not been used successfully with autistic or mentally retarded clients. Clients who are able to reason critically and express themselves well verbally are most likely to benefit from this form of therapy. Burks and Stefflre (1979) view the lack of specific change technology as a weakness of reality therapy. They point out that, "In lieu of planned-change expertise, reality counselors rely upon the pooled common sense between themselves and their clients to create necessary plans to help clients alter their behavior," which "could be a glaring weakness for the noncreative counselor" (p. 313).

The reaction to Glasser's rejection of nearly all forms of mental illness is mixed. Those who believe there are causal, pathogenic factors behind many forms of mental illness (i.e., excessive and/or prolonged stress, deficiencies in psychological and social development, trauma, and genetic or biochemical factors) think Glasser's stance is not only naive and superficial but also harmful and denigrating to clients who are truly mentally ill. Those who hold that mental illness is a myth, that abnormal or pathogenic behavior is chosen by clients as an excuse to act irresponsibly or to deny reality, applaud his stand. Far more, I believe, disagree with both extremes. Certainly some clients find it advantageous to behave consciously in an abnormal manner. Living in a world of their making excuses their inability to face the difficulties of reality, and society often will not hold them accountable for their actions. Still, to say that all mental illness is a myth seems an oversimplification of an extremely complex problem.

Glasser has developed a relatively uncomplicated, short-term therapy that holds the promise of making an even broader impact on mental health professionals in the decade ahead. Its emphasis on involvement, relevance, thinking, and problem solving makes the principles of reality therapy especially practical and useful for working with a variety of group and social problems, as well as for individual therapy.

REFERENCES AND SUGGESTED READINGS

Barr, N. February, 1944. The responsible world of reality therapy. *Psychology Today*, pp. 64–68.

Bassin, A., Bratter, T., & Rachin, R., eds. 1976. *The reality therapy reader*. New York: Harper & Row.

Burks, H., & Stefflre, B. 1979. *Theories of counseling*. 3rd ed. New York: McGraw-Hill.

Glasser, W. 1965. *Reality therapy: A new approach to psychiatry*. New York: Harper & Row.

Glasser, W. 1969. *Schools without failure*. New York: Harper & Row.

Glasser, W. 1970. *Mental health or mental illness?* New York: Harper & Row (originally published 1961).

Glasser, W. 1975. *The identity society*, rev. ed. New York: Harper & Row (originally published 1972).

Glasser, W. 1976. *Positive addiction*. New York: Harper & Row.

Glasser, W. 1981. *Stations of the mind*. New York: Harper & Row.

Glasser, W. 1984. *Take effective control of your life*. New York: Harper & Row.

Glasser, W., & Iverson, N. 1966. *Reality therapy in larger group counseling, A manual of procedure and practice*. Los Angeles: Reality Press.

Glasser, W., & Zunin, L. 1973. Reality therapy. In R. Corsini, ed. *Current psychotherapies*. Itasca, Ill.: F.E. Peacock; 287–315.

Glasser, W., & Zunin, L. 1979. Reality therapy. In R. Corsini, ed. *Current psychotherapies*, 2nd ed. Itasca, Ill.: F.E. Peacock, 302–339.

Glasser, N., ed. 1982. *What are you doing?* New York: Harper & Row (originally published 1980).

Reality therapy: an anti-failure approach. *Impact*, ERIC Counseling and Personnel Information Center 2: 6–11.

8

The Rational-Emotive Therapy of Albert Ellis

DR. ALBERT ELLIS has posited, articulated, and elaborated a cognitive-emotive-behavioristic theory of counseling and psychotherapy. Rational-emotive therapy (RET) is challenging, demanding, and purportedly quite effective, whether we are dealing with the normal problems of daily living or with the inordinately strong emotions and dysfunctional behaviors that keep us from maintaining or reclaiming a solidly rational sensitivity to life and its trials. While Ellis (1974) traces the philosophic origins of his theory to early Stoic writings, granting special recognition to Epictetus and Marcus Aurelius, he has personally applied a modern context to this ancient manner of viewing oneself, others, and the world. He manages this with a distillation and synthesis of ideas from sources as diverse as the phenomenological-existential to the operant conditioning schools of thinking (Ellis, 1974).

Through personal and clinical experiences, Ellis came to believe that we are truly more influenced by what we choose to think about an event than by the event itself. From this basic tenet he developed a humanistic theory of psychotherapy that "squarely places man in the center of the universe and of his own emotional fate and gives him almost full responsibility for choosing to make or not to make himself seriously disturbed" (Ellis, 1974, p. 10).

Ellis views our existence as determined largely by biological predispositions and buffeted constantly by the unpredictable currents of living. He does not, however, maintain that ours is an impossible existence; rather, he claims that we have final dominion over much of the pleasure and pain that life holds for us. He offers us an opportunity to recognize and to challenge our personal brand of irrationality so that we may live our lives in as exciting, as pleasing, and as actualizing a style as we dare choose.

While Ellis may claim that there is little originality in his theory, careful students of RET are quick to point to an originality of organization; an infusion of novel ideas, techniques, and materials; and a unique emphasis on the various cognitive, emotive, and behavioristic components of the theory. They assert that only a creative and radical system of psychotherapy would encourage so much research, attract so many ardent followers, draw such heavy critical fire from so many detractors, or leave so few people neutral after an introduction. Readers may find Ellis and his ideas easy to accept or reject, but ignoring either the man or his ideas could prove difficult.

BIOGRAPHICAL SKETCH

Serious students of psychotherapeutic theories often enhance and expand their understanding of a particular theory by studying the life of the theorist. Even a brief look into the background of Albert Ellis can benefit the student seeking to identify the origin and follow the development of major concepts and hypotheses of RET.

Early Years

Born in Pittsburgh, Pennsylvania, September 27, 1913, Ellis has lived most of his years, including his early childhood, in New York City. Writing a profile of Ellis for *Human Behavior*, Paula Newhorn (1978, pp. 30–35) describes Ellis's father as a very intelligent, opinionated, volatile, energetic, persistent, hard-headed businessman. Ellis's mother is portrayed as a happy, energetic, and often idiosyncratic individual who was bothered little by life's trials, including a divorce that left her to raise three children. Ellis (Newhorn, 1978) attributes his intelligence, drive, and persistence to his father. He credits his early independence of thought and action to his parents' hands-off child-rearing practices.

Ellis was 12 when his parents divorced. It was then that Ellis, who had planned to become a Hebrew teacher, questioned much of his early religious teachings; developed an empirical, scientific approach to life; and rejected a devout belief in any authority.

Education

During junior high school Ellis, determined to become a great novelist, carefully planned his life. He decided to become an accountant, to earn and save enough money to retire comfortably at the age of 30, and once free of financial stress, to concentrate all of his time and energy on writing. While circumstances often dictate revisions of plans formulated in junior high school, Ellis managed to complete the requirements for a baccalaureate degree in business administration and, in 1934, was graduated from City College of New York, despite the ravages of the Depression.

Entering the pant-matching business with his brother, Ellis spent much of his time searching the New York garment auctions for trousers to match his customers' still perfectly good suit coats. His writing endeavors were limited by necessity to his spare time.

Ellis's second venture into the business world lasted 10 years. Beginning as a typist and file clerk for a moderately large gift and novelty house, he quickly advanced to managerial level. During his years with this firm, Ellis (1972) developed bookkeeping, billing, filing, and mail order systems that contributed to the firm's success. As before, Ellis devoted most of his spare time to writing, and by 1941, he had completed nearly two dozen full-length manuscripts. When eight of his novels were rejected, he turned from writing fiction to nonfiction.

A short-lived marriage at the age of 24 led to an intense interest in understanding human behavior, particularly human sexuality. Pursuing this interest, Ellis entered Columbia University in 1942 and, in 1943, was graduated with an M.A. degree in clinical psychology. He began private practice that year while continuing his employment with the gift and novelty firm. During the late 1940s, Ellis taught at both Rutgers University and New York University. He served as senior clinical psychologist at Greystone Park State Hospital in the New Jersey Diagnostic Center and later at the New Jersey Department of Institutions and Agencies.

Ellis received his Ph.D. degree in 1947 and decided to become an analyst. Because psychoanalytic institutes were considering applicants only from the medical profession, he waited until he found an analyst from the Karen Horney group who agreed to work with him. After completing analysis in 1949, Ellis began practicing orthodox psychoanalysis under the direction of his analyst.

Emergence of RET

By the early 1950s, Ellis's faith in psychoanalysis had begun to deteriorate. Initially he moved toward a neo-Freudian stance and then to a psychoanalytically oriented psychotherapy, becoming more active and more directive with each new movement. Still dissatisfied when his patients' perfectionistic, self-damning, and other-directed behaviors remained unchanged (even though they seemed to make great gains in psychoanalytic insight and understanding), Ellis became interested in learning theory and conditioning. With this transition, Ellis became a more effective therapist; however, he discovered also that his patients' behaviors were not the exclusive result of social learning and conditioning. In addition, their behavior appeared to result from biosocial predispositions to retain a number of strong, tenacious, irrational ideas, attitudes, and values.

Ellis began to work diligently toward a rational approach to psychotherapy in 1954. Based more on a philosophical than psychological model, his new and radical system of psychotherapy was elaborated in a series of articles that culminated in 1962 with the publication of *Reason and Emotion in Psychotherapy*. RET and Albert Ellis were on their way to becoming established.

Accomplishments and Awards

In addition to more than 500 papers and articles and numerous instructional tapes and films, Ellis has averaged more than one book per year for the past

35 years. The last count was 47, but surely more will follow. He has served as associate or consulting editor for 10 journals. Ellis is known to work 15-hour days and 7-day weeks, but requests for lectures, consultations, seminars, workshops, professional conferences, and personal appearances on radio and television programs are far too many for any human to meet.

Ellis is founder and executive director of two nonprofit institutes: the Institute for Rational Living, Inc., and the Institute for Advanced Study in Rational Psychotherapy, which is the training and certification headquarters for RET therapists. Branches of these institutes are currently in 10 cities throughout the United States and in Canada, Mexico, Guatemala, the Netherlands, India, and Australia.

In 1971, the American Humanist Association honored Ellis with the Humanist of the Year Award. The Society for the Scientific Study of Sex recognized him for outstanding research in 1972. The APA named Ellis the recipient of their Distinguished Professional Psychologist Award in 1974. In 1976, he accepted the distinguished Sex Educator and Sex Therapist Award of the American Association of Sex Educators, Counselors, and Therapists.

RESOLUTIONS OF THE ELEVEN BASIC ISSUES

Ellis was not involved in the selection of the eleven basic issues presented in this book, and he has not specifically addressed them in any single work. However, Ellis is not one to avoid or ignore any issue, especially a basic issue, and his resolutions are not difficult to find.

Weighting the significance Ellis assigns to each of the eleven basic issues so they might be presented in hierarchical order, however, was difficult. The order presented is a matter of the writer's judgment and, therefore, open to question. There is no guarantee that Ellis endorses this arrangement.

Biological and/or Social Determinants

Because Ellis believes biological and cultural determinants coexist as a dimension of the complex, unified system that is human personality, he resolves this issue by combining its polar opposites. We emerge as biosocial creatures; that is, we are biologically and socioculturally predisposed to perceive, think, emote, and behave in specific and set patterns. And, unless we consciously alter these patterns, Ellis believes that they persist throughout our lives.

While Ellis (1974, 1975, 1977, 1978) does not endow us with the strict and inescapable instincts of lower animals, he does emphasize the biological determinants of our behavior and points to a number of "instinctoid tendencies" or "biologically strong predispositions" that greatly influence us and our modes of perceiving, thinking, emoting, and behaving. Among Ellis's biological predispositions are our tendencies to think rationally and irrationally, to exhibit low frustration tolerance, to be strongly self-evaluating, to seek to survive, to pursue happiness and create misery, to live cooperatively with others, to be overcautious, to think in grandiose and magical ways, to be creative and innovative, to procrastinate and be prone to laziness, to be sensuous and sexual, to love, to benefit from some mistakes and to repeat others endlessly, to be short-range hedonists, to shirk responsibilities, to be perfectionistic, to use and abuse language—thus, to be potentially self-actualizing and self-limiting.

Students of RET will recognize that this listing hardly exhausts Ellis's. Ellis sees these biological predispositions as propensities toward rational (positive, healthful) or irrational (negative, harmful) belief patterns. We are thus born into the world with tendencies to act and to react in a certain pattern. More, we are inclined to perpetuate this pattern regardless of the nature of the stimuli introduced or the individual growth or stagnation we experience.

Our biological predispositions exert a great influence on the development of our personal value systems. Ellis asserts that we function uniquely as a result of our biological heritage, but he also asserts that, because we share enough common biological predispositions with others, there exists a predictable commonality of thinking, feeling, and behaving. Widely held irrational ideas or beliefs have been identified, challenged, and disputed (Ellis, 1975; Ellis & Harper, 1975).

Ellis recognizes that each of us is conditioned by the society and culture in which we grow to maturity, by the types and quality of the early and ongoing relationships we experience, and by the language (symbols and signs) we learn to communicate with ourselves and with others. Our socioculturally acquired tendencies are inseparably linked to, influenced by, and reinforced by our hereditary biological predispositions.

As members of a society, we are conditioned to accept and discouraged from questioning the absolutes that perpetuate that society. Ellis (Ellis & Whiteley, 1979) often refers to our absolutistic societal beliefs as "mustabatory ideas," the "shoulds, oughts, musts, have tos and can'ts" that contribute a great deal to our irrational and maladaptive experiences. In addition, our stronger biological predispositions are often facilitated by sociocultural experiences that reinforce these predispositions.

Our interactions with all significant others strongly influence the way our value systems develop. We naturally assimilate or introject some of the values of these individuals and groups, particularly during our early developmental years. Indoctrination to a particular language begins practically at birth and, as a product of symbolic interaction, we learn early to build a belief system with symbols. Once accomplished, we have the ability to create nearly every human emotion and to initiate a large repertoire of physiological sensations.

In summary, that this biosocial combination of innate and acquired pre-dispositions can lead to difficulty for us is hardly surprising, particularly when our uniquely human thinking ability is added to an already complicated picture. Ellis views us in some degree of precarious balance between the in-nate tendencies and the environmental forces and influences. On the one hand, we are inclined to act in a certain manner because of cognitive-emotive-behavioral propensities that are not easily defined or directly observed but that are engrained in the biological and psychic fiber of each of us. On the other hand, we are faced with the mountains of true and false beliefs and con-ditioned expectations that society provides us from the moment of birth via a language that often seems to contribute to irrational thought. However pre-carious this balance, Ellis holds to the belief that with hard work and long practice we possess the capacity to weight the balance in favor of rational sensitivity.

Conscious and/or Unconscious Determinants

As noted in Chapter 1, when a basic issue is viewed as a polarity, theorists may begin their search for a resolution by selecting one end of the polarity and working to define it, either by determining what it is or by determining what its polar opposite is not. When addressing the polarity of conscious and/or unconscious determinants of behavior, Ellis seems to favor the latter ap-proach and often begins his resolution of human consciousness by explaining what the unconscious, its polar opposite, is not.

Ellis (1975) does not accept the structure of personality proposed by classical psychoanalytic theorists. Thus, Ellis rejects the concept that there exists any part of human personality that can be labeled the id or the uncon-scious. Ellis would view such definitions or terms as mysterious or metaphysi-cal and not of concern to rational students of personality. In fact, Ellis op-poses any theoretical concept built on the idea of an inherited personality arena wherein innate instincts are housed or in which repressed, unexpressed feelings are accumulated and held inaccessible, beyond potential awareness.

Ellis believes that we have developed in our evolution to the point where we possess few, if any, innate instincts so hidden and so powerful that they singularly account for our thoughts, motivations, feelings, and actions (see "Biological and/or Social Determinants"). In addition, Ellis (1974) finds no evidence to show how repressed feelings can exist. Bringing the unconscious or preconscious of the psychoanalysts into awareness is, for Ellis, nothing more than becoming aware of our self-talk, that inner dialogue we constantly exercise.

Although few innate instincts remain with us, we do possess a number of biosocial predispostions or tendencies that, directly and indirectly, contribute to or inhibit our self-awareness:

1. We are holistic beings by virtue of our natural tendency to perceive,

think, emote, and act or react simultaneously, interactionally, and transactionally (Ellis, 1975). When we perceive an event or object, we think about it, we experience a feeling toward it, and, finally, we act or react in accordance with our feelings.

2. Because we inherit a highly developed brain, we are naturally predisposed to think. More important, we are capable of thinking about our thinking. Perhaps most important, we can, and often do, think about what we think about our thinking (Ellis, 1975). Our thinking may be either rational or irrational because we have strong innate tendencies for both.

3. Because of our ability and tendency to think either or both rationally or irrationally, we naturally develop ideas, attitudes, and habitual patterns of thought that tend to perpetuate. From these ideas, attitudes, and patterns of thought, we construct highly personal and unique systems of values and beliefs that in turn come to influence our ideation, attitude, and pattern of thinking.

4. While we think through imaging, fantasy, and dreams, we also exhibit a natural and acquired predisposition to learn and to use language in the form of words, phrases, and sentences that enhances or limits our thinking and our communication with others and ourselves. Our imaging, fantasy, dreams, words, phrases, and sentences contain clear, cognitive, mediating messages that directly and significantly contribute to our emotions and behaviors.

5. We are experiencing beings, but we are not limited to our experience; we can and do conceptualize about our experiences. When something happens to us, we have a natural predisposition to think and to "talk" to ourselves about it. Ellis (1962) refers to this special thought process as "self-talk." Beck (1976), a cognitive theorist, labels it "parallel thinking." Regardless of the descriptor for our inner-dialogue process, the "voice of our value system" is strong enough to cause us to feel and act very much as we talk to ourselves about the events in our lives.

6. Our thinking, then, creates most of our feelings and greatly determines how we will act or react in any particular situation. Our self-talk (beliefs, attitudes, and values) mediates between a given stimulus, whether internal or external, and our response to the stimulus, thus determining how we will feel about an experience and how we will act during or following an experience. Feelings and emotions are neither automatic nor autonomous; they are self-created to fit in harmony with the value systems we are living.

7. With little effort, we can recall most of our self-talk. Even the most repeated and integrated or habituated self-talk rests just below the surface of our constant awareness and is subject to recall.

In summary, as we view our consciousness through the window provided by RET, we can see ourselves as very conscious beings with the potential to be essentially conscious. Although we are innately predisposed to think and to act irrationally and are thrown into an environment that often encourages our irrationality through language and cultural indoctrination, we possess the capability of self-awareness and the potential to create consciously

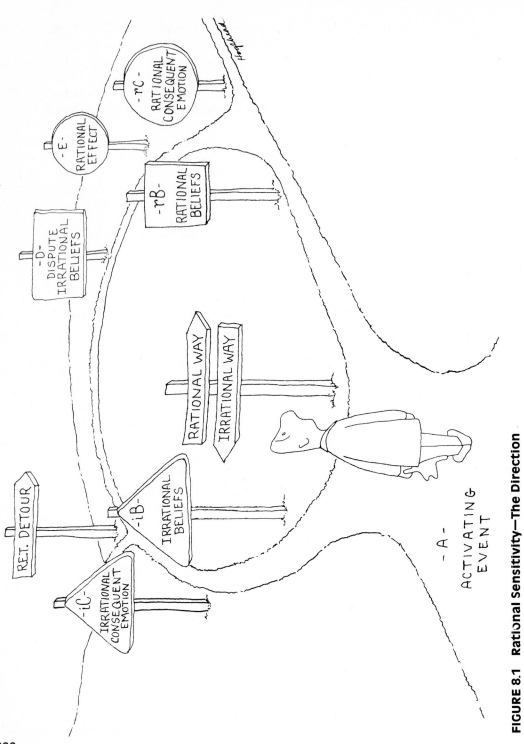

FIGURE 8.1 Rational Sensitivity—The Direction

and perpetuate the present meaning we choose to give our experience. We are largely our own productions.

Importance of Role Assigned to Self-Concept

Ellis is not likely to be numbered among the self-theorists in the field of counseling and psychotherapy, but he does list self-conceptualizing with the biological predispositions and the environmentally bolstered tendencies we share as human beings (1972, pp. 101–102). Ellis recognizes that the concepts we hold of our selves at any particular time will exert a significant influence on the way we feel and act. However, unlike the majority of the self-theorists, Ellis defines our self-conceptualizing as irrational thinking, a process involving self-ratings, self-judgments, and self-justifications, resulting in global positive or negative affect with respect to our feelings of self-worth and intrinsic value.

Ellis not only doubts the rationality of attempting to rate a process, but also questions the possibility and desirability of an accurate global self-rating. He reminds us that in so doing we are attempting to measure and quantify abstract values and concepts. Further, he notes that we would somehow have to include all our traits, potentials, motives, and behaviors in our self-rating.

When our worth or our intrinsic value depends on our rating of our performances, we feel good about ourselves only when we can rate our performances highly. Unfortunately, anything less than a high performance rating results in a poor self-conceptualization, often accompanied by anxiety and depression and the tendency to avoid opportunities and tasks that hold any risk of failure. Because we rate our performances with the performances of others, we can rate ourselves highly only by rating others less highly or, better still, poorly. Those we rate highly are in a position to threaten our self-ratings, and we often find ourselves spending valuable time and energy seeking weakness in their performances while justifying our own. Concern and anxiety become our constant companions. Every new task, project, or assignment carries the possibility of poor performance or failure, thus perpetuating low self-rating, injured self-esteem, still greater anxiety, and even greater depression.

Ellis (Ellis & Harper, 1975; Ellis & Abrahms, 1978) affords us two separate and distinct approaches to the question of the importance of the role assigned to the self-concept. The first, defined as the inelegant approach, is offered to those of us who seem unable to avoid self-rating. During the early development of RET, Ellis referred to the idea of self-concept as a purely tautological and definitional construct in the personality make-up of the individual. Essentially this means, at least for those of us whose definitions are in good order, that we are worthy because we exist, that there is an intrinsic value in being and choosing to remain alive.

Realizing that a definitional approach could neither be validated nor invalidated since our very existence may have made us evil, Ellis moved toward a more elegant and rational approach to the question of self-concept as an important variable in our mental well-being. Ellis asserts that it is far better to avoid self-rating entirely. While he affirms that it is important for us to be aware of our levels of functioning and competence, he cautions us to avoid applying good-bad or right-wrong judgments to our thoughts, feelings, and actions. For Ellis, we do not develop a self; we develop traits and competencies.

Ellis is convinced that as we identify and integrate rational self-acceptance into our psychic repertoire, we become healthier and happier and avoid the many pitfalls of judgmental thinking. Ultimately, we are human. With our humanness comes the fallibility, the flexibility, the complexity, and the propensity to err and to succeed. This is the foundation of our uniqueness. Unconditional acceptance of our humanness, of our selves, will greatly influence how we think and, therefore, how we feel and act toward ourselves, others, and encounters we have in our world.

Ellis's argument against self-rating appears to center on the questions of who we are versus what we are. Throughout his writing, Ellis repeatedly provides his definition of *who* we are as human beings. We are fallible, conscious, self-determining, cognitively-emotionally-behaviorally active, biologically and socially influenced, and habit-prone individuals. If we can accept ourselves unconditionally and rationally function within this structural arena, we can gain a considerable measure of personal freedom and fulfillment. If, however, we are perpetually in search of the perfect, therefore nonexistent me-ism, Ellis believes we are dooming ourselves to a pitiful life of ceaseless disappointment and inevitable failure. Ellis does not discourage our quest for better and more efficient selfhood. However, he frankly asserts that if this quest is tainted with perfectionist or absolutist expectations and demands, it can, and in all probability will, produce a great deal of trauma and personal disillusionment.

Ellis recognizes that many of us define ourselves through our accomplishments and our positions in this world. This posture reflects the *what* of our existence. While it is certainly important for us to achieve, to prosper, and to succeed in a rational manner, we are encouraged not to allow success or failure in the external world to affect our level of self-acceptance. Ellis (Ellis and Abrahms, 1978) identifies this functional area of our being as the "work-confidence" area.

Ellis (Ellis and Abrahms, 1978) defines another area that is directly related to our self-acceptance. This area is "love-confidence" and includes the number, quality, and characteristics of the relationships we have with other individuals and groups. Ellis cautions us to see relationships in a rational perspective and to avoid making ourselves discontented or depressed by demanding that we be accepted and loved by even a single significant other.

As indicated, Ellis views the concept of self-acceptance as a prerequisite to stable and positive mental well-being. Our level of self-acceptance has much to do with how well we function as self-facilitating individuals. To acquire and maintain a rational self-acceptance, we must work diligently to view ourselves in a rational perspective. Such a life stance allows us to move forward without downgrading and damning ourselves for each setback or disappointment we may experience.

Conditioning and/or Freedom to Choose

Again, Ellis positions himself near the center of this polarity. He recognizes the existence of causal factors that are beyond our individual wills and efforts to control or to escape. Those behavioral determinants are deeply rooted in our instinctoid tendencies and in our personal-societal-environmental life histories. But just as certainly, Ellis vows that we possess the potential for a wide range of existential freedom and can, therefore, choose to develop rational sensitivity that, at least to a limited degree, permits us to transcend our biological and experiential antecedents.

While Ellis (1972, 1979) affords us the freedom to choose rational sensitivity, he cautions us that our freedom is conditional because it does not automatically or implicitly guarantee rational thinking. He reminds us that we are innately inclined to think irrationally as well and that only our persistent, uncompromising attention to and expression of our freedom to choose rational sensitivity can sustain rational thoughts, feelings, and behaviors.

While we are conditioned by biological and societal influences, Ellis proposes that we condition ourselves via our so-called self-talk network. Ellis believes that within each of us exists a cognitive dialogue that largely affects how we feel and behave in any given experience. From earliest childhood, our self-talk and the incumbent belief or value system upon which it is founded come under the influence of significant others and external groups.

As children, we inculcate the values of our parents, our teachers, our friends, and all other people whom we encounter significantly. As this occurs, our evolving self-talk network takes on characteristics of those individuals and groups with whom we most closely associate regularly. If the values these individuals and groups hold are rational, we learn to express rational self-talk based on realistic values. The opposite is also the case; thus, our self-talk network contains elements of both rational and irrational thought.

Beyond the valuing influence of individuals and groups, our value systems—hence, our self-talk networks—are perpetually molded and shaped by collective societal and societal system's values. We are provided with valuing alternatives from political rhetoric, the counterculture, the educational establishment, the church, the media, government bureaucracy, and other lesser societal forces. There is no guarantee that the conditioned values we encounter are rational and healthy or in our personal best interests. Television may serve as a good example of this point. The television invites us to tune in to the self-talk network of the masses and to accept the current popular, although often transient, ideals and values. It would seem practically impossible for us to avoid this onslaught of value, belief, and attitudinal conditioning and to grow to maturity devoid of numerous irrational beliefs and priorities imposed by society, particularly when we are biologically predisposed to do just this.

While this situation is and will likely remain reality, Ellis suggests that we can transcend these negative social experiences through development of a keen critical attitude and awareness. Ellis recognizes that the cultivation of rational sensitivity is not easy. However, he believes it to be the most effective way for us to live rationally and to prosper in the present. As we accomplish this, we can express one of the strongest of our natural predispositions—that is, our freedom to choose what we believe and how we behave in our daily lives. Through the confrontation of those ideas that promote irrational thinking and living, we are choosing to consider and eliminate negative valuing influences. We can recreate and maintain a rational value system and a network of self-talk that minimizes personal dysfunction while providing the best ways and means to long-term gratification of our realistic and nongrandiose goals and aspirations.

In the RET ideal, we can and do choose for ourselves what life means to us, how we can and will react to life and to others, and how we use our values, thoughts, emotions, and actions to accept or to alter our circumstances at any given choice-juncture in our lives. Ellis believes that the freedom to choose rational sensitivity is available to each of us, but he allows us to decide whether we shall be governed by our self-conditioning and the conditioning elements of society or whether we shall choose to become more self-determining, self-aware, self-disciplined, active, and striving—thus, more alive and fully functioning human beings.

Explanation of Learning

Ellis readily admits that we are experiencing beings; however, he is quick to demonstrate that we are not limited to our experiences. Our abilities to think, to think about our thinking, and to think about what we think of our thinking permit us to conceptualize our experiences. Essentially, Ellis informs us that we are naturally predisposed to learn and that learning is an important, integral part of our life process and our movement toward more rational living. Thus, for Ellis, learning is central in both the theory and the therapeutic process of RET.

Ellis (1974) accepts many of the main postulates of the learning theorists. He recognizes that sensory data, whether organismic or environmental, can impress and influence each of our minds. However, he insists that our minds, sifting that sensory data through a priori value-laden belief systems, determine the meanings we attribute to our experiences, as well as to our emotional and behavioral responses. Were our belief systems comprised only of rational beliefs, our emotional and behavioral responses would nearly always be appropriate and effective. Unfortunately, our belief systems begin to form during those impressionable early years when we are particularly susceptible to the influence of other people, society, and the environment. Because of our dependence and lack of critical awareness, we tend to accept and internalize those values we hear and observe with little discrimination of their rationality. We live in a social world, and it is natural, although sometimes irrational, for us to share the values of that world.

Our belief systems emerge in the form of self-talk, the declarative and imperative sentences we tell ourselves as we experience ourselves, others, and the world. However, Ellis reminds us that while self-talk crystallizes early and is reinforced constantly in our lives, it is nearly always amenable to change. We are potentially and consciously equipped to transcend these conditioned patterns of valuing and thinking and, with hard work and practice, to move beyond them into a more effective realm of self-facilitaton. We can learn to become more rationally sensitive. Ellis's concept of restructuing our self-talk is an exercise in personal self-awareness that allows us to function more effectively and happily.

In conclusion, RET is primarily a teaching process. RET therapists actively and directly teach their clients the logico-empirical method of questioning, challenging, and debating values, attitudes, and beliefs. This process is directed toward cognitive-emotive restructuring and toward greater rational sensitivity and more effective living.

Psychological and/or Reality Environments

Ellis has established RET as a rational psychotherapeutic theory and practice. This point alone seems to imply that he believes that a reality exists beyond the phenomenological stance of the individual. Further, he encourages us to come to terms with this reality, particularly in accepting the imperfections of ourselves, others, and the world.

Ellis's firm stance against any supernatural or visionary cajolery, against almost any infinites, absolutes, or perfectionism, indicates clearly that he has rooted his theory in the reality of empirical verifications. RET does not allow us the luxury, except in magical, philosophical wonderings, to consider how the world should be; rather, we are taught to accept the world as we encounter it in the present. Reality, RET teaches us, is always as it should be.

While it is clear that Ellis identifies with a reality environment, he affords us both the opportunity and the right to make personal statements about the way things are for us. He stresses that our statements, our self-talk, will have an immense effect on our ability to function in the world and with other people.

It is important to note at this point that when we accept the world as it is, we do not automatically relinquish the right to hope, dream, and act in a manner that promotes the collective betterment of that world. In fact, Ellis states that the healthy individual rationally transcends self and moves into an arena characterized by rational interest in the betterment of the world. We are not victims of cruel fate or ominous, foreboding demons, devils, or gods. We are able, when rationally sensitive, to choose for ourselves how externals will affect us, to choose our attitude toward our world.

As we accept our fallibililty, without judging this as good or bad, and as we accept the imperfections of reality, regardless of the insanity we may witness, we are placing ourselves on a sounder mental footing. As we approach a position of rational equilibrium, we move closer to an existential stance that puts us largely in control of our attitudes and values and, finally, our actions.

Early and/or Continuous Development: Critical or Significant Life Stages

The socialization process begins, and is most effective, during our early years when we are most impressionable and vulnerable, and when we are least equipped to discriminate between the real and the unreal or the sensible and the insensible. It is then, too, that we initiate the formation of our personal value systems. We are encouraged and, in many instances, pressured to accept and to internalize the attitudes, beliefs, and values of our families, our friends, and our teachers. Unfortunately, much of what they pass along is irrational and inappropriate for adult life. In fact, many of our neurotic or pseudoneurotic eccentricities are established during this early developmental period. Still, as important as our early childhood years are, Ellis postulates no critical life stages. We are not doomed to live by the irrational beliefs and values learned in childhood for the remainder of our lives.

Although, as children, our personal belief systems almost surely become tainted by the cognitive-behavioral irrationalities of those around us, RET is based on a unitary, holistic theory of personality and has little use for an approach to development in terms of stages. Ellis asserts that we can choose to transcend our pasts any time that we become determined enough to acknowledge that (1) as children, we created emotional disturbance and discontinuity by our irrational thoughts about events; (2) our continuous reindoctrinations and habituations of these same irrational beliefs are responsible for keeping us upset today; and (3) the only way we are likely to minimize or extinguish our continued disturbance over a past event is by repeatedly confronting and challenging our irrational beliefs while repeatedly acting to undo them. Ellis (1979) warns us that insights (1) and (2) are not enough, that it requires (3), hard work, and long practice to correct early learned, long-standing emotional disturbances and to keep them corrected.

We thus have the tendency to perpetuate early learned patterns of irrational beliefs. We are prone, also, to perpetuate the intensity of our irrational beliefs or thought patterns in proportion to the weight or value we assign to them in our present circumstances. The more value we attach to a belief, the more difficult it will be for us to confront and to change that belief.

There is, then, according to Ellis, a connection between adult dysfunctional behaviors and learning experiences as children. However, he strongly affirms our ability to move beyond the influences of the past. In fact, in therapy Ellis would not likely tolerate our lingering in the past or looking for childhood experiences that cause us to think, feel, or behave in presently self-defeating ways. He would assert, rather early in the therapeutic process, that nothing we encountered in the past is causing us difficulty. He would inform us that our current manner of thinking is the root of our problem and that anything experienced in the past can be changed in intensity or influence by a change in our attitude toward it.

Ellis clearly supports the idea of continuous development since he views rational living as a philosophy and a life-style, as well as a psychotherapeutic theory. The more rationally we are able to think, the better we shall feel. Likewise, our behaviors will become less counterproductive and the cycle of rational living will become a part of our ongoing development. Truly, for Ellis, we are not victims but rational creators of our effectiveness.

Uniqueness and/or Commonality

Ellis maintains that we have the resources and the ability to assert and express a unique approach to dealing with the circumstances we create and encounter in life. Our uniqueness is something we largely discover and unfold as we become aware of our potential to choose freely our destinies. Our uniqueness is an integral part of the value systems to which we adhere and live. Our value systems give character to our every thought, feeling, intuition, and action. This character sets us apart from any other individual in the world and affords us the opportunity to make completely unique contributions to our happiness and to those individuals and things we value in life. However, it is impossible to say that Ellis ignores the fact that we all share many common biological predispositions and socialization patterns and that these influences play a significant role in how we shall come to know, or even if we shall come to know, our uniqueness. Surely, the commonality of similar childhood backgrounds, educational experiences, and sociocultural expectations indoctrinates us with a common heritage of thoughts, feelings, and behaviors. We are like our fellow humans because we share so much biological and experiential input with them. Ellis believes that what we do with this input determines whether we come to realization, expression, and functioning at the level we are uniquely capable of attaining. Perhaps it is easiest to express Ellis's conception of this dichotomy by saying that we have the potential to function uniquely within the commonality of humankind.

Again, what we do with what we inherit and experience is important to Ellis because he believes that this activity of self-destiny most explicitly defines us as unique. Finally, Ellis believes that our uniqueness arises also from the degree of development that we may naturally have in a particular or several different activities or abilities. Not everyone is endowed with the same mental and physical prowess, but we all have at our disposal, by choice, the potential to become as fully functioning and well adjusted as our limitations allow.

Importance of Group Membership

Although primarily a responsible hedonist, Ellis sees us as innately gregarious and relationship prone. He reminds us that, from a responsible hedonistic viewpoint, we are usually much happier when we are integrated members of a human community and active participants in intimate relationship with a few selected members of that community. At the same time, Ellis (Ellis & Harper, 1975) repeatedly cautions us to desire rather than to demand the approval and love of others. It would seem, therefore, that Ellis would likely assert that the importance of group membership is a point that we decide for ourselves and that we had better, for our own long-range benefit, use all the rational sensitivity we can muster when we make that decision. We can, as rationally healthy individuals, learn to transcend singular self-interest and become involved in the well-being and development of others and the community.

As chidren, we are certainly influenced and shaped by our early group affiliations (see "Early and/or Continuous Development"). Our childhood friends, peer groups, and family members beyond the nuclear family provide us with a sense of group membership. As adults, we come under the influence of groups at our place of employment, in our community, and within our social circle that can influence our thinking and our behavior. Ellis would likely advise us to choose our group affiliations rationally so we interact with those groups that have the best influence on us. This implies that we take a rationally critical view of our present affiliations and carefully scrutinize any future affiliations. In the final analysis, we must decide for ourselves what is best for us. This is a power that can work for or against our rational approach to living.

Number and Weight Assigned to Motivational Concepts

As stated earlier, Ellis believes that a rational approach to life is responsible hedonism and that the nature of our choices of thought, feeling, and action, therefore, had better enhance both our short- and long-term search for effectiveness and life satisfaction. Thus, Ellis seems to see long-term self-interest as the major source of motivation for us. Ellis asserts that we are, or at least have the potential to become, positively self-interested. Corollary motivational concepts such as wealth, fame, solitude, and security are supplementary to the overriding motivation of self-interest. Ellis implies that, as individuals solidly founded in rational sensitivity, we will discover that many of our corollary motivational concepts are realized because we more effectively begin to live in, operate within, and benefit from the world in which we exist.

Ellis believes that we naturally seek to avoid pain and to maximize pleasure. This idea possibly arises from Ellis's training in psychoanalysis, but it is not quite as Freudian as it may first appear. As we live rationally, we learn to avoid the pitfalls of irrational thought and action that tend to be painful. As we avoid pain, we begin to have more confidence in our abilities to live effectively. While the Freudian pleasure versus pain dichotomy is rather rigid, Ellis's apparent interpretation of this concept equates effective living with pleasure and ineffective living with pain, thus providing for a wide range of cognitive and behavioral choices at our disposal. More important, Ellis allows us the right to decide for ourselves exactly which and to what degree of these approaches we take to life.

It is safe, then, to assume that Ellis is allowing us to choose our motivational purposes. He does, however, encourage us to be as certain as possible that the things we choose can be rationally achieved, earned, or gained. Ellis does not recognize desires, preferences, hopes, or aspirations as concepts we can rationally categorize as needs since the only true needs we have are those required for survival. Having and retaining certain traits, skills, relationships, or material possessions may contribute to a more pleasant, simpler, and securer life for us, but we are instructed to avoid escalating these personal preferences into the status reserved for need.

In day-to-day living, our choices of motivation remain patently ours. We can learn to identify and to determine whether we are motivated by things that contribute to or inhibit our rational life-styles. One of the aspects of rational living is that we learn to choose those things that provide for our happiness and well-being over both the short and long term. As long as we are motivated by irrational ideas, we will perpetuate irrational thinking and behaving because we will always be pursuing things that are not essential to our betterment. Ellis cautions that our innate low tolerance of frustration can lead us to demand immediate gratification. However, we can, with hard work and practice, re-educate ourselves to think, feel, and act in terms of our best interest so we avoid becoming mired in situations and circumstances that are purely transient and nonessential to our rational approach to and expression of living.

Importance of Reward

It seems evident, with even a cursory look at the philosophic stance of RET, that Ellis considers reward both an important ingredient of rational, healthful living and an integral part of psychotherapy. As mentioned earlier, RET is based on a theory of personality that, when viewed over the long term, is frankly hedonistic as well as humanistic. It begins with the premise that humans naturally prize and pursue pleasure, joy, creativity, and freedom and that their attainment or enhancement is very rewarding. Conversely, we find pain, joylessness, creative stagnation, and bondage naturally aversive. Hence, we are rewarded each time we manage to rid ourselves of them, to minimize their intensity or duration, or to confront and overcome the defensive and dysfunctional behaviors we employ to deny or avoid them.

Hedonism, as practiced in RET, is not considered merely the pursuit of pleasure and the avoidance of pain because this alone is unlikely to reward us with continued enjoyment. Ellis (1974) asserts that rationally sensitive individuals practice responsible hedonism that "emphasizes both the releasing pleasures of the here-and-now and the longer-range goals of future gain through present-day discipline" (p. 13). The goals of RET, therefore, reflect beliefs and habits congruent with this concept (Walen, DiGiuseppe, and Wessler, 1980): survival, achieving satisfaction with living, affiliating with others in a positive way, achieving intimate involvement with a few others, and developing or maintaining a vital absorption in some personally fulfilling endeavor. Again, these are all rewarding pursuits and may be attained in a wide variety of ways (see "Therapeutic Process").

Although RET, particularly in its elegant form, concentrates primarily on restructuring our belief or value systems by teaching us to recognize, dispute, and change those ideas and attitudes that lead to inordinately strong emotions and ineffective, maladaptive, or dysfunctional behaviors, our new, more rational beliefs must be subjected to the trial of practice if they are to be meaningful or lasting. To this end, RET includes many conditioning, deconditioning, and self-conditioning techniques to reward and reinforce independent and creative thinking. Further, with RET we are taught to construct our own reinforcement schedules and to use these schedules to enhance our personal styles of living.

In summary, reward, especially self-reward, plays an important part in RET. It is rewarding to be less perfectionist and absolutist; to minimize our dire need for love, approval, and success; to accept rather than damn ourselves, others, and the world; to be less procrastinating and more productive; to become more involved with others; to risk new and once frightening behaviors; to rid ourselves of the magical thinking of superstition and prejudice; to become committed to a vital interest or project; thus, to minimize the pain and maximize the pleasure of living.

GOALS OF THE RATIONAL-EMOTIVE THERAPIST

The essence of RET is "that it is possible to achieve maximum actualization through the use of cognitive control of illogical responses" (Morris & Kanitz, 1975, p. 8). The ultimate goal of the elegant or preferential form of RET is personality change or reorganization through cognitive awareness and philosophic restructuring and the acquisition of a logico-empirical method to maintain that change.

To avoid some of the common misunderstandings or misinterpretations concerning the goals of elegant RET, it is important to note the following:

1. In addition to the elegant, or preferential, form of RET , which makes RET unique among the cognitive therapies, there is the inelegant, or general, form, the goals of which are specific and indistinguishable from other forms of cognivite therapy.

2. While the two forms of RET therapy have different implications for therapeutic goals, they are not completely distinct and separate. The goals of inelegant RET (often expressed as resolving a problem, making a decision, reducing the pain of a symptom, or changing a behavior) may occur through the practice of elegant RET. Conversely, although much less likely, personality change or reorganization can occur through the practice of inelegant RET.

3. The RET therapist seldom employs the elegant form of RET exclusively. Ellis and Whiteley (1979) define the RET therapist "as one who *generally* does CEB [cognitive-emotive-behavioral] therapy and who also *specifically* does rational-emotive therapy" (p. 246, emphasis in original). The elegant form of RET is preferred because the objective of this form of therapy is not only to help clients eliminate their existing disturbances but also to help them learn a logico-empirical problem-solving process to prevent extreme, sustained, negative emotions and dysfunctional behaviors in the future.

4. While RET therapists will, whenever feasible, actively and directly encourage their clients to recognize and dispute their irrational beliefs so they might gain control of their inordinately strong negative emotional responses, they do not impose any absolutist criteria of rationality. In discussing the term, *rational*, as it is used in RET, Ellis and Whiteley (1979) tell us that it "refers to people's (a) setting up or choosing for themselves certain values, purposes, goals, or ideals, and then (b) using efficient, flexible, scientific, logico-empirical ways of attempting to achieve such values and goals and to avoid contradicting or self-defeating results" (p. 40).

It is apparent from the resolutions presented earlier (see "Conditioning and/or Freedom to Choose" and "Uniqueness and/or Commonality") that RET therapists value highly and accept fully their clients' prerogative to decide their own direction. The RET directive that goal priority rests with the client is possibly best expressed by Walen, DiGiuseppe, and Wessler (1980) when they remind RET therapists that they are not there to stamp out all irrational beliefs in their clients but to help their clients change what they want to change (p. 35).

5. RET supports a philosophy of responsible hedonism: "Go for the pleasures of the moment, but weigh those pleasures against future consequences" (Wessler & Wessler, 1980). RET clients are encouraged to evaluate their decisions, plans, and actions from both a short- and long-range perspective

and to assess the consequences within their value systems. The route to adjustment is enlightened self-interest.

While RET therapists are continually striving to achieve the ultimate goal of elegant or preferential RET, they may approach the ultimate via the accomplishment of the following subsidiary goals:

To communicate high credibility, professional competence, mutual respect, and a genuine interest in, and commitment to, helping their clients change;

To communicate unconditional acceptance of their clients;

To communicate a faith in their clients' abilities to reconstruct their belief systems;

To help their clients become aware of their natural predisposition to think and to talk to themselves about nearly everything that happens to them and that this inner dialogue creates most of their feelings and determines how they will act or react in any particular situation;

To demonstrate to their clients that they can recall most of their self-talk when they choose to do so;

To help their clients become aware of how their language contributes to irrational perceptions, thoughts, emotions, and actions;

To encourage their clients to question and dispute their irrational beliefs, particularly the absolutist beliefs—the shoulds, oughts, musts, have tos, and can'ts;

To teach actively and directly their clients a logico-empirical method of questioning, challenging, and disputing values, attitudes, and beliefs;

To convince their clients that they can, with hard and diligent work, weight the balance of their inherent tendency to think both rationally and irrationally in favor of rational thought;

To demonstrate to their clients that past experiences can only continue to disturb them as long as they actively continue to reinforce and reindoctrinate themselves with the same irrational self-talk that created their disturbances in the first place;

To encourage their clients to come to terms with reality, particularly to accept without blame the imperfections of themselves, others, and the world;

To encourage their clients to avoid escalating their personal preferences, wants, and desires into the status reserved for needs;

To help their clients accept the fact that they are only, but totally, human and, as humans, fallible;

To demonstrate to their clients the futility of self-conceptualizing, which results in global positive or negative affect with respect to feelings of self-worth and intrinsic value;

To acquaint their clients with irrational beliefs commonly held by large segments of the population.

THERAPEUTIC PROCESS: METHODS AND TECHNIQUES

Before looking into the tharapuetic process of RET, consider the following two important points: (1) RET is not a set of methods or techniques, as implied in the heading of this section, and (2) because it is not a set of methods or techniques, there is no set way to practice RET, including the way demonstrated by Ellis.

We know that it is impossible to distinguish between effective and ineffective therapists solely on the basis of the methods they use or the techniques they employ. It seems that many of the methods and techniques of the experts work only because the users are experts. It is a mistake, then, to assume that the methods and techniques of experienced and effective RET therapists can be taught directly to the novice. The methods and techniques of RET are applied with knowledge and skill; there is no substitute for experience.

Therapeutic Relationship

Practitioners of RET contend that, since people have drastically changed their personalities through a wide variety of direct and vicarious experiences, there probably are no necessary and sufficient conditions for psychotherapy or for the psychotherapeutic relationship; that is, no absolutes guide RET therapists as they attempt to establish a therapeutic relationship with their clients.

Wessler and Wessler (1980) remind therapists, however, that the absence of absolutes does not diminish the importance of establishing a sound working relationship with their clients. The process of therapy is a partnership: two persons working together in pursuit of common goals. There are, then, desirable conditions that seem to facilitate therapeutic collaboration. Walen, DiGiuseppe, and Wessler (1980) believe that the development of a good rapport between client and therapist is an important ingredient in maximizing therapeutic gains. They remind us that the initial approach in RET therapy requires "patience, encouragement, and gentle confrontation" (p. 28). In a paper presented at the First National Conference on Rational Psychotherapy, Young (1981) views relationship building "as a primary consideration in any attempt to practice RET with young people," and presents 10 specific expressive techniques that he found particulary helpful in establishing a "trusting, accepting, interpersonal relationship" with the reluctant or frightened adolescent client (pp. 1–3).

Patterson (1980), believing that Ellis clearly communicates a genuine interest in, and concern for, his clients, suspects that Ellis's results are more influenced by the relationship he establishes with his clients than Ellis cares to admit (p. 94). The implication of Patterson's position is that the counseling relationship is, in and of itself, therapeutic, a position unacceptable to Ellis and to most RET therapists who view the relationship they establish with their clients as a means to an end, not an end in itself.

As with most therapeutic theories, there are minimal conditions that had best be met if the therapist expects to see the client more than once. Of course, these conditions will vary somewhat from client to client. However, the therapist had better seek to communicate high credibility, professional competence, mutual respect, and a genuine interest in, and commitment to, helping the client change. Experienced therapists will tailor the emphasis they place on each of these conditions according to their assessment of their clients, as well as to their clients' expectations of therapy.

Because RET therapists believe all humans are fallible, they not only accept fallibility in their clients, but also encourage maximum understanding of, and tolerance for, human error and frailty. They specifically and vigorously oppose all types of blaming, including self-blame. They fully accept their clients as human beings, regardless of how objectionable or dysfunctional their clients' behavior. In addition to accepting their clients' fallibility, RET therapists communicate a faith in their clients' abilities to reconstruct their belief systems; to perceive, think, and act more rationally and effectively; and to accept the responsibility for their choices. Thus, while seldom communicating warmth or love, RET therapists regularly communicate unconditional acceptance of their clients. The therapeutic relationship of RET does not often produce transference, but should it occur, it is quickly analyzed (via the client's self-talk) and uprooted.

Initial Procedures and Strategies

With the absence of absolutes, no set or prescribed structure is available for the RET therapist to follow when initiating therapy. Although it is possible to learn from experienced therapists, remember that RET therapists not only differ from each other in manner and style but also often vary their therapeutic approach from one client to another or from one session to another with the same client. Each client is unique, and each presents a unique set of conditions or circumstances for the therapist to assess and deal with creatively. Still, RET is an active-directive therapy, and although the client determines the content of the session, the structure, flexibly adjustable to variations in clients, is decided by the therapist.

Initiating Therapy.   As with most therapies, the therapeutic relationship of RET is initiated with the first communication between client and therapist. The tone for what is to come is set. First impressions and statements are important. If opening remarks are inane, amounting to little more than the usual social icebreakers, they serve no purpose and, if prolonged, may prove ineffectual or even dysfunctional. The beginning of the session portends the expectations of therapy. The professional, businesslike opening is much more likely to instill client confidence and encourage the client to begin working on the antecedent concerns that have brought him or her to therapy.

Initial rapport building can usually be accomplished fairly quickly with most clients, but others require more time. The referred client, the frightened client, and the adolescent client are often reluctant clients. They may have little or no confidence in either the therapist or the therapy and may be unable or simply reluctant to talk about themselves. Until their fears and uncertainties have been reduced, any attempt to move into therapy proper is met with resistance.

Client Expectations. RET therapists are seldom interested in an extensive history of their clients, but many want to know whether their clients have ever been in therapy and, if so, the type of therapy they experienced. They may collect this information prior to therapy or during the first session, and its purpose is to assess their clients' expectations of and experience with therapy. Congruent expectations of the client and therapist enhance the therapeutic effect. Conversely, incongruent expectations diminish therapeutic efficacy and often lead to the client's decision to leave therapy or to resist it. An accurate assessment of client expectations may help the therapist avoid unnecssary mistakes, as well as wasted time and effort.

Structuring. When the client is experiencing therapy for the first time or when the therapist's assessment of the client's expectations reveal disparity, structuring may be in order. Intent on identifying and disputing their clients' irrational ideas and beliefs, many RET therapists—the inexperienced, in particular—overlook the advantages of structuring when initiating therapy. These therapists tend to move into therapy before their clients are prepared to follow. In addition to an assessment of client expectations to uncover disparities in client and therapist goals, at least some assessment of client readiness for therapy seems advisable. Structuring not only provides a clear definition of RET for the client but also often helps to reduce the client's uncertainties, concerns, and fears about entering therapy, thus facilitating the initiating process and the client's expectation for change.

Structuring, or defining, the therapeutic process of RET typically includes an introduction to the ABC anatomy of emotion, a delineation of therapist and client behaviors and responsibilities, and a specification of and rationale for the goals of therapy. In addition, limits are clearly defined. Therapy schedules and fees are outlined and agreed to. Confidentiality is assured, especially when there is evidence of the vested interest of a third party—for example, the client's parents or a referral agent or agency. Further, many RET therapists use the initiating phase to inform their clients that therapy is not limited to the therapeutic session but that they will often be required to complete difficult assignments between sessions. To emphasize this point, specific readings, designed to define RET further and emphasize the importance of working and thinking about therapy between sessions, may be assigned during the first session. Carefully selected readings, tapes, and films or filmstrips can be used to persuade clients that thoughts are responsible for

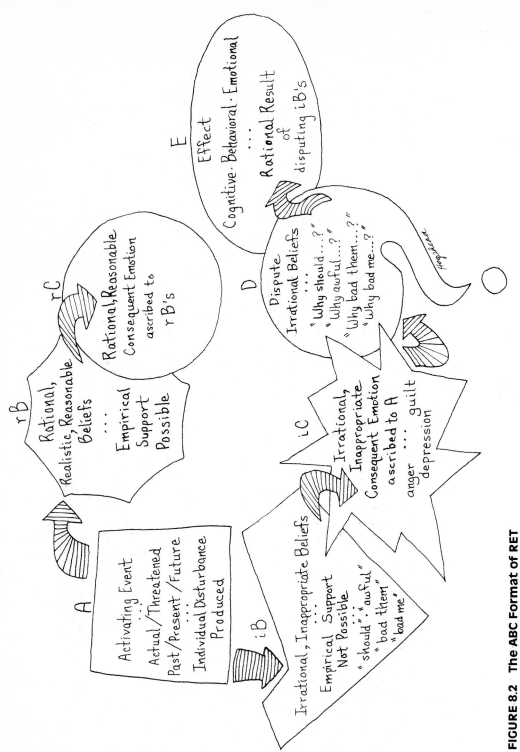

FIGURE 8.2 The ABC Format of RET

most emotions. Such supplementary homework assignments may save a great deal of time in future sessions.

RET therapists may judge their attempts at initiating therapy successful when their clients leave convinced that their decision to enter therapy was a good one, that there is a distinct possibility they will receive the help they seek, and that they have a fairly clear idea of what is expected of them and what they can expect from therapy.

Course of Therapy

Problem Assessment.   An early task of the RET therapist is to encourage the client to articulate and clarify problems and concerns. Wessler and Wessler (1980) warn us of the inadvisability of making blatant assumptions when assessing problems and strongly recommend a probing exploration while employing the ABC format of RET: "Starting with C, tie C to A, get B" (p. 85). In Figure 8–2, the ABC format is regarded as the format for rational self-analysis—the anatomy of emotional disturbance, or the structure of RET.

Although RET is primarily interested in the elegant solution and employs the DIBs technique (Disputing Irrational Beliefs) with nearly every client, any technique used in accordance with the theory is legitimate. RET therapists, then, may employ a wide variety of cognitive, emotive-evocative, and behavioral techniques individually selected for a particular client.

Cognitive Disputation Techniques.   Undoubtedly the most common and most fundamental rational-emotive technique of RET, since RET would be indistinguishable from the other cognitive therapies without it, the DIBs technique is initiated early in therapy by practically all RET therapists.

Following the therapeutic model outlined here, RET therapists work to assist their clients to gain and apply three separate but related insights. First, Point A is not the cause of Point C. Rather, clients feel disturbed and demonstrate inappropriate and self-defeating behaviors because of Point B, their irrational thinking (beliefs, values, attitudes, personal philosophies) and self-talk about Point A; that is, they make themselves disturbed, and they alone are responsible for their self-defeating behavior. Second, clients are not presently disturbed because of their past conditioning to think irrationally. Rather, they create their own distress now and continue to feel distressed because they are actively reinforcing their past irrational thinking. Third, since they are responsible for their past disturbed feelings and continue to reinforce their past irrational thinking, only repeated work and long practice can extinguish their irrational belief patterns of attitudes and values. Realizing that A does not cause C is not enough. Accepting responsibility for disturbing emotions and self-defeating behavior is not enough. Only the repeated disputing of irrational beliefs and earnest practicing of new and actualizing behaviors are likely to bring about positive change in thoughts, feelings, and behaviors. One method of encouraging this necessary repetition is rational self-analysis.

When working with a client who describes himself as having an uncontrollable temper and who has been arrested numerous times for assault and battery, an RET therapist attempts to demonstrate to the client that not only is his temper controllable but also that he creates and is responsible for his emotions. The following excerpt occurs about mid-way into the initial session.

Client I can't help it. When he called me a son-of-a-bitch, I just lost all control. It took four men to pull me off him. I think I would have killed him if they hadn't stopped me. There are just some things I can't stand, and that's one. No one—I mean no one—calls me that and gets away with it. No one has the right to say that to me. (Client's anger is obvious: face flushed, breathing rapid, fists clenched, etc.)

Therapist You were more than angry; you were enraged. You're angry now just thinking about it. But isn't this exactly what we discussed earlier? We might use this incident as an example of how we create our own emotions.

Client: You mean you're going to sit there and tell me I made myself angry? Come on, *he's* the one who called *me* names. I felt fine until he called me a son-of-a-bitch. That's when I lost it.

Therapist: That's true. He did call you a son-of-a-bitch, but how can that automatically or magically make *you* feel enraged? You made yourself feel enraged by what you told yourself about what he called you. While *son-of-a-bitch* is certainly no term of endearment, neither is it a term of magical quality that can create emotion in you.

Client: (Silent, glaring at the therapist.)

Therapist: O.K., I can see you're having some trouble with that. Let's look at it another way. Suppose I were to call you a carrot. How would that make you feel?

Client: (Nervous laughter, almost a giggle.) That wouldn't make me feel anything. That's not serious. It's silly.

Therapist: But suppose I were very serious and I seriously called you a carrot. How would you feel?

Client: (Laughing, this time in a more relaxed manner.) It would be even sillier if you were serious. I'd just think you were nuts and walk away.

Therapist: Doesn't that demonstrate the very point I was trying to make earlier? "Carrot," like "son-of-a-bitch," is only a word, nothing more. How can a word make you feel anything? Your feeling or emotion will arise only after you first tell yourself something about that word. What did you tell yourself when this person called you a son-of-a-bitch?

Client: I don't think I told myself anything. I just hit him.

Therapist: Some of our self-talk occurs very rapidly, especially following events in our lives that appear to have caused strong emotions in us over the years. Still, it's not hard usually to recall that self-talk if we try. What do you say to yourself when you hear the term, *son-of-a-bitch*?

Client: No one has the right to call anyone that. It's a terrible thing to say to anyone. When someone says that they should really be clobbered.

Therapist: O.K. Good. Now, what did you tell yourself when this man called you a son-of-a-bitch?

Client: There's no excuse for that. He can't call me that. I can't stand anyone calling me that. No one is ever going to call me that and get away with it.

Therapist: Good. Let's take a closer look at that. First, your statement, "There's no excuse for that." There is no excuse. Calling anyone that is both ill mannered and insensitive. At the very least it is in very poor taste. But how about the statement, "He can't call me that"?

Client: No one can call me that.

Therapist: Remember, we said earlier that when a belief is rational there is evidence for its validity. Where is your evidence that no one can call you that?

Client: Well, I suppose they can, but they will be damned sorry if they do.

Therapist: That may well be, but your self-talk was that no one could call you that. The reality of this situation is that anyone who can pronounce the word has the ability to call you a son-of-a-bitch. Isn't telling yourself that no one can, when in fact nearly anyone can, a denial of reality?

Client: (Nods affirmatively and responds in a low voice.) I guess.

Therapist: Unfortunately, there are a great many people in this world who are ill mannered, who don't consider the feelings of others when they speak, and while you may force them to regret calling you names, there is really no reason why they can't do so if they wish. You also said, "I can't stand anyone calling me that." Certainly, there is no reason for you to like it, but why can't you stand it?

Client: I just can't. That's an awful thing to call anyone.

Therapist: I can see that you *won't* tolerate someone calling you a son-of-a-bitch, but again, where is the evidence that you *can't stand* it?

Client: Well, I suppose I could stand it, but I see no reason why I should.

Therapist: There is no reason why you should or why you must, but aren't there many sound reasons why you would be much better off if you had stood it? Where did not standing it get you?

Client: (Soft voice) It got me arrested.

Therapist: Right. While acting on an irrational belief, like "I can't stand something," may give you some immediate satisfaction, it will seldom be good for you in the long-range scheme of things. You might receive immediate gratification for punching a person who is ill mannered or who uses poor judgment, but it led to your arrest and you're now facing a trial and a possible jail sentence.

Client: But why should I have to take something like that from anyone?

Therapist: Better, still, why shouldn't you? As I said before, there is no reason why you should, if you are using should to mean must. If you are using the word, *should*, rationally, in the sense that it would be better for you if you did, I can think of numerous reasons. Suppose you had said to yourself, "I don't like to be called a son-of-a-bitch." How would you likely have felt then? Would you have felt enraged?

Client: I would have felt a little ticked off.

Therapist: Right. You would have found this person annoying, a real pain in the neck, but chances are you would have ignored him or simply walked away. Suppose rather than telling yourself that you couldn't stand his calling you a son-of-a-bitch, you had said, "There are a lot of ill-mannered people in this world, and this is my night to run into one of them." Would you have felt enraged? Do you think it would have taken four men to pull you off him?

Client: No, I guess not.

Therapist: Would you have felt the need to do him bodily harm?

Client: If I had said that to myself, I probably would have just brushed it off and walked away.

Therapist: So, no word has magical qualities that can force you to feel anything. No word is inherently good or bad, awful, terrible, or horrible. A word is a word is a word. Only you can give a word power over you by telling yourself something about that word. Ill-mannered and insensitive people *can*, as long as they have the ability to pronounce it, call you anything. You many cause them to regret doing so, but they *can* do it. And while you may not enjoy it, you *can stand* most anything.

The DIBs technique is a process of questioning. RET therapists often employ a Socratic method of questioning to teach their clients a logico-empirical approach to knowledge and to rational sensitivity:

1. What *evidence* do you have for this belief?
2. How do you *know* your belief is true?
3. Why *must* that be so?
4. How would that be so *awful*?
5. How does that belief make you *feel*?
6. Would that really be so *horrible*?

By asking clients for proof or justification, a Socratic dialogue guides them through sentence-by-sentence disputations of their irrational beliefs. Because neither proof nor justification exists for an irrational belief, RET clients learn to replace their irrational beliefs with rational beliefs.

Imaginal and Behavioral Disputation Techniques. Once clients have successfully challenged and disputed their irrational beliefs, RET therapists may employ imaginal and/or behavioral disputation techniques. The imaginal technique asks clients to return to Point A in their imaginations, then to reveal Point C, their feelings. If their feelings have indeed changed as a result of their cognitive disputations, they are asked to review their current self-talk to reinforce their new, more rational beliefs. Conversely, if Point C is the same, there may be irrational beliefs not covered in the cognitive disputation, and the imagery exercise may help to bring them to awareness. When this is the case, the DIBs technique may be repeated.

Rational-emotive imagery is another imaginal technique sometimes employed by the RBT (Rational Behavior Therapy) therapist (Maultsby, 1975). Clients are asked to close their eyes to try to experience one of the negative feelings at Point C and are asked what thoughts accompanied their negative feelings. They are then asked to shift to a more moderate feeling. Again, they are asked to review the thoughts they employed to achieve that emotive shift. The purpose is to show clients that their irrational beliefs create strong negative emotions and that rational beliefs result in moderate manageable emotions. Behavioral disputation techniques are usually in the form of homework assignments in which clients are asked to challenge their irrational beliefs by behaving in direct opposition to them.

Homework Assignments. Homework is a significant component of RET. Therapists make use of assignments specifically designed to urge their clients to think about and work on therapy between sessions, to encourage their clients to challenge and dispute their irrational ideas and beliefs, and to press their clients to practice their newly acquired rational sensitivity. Walen, DiGiuseppe, and Wessler (1980) discuss four important characteristics of the RET homework assignment: "Consistency, Specificity, Systematic Follow Through, and Large Steps" (pp. 216–217). Homework is consistent with the work of the session in which it is assigned. It is both clear and concise; it is structured to provide for systematic follow-through, usually at the beginning of the next session; and it encompasses large steps that are considered more effective in cognitive restructuring than gradual shaping.

The homework assignments of RET may be cognitive, emotive, and/or behavioral, and they may include one or any combination of the following: reading, listening, viewing, writing, thinking, imagining, conditioning, and acting or behaving.

Experienced RET therapists have discovered that specific homework assignments using reading or audio/visual materials can save a great deal of time and effort early in the therapeutic process. A number of excellent materials are designed specifically to introduce the new client to the basic principles of RET (see, for example, Ellis and Harper, 1975; Lembo, 1974; Maultsby, 1975; Young 1974; and Young and Young, 1976). In addition to tapes of the client's sessions, the following three tapes by Ellis may prove helpful: "Solving Emotional Problems," "Twenty-one Ways to Stop Worrying," and "Rational Living in an Irrational World." Many RET therapists provide each client with specially prepared packets of materials from which these early assignments are drawn. Some therapists require their clients to tape every session so selected tapes may be assigned for review between sessions.

As therapy advances, so do the homework assignments. Writing assignments are fashioned throughout therapy to suit the particular situation of the client, but they usually take one of three forms: rational self-analysis, which follows the ABC format described earlier; the essay, a written debate of one or more of the irrational ideas or beliefs expressed by the client; and the diary or log, a record of specific events that is used to assess the accuracy of the client's perceptions and predictions ("I never do anything right") or to identify antecedents and consequences of a client's disturbing or maladaptive behavior. Clients unable to complete writing assignments may be persuaded to do the same assignment using a tape recorder.

Therapists may teach their clients imaginal disputation or imaginal desensitization so they might rehearse new cognitions that promote change and awareness between sessions. Clients may be taught to use their imaginations to project themselves forward in time and to view their "awfulizing," feelings of hopelessness or loss, in a more rational perspective. Imaginal assignments may also involve teaching the client to pair stimuli with aversive or noxious images to assist in the extinction of ineffective or dysfunctional behavior.

Action or homework assignments are usually selected by the therapist to encourage clients to dispute their irrational ideas behaviorally. These assignments nearly always involve some degree of risk since the clients are often asked to do the very thing they most fear. For example, clients who demand self-perfection may be instructed to select three tasks during the next week and intentionally do them poorly. Clients who anticipate the rejection of others are told to collect at least three rejections a day for three consecutive days and to note their self-talk immediately after each attempt. In every instance, the risk to the client should be assessed carefully by the therapist before giving the assignment. The consequence of the behavior assigned should be neither harmful nor damaging to the client (i.e., result in the client's being fired from his or her job or being arrested). The purpose is to challenge the clients' irrational beliefs, not to reinforce them.

In addition to the techniques already discussed, RET therapists may employ operant conditioning, self-management, problem-solving, and contracting procedures; teach assertiveness and paradoxical intention; make use of biofeedback or instruct their clients in methods of thought stopping and focusing on nondisturbing or peaceful ideas; or give their clients lessons in general semantics and employ confrontive humor. It is apparent that the methods and techniques of RET are limited only by the creativity and ingenuity of the therapist.

ASSESSING PROGRESS

Initial and specific goals of therapy are determined by the client and therapist early in the therapeutic process. Specific emotional and/or behavioral changes are often targeted at this point. However, because the basic premise of RET is that thinking creates emotions and significantly affects behavior, the goal of therapy is to change the client's thinking so the targeted emotional and behavioral changes consequently will occur. Further, as explained earlier, RET provides the therapist with the structure for achieving this goal. This same structure may be employed by the therapist to assess progress.

Unless therapists experience difficulty establishing a therapeutic alliance with their clients, progress through the early stages of RET (start with C, tie C to A, get B) proceeds rather rapidly. Initial therapy sessions usually open with clients telling their therapists how they feel, and since most clients enter therapy convinced that their feelings are externally caused, identifying Point A proves equally easy. An exception, of course, may be the client who is experiencing symptoms of a free-floating anxiety.

The inital insight, that humans create their emotions by the declarative and exclamatory sentences they tell themselves about their perceptions, is usually fairly easy to reach because of the numerous and frequent examples readily available from the life experiences of both the client and the therapist. Here, again, there are exceptions, and this is the point at which RET therapists may first meet client resistance. Clients who have been miserable for a long time or who have nearly always blamed others for their misery may find it very difficult to accept this explanation. Recognizing that they create their emotions means accepting responsibility for weeks, months, or even years of feeling miserable.

Point D, disputing irrational ideas, can prove especially difficult for many clients. Their resistance to therapy is likely to increase significantly, slowing progress. Reasons for client resistance at this stage in therapy vary. An assessment of progress at this point may reveal that any one of them may block therapy or end it.

First, clients may be unaware of their irrational beliefs because they have held them so long and repeated them so often that they are deeply internalized, highly valued, automatic, and habitual. Second, some of their irrational beliefs may be shared so widely by others around them that the possibility that their beliefs are irrational is seldom, if ever, considered and, thus, neither recognized nor challenged. Third, and perhaps one of the more difficult resistances to overcome, clients progressing to this point in therapy are often rational enough to look ahead, and they see, although initially they may deny it, that surrendering their irrational thinking will result in a loss of focus that has served them well over time. Only as long as their irrational beliefs remain intact can they continue to be employed to avoid and deny many of life's difficulties. They recognize, consciously or unconsciously, that they are about to lose the numerous secondary gains their irrational beliefs provide. When irrational beliefs are extinguished and dysfunctional behaviors are minimized, clients lose nearly all their supposed needs since needs are limited to those necessary for survival. They lose their guiding and limiting absolutes because rationally few, if any, concepts or rules are beyond revision. Their blaming is diminished, also, and this leads to the elimination of most feelings of depression, guilt, self-pity, anger, and the desire to punish or seek revenge. Finally, they lose their magical thinking, which nullifies nearly all prejudices, superstitions, and demands they have used to manipulate and control self, others, and the environment.

At some point in their therapy, many clients become aware of the determination, commitment, hard work, and long practice that progress in therapy requires of them, and they may, unless confronted with their irrational thinking, decide that they are incapable or that they cannot presently afford the necessary time and effort.

There is another point in the therapeutic process at which RET therapists have learned to expect client resistance. As their clients successfully dispute their irrational thinking and begin to develop rational sensitivity, they realize that they are expected to practice new, often frightening, risk-taking, self-directing behaviors. They realize that rational sensitivity leads to tolerance, responsibility, involvement, commitment, and an uncon-

FIGURE 8.3 A Schematic Analysis of Ellis's Stand on the Basic Issues

Biological Determinants	▬▬▬▬	Social Determinants
Unconscious Determinants	▬▬▬	Conscious Determinants
Early Development	▬▬▬	Continuous Development
Psychological Environment	▬▬▬▬	Reality Environment
Conditioning	▬▬	Freedom
Commonality	▬▬▬	Uniqueness
Importance of Group Membership	Group affiliation shapes and influences our development. We are naturally gregarious, but Ellis cautions us to desire, not demand, the approval and love of group members. Active participation within a group facilitates greater degrees of personal happiness, but the importance given to group membership rests with our rational sensitivity.	
Explanation of Learning	We are naturally predisposed to learn, cognitively attributing personal meaning to experiences, as well as emotions and behavior repsonses. Developed early under the rational or irrational influence of others, belief systems emerge as self-talk. Through restructuring our belief systems, we can develop greater rational sensitivity and self-facilitative capabilities.	
Number and Weight Assigned to Motivational Concepts	Ellis advocates responsible hedonism as the rational approach to life. Long-term self-interest is his primary concept, and within the parameters of pain avoidance (ineffectual living through irrational thinking) and pleasure (effective living through rational thinking), we choose our motivational purposes. Rational sensitivity facilitates realization of desires and prevents the irrational transformation of desires into needs.	
Importance of Reward	Reward is experienced with the realization of here-and-now pleasures and the attainment of long-range goals achieved through day-to-day discipline. Effective living—affiliation, intimacy, and fulfilling activity—is itself rewarding.	
Importance or Role of Self-Concept	Self-conceptualizing, a biological predisposition, exerts significant influence on behavior; but when self-conceptualizing includes global self-rating based on behavior, it is irrational. So, while Ellis encourages rational self-acceptance which promotes self-facilitation, he discourages self-rating. For Ellis, self-acceptance is prerequisite to stable and positive mental health.	

ditional accceptance of self, others, and the world. In brief, they learn that they are expected to confront and practice the very behaviors they have been striving so hard to avoid.

FINAL COMMENTARY

Following the basic-issues approach presented in Chapter 1, Ellis receives high marks for developing a comprehensive, clear, and heuristic theory of counseling and psychotherapy. Moreover, RET is the theory of choice for a large number of counselors and therapists and is firmly established as one of the major systems of counseling and psychotherapy in use today.

RET is comprehensive. It is evident that Ellis responds in some depth to each of the eleven basic issues. Included in his resolutions are assumptions and hypotheses that can be applied to a variety of situations, settings, and age groups. As a consequence, RET practitioners can be found working successfully in elementary and secondary schools, colleges and universities, hospitals and clinics, rehabilitation centers, mental health centers, public health departments, probation and law enforcement agencies, crisis intervention centers, suicide prevention centers, child abuse centers, drug and alcohol abuse centers, and the personnel offices of some businesses and industries. RET practitioners are working with children, adolescents, young adults, adults, and the elderly. They work with the handicapped, the chronically ill, people in crisis, people under stress, parents and parent groups. Although initially employed as a therapy for the emotionally disturbed, RET today is also used as a growth therapy, a preventive mental health practice, and a self-help approach.

RET is easily understood and communicable. There are no evident contradictions in Ellis's resolutions of the eleven basic issues. Certainly RET offers counselors and therapists one of the clearest and most consistent attempts to explain the role of cognitive processes in the development of emotional disturbance, as well as the recognition and impact of commonly held irrational beliefs. The goals of RET are clearly stated; moreover, the methods and techniques are multiple, specific, and consistent with the theory. The theory of RET is functional, giving practitioners clear direction. It tells them why, how, and when to apply a particular method or technique and then predicts what they can expect. Thus, it clearly points out the relationship between means and ends.

RET is heuristic; it encourages further testing of its efficacy. Ellis (Ellis & Grieger, 1977; Ellis & Whiteley, 1979) presents a summary of research data that he believes confirms the 32 major clinical and theoretical hypotheses of RET in particular and cognitive-behavioral therapy in general. Because RET employs criteria of rationality and effective living that stress scientific investigation, Ellis firmly believes not only that his theory will stand up under rigorous investigation but also that additional testing will result in empirical confirmation and dispel some of the existing misconceptions and doubts.

RET has its critics, but this cognitive-emotive-behavioral therapy has made a significant impact on professionals in mental health and has emerged as a widely accepted and effective system of counseling and psychotherapy.

The phenomenon of RET may best be summarized by Ellis (1979): "It is what its name implies: rational *and* emotive, realistic *and* visionary, empirical *and* humanistic. As, in all their complexity, are humans" (p. 226).

REFERENCES AND SUGGESTED READINGS

Beck, A.T. 1976. *Cognitive therapy and the emotional disorders*. New York: International Universities Press.

Ellis, A. 1957. *How to live with a neurotic at home and at work*, rev. ed. New York: Crown Publishers.

Ellis, A. 1972. *Executive leadership: A rational approach*. Secaucus, N.J.: Citadel Press.

Ellis, A. 1974. *Humanistic psychotherapy: The rational-emotive approach*. New York: McGraw-Hill (originally published 1973 by Julian Press, New York).

Ellis, A. 1975. *Reason and emotion in psychotherapy*. Hollywood: Wilshire (originally published 1962 by Lyle Strart, New York).

Ellis, A. 1977. Rational-emotive therapy: Research data that supports the clinical and personality hypotheses of RET and other modes of cognitive behavior therapy. *The Counseling Psychologist* 7: 1.

Ellis, A. 1979. Rational-emotive therapy. In R. Corsini, ed. *Current psychotherapies*, 2nd ed. Itasca, Ill.: F.E. Peacock.

Ellis, A., & Abrahms, E. 1978. *Brief psychotherapy in medical and health practice*. New York: Springer Publishing.

Ellis, A., & Grieger, R. 1977. *Handbook of rational-emotive therapy*. New York: Springer Publishing.

Ellis, A., & Harper, R.A. 1975. *A guide to rational living*. Englewood Cliffs, N.J.: Prentice-Hall.

Ellis, A., & Knaus, W. 1977. *Overcoming procrastination*. New York: Institute for Rational Living.

Ellis, A., & Whiteley, Jr. 1979. *Theoretical and empirical foundations of rational-emotive therapy*. Monterey, Calif.: Brooks/Cole.

Goodman, D.S., & Maultsby, M.C. 1978. *Emotional well-being through rational behavior training*, rev. ed. Springfield, Ill.: Charles C Thomas.

Grieger, R., & Grieger, I., eds. 1982. *Cognition and emotional disturbance*. New York: Human Services Press.

Lembo, J. 1974. *Help yourself*. Niles, Ill.: Argus Communications.

Maultsby, M.C. 1975. *Help yourself to happiness*. New York: Institute for Rational Living.

Morris, D.T., & Kanitz, H.M. 1975. *Rational-emotive therapy*. Boston: Houghton Mifflin.

Newhorn, P. January, 1978. Albert Ellis. *Human Behavior*, Vol. 7, pp. 30–35.

Patterson, C.H. 1980. *Theories of counseling and psychotherapy*, 3rd ed. New York: Harper & Row.

Walen, S.R., DiGiuseppe, R., & Wessler, R.L. 1980. *A practitioner's guide to rational-emotive therapy*. New York: Oxford University Press.

Wessler, R.A., & Wessler, R.L. 1980. *The principles and practice of rational-emotive therapy*. San Francisco: Jossey-Bass.

Weinrach, S.G. November, 1980. Unconventional therapist: Albert Ellis. *Personnel and Guidance Journal*, pp. 152–160.

Young, H. 1974. *A rational counseling primer*. New York: Institute for Rational Living.

Young H.S. 1981. Rational counseling with resistant adolescent clients: Joining forces against a common enemy. *RET Work*, 1 (2), pp. 1–4.

Young, H., & Young, M., producers. 1976. *Understanding and overcoming emotional upset* (filmstrip). New York: Institute for Rational Living.

9

The Social Learning Theory of Albert Bandura

THEORETICAL AND EXPERIMENTAL advances in the field of social learning convinced Bandura (1969, 1977 a and b; Bandura & Walters, 1963) that traditional learning theory, with its emphasis on external reinforcement and experimentation with lower animals, was too circumscribed to explain adequately the acquisition, maintenance, and modification of complex human behavior. In his attempt to develop a unified theoretical framework for analyzing human thought and behavior, Bandura (1977a) directed his efforts to extending and modifying many of the existing perspectives in learning. The result is a so-called sociobehavioristic learning approach based on human social interaction that departs substantially from the traditional learning theories.

Bandura believes practically all human behavior is learned, but he places special emphasis on observational learning. Further, he recognizes human cognitive processes as agents that mediate the direction of our actions by giving us the capacity to perform both insightful and foresightful behavior (Bandura, 1977a). Bandura asserts that most of our behavior is learned through example, by observing the actions of others and modeling our behavior after them, although he contends that learning can occur without emitting a response and receiving positive or negative reinforcement for it. In fact, he suggests that operant conditioning, because it is both rare and ineffective in human learning, should be assigned the role of regulating performance of behavioral sequences after such sequences have been learned through modeling.

Although influenced by external stimuli, we are not helpless respondents. Our responses are not triggered automatically by external stimuli. Because we are able to observe, symbolize, and interpret the consequences of our behavior, we form expectations and anticipate that specific actions will result in reward or punishment. Certainly we are influenced by external forces, but we are also able to regulate and guide the extent and direction of these influences. Bandura (1977a) expresses it best in the "Preface" to *Social Learning Theory:* "The extraordinary capacity of humans to use symbols enables them to represent events, to analyze their conscious experience, to communicate with others at any distance in time and space, to plan, to create, to imagine, and to engage in foresightful action" (p. vii).

Self-regulatory processes are assigned a central role in Bandura's social learning theory. He sees a continous reciprocal interaction between cognitive, behavioral, and environmental determinants (Bandura, 1969, 1977a). Although external factors at times exert powerful constraints on our behavior, there are also occasions when personal factors are the major determinants of the course of environmental events, when symbolic, vicarious, and self-regulatory processes assume a prominent role. Our unique human capacity to use symbols gives us the means to process and preserve our experiences in representational forms that, in turn, serve as guides for our future behavior and courses for long-term goals. According to Bandura (1977a), "cognitive factors partly determine which external events will be observed, how they will be perceived, whether they leave any lasting effects, what valence and efficacy they have, and how the information they convey will be organized for future use" (p. 160).

Based on rigorous scientific investigation, Bandura's innovative theory of social learning promises to become an exciting force in counseling and psychotherapy. The number of counselors and therapists receiving training in the theory and application of his approach to social learning grows steadily. Bandura's concepts have already made a forceful impact in the field of personality development. His theory is being accepted both as a method of researching and as a means of changing complex human behavior.

BIOGRAPHICAL SKETCH

Early Years

Born December 4, 1925, to Joseph and Jessie (Berazanski) Bandura, Albert Bandura grew up in the small northern town of Mundare in the province of Alberta, Canada. His parents were wheat farmers.

Education

Bandura was 1 of 20 students in a high school that had only two teachers and few resources. As a result, Bandura learned early to rely on his own academic initiative. After graduating he matriculated at the University of British Columbia in Vancouver. He received his B.A. degree in 1949 with the Bolocan Award in psychology. He immediately began graduate work in psychology at the University of Iowa, receiving his M.A. degree in 1951. Bandura received his Ph.D. degree the following year under the direction of Arthur Benton. It was at Iowa that Bandura met his future wife, Virginia B. Varnes.

Emergence of Social Learning Theory

After a year at the Guidance Center in Wichita, Kansas, Bandura was appointed to the faculty of Stanford University, a position he has held for more than 30 years. He was granted a full professorship in 1964 and chaired the Department of Psychology from 1976 to 1977. Always a productive scholar, Bandura has published his research in numerous professional and scientific journals. His earlier books, *Social Learning and Personality Development* (1963, written in collaboration with Richard H. Walters), *Principles of Behavior Modification* (1969), and *Agression: A Social Learning Analysis* (1973), culminated in his best known work, *Social Learning Theory* (1977a), in which he clearly presents the basic theoretical constructs of social learning.

Accomplishments and Awards

Bandura spent the year, 1969 to 1970, as fellow of the Center for Advanced Study in the Behavioral Sciences at Stanford University. He was the recipient of the Guggenheim Fellowship in 1972. That same year, he received the Distinguished Scientist Award from Division 12 of the APA. In 1973, he accepted the Distinguished Scientific Achievement Award from the California Psychological Association. He was awarded an endowed chair, the David Starr Jordan Professor of Social Science in Psychology in 1974. Bandura was further honored that year by being elected president of the APA. In 1977, he received the James McKeen Cattell Award. The University of British Columbia recognized his achievements in 1979 by conferring an honorary doctor of science degree. In 1980, Bandura received the Distinguished Contribution Award from the International Society for Research on Aggression, was named a fellow of the American Academy of Arts and Science, and was honored by his peers again with the Distinguished Scientific Contributions Award, one of the highest awards bestowed a member of the APA.

In addition to his teaching and research, Bandura has served as a consultant to government committees and organizations, including the Veterans' Administration. Further, he has served on the editorial boards of approximately 20 professional journals, including a lengthy assignment as series editor of social learning for Prentice-Hall. Bandura has seen his work accepted by increasing numbers of psychologists, therapists, and counselors throughout the United States and Canada, perhaps the greatest recognition granted any theorist.

RESOLUTIONS OF THE ELEVEN BASIC ISSUES

Like the majority of theorists selected for presentation in this book, Bandura has not specifically addressed the eleven basic issues. The following

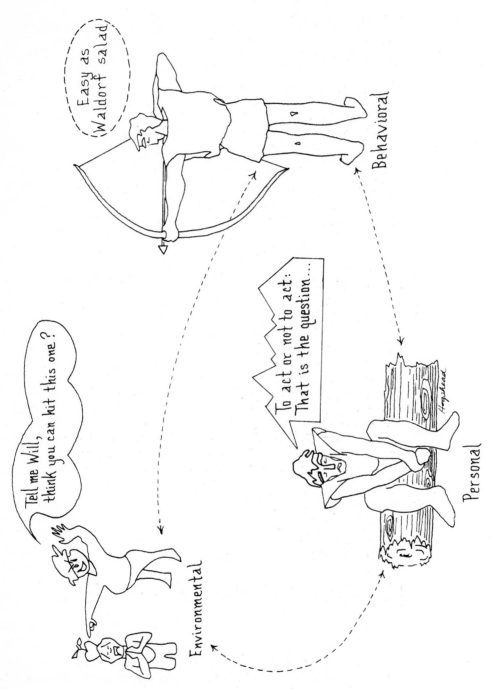

FIGURE 9.1 Triadic Interaction

resolutions are this writer's interpretations of Bandura's response to each issue. Although each resolution was formed only after careful review of his major works, there is no guarantee that Bandura would grant full endorsement or that he would agree to the writer's hierarchical arrangement.

Most of Bandura's books were included in the search for issue resolution; however, heaviest reliance was placed on *Social Learning Theory* (1977a) since in this work Bandura presents his readers with a most succinct, yet comprehensive, view of his unique approach to human learning and personality development.

Biological and/or Social Determinants

Except for our basic reflexes, Bandura believes that nearly all behavior is learned and that our learning occurs as a result of continuous and reciprocal triadic interaction between personal, behavioral, and environmental determinants. Never do these determinants function independently, and never is any one the sole determinant of our behavior; rather, they are reciprocally interlocking, each influencing the others synergistically.

As beings in the world we cannot be separated from our environment. We influence and, in turn, are influenced by it. Likewise, we cannot be considered independent of our behavior because our behavior generates experiences that also influence what we subsequently do and what we become. Further, our present behavior will affect the patterns of our future behavior. Viewed from Bandura's rather optimistic perspective, we are individually portrayed as a vast potentiality that can be modeled by direct and vicarious experience into a diversity of forms within the boundaries set by our biology.

We are neither unconsciously driven by inner impulses or needs nor helplessly battered by environmental stimuli. Within the social learning approach, covert symbolic, vicarious, and self-regulatory processes provide an internal deterministic triad of possible behavioral alternatives to given environmental stimuli or circumstances. We have the ability to encode and symbolize environmental events and to anticipate, from experience, what particular behaviors will result in specific consequences.

Bandura (1977a) acknowledges that our biology largely defines the limits of what, when, and how adequately we can learn. In addition, he recognizes numerous physiological conditions that can motivate us to act. Pain is a good example, as is the aversive stimulation that arises from tissue deficit. Further, Bandura is aware that our heredity can determine physical characteristics that influence the kinds of reinforcements we receive from others in a particular culture, especially the reinforcement we receive during the important early years of development and the initial formation of self-efficacy. Still, most of our behavior is learned, and genetic factors are assumed to have a relatively minor role in the overall and ongoing learning process.

While Bandura places greater emphasis on environmental than on biological determinants, he recognizes that our responses, whether affective or physical, are not dependent solely on external stimuli. Our thoughts about environmental events can regulate our responses. We are not simply passive reactors to external influences; there is potential in Bandura's theory for at least some intentional behavior.

We not only act but also are aware of the effects of our actions. Our ability to symbolize and to represent actions and consequences symbolically also extends to the selection, organization, and transformation of the external stimuli that impinge on us. Some influences, then, are self-produced. In brief, behaviorally, we have a reciprocal interaction with our environment. Reinforcement, whether direct or vicarious, is not necessary for learning to occur initially in many instances. We acquire, maintain, and change many behaviors through emulation of models, by witnessing the actions and consequences that others experience. We also choose and shape many of our behaviors to attain anticipated rewards or to avoid expected pain, thus using our expectations as criteria for behavioral selection or modification.

In summary, Bandura's stance on this issue is one of *reciprocal determinism*. Our biology, actions, and environment are potentialities that interact reciprocally, each determining the other.

Explanation of Learning

Bandura's theory is founded on the phenomenon of learning. However, once he moves beyond the assumption that practically all behavior is learned, he parts from the ranks of both radical and moderate behaviorists. Although Bandura does not deny the effect of external reinforcement on learning, by stressing the intervening influence of our cognitive processes, he relegates external reinforcement to a facilitative rather than a necessary role in the learning process. He contends that factors other than response consequences often influence what we attend to and assigns external reinforcement to a role compatible with a cognitive orientation and the broad effects of modeling.

Bandura and Walters (1963) and Bandura (1969, 1977a) have demonstrated repeatedly that we can and do learn novel behavior simply by attending to the performance of another person who serves as a model. Further, they maintain that much of what we learn through modeling is acquired in large segments or in total without either an overt response to the witnessed behavior or the administration of external reinforcement. In fact, because of our ability to symbolize, modeling often is symbolic rather than behavioral. We can model a behavior by reading or listening to a description of it. We can translate a visual image into symbols that can be stored into memory far more efficiently than visual images alone.

Once a modeled behavior is symbolized, we can cognitively relate anticipated consequences of that behavior to our personal standards, values, and goals. We can, through the use of symbols, rehearse dangerous or feared behaviors before attempting them or solve complex problems by cognitively testing alternatives and their anticipated consequences, executing only favored symbolic actions and solutions. A large portion of our learning is not only the result of modeling but also is mediated by cognitive factors.

According to Bandura (1969, 1977a; Bandura & Walters, 1963), certain interrelated cognitive-perceptual processes must occur for modeling to be effective:

Attention processes: Exposure to a model is insufficient unless we attend to the model's behavior, perceive accurately, and select the most relevant stimuli. Learning thus is first a perceptual process; discriminative observation is a requisite condition to the appearance of modeling.

Retention processes: We must encode and represent symbolically what we observe. Symbolic images are more permanent and easier to recall. It helps, for example, to talk ourselves mentally though the sequential stages of the modeled behavior.

Motor reproduction processes: Motor reproduction can occur on two levels: (1) actual practice of the modeled behavior, including feedback regarding accuracy, and (2) internal, or silent, rehearsal of the model's behavioral sequence.

Incentive and motivational processes: Vicarious or anticipated positive reinforcement, although unnecessary for learning to occur, can increase the likelihood of actual performance. Conversely, vicarious or anticipated negative reinforcement or punishment tends to inhibit actual performance.

Bandura and Walters (1963) and Bandura (1977a) point to other factors that may also influence our tendency to perform the modeled behavior we learn. These influences include our perceptions of the characteristics of the model and our self-attributes, our personal standards and valued goals, the complexity of the behavior, and the external, vicarious, and anticipated reinforcements we receive.

We are likely to repeat a behavior we learn when the model we observe is someone similar to ourselves in sex, age, background, and appearance. We are also prone to reproduce the behavior of a model we respect and admire and to whom we grant a position of prestige or status. We tend to imitate a model when our self-confidence and self-esteem are low. We are likely to model behaviors we have observed that are congruent with our personal behavioral standards and valued goals. And, we are prone to repeat behaviors that have been reinforced, whether that reinforcement is external, vicarious, or anticipated.

According to Bandura (1977b), we function as active agents "who transform, classify, and organize modeling stimuli into easily remembered

*Motor reproduction of modeled behavior can occur
via actual practice or via internal rehearsal.*

schemes rather than as quiescent cameras or tape recorders that store isomorphic representations of modeled events" (p. 199). We think, aspire, value, plan, and anticipate. We do not become mere accumulations of conditioned responses. By recognizing the mediating role of cognition in the acquisition, retention, and expression of behavior, social learning theory increases the dimension of our learning processes to include social behaviors and social reinforcers, as well as the more abstract concepts of language, conversation, personal values and standards of moral reasoning, and the functional influence of our precepts of self-efficacy.

Unconscious and/or Conscious Determinants

Bandura believes behavior is learned and experience must be conscious for learning to occur. He finds neither need nor reason to ascribe any human behavior to elaborate, unconscious conflicts, impulses, or motivations that require exposure or alleviation (Bandura & Walters, 1963; Bandura 1977a). We are not, then, driven by mysterious, prohibitive, inner forces or pulled by any innate actualizing tendency; rather, we are largely conscious, thinking beings. We cognitively select, organize, and transform the stimuli that we encounter. Further, we have the capacity to observe and interpret the effects of our behavior and the behavior of others, to form expectations, and to anticipate behavioral outcomes. We develop personal sets of rules and standards against which we evaluate our actions and gauge the value of both external and self-rewards (Bandura, 1977a, 1982a).

Unlike either the classic psychodynamic or behaviorist approaches, social learning theory acknowledges self-awareness and other forms of internal regulatory influences on behavior: "Human functioning, in fact, involves interrelated control systems in which behavior is determined by external stimulus events, by internal information-processing systems and regulating codes, and by reinforcing response-feedback processes" (Bandura, 1969, p. 19).

Not only does Bandura (Bandura & Walters, 1963) oppose any concept of an omnipotent entity in the form of an unconscious mind, he also argues that preoccupation with internal response-producing agents results in the neglect of external variables that have been demonstrated experimentally to influence control over learning and overt social behavior.

Early and/or Continuous Development: Critical or Significant Life Stages

Bandura (1977a) rejects the idea that our early childhood experiences function as permanent determinants for all our future behavior. We can and do replace early learning with new learning and revised behavioral standards. Further, Bandura believes that thinking in terms of critical life stages is counterproductive in the study of human development. Stages as concepts have no existence in reality. However, adherents of stage theories tend to categorize their clients according to a fixed sequence of cognitive stages and, once categorized, view their clients in terms of stereotypical category rather than as individuals with unique thoughts, feelings, and actions.

Although he does not hold to critical life stages, Bandura (1977a) does note the significance of early childhood experiences. During our early years, we develop the ability to use symbols that greatly facilitate observational learning, the formation of perceptions of self-efficacy, and the establishment of internal performance standards.

According to Bandura (1977a, 1982b), three main factors contribute to our development: (1) physical maturation, (2) experience with the social world, and (3) cognitive development. Physical development is considered the least important of the three factors. We must, of course, have the physical maturity to reproduce the motor responses if we are to repeat the observed behavior.

Experience with the environment facilitates our social development in two ways. First, as children we acquire a repertoire of behaviors. We encounter a social world constituted of models to observe and people who will apply both positive and negative reinforcements. By experiencing external reinforcements in various situations, we learn which of our behaviors are deemed appropriate and inappropriate within the societal framework. These reinforcements motivate us to behave in ways that are socially approved. Second, we encounter different social environments at different ages, and the changes we experience facilitate our development as we move into greater participation with society.

During early childhood in particular, we undergo extreme changes in cognitive development. Our attention, memory, and cognitive organization evolve both rapidly and importantly. For Bandura (1977a, 1978a, 1982a), one especially significant developmental change is our growing capacity to translate observations into symbols. Our cognitive development makes learning more flexible, efficient, and lasting. We can now use symbols to rehearse and store in memory what we observe. Further, we have the ability to recombine these symbols to form hypotheses. Both physical and social events can be abstracted, formulated, and tested. We no longer have to see a specific behavior modeled to learn it: we can read a description of a behavior and reproduce it. We can listen to instruction and carry it out. Further, we are predisposed to represent future consequences symbolically and to compare anticipated behavior and consequences with our personal goals and behavioral standards, thus giving us the criteria to measure disparities between actual outcomes and the likelihood of a desired outcome.

Our families, particularly our parents, play a major role in our early development. We repeatedly observe and learn most thoroughly the behavior of our family members. We are socialized into the ideologies and life-styles of our families through constant, complex networks of rewards and sanctions. Still, as influential as our families are, once we develop the capacity for observational learning, we learn what we see, and with television especially, much of what we see, even as very young children in our own homes, is not always good.

To complicate the process further, the examples that adults present us are often incongruent with the behaviors and ideas they endorse as ideal or optimal. We must learn as children to discriminate from differential modeling cues and differential patterns of reinforcement those behaviors we eventually perform because of their applicability to our goals. Moreover, as we observe the effects of our actions in any particular situation and in relation to the outcome of that situation, we develop efficacy expectations that constitute major regulatory influences on our future behavior.

Self-control begins in early childhood. The greater our cognitive abilities, the more active we are in accepting and resisting the reinforcements applied to us and in engaging in self-control that mitigates the effects of these reinforcements. As we mature, we do not passively receive information and meaning from outside; rather, we actively develop encoding strategies, expectations, reinforcement values, and plans. We endeavor to buffer externally imposed reinforcements and exercise considerable self-control by identifying personal goals and strategies and by selecting consequences that reinforce our actions.

Importance of Role of Self-Concept

As with all causal processes in social learning theory, the self is conceptualized in terms of reciprocal determinism (see "Biological and/or Social Determinants"). Bandura (1977a, 1978a, 1982a) assigns self-referent and self-regulatory influences a central role in his theory but does not regard the self-concept as an autonomous psychic entity with unidirectional control over our behavior. Further, assuming that "a postulated internal determinant cannot be less complex than its effects," Bandura (1978a, p. 348) discards any global view of a self-concept. He believes self-influences are cognitive, contributory influences in a reciprocally interacting system of personal, behavioral, and environmental influences. The self-system in Bandura's theory "refers to cognitive structures that provide reference mechanisms and to a set of subfunctions for the perception, evaluation, and regulation of our behavior" (1978a, p. 348).

Acknowledged in the self-system of social learning theory are self-precepts including self-awareness, self-inducements, and self-reinforcements—all of which can influence our thought patterns, actions, and emotional arousal. We form efficacy expectations from both actual and vicarious experiences. Collectively, our efficacy expectations constitute our sense of self-efficacy that, in turn, exerts significant influence on our choice of and persistence in coping behaviors. The stronger our efficacy expectations, the greater our effort and the longer our persistence in coping with life tasks; hence, the higher the probability that we will accept risks and deal successfully with threatening situations. Conversely, the weaker our self-efficacy, the less likely we are to exert maximum effort and to persist until we succeed when tasks are difficult or frightening.

Bandura (1977a) is convinced that most of our behavior is maintained by anticipated rather than immediate consequences. Anticipated consequences, our capacity to represent future consequences in symbolic form, will partly determine which events we observe, how we will perceive them, what events motivate us or are efficacy reinforcing, and how we will organize the information they convey for future use (Bandura, 1977a, 1978a). Our symbolizing and self-reactive capacities make us less dependent on immediate external reinforcment for our behavior. For example, we set specific goals and standards that define conditional requirements for positive self-regard, and we often deny immediate external reinforcement for behavior that falls below our standards rather than risk the pain of self-disapproval and the resulting loss of self-efficacy.

Our appraisal of the determinants of our behavior affects our reactions. We take pride in accomplishments only when we can attribute success to our own efforts and abilities. We derive little personal satisfaction from any performance that is heavily dependent on external factors. We respond self-critically to inadequate performances when we feel responsible. We do not, in contrast, judge ourselves critically when we attribute poor performance to unusual circumstances or when we consider the task beyond our capabilities. Moreover, we have little concern for any accomplishments we assign little or no significance.

We are not, then, simply perceivers, knowers, and actors. Our cognitive abilities to think and to symbolize give us the capacity for reflective self-awareness and self-reaction. We can predict outcome and anticipate consequences in relation to our perceived self-efficacy. We can set standards and goals and, using these as guides, generate self-inducements and conditional reinforcements. Our self-concept must be considered a significant, contributory factor in the complex process of reciprocal determinism; thus, its role cannot be overlooked when predicting our behavior.

Conditioning and/or Freedom to Choose

Bandura's stance on conditioning and/or freedom to choose also is one of reciprocal determinism. True, we are influenced by the antecedents and consequences of our behavior, but we, in turn, mediate the influence of these antecedents and consequences through our cognitive processes. Our cognitive processes influence which of the numerous environmental events we attend to, as well as how we perceive and respond to these events.

We can be considered neither causes independent of our behavior and environment nor simple reactors to environmental influences. To the degree that we can influence future conditions by cognitively anticipating the future consequences of our actions, by regulating our present behavior, and by administering self-reinforcing consequences to sustain it, we are causal contributors to our life paths.

Our cognitive capacity and ability to work with symbols allow us to create as well as to select our environments. Moreover, the capability of intentional action is rooted in our symbolic activity. We have the ability to plan, imagine, and engage in foresightful action. We select, organize, and transform the stimuli that impinge on us. We develop values and set behavioral standards and goals to guide our direction and determine our persistence. We develop a sense of personal efficacy that has considerable functional value. Thus, our behavior is at least partially determined by self-produced and self-regulating influences. We can and do, with the effective tools of personal agency and social support, give incentive, meaning, and worth to what we do.

Bandura (1974) believes that reflexive conditioning in humans is largely a myth. From a social learning perspective, conditioning is "simply a descriptive term for learning through paired experiences" (p. 859). The assumption that conditioning occurs automatically is in error. Rather, conditioning in humans is cognitively mediated. Our so-called conditioned reactions are, for the most part, self-activated rather than automatically evoked. It is not so much that events occur together in time, according to Bandura (1974), but that we learn to predict them and to rally appropriate anticipatory reactions.

Bandura (1974, 1977a, 1982a, b) does not view freedom as an act of will; he defines freedom as the number of options available to us at any particular time and our right to exercise them. Viewed from this reciprocal perspective, we have the ability to expand our freedom by extending and perfecting our coping competencies and eliminating our dysfunctional self-restraints. The greater the number of our behavioral alternatives, personal skills, and rights as individuals and the fewer our self-restraints, the greater our freedom. The greater our sense of personal efficacy, the more likely our behavior is under our anticipatory control.

Importance of Reward

As indicated in "Explanation of Learning" and "Conditioning and/or Freedom to Choose," the reinforcement construct in social learning theory incorporates a wider range of influences than do the more traditional theories of learning. Certainly, we are subject to the immediate reinforcement influence of environmental consequences. However, because we possess the unique human capacity of anticipatory thought, environmental consequences neither are singular determinants of our behavior nor do they operate automatically and unconsciously. Bandura (1974, 1977a, 1978a, 1982a) argues that our behavior is affected minimally by external reinforcements of which we are unaware.

According to Bandura (1974, 1982a), we have the ability to shape conditions for our purposes. By cognitively bringing future consequences to bear on our present behavior, we are in a position to choose anticipatory or delayed reinforcement over immediate environmental consequences. "The idea that behavior is governed by its consequences fares better," according to Bandura, "for anticipated than for actual consequences" (1978, p. 356). We further shape our conditions by establishing personal goals and behavioral standards that carry qualitative expectations and conditional reinforcement values. Reinforcement, then, becomes internal and involves a personal sense of self-esteem and self-regard.

Our actions are often based on foresight, and our most influential reinforcements are often vicarious and self-generated consequences (see "Conditioning and/or Freedom to Choose"). Environmental consequences exert their greatest influence on our behavior when they are compatible with those consequences under our anticipatory control. As we mature, externally imposed rewards become less important than our sense of self-regard, and immediate gratification becomes less significant than the achievement of our long-range goals or the accomplishment of our self-imposed level of performance. We can, through foresight, proficiency, and self-influence, transcend external reinforcement and control. It should be noted that determinism is not in question because in the view of social learning theory, all behavior is caused. Bandura's stance of reciprocal determinism means there is a reciprocal interaction of environmental and personal influences.

Number and Weight Assigned to Motivational Concepts

As Bandura (1977a) points out, there are inherent problems in constructing and testing a theory of motivation "when the existence of that motivation is inferred from the very behavior it supposedly causes" (p. 109). From a social learning perspective, Bandura believes it is preferable to explore how positive incentives, whether external or cognitively formulated, facilitate the development of competencies and interests that serve as enduring sources of personal satisfaction and contribute to a sense of self-efficacy. Following this approach to motivation, reinforcements are viewed as anything we value under existing circumstances. From this perspective, reinforcements become incentives rather than implanters of behavior. We are motivated to act by reinforcement only when we believe our action and the reinforcement we receive for it are meaningful and useful. We discontinue action and disregard reinforcements that offer no incentive.

Bandura (1963, 1977a) recognizes that adversive stimuli, both internal and external, can motivate action. Examples include the internal adversive stimuli that arise from tissue deficit such as hunger and thirst and external adversive stimuli such as pain. However, he asserts that the major sources of human motivation are those stimuli that arise from cognition and that include properties that are both dynamic and structural. We develop anticipatory capacities that enable us to be motivated by expected consequences. "By representing foreseeable outcomes symbolically," Bandura claims, "people can convert future consequences into current motivators of behavior" (1977a, p. 18).

We have the self-reactive capacity to move from immediate to anticipated consequences once we develop specific standards and goals against which we can measure our performance. We specify conditional requirements for self-efficacy. External reinforcement matters little if we fall below our conditional requirements and is unnecessary if we meet them. Success can be motivating because self-satisfaction is seldom lasting. Once we attain our goal, we raise our sights to even higher levels of performance. The higher our goals, the higher the performance level and the greater the enhancement of our self-efficacy. Cognitive motivation, then, operates through the intervening influence of personal standards and self-evaluation. We judge our performance against others or against our past performance. When we can ascribe successful goal attainment to our abilities and efforts, we feel an increased sense of self-efficacy and are motivated to continue and quite often to increase our effort. Conversely, we deny both external and self-reward rather than risk self-censure and the loss of self-efficacy.

Because of the capacity for reciprocal influence, our motivating contingencies are at least partly of our own making. Self-generated incentives are motivating when they are designed to enhance or authenticate personal efficacy. We can, therefore, learn to rely extensively on our goals and approval as motivation for our direction and behavior.

Importance of Group Membership

As indicated earlier (see "Early and/or Continuous Development"), we are indoctrinated into the ideology and life-style of our particular family group where, during our most formative years, we observe repeatedly and learn most thoroughly the behavior modeled by family members. Also during this period we begin to form our personal systems of preferences, values, and behavioral standards, as well as our precepts of personal efficacy. Although our opportunities for group affiliation expand significantly as we develop, we appear to have a natural tendency to move toward those groups whose members we perceive share our interests and values. In brief, we give and receive mutual reinforcement to preexisting bents through our group affiliations.

The skills and interests we develop also influence our activities and relationships. The particular social milieus to which we have access are at least partly determined by the potentialities we cultivate and actualize.

In addition to our skills, values, interests, and behavioral standards, the strength of our personal agency will influence our choice of group affiliation. According to Bandura (1982a, 1982b), when we develop competencies, self-precepts of efficacy, and self-regulatory capabilities—that is, strong personal agency—we are more likely to be attracted to groups that offer incentive, meaning, and worth to what we do. Conversely, when healthy social affiliations are lacking, we become vulnerable to coercive or communal groups that offer friendship in exchange for conformity (Bandura, 1982b).

Induction into a group not only brings us into contact with new incentive systems, but also "furnishes a distinct symbolic environment as well"

(Bandura, 1982b, p. 752). In addition to feelings of affinity and solidarity, group symbolic systems, whether healthy or unhealthy, help shape members' ideological perspectives on life and living.

Bandura (1977a, 1982a, 1982b) asserts that the greatest protection we have as individuals rests with groups and organizations whose members have a sense of collective efficacy and can mobilize their efforts and resources to protect individual rights. We are not, according to Bandura (1982a), forced to live our lives as social isolates. We can gain strength in groups. Further, our perceived collective efficacy will influence what we do as a group, the effort we expend as a group, and the length of time we continue to work as a group when the group's efforts fail to produce immediate results. Moreover, he claims, "the higher the perceived efficacy, the greater the propensity to social activism" (Bandura, 1982a, p. 143).

Psychological and/or Reality Environments

According to Bandura (1974, 1977a, 1982b), we form perceptions about ourselves and our world by observing and extracting regularities and uniformities of events in our particular environments. By encoding direct and vicarious experiences symbolically, we gain knowledge about priorities and relationships. We anticipate consequences and predict outcomes. We formulate standards and rules and develop incentives and logical verification procedures. We naturally generate perpetuating ideas, attitudes, and habitual patterns of thought. And, most important for this issue, we sift all our new experiences of the environment through our current understanding and expectations about ourselves, our behavior, and the world.

Our capacity to symbolize events and our self-evaluative and self-regulatory reactions play prominent roles in influencing our perceptions of our world. The concepts we hold at any particular moment exert significant influence on our perceptions of present experiences. Although we are rooted in the reality of observables and ponderables, we can act on that reality. We have a hand in the creation of what that reality is for us. We have the capacity and we can create the incentive to assert and express ourselves on the world we conceptualize and encounter. We interpret our perceptions and act on our images of reality. In short, we develop a personal integrity that, in turn, influences our perceptions of ourselves, others, and the world.

Uniqueness and/or Commonality

Bandura has not addressed this issue in the material reviewed, but his firm stance on reciprocal determinism makes it clear that he views us as unique individuals. Not only are our experiences, whether actual or vicarious, both numerous and varied, but also we develop highly personal systems of cognitive processes, opening our conceptualizations of every experience to an infinite variety of individual, creative, interpretive shadings. Our realities are subjectively determined images of the world we encounter. Our feelings and actions during and following any experience are uniquely our own. We are, then, neither predictable nor typical. Rather, we are each unparalleled with innate potentials, creative perceptions, and personally constructed attitudes, values, goals, and behavioral strategies.

GOALS OF SOCIAL LEARNING THERAPISTS

Unlike the therapies of Rogers, Ellis, Perls, and May, few accepted social learning therapeutic goals apply to all clients. The focus of social learning therapy is instead on the individual client's present behavior or behavioral patterns. Although social learning therapists assist their clients to learn desired or required behaviors and to extinguish maladaptive behaviors that lead to grief, difficulty, or negative consequences, the specific goals of therapy vary from client to client.

Clients in social learning therapy play a major role not only in determining the nature and direction of therapy but also in delineating the specific behavioral changes to be produced. The primary role of the therapist initially is to assist the client to view desired outcomes in terms of specific performance objectives, preferably objectives that are both observable and measurable.

When clients are uncertain about what they want from therapy or when they express goals that are obscure or general rather than specific, social learning therapists may have to assist in a review of the alternative courses of action available to their clients, as well as in an exploration of the probable consequences of following any of them. The goals of social learning therapy are the clients'; however, only when goals are clearly defined in terms of observable, measurable behavioral change can the client and therapist arrive at decisions regarding experiences most likely to produce the outcomes desired. Poorly defined goals leave the client and therapist without any rational, meaningful basis for selecting an appropriate treatment plan and behavioral strategies or for evaluating the effectiveness of therapeutic effort.

Once clients are able to express their problems, social learning therapists often assist with the assessment process before devising goals or plans of intervention or action. For example, when, where, and with whom is the problem behavior exhibited? How pervasive and frequent is the behavior? What are the antecedents and consequences of the behavior cited? What were the conditions when the problem behavior originated? Who were the client's role models? How is the behavior maintained? Are there situational factors in the client's living conditions that may be helpful in effecting change? How might these factors be utilized in a program to modify the inappropriate behavioral patterns? Would it be helpful to secure the client's permission to interview other people influential in the client's life who might serve as models of the desired behavior? It may be helpful, also, to specify the conditions under which the desired outcomes may be expected to occur.

When behavioral outcomes are complex, they may be divided into a number of subgoals or steps and sequenced in hierarchical order to ensure optimal progress. Intricate modes of behavior are often best achieved by modeling progressively more complex responses and reinforcing (directly or vicariously) gradual response elaboration.

THERAPEUTIC PROCESS: METHODS AND TECHNIQUES

For Bandura (in Bergin & Garfield, 1971), any therapeutic process that focuses on the interview or the relationship as the major method for producing therapeutic change places severe and unnecessary limitations "on the quality, range, and intensity of the experiences that could be created in the therapeutic setting" (p. 653). Convinced that nearly all human behavior is learned and that practically all learning that occurs from direct experience can occur vicariously as the result of observing the behavior of others and its consequences for them, the therapist produces a process of therapy significantly different from the processes of interview and relationship therapies. These differences are evident in the content and focus of therapy, as well as in the agents of treatment.

While skillful interview and relationship techniques may facilitate behavior assessment, goal alignment, and acceptance by the client of the therapist as a model, the focus of social learning therapy is on the specific client behaviors requiring modification rather than a series of interviews in which these behaviors, or feelings about these behaviors, are only discussed. Further, rather than confining the therapy session to the office of the therapist, much of the therapeutic process of social learning therapy occurs in the setting in which the client's problem behaviors evolve. While the social learning therapists may serve as models, the agents of therapy are often carefully selected individuals and groups who already have intensive contact with the client or who possess the behavior repertoire necessary to serve as effective models.

Bandura accepts most modes of therapy based on learning principles (see Chapter 10). However, the emphasis in this chapter is on those specific behavioral enactment methods that are based on modeling principles, methods which have been demonstrated as effective and economical whether acquiring new patterns of behavior, strengthening or weakening inhibitions of responses that already exist in the client's repertoire, or facilitating the client's perceived self-efficacy.

Therapeutic Relationship

Social learning therapists recognize that a sound professional therapist-client relationship can enhance the value of the therapist as a model and as a dispenser of positive or negative reinforcement (see "Explanation of Learning"). However, Bandura (Bandura & Walters, 1963), citing numerous examples where both children and adults learned complex behavioral patterns by observing models with whom they had no prior relationship, flatly rejects the notion that the therapeutic relationship is either the requisite or the essence of therapy.

While the therapist's expression of warmth, concern, empathy, authenticity, as well as the manifestation of authority, prestige, self-confidence, and self-assurance, is viewed as desirable in social learning therapy, such expressions and manifestations are considered insufficient. In fact, Bandura (Bandura & Walters, 1963; Bandura, 1969, 1977a) contends that the acquisition or modification of client behavior so often attributed to the therapeutic relationship is the result of inadvertent applications of essential learning principles by the therapist. Thus, while social learning therapists do not neglect relationship variables, they do minimize the importance of personal and interpersonal elements of the therapeutic relationship and focus on deliberate and carefully planned applications of experimentally derived learning principles with demonstrated effectiveness.

Initial Procedures and Strategies

Initiating Therapy. Therapy begins with problem definition and assessment. The importance of this initial assessment process in social learning therapy cannot be overemphasized because decisions regarding therapeutic approach, strategies, or action plans are based on this definition. Accurate problem definition involves more than identification of the presenting problem. It includes the determination of whether the presenting problem represents all the client's concerns. If the therapeutic process is structured to meet the client's needs, and that is the major purpose of therapy, a thorough problem assessment must be conducted by the client and the therapist to identify all client concerns, including those that, for whatever reasons, may be withheld or those that are not readily recognized by the client. Initial problem presentations are often vague and emotion laden, so clarification is necessary to eliminate ambiguity. Clear and accurate specification of problem behaviors is the basis for therapeutic purpose and goal formulation, as well as selection of strategies. Furthermore, conceptualizing the client's problem in terms of specific problem behaviors not only offers both client and therapist a clear and consistent view of the problem but also provides a baseline for future progress assessment.

Clients of social learning therapists are neither categorized with any preconceived diagnostic lables like those listed in the *Diagnostic and Statistical Manual of Mental Disorders* (1980), nor identified as possessing any generalized or global traits or characteristics like those provided by scores on certain standardized tests; rather, social learning therapists and their clients work together to define their clients' problems operationally. A clear operational definition not only has the advantage of focusing on specific problem behaviors and the conditions (antecedents and consequences) contributing to them but also avoids the negative global inferences of diagnostic labels and vague traits. Further, operational definitions are much less likely to carry bias into the treatment procedure, thus affecting the way others relate to the client.

Client Expectations. Clarification of initial client expectations occurs within the highly interactive process of problem assessment. As the client's behaviors are operationally defined and the most pressing and stressful of his or her concerns are specified, both the client and therapist become aware of what can and cannot be accomplished in both the short and long term of therapy. Although both client and therapist are active participants in the process of therapy, goals are ultimately determined by the client. Furthermore, because the client's desired outcomes are specified clearly in observable and measurable terms, both the client and therapist can readily determine where the client is in the therapeutic process, as well as what he or she has to accomplish.

Client expectations are seldom permanent. After working on a problem area for a time, the client may reveal new concerns that are even more pressing. New behavioral alternatives and their consequences must be explored and evaluated. Initial goals and strategies are to be viewed as temporary. Reevaluation by the client is a constant in the assessment process.

Structuring. Structuring in social learning therapy entails explanation of the rationale for each step of the therapeutic process. The client is informed why his or her concerns are to be defined behaviorally and operationally; the purpose of goals is explained, and all strategies, interventions, and treatment rationales are clarified. Structuring not only facilitates the therapeutic process by focusing on the responsibility of the client but also helps to keep the therapist aware of the client's needs and choices in the process of therapy, as well as his or her own values, skills, and limitations. Bandura (1969) contends that redefinition of the client's desired outcomes by the therapist is an ethical issue and one too often largely ignored (p. 103). Re-evaluation in social learning theory is to be an option only when the client fully understands and consents. Any therapist influence in the re-evaluation process is to be open and explicit.

Course of Therapy

Modeling is the major technique used in social learning therapy. It may be used as the single therapeutic technique in certain instances, but modeling, in most cases, is the dominant component in a more inclusive strategy or action plan designed to demonstrate the client's desired goal behaviors. Models can be live, symbolic, or, in the case of covert modeling, imaginal. When part of a larger program, modeling may be supplemented with verbal sets explaining the rationale of strategy, rehearsal sessions in simulated or natural settings, coaching and induction or support aids, client self-directed practice, feedback, homework assignments, and postevaluations or progress assessments.

The course of social learning therapy involves some form of observational learning, or modeling, in which desired behavioral sequences and outcomes are demonstrated either in the client's natural environment or symbolically. The modeling process is usually followed by some form of client rehearsal that is often accomplished by coaching and/or feedback from either the therapist or a designated helper who possesses the required behavioral repertoire being considered. To facilitate the transfer of learning, the client is asked to demonstrate the newly acquired goal behaviors by completing a homework assignment or by engaging in self-directed practice in his or her natural environment. To assess the efficacy of therapy, both short-term and long-term follow-up at selected intervals following termination is strongly recommended. In addition to communicating the therapist's continued interest in the client's welfare, the information gathered through follow-up can be used to determine the extent to which the client is continuing to perform the desired goal behaviors without therapeutic support. Bandura (1969) asserts that therapy can be determined successful only when viewed over the long-term.

Methods and Techniques

The brief descriptions of four modeling approaches that follow are not to be viewed as a set of decisive or inflexible techniques. Modeling experiences are individually determined by the client and therapist, the specific problem behaviors selected for change, the desired behavioral outcomes or therapeutic goals, and the particular setting and circumstances in which the problem behaviors evolve. Variations of the content and sequence of these modeling approaches are limited only by the creative ability of the therapist.

Live Modeling. Certain characteristics of the model may enhance the learning process (see "Explanation of Learning"), but live models may be anyone with the capability to demonstrate the desired behavior to the client. Consider the following example. The client's goal behavior is to be more assertive with a supervisor who takes advantage of his compliant response to unfair requests. In this example, the therapist elects to serve as a model. Since this is a case of deficit behavior, the therapist begins with role reversal, asking the client to play the part of the supervisor while the therapist plays the part of the client.

Therapist: For the next few minutes, I'd like you to imagine that you are the supervisor. I want you to act exactly as he does when he asks you to do something you consider unfair. I'm going to imagine that I'm you; however, rather than reacting compliantly to your request, I'm going to respond in a more assertive manner.

Client: I know it's nearly time to punch out, Old Buddy, but I want you to stay over for a few hours and help me with a report I have to write.

Therapist: Sorry, Tom. I'd like to stay and give you a hand with your report, but I've made other arrangements for tonight, and it's too late now to change them.

Client: Oh, come on Old Buddy; you can always call her up and give her a rain check. I really need your ideas for this report.

Therapist: I might have been able to make other arrangements if you had just asked me sooner, but this evening is set, and I'm committed. I'd be glad to help you with it tomorrow. Perhaps we can find time to work on it during the day. I've really got to run now. See you first thing in the morning.

Once the behavior has been successfully demonstrated, the therapist may ask the client to review his or her perceptions of what just happened. This review assists the client's coding of the modeled behavior to make recall easier and to select for practice those modeled responses the client believes he or she can perform comfortably. Modeled behavior is only suggested behavior, and the client should be encouraged to adapt the responses to his or her style.

Therapist: Suppose we stop now and talk about what just happened. Were you able to capture the way your supervisor acts?

Client: Yeah. He'll breeze in just before quitting time and tell me that he wants me to work late without any consideration of how I feel about it. He's always calling me "Old Buddy," too, and I really hate that.

Therapist: We might work on the "Old Buddy" later, but, for now, let's concentrate on what we just did. What did I do when asked to work late?

Client: Well, you didn't get nasty or anything. You just said that you were sorry but you had made other plans. Oh yeah, you offered to help him the next morning.

Therapist: If you remember, I also told him that I might have been able to make other arrangements if he hadn't waited until the last minute to tell me that he needed my help. Do you think you might be able to respond somewhat as I did the next time your supervisor makes a request you consider unfair?

Client: Yeah. I think I might.

Therapist: O.K. Let's give it a try. This time I'll play the part of the supervisor; you just be yourself. It's 5 minutes until quitting time.

Hey Old Buddy, I'm going to need you to work over tonight and give me some of your ideas on the Baker account. We ought to be able to wrap it up in a couple of hours.

Client: Sorry. I can't do it tonight. I've promised to meet someone right after work and it's too late to make other arrangements. I'll be glad to get together with you first thing in the morning though. How about 8 o'clock?

Therapist: Very good! I especially liked the way you set a specific time to meet with him the next morning. You remained calm, and you held your ground. You also reminded him that you have a life outside the office and last minute requests can't always be honored. Would it help if we tried it again, or do you feel comfortable with your response?

Client: I'm a little nervous about how he might react, but I feel comfortable enough with telling him I can't stay over.

Therapist: I'm going to give you a little homework assignment. Between now and our next appointment, I want you to find a few minutes once each day when you can be alone and imagine your supervisor making an unfair request. Then, still using your imagination, answer him in a way that informs him that he can't take advantage of you and that you are willing to cooperate when his requests are fair. Keep in mind that the goal is assertiveness, not anger. We'll practice more of this next week.

Participant Modeling. According to Bandura (in Krumboltz & Thoresen, 1976), there are four major components in participant modeling: (1) explanation of the rationale and instruction, (2) modeling, (3) guided participation, and (4) successful experiences. When the desired behavioral outcome is complex or highly threatening to the client, it is divided into a series of behavioral responses or approximations of the desired behavioral pattern and arranged in order of difficulty. It is important that the first outcome demonstrated is one the client can observe without threat and, with direct support and guidance, complete successfully. The object of participant modeling is to promote client competence and, in turn, enhance the client's perceived self-efficacy (Bandura, Reese, & Adams, 1982).

Selection of an appropriate model is important (see "Explanation of Learning"). The therapeutic context may make the therapist the most likely model selection. However, greater gains may accrue by using multiple models or, in the case of strong or disabling avoidance behaviors, coping models—that is, persons who have successfully overcome their fears by employing the participant model approach in therapy.

In participant modeling, the model demonstrates a single behavioral response. The demonstration may be repeated by the same model or, when feasible, by several different models. Multiple modeling of a goal response lends both variety and credence to the demonstration.

Following the demonstration of each modeling sequence in the modeling hierarchy, the client is given the opportunity for guided participation. Guided participation includes direct assistance and support while the client performs the behavior modeled. Each practice attempt by the client is accompanied by feedback from the therapist about his or her performance, reinforcement for successful attempts, and when appropriate, suggestions for improving the next practice attempt.

Induction aids are often selected to support and encourage the client during initial practice sessions. The therapist or model may elect to assist or participate directly in the early practice attempts. For example, working with a client who experiences inordinately strong fear of and avoidance behaviors with snakes, the therapist or model may, at the point at which the client is first asked to touch the snake, hold the head and tail so the client can touch the body. If still hesitant, the client may be provided with a pair of thick gloves. As therapy progresses, the induction aids are gradually withdrawn. Eventually, the client is expected to perform each behavioral sequence without aids or assistance. In addition, the practice attempts should move from the low-risk situation of the therapeutic interview to the client's natural environment where the risk encountered is often greater. Finally, the client is assigned a series of progressively more difficult homework assignments.

Symbolic Modeling. Because of our ability to symbolize, models may be presented symbolically through films, audio or video recordings, photographic slides, imagery scripts, or written and printed materials. Film or video models are used in therapy in much the same way live models are used and can become the major component of a more complex strategy or used independently by clients for self-directed improvement. Bibliotherapy is a form of symbolic modeling and has proven particularly effective when model and reader are similar in race, sex, cultural background, and experience or when involved in similar situations.

Symbolic modeling has been demonstrated as a practical and efficacious modeling approach in therapy. It is a highly versatile and, when used repeatedly over time, cost-effective treatment method. The particular medium selected for symbolic modeling will depend on the client or group of clients for which it is designed, the specific goal behaviors to be acquired by those who use it, as well as where and how the medium is to be used. As with other forms of modeling, the effects of symbolic modeling are likely to be enhanced when the presentation or display is followed with instruction and explanation of the rationale, guided practice opportunites, immediate feedback, and evaluative follow-up.

Self as Model. When others are viewed as models, the possibility exists of negative effects for the observer (Bandura, 1969). Even when the model is carefully selected and possesses many of the favorable model characteristics (prestige and status, same sex and age, and similar cultural and ethnic background), the client still may react negatively. Bandura informs us that modeling characteristics exert a differential influence on various observers.

For some clients, self as model can result in closer attending and coding. Seeing or hearing themselves perform and practice the goal behavior not only facilitates the modeling process—hence, the likelihood of correct performances—but also offers clients the unique opportunity to learn how they cope with formerly threatening and difficult situations. This experience can enhance the clients' perceptions of self-efficacy and can result in greater willingness to risk new or anxiety-producing behaviors.

Initially, self-as-model tapes that can be used for modeling purposes may be difficult to obtain. Therapists may be forced to edit carefully tapes of the client's early modeling attempts, keeping only those portions in which the client demonstrates appropriate goal behavior. The edited version, then, becomes the model tape and is played for the client who sees or hears him- or herself practicing the behavior he or she wants to acquire. To reinforce correct behavior and encourage further rehearsal, the therapist may stop the tape at appropriate intervals to praise a satisfactory performance by the client or to coach the client on ways to improve a particular behavior. To achieve the benefits of repeated modeling, the therapist may ask the client to take the tape home so he or she may view or listen to it outside the therapy session, preferably at specified times each day for an agreed on period. The client may also be asked to record at least one short practice tape immediately after viewing or listening to the modeling tape. As with other modeling approaches— participant modeling, for example—the client is encouraged to transfer gradually the newly acquired goal behaviors to his or her natural environment.

ASSESSING PROGRESS

When the client's therapeutic goals are defined operationally in terms of explicit behavioral change or changes, progress assessment automatically becomes a continuous therapeutic process. Even when the desired behavioral goal is complicated or threatening, it is divided into a number of smaller, manageable behavioral subtasks, gradually increasing in complexity or risk. Both client and therapist continuously monitor and assess therapeutic progress.

Final assessment of therapeutic success must wait until some time after termination of therapy. If, after an acceptable time period, the client is still

FIGURE 9.2 A Schematic Analysis of Bandura's Stand on the Basic Issues

Biological Determinants	▉▉▉▉	Social Determinants
Commonality	▉▉▉	Uniqueness
Conditioning	▉▉▉	Freedom
Early Development	▉▉▉	Continuous Development
Psychological Environment	▉▉▉	Reality Environment
Unconscious Determinants	▉▉▉	Conscious Determinants

Importance of Group Membership	Particularly in our formative years, the group facilitates formulation of personal preferences, values, standards, and a sense of efficacy. As our social milieu broadens, we tend to move to those groups espousing similar interests and values. Group affiliation promotes mutual reinforcement of preexisting inclinations.
Explanation of Learning	Learning occurs via modeling and effective modeling entails attentional, retentional, motor reproduction (actual practice or internal rehearsal), and incentive and motivational processes. External reinforcement is relegated to a facilitative rather than a necessary role in learning.
Number and Weight Assigned to Motivational Concepts	Only those reinforcements experienced as personally meaningful become incentives for behavior. Positive incentives (formulated cognitively or externally) facilitate development of competencies and interests that are personally satisfying and that promote self-efficacy.
Importance of Reward	Anticipatory reinforcement carries more weight than immediate, environmental reinforcement. Anticipatory reinforcement is internal, transcending external reinforcement and control and fostering a personal sense of self-esteem and self-regard.
Importance or Role of Self-Concept	Conceptualized in terms of reciprocal determinism, the self acts as a cognitive contributory influence that interacts reciprocally within a system of personal, behavioral, and environmental influences. An autonomous psychic entity with unidirectional control is disregarded.

practicing the desired new behaviors in his or her natural environment, then social learning therapy may be considered successful. The assessment process in social learning therapy begins when therapy is initiated and ends 6 months to 1 year after therapy has been terminated.

FINAL COMMENTARY

Initially identified with moderate behaviorism, Bandura's recent interest in the essentially cognitive structure—hence, covert role—of self-regulating and self-motivating influences has virtually led to the severance of his ties with the behavioral arena. Patterson (1980), an astute student of the theories of counseling and psychotherapy, remarks on Bandura's role in the demise of orthodox behavior therapy: "If one were to date the onset of the terminal illness of behaviorism, Bandura's 1974 presidential address to the American Psychological Association might well be chosen" (p. 640).

Based on an impressive outpouring over the years of carefully controlled experimental research, Bandura's theoretical concepts are innovative, current, relevant, and concise. His tendency, however, to shift the focus of his research efforts to cover a wide variety of content areas (e.g., from reciprocal determinism, observational learning, and aggression to self-regulation, self-motivation, and self-efficacy) has resulted in a psychotherapeutic approach that is rather loosely organized. While his concepts are both contemporary and relevant, they lack theoretical integration. There is no comprehensive theoretical construct to bind his many concepts into a gestalt. Bandura has contributed a great deal to our understanding of how the human personality is formed and changed, but he has not clearly explained its structure and organization. His theory is more descriptive than explanatory.

For a relative newcomer to the theoretical arena, Bandura has exerted a tremendous impact on both the experimental and applied fields of counseling and psychotherapy, particularly in educating prospective counselors and therapists where modeling is employed extensively in teaching therapeutic skills. Moreover, because the theory of social learning is highly flexible, thus constantly evolving in light of new research, it seems reasonable to assume that Bandura's approach to therapy has not reached its full potential and that we shall witness a considerable influence of his theory.

REFERENCES AND SUGGESTED READINGS

Awards for distinguished scientific contributions: 1980. January 1981. *American Psychologist* 36: 27–42.

Bandura, A. 1969. *Principles of behavior modification.* New York: Holt, Rinehart & Winston.

Bandura, A. 1973. *Aggression: A social learning analysis.* Englewood Cliffs, N.J.: Prentice-Hall.

Bandura, A. 1974. Behavior theory and the models of man. *American Psychologist* 29: 859–869.

Bandura, A. 1976. Effecting change through participant modeling. In J.D. Krumboltz & C.E. Thorensen, eds. *Counseling methods.* New York: Holt, Rinehart & Winston.

Bandura, A. 1977a. *Social learning theory*. Englewood Cliffs, N.J.: Prentice-Hall.

Bandura, A. 1977b. Analysis of modeling processes. In E.M. Hetherington & R.D. Parke, eds. *Contemporary readings in child psychology*. New York: McGraw-Hill, pp. 191–207.

Bandura, A. 1978a. The self system in reciprocal determinism. *American Psychologist* 33: 344–358.

Bandura, A. 1978b. Social learning theory of aggression. *Journal of Communication* 28: 12–27.

Bandura, A. 1982a. Self-efficacy mechanisms in human agency. *American Psychologist* 37: 122–147.

Bandura, A. 1982b. The psychology of chance encounters and life paths. *American Psychologist* 37: 747–755.

Bandura, A. 1982c. The assessment and predictive generality of self-percepts of efficacy. *Journal of Behavioral Therapy & Experiential Psychiatry* 13: 195–199.

Bandura, A. 1983. Temporal dynamics and decomposition of reciprocal determinism: a reply to Phillips and Orton. *Psychological Review* 90: 166–170.

Bandura, A., & Walters, R.H. 1963. *Social learning and personality development*. New York: Holt, Rinehart & Winston.

Bandura, A., Adams, N.E. & Beyer, J. 1977. Cognitive processes mediating behavioral change. *Journal of Personality Social Psychology* 35: 125–139.

Bandura, A., Reese, L., & Adams, N.E. 1982. Microanalysis of action and fear arousal as a function of differential levels of perceived self-efficacy. *Journal of Personality and Social Psychology* 43: 3–21.

Bergin, A.E. & Garfield, S.L., eds. 1971. *Handbook of psychotherapy and behavior change: an empirical analysis*. New York: John Wiley & Sons.

Carroll, W.R., & Bandura, A. 1982. The role of visual monitoring in observational learning of action patterns: making the unobservable observable. *Journal of Motor Behavior* 14: 153–167.

Diagnostic and Statistical Manual of Mental Disorders, DSMIII, 3rd ed. 1980. Washington, D.C.: American Psychiatric Association.

Maddi, S.R. 1976. *Personality theories: a comparative analysis*, 3rd ed. Homewood, Ill.: Dorsey Press.

Meichenbaum, D. 1977. *Cognitive behavior modification*. New York: Plenum.

Patterson, C.H. 1980. *Theories of counseling and psychotherapy*, 3rd ed. New York: Harper & Row.

Rotter, J.B., Chance, J.E. & Phares, E.J. 1972. *Application of a social learning theory of personality*. New York: Holt, Rinehart & Winston.

10

The Operant Behaviorism of B. F. Skinner

UNLIKE MOST OF the theorists selected for inclusion in this book, the data for Skinner's behavioristic approach to therapy did not emerge from personal experiences in the therapeutic setting. A dedicated experimental psychologist and ardent radical determinist, Skinner's work setting was the laboratory. Furthermore, convinced that the laws of learning apply to all organisms, Skinner's early subjects were selected from infrahuman species, usually rats and pigeons. Skinner holds steadfastly to the belief that advances in science occur progressively from the simple to the diverse and complex.

Committed to a nontheoretical, scientific approach, Skinner concentrates on carefully controlled observations of the overt, measurable behavior of a single subject. Furthermore, he sees no reason for formal theorizing and objects strongly to introspection as a method for gathering theoretical data. Skinner is certain that when sufficient facts are known, cause and effect become obvious. Looking for internal motivations (such as instincts, needs, drives, and traits) and underlying causes (such as conscious, unconscious, or actualizing forces) has, according to Skinner, only held back the scientific approach to the prediction and control of human behavior. Not only are mentalistic and intrapsychic concepts and constructs objectively unobservable—hence, unverifiable—they also have no direct reference to natural events. This idea, along with the reinforced illusion of freedom held by so many in democratic countries, Skinner believes, keeps us from formulating a behavioral technology necessary to promote fully the development of our species and society. For Skinner (1971), our struggle for freedom is not due to an inherent free will but to the avoidance of aversive environmental stimuli. He warns us repeatedly that wise decisions and careful planning are necessary for our survival as a species and culture but highly unlikely to be realized as long as we continue to believe that we are not controlled by the contingencies of our environment (see "Biological and/or Social Determinants" and "Conditioning and/or Freedom to Choose").

There is little doubt that Skinner is one of the most influential psychologists in the Western world today and even less doubt that he is one of the most controversial. While his contibutions to the explanation, prediction, and control of behavior have gained him the recognition and respect of experimental psychologists and scientists throughout the world, he is also the target of severe criticism. Psychoanalysts and humanists, in particular, find his revolutionary ideas frightening, and poets, philosophers, and theologians have expressed outrage. His call for a technology of behavior, a systematic, scientific program to redesign our culture to shape and control our behavior for survival, challenges many of our most sacred ideals and questions any concepts of free will and creativity (Skinner, 1971, 1972, 1974). Thus, Skinner leaves few who hear his plan for a better world unaffected. Because Skinner's scientific technology of behavior involves control and controllers, it has resulted in much discussion and debate, the most well known of these perhaps are the Rogers and Skinner debates (audiotapes of these debates are available through the American Association of Counseling and Development, AACD, formerly APGA).

BIOGRAPHICAL SKETCH

The ease with which biographical material can be located for the theorists whose ideas are presented in this book appears directly related to the theorist's stance on the basic issue, early and/or continuous development. Those who see little or no relationship between their early years and later accomplishments are not likely to disclose their early histories. Conversely, those who espouse causal theories are inclined to discuss the early childhood events and experiences they consider to be critical or significant in their personal development. Skinner, a radical determinist, provides us with a three-volume autobiography: *Particulars of My Life* (1976), *The Shaping of a Behaviorist* (1979), and *A Matter of Consequence* (1983b). In addition, although the entries are not dated, Epstein's edited volume, *Notebooks, B.F. Skinner* (1980), offers insights into the development of Skinner's personality and theory that can be found nowhere else. As with the biographical sketch of Freud (see Chapter 2), pertinent information about Skinner's life is both abundant and readily available. The difficulty here is being constantly confronted with the task of deciding what material to exclude.

Readers who identify with Skinner's ideas are almost certain to find his autobiographical works fascinating, and I recommend they read them. However, I especially recommend these works to readers who are strongly opposed to the idea of behavioral control. As stated in Chapter 12, the exercise of crossing swords with an expert from the opposing camp can be a most beneficial experience.

Early Years

Born 1904 in Susquehanna, a small Pennsylvania railroad town located close to the border of New York, Burrhus Frederick Skinner was the eldest son of

William Arthur Skinner and Grace Madge (Burrhus) Skinner. His brother, Edward James, 2 years his junior, died suddenly at the age of 16. Skinner (1976) remembers his early family life as warm and stable. Until he left for college, he lived in the house in which he was born. While he cannot recall ever being punished physically by his parents (with the exception of an occasion when his mother washed his mouth with a soapy washcloth for repeating a bad word), he considers his parents' disciplinary methods effective in shaping his early behavior.

There was never any doubt in Skinner's mind regarding what was expected of him. His mother's standards of right and wrong were both rigid and consistent. The consequences of breaking the law was instilled in him early when his father, an attorney, took him to the county jail to see firsthand the treatment of those convicted of a crime. He reports a vivid recollection of his grandmother's forcing him to look into the red embers of the coal stove so he might have some idea of hell and eternal hell fire. He knew that learning was valued highly because it was both encouraged and reinforced in his family.

Skinner (1976) was taught to appreciate music by his father, "a competent performer on the cornet" (p. 11), and his mother, who "played piano in an orchestra and accompanied singers in recitals"(p. 18). He learned to play the saxophone and earned money while in high school as a member of a jazz band that performed twice each week in the local theater.

Always mechanically inclined, Skinner spent much of his leisure time as as a child constructing, among other things, roller skate scooters, steering mechanisms for wagons and carts, a steam-powered blow gun that could fire potato and carrot plugs over the roofs of neighboring houses, kites, model planes powered by rubber bands, a perpetual motion machine that refused to work, and a room filled with Rube Goldberg–type contraptions. His interest in mechanical devices remained with him, culminating in the so-called Skinner box, the cumulative recorder, the teaching machine, and the air-crib.

It was in high school that Skinner, setting out to prove to his English teacher that Francis Bacon was the author of Shakespeare's plays, first came under Bacon's influence. This influence proved lasting and is expressed in both Skinner's thinking and writing.

Education

Determined to become a writer, Skinner entered Hamilton College, a small liberal arts school in New York. He did well academically, earning a Phi Beta Kappa key, but he never adjusted fully to campus life, He was a member of a fraternity but not a very active participant. Inept in sports, he avoided most athletic activities. Along with a number of his fellow students, Skinner considered many of the college curriculum requirements irrelevant and objected strenuously to being forced to complete them. During his senior year, his objections became more overt, and he took an active part in a number of student activities designed to humiliate certain faculty members believed to be pompous and arrogant in their relations with students. Although threatened by the college president with expulsion, he was permitted to graduate and received his A.B. degree in 1926.

Armed with determination and an encouraging letter from Robert Frost, who had generously critiqued three of his short stories, Skinner returned to his family home, set up an attic studio, and proceeded to pursue his career in writing. After a year, with nothing of substance to show for his effort, he decided he would benefit from contact with other writers and moved to Greenwich Village. Here, again, he accomplished little writing, although he did read extensively. He was particularly influenced by Bertrand Russell and Francis Bacon and, through them, was introduced to the works of Pavlov and Watson. This was his first taste of psychology since he did not take courses in this discipline while in college. From Greenwich Village he spent the remainder of the year in Europe and, discovering that he had nothing important to write about, decided to give up writing as a career and continue his formal education, this time in psychology.

He entered Harvard University, and by leading a Spartan life and reading only in the fields of psychology and physiology, he completed all degree requirements in an amazingly short period of time: the M.A. was awarded in 1930 and the Ph. D. in 1931. His postdoctoral training for the next 5 years included work as a National Research Council fellow and later as a junior fellow in the Harvard Society of Fellows, Harvard's most prestigious award for young scholars. In 1936, Skinner married Yvonne Blue, an English major at the University of Chicago.

Skinner accepted his first academic postion at the University of Minnesota. In 2 years he published his first book, *The Behavior of Organisms* (1938), which, incidentally, he considers his most important work. It was here, too, that he began work on a novel, *Walden Two* (1948), a story of a utopian commune governed by operant principles. During the 9 years he spent at Minnesota, Skinner was remarkably prolific, establishing himself as one of the country's leading experimental psychologists.

From Minnesota, Skinner moved to the University of Indiana where, for a brief period, he served as professor and chairperson of the department of psychology. In 1947 he delivered the William James Lectures at Harvard, and the following year he joined Harvard's Department of Psychology as a full professor.

Emergence of Operant Conditioning

With the publication of *The Behavior of Organisms* (1938), Skinner presented his early principles of operant conditioning. *Walden Two* (1948), Skinner's only published novel, was an early application of his theory that drew heavy response and inspired the establishment of several experimental communities, as well as a national conference. *Science and Human Behavior* (1953) introduced us to a variety of applications of these principles. In *The Technology of Teaching* (1968), Skinner proposed a revolutionary approach to learning in the school setting. He presented his scientific position in *Contingencies of Reinforcement* (1969) and explained its relevance for a wide band of social problems. After the publication of *Beyond Freedom and Dignity* (1971), Skinner drew heavy criticism for asserting that present illusory concepts of human freedom and dignity block scientific planning for a better world. *About Behaviorism* (1974) is a summary of his views of psychology. His most recent publication, *Enjoy Old Age* (Skinner & Vaughan, 1983), concerns the application of his principles to aging.

Accomplishments and Awards

In 1941, Skinner was the recipient of the Guggenheim Fellowship and wrote the initial draft of *Verbal Behavior* (1957). The Society of Experimental Psychologists awarded Skinner the Warren Medal in 1942. In 1951, an honorary doctor of science degree was conferred by his alma mater, Hamilton College. Since then, he has received about a dozen others, including the Sc.D. from the University of Chicago in 1967; the University of Execter, England, 1969; McGill University, Montreal, 1970; and Ohio Wesleyan University, 1971. He received the Distinguished Contribution Award from the APA in 1958. The highest public award for scientific contribution, the National Medal of Science, was presented to Skinner in 1968; only three behavioral scientists have received this award. In 1971, he was the recipient of the APA Gold Medal and the Joseph P. Kennedy, Jr., Foundation Award.

When asked during an interview how he felt about the numerous awards he had received, Skinner's response was, "By denying creativity and freedom, I have relinquished all chances of being called a Great Thinker" (1983a, p. 32). He was often depressed or frightened by the honors conferred on him and attempted to refuse those that would either take time from his work or unduly reinforce specific aspects of it.

RESOLUTIONS OF THE ELEVEN BASIC ISSUES

For the most part, Skinner's resolutions of the eleven basic issues are strong and explicit, reflecting a belief in and commitment to elementalism, environmentalism, objectivity, reactivity, determinism, knowability, and controllability. There are, however, a number of issues that are not applicable to Skinner's position since he rejects internal cognitive-perceptual variables as causes of behavior. Our behavior, according to Skinner, is the direct result of specifiable, unique conditioning histories.

Biological and/or Social Determinants

Skinner (1969) does not deny the influence of biological determinants on our behavior. This issue appears at the top of the hierarchy because he ascribes the propensity for reinforcement to genetics. For Skinner, the process of evolution shapes innate behaviors in much the same way the environment shapes learned behaviors (see "Explanation of Learning"). Our inherent sensitivity to reinforcement, then, evolved because of its especially strong survival advantage. Life-maintaining and life-enhancing behaviors are reinforced behaviors selected within the environment for survival. Skinner recognizes, too, that some behaviors may be entirely genetic, thus unaffected by external stimuli.

While Skinner does not claim that behavior is singly a product of the environment, he does de-emphasize the practical importance of biological determinants. Skinner is interested in a scientific study of behavior, and biological variability that cannot be directly observed, measured, manipulated, or controlled does not lend itself well to this rigid, functional, experimental analysis. His focus, then, is exclusively on environmental stimuli that can be manipulated—hence, controlled—in the laboratory setting.

Skinner consistently focuses on the whole-body behaviorism of individual organisms as they interact with their environment. For Skinner, behavior is always the function of existing environmental contingencies. Our behavior always occurs in, and has an effect on, the environment. As our behavior changes, the contingencies of the environment also are altered. While there may be internal contingencies influencing behavioral selection patterns, Skinner excludes or rejects internal causes and focuses exclusively on the more easily observable and manipulatable environmental events. He emphasizes the modification, prediction, and planned control of behavior by developing a behavioral technology to change society and culture.

Importance of Reward

The principles of operant reinforcement—that is, reinforcement of a behavior that operates on the environment controlling it and, at the same time, being controlled by it—are at the base of Skinner's theory. Stated simply, when a given behavior is followed closely by a reinforcer (a reward), the emitting organism tends to increase the frequency of that behavior under identical or similar circumstances. An operant reinforcement is associated with and immediately follows the emitted response rather than immediately preceding the stimulus that elicits the response, as in the case of respondent conditioning.

A reinforcement may be either *positive* (a rewarding stimulus) or *negative* (the withdrawal of an aversive stimulus, which is also rewarding). It may be either *primary* (an unconditioned reinforcer such as food, water, attention, or sex) or *secondary* (a conditioned reinforcer such as money or tokens). When reinforcement is withheld, interrupted, or stops, a conditioned behavior diminishes in a process known as *extinction*. Reinforcement, then, is essential for both the acquisition or the maintenance of respondent behavior.

Focusing on variables that increase or decrease the probability of a response occurring over time, Skinner (1938, 1953, 1974) discovered that different schedules of reinforcement (the contingencies under which reinforcement is delivered) had different effects on respondent learning. Continuous reinforcement involves reinforcing the organism each time it emits the desired behavior and is usually employed at the onset of most operant conditioning. There are, however, a variety of intermittent schedules of reinforcement in Skinner's system, falling into two general classifications: (1) reinforcement after a regular or fixed time interval, called *interval reinforcement schedules,* and (2) reinforcement after an irregular or fixed number of responses, called *ratio reinforcement schedules.* These two general classifications provide four basic schedules of reinforcement:

1. *Fixed-ratio schedule:* A schedule in which the reinforcement is given only after the subject has emitted a predetermined or fixed number of responses. This schedule generates high operant levels since the more the subject responds, the more reinforcement he or she receives. The fixed-ratio schedule is used effectively in industry, where the employee is paid for the number of pieces produced or operations performed. Sales commissions are based on fixed-ratio schedules. Academic promotions and salary increases based on publication of a specified number of research articles or books over a fixed time period is another example of a fixed-ratio schedule of reinforcement.

2. *Fixed-interval schedule:* A schedule in which reinforcement is given only after an established or fixed period of time without regard to the number of responses. Examples of this schedule are paying for work done by the hour, day, week, or month; giving a child a weekly allowance; and administering mid-term and final examinations. Response increases over time with a sharp increase immediately preceding the time for reinforcement. In addition, there is often a low rate of response immediately after reinforcement.

3. *Variable-ratio schedule:* A schedule in which the number of responses for reinforcement is varied randomly around a specified average value. On a variable-ratio schedule of 15, the subject is reinforced for every fifteenth response on the average, but rather than coming at the fixed internal of 15, the response receiving reinforcement is randomly selected. This schedule produces a high and constant response rate, and extinction is often slow because the subject does not know when the next reinforcement will be forthcoming. The slot machine serves as a good illustration of this schedule.

4. *Variable-interval schedule:* A schedule in which reinforcements are presented on some stated time interval, but the intervals between reinforcements are irregular and impossible to predict. While reinforcement is solely based on time, the subject must make the appropriate response after the interval is over. For example, when performing on a 5-minute schedule, reinforcement

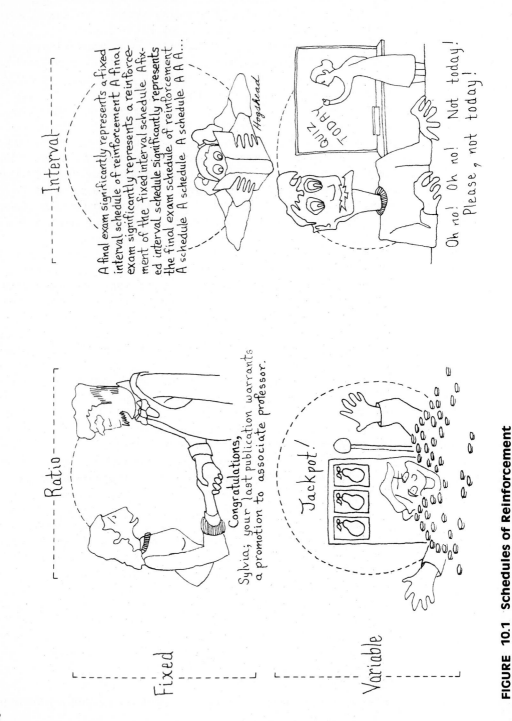

FIGURE 10.1 Schedules of Reinforcement

may be given after 8 minutes, 2 minutes, 6 minutes, and 4 minutes. With this schedule, short time intervals generate a high rate of response, and long time intervals, a low rate. Nevertheless, response rates tend to be steady and are difficult to extinguish. Surprise quizzes may be effectively employed on a variable-interval schedule to ensure a relatively stable rate of student preparation and study.

Explanation of Learning

For Skinner, learning, like knowledge, is an aspect of behavior attributable to the contingencies of reinforcement. Most of the behavioral responses we emit, whether in the form of thoughts, feelings, or overt actions, are the product of learning, which is a direct response to environmental contingencies. In the most simplistic terms, what we learn is dependent on environmental contingencies that consist of a myriad of stimuli, responses, and consequences. Moreover, practically all learning is purposive in the sense that we learn to satisfy certain contingencies of reinforcement.

Environmental stimuli are events and situations we encounter in the experience of daily living. They are the part of the environment that touches our senses and from which, through the processes of generalization and discrimination, we define our world, the beings we encounter in it, and ourselves. We must learn to discriminate environmental stimuli accurately if we are to respond appropriately. Moreover, stimuli must be associated with a response, a covert or overt physiological reaction, which may take the form of thought, emotion, or action and must be followed by a consequence.

The consequence of an appropriate response is reinforcing and increases the probability of a similar response under similar future contextual stimuli. We learn, then, by way of our operant responses to stimuli in the environment, conditioned response patterns that, in turn, are reinforced or punished by the environment. The contingencies of the environment are reciprocal. We learn early in life that there is a natural relationship between our environment, how we respond to our environment, and the consequences we experience as a result of our environment. While this knowledge promotes appropriate adjustment, it can be disadvantageous because past learning can interfere with present learning. Extinction of the old ways of responding is essential if new and more appropriate ways are to be learned.

A further condition of learning is the degree to which we are able to define the parameters involved in the environmental contingencies. Genetic limitations, misperception of stimuli, and poorly learned problem-solving behaviors may lead to faulty learning. Because learning is cumulative in the sense that all forms of learning seem to build on one another, faulty learning can predicate later difficulties. We first learn to respond to our environment on a rather basic level. As we grow and mature, we develop more complex patterns of responding. There is a transition from learning based on natural consequences of perceiving and responding to learning based on culturally transmitted, rule-governed behaviors. Witnessing, hearing, or reading the consequences of a particular response may eliminate the necessity of having to experience the consequences of that response.

Thus, learning is the basis on which behaviorism is founded. It is a continuous, complex physiological process defined in relation to the contingencies of reinforcement (see "Importance of Reward") and the ways in which our reinforcement history continually influences our behavior.

Conditioning and/or Freedom to Choose

Skinner's stance on this issue is clear. All behavior, including all human behavior, conforms to causal laws. Our behavior is determined by antecedent factors, our individual reinforcement histories. According to Skinner (1969), free will and autonomy are illusions, mere philosophical notions, that have been reinforced in our past and hold no place in a scientific approach to the study of behavior. We are always subject to the control of variables outside ourselves. Our behavior is always determined by our genetic endowment and environmental contingencies.

It is neither, as Skinner is often accused, that he is against freedom and human worth nor that he advocates imposing control; rather, he (1971; Epstein, 1980) argues that control exists. Control is a constant. Further, he warns, control is capricious and will remain so as long as we continue to hold the illusion of freedom and do nothing to influence that control.

While we are not, in Skinner's view, free agents, neither are we passive organisms. We operate on the environment that controls us. By giving up our destructive illusion of autonomy and understanding and accepting the principles of behavior, we are in a position to develop a behavioral technology that will permit us to plan for and generate controlling environmental stimuli. We can visualize the good life by examining and analyzing our feelings, but we can only achieve our visualizations by arranging the environmental contingencies that control our behavior. In brief, we are masters of our destiny only to the extent that we can manipulate the controlling environment contingencies.

Importance of Group Membership

Skinner (1953), who believes that "it is always the individual who behaves" (p. 311), rejects common explanations that personify groups as if they were individuals. He dismisses concepts such as the group mind, the herd instinct, and national character as weak attempts to support an unscientific approach to the study of groups.

Skinner admits, however, that while it is the individual who acts, it is the group that possesses the stronger effect. We can, as individuals, increase both the probability and the strength of reinforcement by joining a group because the reinforcement contingencies of the group easily outweigh the total consequences that can be generated by its members acting individually. Within a group there is an intensification of effect. Reinforcement for the individual becomes stronger when he acts in concert with others.

The larger the group, the more powerful its effect on the individual and the environment. Society, therefore, plays an important role in the establishment of reinforcement consequences essential for the definition, transmission, and maintenance of desired behaviors among its members. Skinner (1953, 1971, 1974) asserts that when behavioral definitions are carefully planned (through functional analysis, for example) and effectively reinforced (through positive reinforcement contingencies), their effect on the individual and the environment are not only immediately beneficial but also contribute to the survival of the species and the culture. Whether a family or a culture, the group is of maximal importance in transmitting rule-governed behavior into its members' personal and unique repertories of responding. It is crucial that the child learn the values, first of its particular subgroup and, later, of its culture, to live an effective life as an adult.

Conforming is also a concern in behaviorism. Because some individual responses in a group are positively reinforced while others are ignored or punished, a response conformity is established in a group. Skinner believes this conformity may be partially explained by an analysis of imitation. Imitation is likely to be reinforcing. In contrast, membership in several groups, where the behavioral repertoire learned in each does not generalize to the others, often results in several different repertoires—hence, several different personalities (see "Importance of Role of Self-Concept"). We thus develop separate selves, each appropriate for participation in a particular group. We behave one way in our family group, another way in our professional group, and another way in a group of close friends.

While Skinner has done little in the area of group dynamics, he is convinced that group interchange and heightened effect of the group on the environment can be studied most effectively within the framework of natural science. Indeed, he argues, this approach should be used fully before we decide to accept the constructs of social units, forces, and laws that require methods of a different nature (Skinner, 1953).

Early and/or Continuous Development

For the operant behaviorist, growth or development is simply the acquisition of a growing repertoire of behavior. If a child's behavior differs from that of a year earlier, it is not only because the child has grown but also because the child has acquired a larger repertoire of behavior through exposure to new contingencies of reinforcement. More specifically, the environmental contingencies affecting the child are different at different ages. Behavior reinforced at one age may be ignored or even punished at another. Skinner (1974) reminds us, "the child's world 'develops,' too" (p. 67).

For Skinner (1953, 1974), the discovery of developmental stages does not explain overt behavior; rather, it is more behavior to be explained. In *About Behaviorism,* Skinner expresses little regard for the structural concepts of the developmentalists:

> Compared with the experimental analysis of behavior, developmental psychology stands in the position of evolutionary theory before Darwin. . . . It remained for Darwin to discover the selective action of the environment, as it remains for us to supplement developmentalism in behavioral science with an analysis of the selective action of the environment. [1974, p. 68]

While a carefully compiled record of topography may help us predict behavior, Skinner (1974) asserts control is another matter. We need, in addition, an equally detailed record of the conditions under which the behavior described is acquired. Developmental stages presently defined in terms of feelings and states of mind are, according to Skinner (1974), really stages in the development of the world and in the changing contingencies generating the conditions felt or introspectively observed by the individual. While learning (growth) is considered a continuous process, behaviors learned during our earliest years are significant, particularly since new behaviors are often dependent on unlearning old behaviors.

In summary, growth or development is nothing more than the acquisition of a behavioral repertoire. Learning is development for the individual, and this development is dependent on the limitations of genetic endowment and the existent and potential contingencies of the environment. Physiological development is additionally important because some of the mechanisms necessary for more complex behavioral responses are not present at birth. It is, however, the contingencies of reinforcement that play the major role in development.

Number and Weight Assigned to Motivational Concepts

In a theory that focuses exclusively on observable behavior and in which all behavior can be traced to external causes, inner motivational constructs such as instincts or drives are not only considered unnecessary but also wasteful and confusing explanations. Operant responses are emitted, reinforced, and strengthened. What appears to be inner motivation is, for Skinner, nothing more than probability of response. Moreover, he asserts that differing probabilities of response can be accounted for by variables such as degree of deprivation or satiation. Hunger and thirst, then, are not inner motives or instinctual drives but aversive stimuli brought about by deprivation of food and water. Removal of aversive stimuli (eating and drinking) is reinforcing. Skinner's pigeons were held at 85 percent their normal body weight, making food pellets and water reliable reinforcers for shaping desired behavior. Thus, the greater the deprivation, the stronger the aversive stimulus and the more certain the reinforcer—hence, the greater the probability, predictability, and controllability of that behavior.

While Skinner recognizes that a single inner motivational construct (a sovereign drive for actualization, striving for perfection and completion, individuation, or the instinctual drives of an id, for example) could be used to explain a myriad of behaviors, he is convinced that inner constructs are both unscientific and dangerously misleading. Inner motivational constructs contribute nothing to the prediction and control of behavior and keep us from looking for external, objective factors that are the true cause of behavior.

Conscious and/or Unconscious Determinants

Skinner flatly rejects either conscious or unconscious entities like those proposed by Freud. Indeed, he rejects all intrapsychic agents. He believes, by turning to the facts on which these inner constructs are based, "it is usually possible to identify the contingencies of reinforcement which account for the intrapsychic activities" (Skinner, 1974, p. 154).

For Skinner, consciousness is a social product resulting from a verbal community that arranges contingencies under which we not only see an object or event but also see that we see it. We are a part of a verbal community that insists that we become aware of what we are doing and why we are doing it. Further, the verbal community insists that we talk about it. We are conditioned to observe ourselves; otherwise, we would have no reason to do so. "Our physical world, then, generates both physical action and the physical conditions within the body to which an individual responds when a verbal community arranges the necessary contingencies" (Skinner, 1974, p. 220).

We are conscious in the sense of being under stimulus control. As with all other animals, we feel the pain caused by a painful stimulus. However, we are conscious—aware that we are feeling the feeling of pain—because of verbal contingencies. Different verbal communities reinforce different kinds and degrees of consciousness in its members.

In a sense, all behavior is unconscious until it is observed and analyzed. Moreover, unconscious behavior need not be observed to be effective. We may be unconsciously in pursuit of certain consequences, but our behavior is, nevertheless, best understood with reference to its consequences rather than its conscious or unconscious nature. The causality in behavior does not depend on awareness, so it makes little difference to the behaviorist observing a behavior whether that behavior is conscious or unconscious.

Importance of Role of Self-Concept

For Skinner, what many theorists refer to as self or personality is nothing more than a learned repertoire of behaviors, responses acquired through conditioning that are characteristic of a particular individual. Differences in self or personality are nothing more than differences in observed behavior. While complex, each self or personality is constructed, element by element, over a period of time. Skinner's view of the self or personality is elementalistic and in sharp contrast to the holistic views held by Rogers, May, and Perls (see Chapters 4, 5, and 6). For Skinner, subjectivity is irrelevant and nothing other than an explanatory fiction.

"The 'role a person plays in life' is a repertoire of behavior, not a 'self' or 'personality.' It is more than a structural concept because it implies an effect" (Epstein, 1980, p.154). It is clear from this statement that, while Skinner (1953; Epstein, 1980) accepts the phenomenon of self-awareness or self-knowledge, he does not attribute this phenomenon to introspective observation; rather, our knowledge of emotions, attitudes, values, and internal states consists of the inferences we draw from our direct observations of our overt behaviors and/or from the particular situational context in which these behaviors occur. Self-awareness or self-knowledge, then, is a description of our overt behavior—hence, a function of our reinforcement history—and self-concept is neither a construct nor structure of personality but a label we employ to describe our observations. Our self-concept will change as we add new behaviors to our repertoire. When, for example, a certain behavior is consistently reinforced, we are likely to emit that behavior and then begin to see ourselves as persons who are likely to engage in that behavior.

The idea of a self-concept is unnecessary in the functional analysis of behavior. As a mentalistic concept—that is, neither observable nor controllable—it is better ignored or, at best, viewed with caution because it can be misleading and used to account for variability that can be discovered more accurately in the contingencies of reinforcement. As an empiricist, Skinner is unwilling to grant a role to unseen and unseeable hypothetical constructs. He prefers to limit his study to manifest behavior.

Psychological and/or Reality Environments

Skinner's stance on this issue is both strong and explicit. Perceiving is considered a behavior, and behavior can be explained solely in terms of objective cause-and-effect relationships. To introduce subjective experience—the way we think and feel about incoming stimuli or outgoing responses—is to supplant the external cause of behavior with an explanatory fictional concept. Causality in behavior does not depend on perception. Subjective inner experience is not only irrelevant in Skinner's approach to behavior but also a major source of confusion in contemporary psychology. Once an inner subjective experience is accepted as an explanation for behavior, there is no longer any motivation to look further for the true external causes.

In short, Skinner's commitment to objectivity is unequivocal. We learn to perceive in the same way we learn to respond to other stimuli: because of the environmental contingencies of which they are a part.

Uniqueness and/or Commonality

Accused of dehumanizing humans, Skinner (1971) reminds his accusers that "no theory changes what it is a theory about; man remains what he has always been" (p. 206). In *About Behaviorism* (1974), Skinner tells us, "Nothing about the position taken in this book questions the uniqueness of the human species, but the uniqueness is inherent in the sources" (p. 225). We are, in every sense, the locus of these sources, that "point at which many genetic and environmental conditions come together in joint effect" (Skinner, 1971, p. 168).

Every cell in our body is uniquely our own, and we share our personal histories with no other organism. We have each occupied a unique space in this world, making it impossible for anyone else to be subjected to exactly the same reinforcements. Moreover, the gap that exists between each one of us and all others grows with time. With each hour, day, week, and month, we become more uniquely ourselves. Taken a step further, because we act on the environment in our unique ways, we make a difference to the world; we are important.

GOALS OF BEHAVIOR MODIFICATION

The operant behaviorists' approach to counseling and psychotherapy is based on clinical applications of Skinner's principles of behavior. While these applications have moved from the laboratory to various clinical, agency, school, and industrial settings, their goals and methods are the same as those established by Skinner in the laboratory: the scientific prediction and control of behavior through contingency management. Behavior modification as a therapy, then, is a compilation of principles and techniques about how to change behavior. It is not a comprehensive therapeutic theory. Further, the principles of learning are value-free, giving the therapist no specific directions about what behavior should be modified or who should do it. These principles also do not answer the questions of why or when behavior modification should occur. For those in the field of therapy, these questions center on individual and cultural values, and the answers must come from the therapist and that individual's professional organizations (the APA or American Association for Counseling and Development (AACD), formerly APGA, for example) or state licensing boards.

For most behavior modification therapists, the client, in a highly interactive process with the therapist, ultimately decides the desired outcomes or goals of therapy. As in most therapies, active client participation is essential. The goals of operant therapy must be explicitly defined in terms of concrete, overt, measurable behaviors, and the process of translating the amorphous feelings of anxiety, depression, helplessness, anger, guilt, fear, and frustration into clearly defined goals for behavioral change can be difficult, especially for those clients who attribute the source of their problems to their feelings.

After an effective relationship has been established, problem assessment and formulation are usually the first steps in therapy proper and involve high degrees of listening and empathy skills on the part of the therapist (see "Therapeutic Relationship"). A thorough understanding of a client's problem, as outlined by Cormier and Cormier (1979), includes the following points:

Some structuring: An explanation of the purpose of problem formulation (see "Structuring and Client Expectations");

Identification and selection of problem concerns: A discussion of general problem situations to obtain a complete picture of the problem, followed by a selection of the concerns that are the most troublesome or difficult, and last, setting priorities and pinpointing the problem that brought the client to counseling;

Identification of present problem behaviors;

Identification of antecedent conditions—overt, covert, past, and present—contributing to the problem;

Identification of consequent contributing conditions—overt, covert, positive, negative, immediate, and delayed;

Identification of client coping skills;

Identification of problem intensity—extent, frequency, and duration of problem behaviors.

When both client and therapist thoroughly understand the client's problem, the process of goal selection begins. The importance of establishing clearly defined goals that accurately reflect specific areas of client concern cannot be overemphasized. Outcome goals not only clarify the client's initial expectations of counseling by delineating what can and what cannot be accomplished in counseling but also specify the direction of therapy. In addition, the goals of therapy establish the techniques, strategies, and evaluation procedures. In the following excerpt, a behavior therapist assists a client in determining and prioritizing the goals of therapy.

Therapist: During our meeting last week, you talked about your dissatisfaction with your life since your husband's death 2 years ago, particularly your difficulty making decisions and your hesitation about going anywhere or doing anything other than the normal daily chores of keeping house and preparing meals. I wonder if today we might begin defining some goals for therapy—specific changes that you think might help you to improve your situation. Goals will give us something specific to work for and help us to measure our progress in therapy. How does that sound to you?

Client: Well, I have to do something. I don't want things to go on as they are now. I just don't know what to do (eyes downcast, voice barely audible).

Therapist: I realize that when I told you last week that ultimately the selection of goals would be your decision, you became rather anxious. One of your problems right now seems to center on your difficulty with making decisions. But there may be other changes you might wish to consider, and I think I can help you with this.

Client: I hope so. I could use some help right now (brief laughter, but appears uncomfortable).

Therapist: Let's begin by focusing on how you would like things to be different. Let's suppose we're successful and you've made the changes you want to make. How would you be different? What would you be doing then that you aren't doing now?

Client: I'm not sure. It was always easier when Jim was alive. If something came up that had to be decided on, we could talk it out. I made most of the decisions then, but I had somebody to talk to. Now I'm all alone. If I have to make a decision now there's no one to talk to about it. I worry all the time that I'm going to make the wrong decision.

Therapist: I know it's very hard for you right now to look beyond the present. Let's see if we can't improve on that. You told me last week that one of your grandsons was married out of state recently and that you couldn't attend. You've never met his wife. Is that right?

Client: Yes, that's right. I've seen some of the wedding pictures and she's written to me, but I've never met her.

Therapist: O.K. Now, what I want you to do is to close your eyes and imagine, as vividly as you can, that one full year has passed. It's now March of next year. We've been successful in therapy and you've accomplished all your goals. Imagine that you're home sitting in your favorite chair. Everything is going well for you now, and you feel rested and relaxed. Have you got that?

Client: Yes, I think so.

Therapist: Good. Suddenly the doorbell rings. It startles you, and you push yourself out of the chair, wondering who it might be. When you open the door, there's a young woman. You can't be certain, but you think it might be your grandson's wife. She says, "Mrs. Gregory?" You answer, "Yes." She smiles, and says, "I'm Mrs. Gregory, too." You realize you were right; she is the young bride you saw in the wedding pictures. She then apologizes for dropping in on you unexpectedly but explains that she was on her way to her husband's new base, and since you were just off the route she was traveling, her husband suggested she stop to see you. Are you still with me?

Client: Yes (spoken softly).

Therapist: Good. Now, here's a person who is meeting you for the first time. She didn't know you a year ago when you were having all those problems. Describe for me, if you will, what she would see you doing. How would you be different? How would your situation be different?

Client: You mean how would I be if I didn't have the problems I have now?

Therapist: That's exactly what I mean. What would she tell your grandson about her visit with you when she saw him again if she had only seen you after you had successfully worked through the problems you have now?

Client: Well, I suppose she would tell him that I was relaxed and that I really seemed happy to see her.

Therapist: Go on. What else would she tell your grandson?

Client: Well, she would tell him that I seemed interested in what they were doing, that I asked a lot of questions about him. She would tell him that I seemed to be very busy and had a lot of friends. She would probably tell him that I took her out to dinner at a nice restaurant so we had more time to talk.

Therapist: O.K. How would that be different than if she dropped in unexpectedly this afternoon?

Client: Well if she came today, she'd find me down—you know, worried and depressed, poor company. I'd be wrapped up in my own problems. I wouldn't be as interested in her or in what she and my grandson were doing. I certainly wouldn't feel like going out to dinner. I wouldn't feel like doing much of anything.

Therapist: All right. Do you see anything from this that helps you to decide what you want out of therapy?

Client: It would help if I didn't worry so much about myself, if I could get interested in something besides my own problems. It would help if every decision didn't seem so big, so hard to make. It would help if I had someone to talk to once in awhile, maybe someone who knows how it feels to be alone. It would help if I got out of the house more.

Therapist: Let's see, I think you've just listed a number of goals we might consider further. First, you would like to worry less about yourself and your situation. Second, you would like to be able to make decisions better than you do now. Third, you would like to cultivate interest in other people and things. Fourth, you would like to get out of the house more. And, fifth, perhaps this is related to four, you'd like to find some-one you could talk to, someone who would understand you. Does that seem about right to you?

Client: Yes. Like I said before, I've got to do something. I don't want to go on like it is now.

Therapist: What do you think are some of the things you would have to do to accomplish some of these goals?

Client: I'm not sure. I suppose I'd have to stop thinking of my problems all the time. I'd have to make decisions and then stop worrying about maybe making the wrong decisions. I'd have to find places to go and things to do that would interest me.

Therapist: I wonder, what might be some of the risks if you decided to work on any of these changes? Would there be any disadvantages to working on any of these goals?

Client: I can't see any disadvantage in not worrying all the time, and I can't see any disadvantage in being able to make decisions without getting so nervous that I feel sick. I'm nervous when I have to decide something, even some little thing, and I'm nervous after I decide for fear that I made the wrong decision. I can't see any disadvantages of having someone to talk to occasionally. My kids are too far away; I can't call them every time something comes up that requires a decision. They have their lives to live, too.

Therapist: I agree, there may be few or no disadvantages, but I can see a few risks. As long as you sit around the house worrying, you don't have to do anything. Let me explain. As long as you worry about a decision, you can postpone having to make that decision. As long as you stay in the house, you don't have to go out and look for something that interests you enough to become involved. By staying in the house, you don't have to look for someone willing and interested in talking to you when you want to talk. The risk I'm referring to here is the risk of changing your recent life-syle. It will require work and effort, both of which you're avoiding right now—rather successfully, too, I might add. Do you think you can do this?

Client: I think I can, if I know what I'm supposed to do. I don't like things the way they are now.

Therapist: Good. I think you can, too. So, let's see if we can't decide on which of the changes you've mentioned we should begin to work on first. Which seems most important to you?

Client: The worry. I would like to begin working on the worry first. I think if I could stop worrying so much I could do some of the other things. I mean, if I didn't worry so much maybe the other things wouldn't seem so terrible.

Therapist: Fine. That's where we will begin.

Characteristics of behavioral outcome goals are explicitness and attainability. It should be remembered, however, that the client has decision primacy in goal selection. The therapist must decide, on the basis of the client's goals and his or her therapeutic skills, whether or not he or she can help the client attain the goals selected. Major reservations at this point could lead to a re-evaluation of the client's goals, referral to another therapist, or termination. In either case, the counselor's reasons should be explicit and fully revealed to the client.

As with problem formulation, the goals of therapy must be behaviorally and individually specific and include the conditions under which the goal behavior is to occur, the level or extent of the behavior, an identification and hierarchical arrangement of subgoals, and client commitment to behavior management efforts.

THERAPEUTIC PROCESS: METHODS AND TECHNIQUES

Therapeutic Relationship

While the behavioristic conceptualization of the therapeutic relationship is different from that of many of the counseling theories presented in this book, it it certainly no less important. The therapeutic relationship is not, for example, the essence of therapy as it is in Rogers's person-centered therapy (see Chapter 4), nor is it sufficient for therapy. It cannot be used to bring about behavior change or solve client problems. Indeed, in one of his notes, Skinner (1980) argues that it cannot be used at all since, if genuine, the relationship cannot be turned on or off at will for reinforcement purposes. For Skinner (Epstein, 1980), "it is the contingencies that establish the relation" (p. 262).

Still, most behavior therapists support the importance of the therapist's demonstration of accurate listening, acceptance, understanding, concern, and respect for the client. Cormier and Cormier (1979) suggest that authenticity and spontaneity are potent characteristics of effective therapists. Indeed, they define effective therapeutic relationships from the counselor's viewpoint as "those in which counselors are able to demonstrate their skills without being preoccupied with those skills or themselves" (p. 10). Preoccupation inhibits relating; spontaneity enhances it. Thus, while the relationship between the client and therapist alone cannot be used to solve the client's problems, it is a potential vehicle to foster trust, increase verbal communication, and enhance reinforcement. Overall, then, it is a facilitative factor in producing client change.

It is essential that the therapist spontaneously demonstrate accurate listening, acceptance, empathic understanding, concern, and respect for the client, particularly in the initial stages of therapy during problem assessment and formulation. Active participation is encouraged and self-management is emphasized. Moreover, the way the therapist delivers these skills appears to be as important as having them.

Initial Procedures and Strategies

Initiating Therapy.   Therapy proper, or the treatment phase of therapy, rests on the foundation built by the client and therapist in the early counseling sessions. During the first phase of therapy, a therapeutic relationship is initiated, the client's presenting problem is functionally assessed and behaviorally formulated, client expectations are explored and clarified, specific behavioral outcomes are defined, and a mutual agreement and commitment to enter the next phase of therapy are confirmed. Client involvement, essential in every phase of operant therapy, is especially crucial in the beginning sessions since these are where the pattern is set for future sessions.

Structuring and Client Expectations.   Experience indicates that initial client expectations can have either a positive or negative effect on the therapeutic process. While a moderately positive level of client expectation can enhance the probability of therapeutic change, extreme expectations, whether high or low, are often deleterious to the outcome of therapy. Excessively high expectations are usually impossible to realize. Excessively low expectations can be an indication of little or no incentive on the part of the client to participate actively and cooperatively in the therapeutic process.

Structuring—carefully delineating client and therapist roles—is one method of clarifying client expectations and may be employed throughout therapy as the need arises. By discovering the antecedent stimuli that cause current maladaptive behavior, explaining how that behavior was learned, and describing how relearning occurs in the therapeutic situation, the therapist can often correct the client's unrealistic expectations.

Establishing the goals of therapy is usually effective in clarifying the client's initial expectations of therapy. Clearly defined behavioral goals may help both the client and therapist anticipate what can and cannot be accomplished through this particular approach to therapy. Again, because client and therapist commitment is a part of the process of goal alignment, increased client motivation is a natural outcome.

Course of Therapy

While therapists who follow an operant behavioristic approach to counseling function as behavior modifiers and researchers, they are obligated by practical considerations of the therapeutic situation that are not present in the laboratory. Unlike experimental psychologists, they are attempting to help a client whose behavior is subject to simultaneous impacts from numerous uncontrolled environmental variables. Under the conditions of therapy, immediate action is often necessary because of their client's situation, whether or not validated techniques exist. The necessity for immediate action forces therapists to combine their knowledge of the principles of behavior with their therapeutic experiences and then act, using both objective data and educated intuition. Following a set of value-free behavioral principles that can exert both immediate and long-range influence on their clients, therapists who have adopted a behavioral approach must continually re-evaluate both the goals and techniques of therapy, not only for therapeutic effectiveness but also for social consequences.

Even though there are recognized differences, the process of therapy is similar to the experimental process. For example, steps may include:

Problem formulation, arrived at through a functional analysis;
Behavioral program planning and therapeutic procedures;
Execution of the plan;
Assessment or evaluation of therapeutic outcome.

While the stages of the therapeutic process of behavior modification appear discrete and separate, there is considerable overlap, and it is often necessary to return to reformulation of the problem and a revision of methods and techinques as the therapeutic relationship matures.

Therapy is terminated when the delineated desired behavioral outcomes are achieved, regardless of whether there is any understanding of how the outcomes were achieved. Control, not understanding, is the goal of behavior modification.

Just as there is no single theory of behavior therapy, there is no single set of behavioral methods or techniques accepted by all behavioral therapists. While operant conditioning is not distinctly separable from other learning theories, Skinner's operant paradigm is treated here as an indepedent therapeutic approach. The methods and techniques described in this section are thus limited to those most commonly employed by therapists who adhere closely to Skinner's operant reinforcement principles.

Behaviorally Oriented Interview. While the interview is not considered an objective method for gathering information required for a functional analysis of the client's behavior (see "Assessing Progress"), the therapist often relies on the interview when it is impractical or impossible to arrange for direct observation of the client's behavior in the natural environment. A fairly standard procedure is for the therapist to instruct the client on demonstrated methods of self-monitoring and directions for recording specific information about the ABCs of behavior control (antecedents, behaviors, and consequences) in a diary or pocket notebook. The client may also be provided a wrist counter or stopwatch to complete a freqency count for baseline assessment of a target behavior.

Self-management. The ultimate goal of every therapeutic approach is to provide clients with the techniques they need to control their behavior so they can be effective self-managers. Behavior modification is no exception. Although in the end all behavior, including self-controlling behavior, must be accounted for with variables from outside ourselves, we control ourselves, according to Skinner (1953, 1971), precisely as we would control the behavior of anyone else: "through the manipulation of variables of which behavior is a function" (p. 123–124). Interested in the client's right to participate actively in all phases of the therapeutic process, operant reinforcement therapists have developed and demonstrated self-controlling strategies for initiating and maintaining changes in a wide variety of behaviors.

Self-control programs are individually formulated to effect change for clients who are engaging in behaviors that are dysfunctional, self-defeating, or injurious or who are engaging in a desired behavior too infrequently. Examples of client problems in the first instance are eating to the point of obesity, excessive smoking or drinking, and indiscriminate sexual activity. Self-control strategies, or operant reinforcement programs, are designed to reduce the probability of these behaviors. Examples of client problems in the second instance are inability to speak on one's behalf, failure to exercise adequately, and fear of initiating social contacts. Self-control strategies here are planned to increase the probability of these responses. In therapy, clients may express the desire to work on a program that includes decreasing one response while, at the same time, increasing another. A self-control program for the obese client may, for example, include decreasing caloric intake by changing eating patterns while simultaneously burning a greater amount of calories by increasing exercise.

Behavior therapists using operant reinforcement are not only interested in how schedules of reinforcement determine behavior (see "Importance of Reward") but also in the role of self-management processes as clients act to alter the variables that affect their behavior. For Skinner (1953, 1971; Epstein, 1980), self-control is an exercise in manipulating the variables that determine one's behavior. Self-controlling manipulations might include behaviors such as physical restraint, physical aids, changing the stimuli that induce unwanted behavior or that make wanted behavior more probable, inducing emotional changes that are likely to assist with desired behavioral outcomes, avoidance of undesirable situations, or rewarding desired behavior while punishing undesired behavior. The self-management techniques are limited only by the number of variables the client and counselor can manipulate successfully.

The obese client discussed earlier may, for example, set a goal to lose two pounds a week for a period of ten weeks. To help himself reach this goal, he plans the number of calories he must reduce from his normal diet, a baseline he established from an earlier assessment of his present eating patterns. He decides to remove all unnecessary food from the house and not to purchase food that might be eaten conveniently or impulsively. He places a lock or an aversive sign on the refrigerator door to remind himself that he is not to eat between meals. He serves his meals on smaller plates, eats slowly, chews each bite thoroughly, and places his fork on the plate between bites. He decides, also, to take one five-minute break during each meal. He manipulates antecedent events by avoiding places or situations where snacking usually occurs. When he feels the urge to snack, he walks—this in addition to his regular exercise plan. He charts his weight every three days, rewards himself when he records a loss, and deprives himself of something he particularly enjoys when there is no loss or when he records a gain. As an additional incentive, he gives someone he trusts $200 he has saved for clothes with instructions to return $10 for each pound he loses toward the twenty-pound goal. In those weeks he has not lost two pounds, his friend donates the $20 to a designated charity.

In this example, both the positive reinforcements and aversive consequences are contingent on a specific weight loss. While the client serves as a contingency manager in most instances, the friend functions in this capacity in the last. Contact with others in the program may be helpful to some clients. Success often depends on accurate baseline data and a realistic plan. Charting progress during treatment may also be used to the client's advantage in this plan. The chart becomes an additional reinforcement when he is successful and a punishment when he is not. Complexity of the program depends on the sophistication and involvement of the client.

Token Economy.   Based on the principles of reinforcement and extinction, the token economy has been demonstrated as an effective operant approach in group environments. It has been employed successfully in institutional settings such as classrooms, resident care facilities, psychiatric hospitals, and correctional facilities.

In the token economy, tokens or points that can be exchanged for consumer items or privileges are presented to clients for specified desired behaviors. Undesirable behaviors go unrewarded or are set up on a cost basis. Initially, target behaviors scheduled for reinforcement focus on order and discipline. For example, single tokens might be awarded to clients who bathe at the designated time, brush their teeth, comb their hair, dress themselves properly, and make their beds. As clients' behaviors improve, reinforcement is increased to a much wider range of socially approved behaviors, and the tokens may be used to purchase a greater variety of goods and privileges. Clients may, for example, use their accumulated tokens to purchase desired consumer goods, acquire greater privacy, attend movies, and participate in field and shopping trips outside the institution.

The initial step in designing a token economy is the identification of clearly specified target behaviors—both those that are desired and to be acquired and those that are undesirable and to be extinguished. Staff involvement at this point is necessary, first to establish baseline behaviors and, second, to facilitate interest and cooperative participation in the program. Step two focuses on the definition of currency. Although usually simple, the resources of the institution and the nature of the group being considered usually dictate the form that tangible tokens will take. Items such as poker chips, points on a tally sheet, punched cards or tickets, and gold stars have been used to establish successful token economies. In the final step, an exchange system is devised. Goods and privileges must be identified and their exchange rate determined. For tokens to maintain their reinforcement and incentive value, their exchange rate and the variety of goods and privileges they may be used to purchase must be increased as clients' behaviors improve.

In addition to improved behavior are the following advantages of implementing a token economy:

1. Once the behaviors have been specified and the program designed, training the staff to participate in a token economy is relatively easy and requires little time and expense.
2. The use of tokens promotes immediacy between the client's response and tangible reinforcement.
3. Tokens serve as positive reinforcements.
4. By manipulating the rate of exchange, clients can be encouraged to work over extended periods of time for single, highly desired reinforcements.
5. By pairing the tokens with verbal reinforcements, the value of intrinsic motivation is enhanced.
6. A token economy is open to—indeed, facilitates—social reinforcement measures.
7. It is possible to select behaviors that are not normally reinforced by society.
8. By targeting behaviors that contribute to both the short- and long-term quality of life, it becomes obvious to clients and staff members that the program accomplishes more than simply controlling undesirable behavior.

9. The program is designed to ensure that modified behaviors generalize to life requirements outside the institutional setting, making the client's transition to the natural environment easier.

ASSESSING PROGRESS

Assessment assumes an especially significant and continual role in behavioral modification. The information, used by the client and therapist to formulate the target problems for therapeutic focus and by the client for goal selection, emerges from a thorough functional analysis of the client's present situation. From this same process the therapist uncovers the information he or she needs to determine the specific methods and techniques of therapy. Finally, the assessment process is used throughout therapy to evaluate the effectiveness of the therapeutic plan. Arguing for the logical relationship of assessment and the objectives of therapy in the initial phase of therapy, Lazarus (1976) informs us: "Faulty problem identification (inadequate assessment) is probably the greatest impediment to successful therapy" (p. 14).

If possible, behavioral assessment is based on direct and objective observations of the client's behavior as it occurs in the natural environment. A number of sophisticated behavioral observation rating procedures have been developed and tested over the years to measure and record the frequency, intensity, and duration of specific behaviors. Many are designed also to record behavioral antecedents (those events immediately preceding the behavior being measured) and the consequences of the behavior, both to the client and all others present at the time. Concentrating on the how, when, where, and what of behavior can assist clients in discovering the behavioral referents necessary to replace their usual global impressions and feelings.

When a client's behavior has been carefully and directly observed and the specific goals of therapy have been behaviorally defined, therapeutic effectiveness is not difficult to evaluate. The severity of the client's target problems at the time of provisional behavioral analysis can be compared with an analysis of severity at any point in therapy, including termination of treatment.

FINAL COMMENTARY

While Skinner's work focused on the behavior of lower animals, his simple and precise reinforcement principles have had significant impact on the thinking and investigations of numerous researchers and practitioners in a variety of disciplines, particularly in the areas of psychopathology, education, and social engineering. Psychiatrists, psychologists, counselors, psychiatric

FIGURE 10.2 A Schematic Analysis of Skinner's Stand on the Basic Issues

Biological Determinants	▮▮▮▮	Social Determinants
Commonality	▮▮▮	Uniqueness
Conditioning	▮▮▮	Freedom
Early Development	▮▮▮	Continuous Development
Psychological Environment	▮▮	Reality Environment
Unconscious Determinants	▮▮▮▮	Conscious Determinants

Importance of Group Membership	Group reinforcement contingencies significantly outweigh individual contingencies, and the larger the group, the more powerful its impact on the individual. Different groups reinforce different response repertoires and each group requires conformity of its members. The group is important in the transmitting of rule-governed behavior.
Explanation of Learning	Environmental contingencies (stimuli, responses, and consequences) determine what we learn; and we learn that which satisfies certain contingencies of reinforcement. Learning is cumulative, and patterns of responses become increasingly complex as we mature. Effective learning entails the ability to discriminate various stimuli and associate particular responses with particular stimuli.
Number and Weight Assigned to Motivational Concepts	Behavior is contingent on reinforcement histories. Inner motivational constructs are unscientific, contributing nothing to the prediction and control of behavior.
Importance of Reward	External reinforcement (that which is associated with or immediately follows an emitted response) influences both the acquisition and maintenance of behavior. Reinforcement may be positive or negative, primary or secondary, and different schedules of reinforcement have different effects on respondent learning.
Importance or Role of Self-Concept	Self-concept is an irrelevant, hypothetical construct that focuses on the unseen, uncontrollable—an introspective observation. Although self-awareness and self-knowledge are acceptable phenomena, they are but functions of reinforcement histories which describe overt behaviors. *Self* and *personality* are merely learned repertoires of behavior.

social workers, nurses, and teachers are attracted to a theory that is firmly grounded in and supported by empirical data, unencumbered by excess concepts and assumptions, and relatively easy to apply in a broad spectrum of human difficulties. As a result, behavior modification became a major force in the helping and teaching professions, reaching full expression about 1965.

Although somewhat conservative and less comprehensive than many of the therapies presented in this book, there is little question regarding the empirical validity, parsimoniousness, and heuristic value of Skinner's theory. And, although attacked by nearly every rival system, Skinner's theory of operant conditioning must also be rated highly for its applied value. In spite of the charges that operant control strategies are dangerous and diminish human freedom, many institutions have integrated Skinner's operant principles into their programs for helping clients change their behavior.

This chapter is limited to Skinner's theory of operant conditioning; however, it should be noted that behavioral counseling, like existential counseling, is not a single system. Certainly all behavior therapists emphasize the principles and techniques of respondent and operant conditioning, but few restrict themselves to these principles and techniques; rather, they draw as well on the theories of social learning therapy (see Chapter 9) and cognitive therapy (see Chapter 4). Lazarus (1976), spokesman for a multimodal approach to behavior therapy, encourages the therapist to reach beyond overt behavior to consider other mediating variables such as affective responses, sensory reactions, emotive imagery, cognitive processes, and the indications of appropriate medication.

REFERENCES AND SUGGESTED READINGS

Cormier, W., & Cormier, L.S. 1979. *Interviewing strategies for helpers, a guide to assessment, treatment, and evaluation.* Monterey, Calif.: Brooks/Cole.

Epstein, R., ed. 1980. *Notebooks, B.F. Skinner.* Englewood Cliffs, N.J.: Prentice-Hall.

Ferster, C.B., & Culberston, S.A. 1982. *Behavior principles,* 3rd ed. Englewood Cliffs, N.J.: Prentice-Hall.

Hilts, P.J. 1974. *Behavior mod.* New York: Harper's Magazine Press.

Lazarus, A.A. 1971. *Behavior therapy and beyond.* New York: McGraw-Hill.

Lazarus, A.A. 1976. *Multimodal behavior therapy* (with contributors). New York: Springer.

Martin, G., & Pear, J. 1983. *Behavior modification, what it is and how to do it,* 2nd ed. Englewood Cliffs, N.J.: Prentice-Hall.

O'Leary, K.D. & Wilson, G.T. 1975. *Behavior therapy, application and outcome.* Englewood Cliffs, N.J.: Prentice-Hall.

Rimm, D.C., & Masters, J.C. 1974. *Behavior therapy: techniques and empirical findings.* New York: Academic Press.

Rogers-Skinner Debates. (audio tapes). AACD, 5999 Stevenson Avenue, Alexandria, Virginia 22304.

Skinner, B.F. 1938. *The behavior of organisms.* New York: Appleton-Century-Crofts.

Skinner, B.F. 1948. *Walden two.* New York: Macmillan.

Skinner, B.F. 1953. *Science and human behavior.* New York: Macmillan.

Skinner, B.F. 1957a. *Verbal behavior.* New York-Appleton-Century-Crofts.

Skinner, B.F. 1957b. *Schedules of reinforcement* (with C. B. Ferster). New York: Appleton-Century-Crofts.

Skinner, B.F. 1968. *The technology of teaching.* New York: Appleton-Century-Crofts.

Skinner, B.F. 1969. *Contingencies of reinforcement, a theoretical analysis.* New York: Appleton-Century-Crofts.

Skinner, B.F. 1971. *Beyond freedom and dignity.* New York: Bantam Books.

Skinner, B.F. 1972. *Cumulative record, a selection of papers,* 3rd ed. New York: Appleton-Century-Crofts.

Skinner, B.F. 1974. *About behaviorism.* New York: Alfred A. Knopf.

Skinner, B.F. 1976. *Particulars of my life.* New York: McGraw-Hill.

Skinner, B.F. 1979. *The shaping of a behaviorist.* New York: Alfred A. Knopf.

Skinner, B.F. September 1983a. Origins of a behaviorist. *Psychology Today,* pp. 22–33.

Skinner, B.F. 1983b. *A matter of consequences.* New York: Alfred A. Knopf.

Skinner, B.F., & Vaughan, M.E. 1983. *Enjoy old age.* New York: W.W. Norton.

11

Conspectus of the Theories

A SINGLE CONCEPTUAL STRUCTURE comprised of eleven basic issues was used in this book to assist you with your examination, understanding, and evaluation of nine major psychotherapeutic orientations. In this chapter, that same conceptual structure serves to uncover similarities and differences in ideology, method, and technique as the theorists' positions on the eleven basic issues are reviewed. Although the focus of this chapter is on the similarities and differences of the nine theories, further comparisons, whether of substance or content, are encouraged and facilitated by a separate Table of Contents that traces each of the eleven basic issues across chapters.

BIOLOGICAL AND/OR SOCIAL DETERMINANTS

Few theorists of psychotherapy grant greater recognition to biology as a determinant of human behavior than Freud. For Freud, human nature is essentially biological. What we become is largely a function of internal dynamics. We are motivated by innate instincts that are largely unconscious and constitute the total psychic energy available to operate all mental processes and functions. In contrast, while Adler, Ellis, Glasser, Perls, and Rogers recognize biological determinants, they believe that through evolution most basic animal instincts, along with their fixed, predetermined directives, have become supplanted by or subordinated to innate possibilities or biological predispositions that need not always be followed and may, in certain instances, require conscious development.

While the belief in a biological predisposition to actualize innate potentials is central to Rogers's theory, he is convinced that actualization can occur only in a facilitative environment. Perls tells us that our innate needs naturally rise to awareness, but like Rogers, he maintains their fulfillment requires contact with others and the world. Glasser also speaks of personalized and controlled needs that must be met responsibly through the reality of the environment. Ellis claims that we inherit a brain that enables us to think both rationally and irrationally but argues that we largely acquire our rational and irrational beliefs and values through social and cultural interaction. May, too, recognizes that we are biological beings; however, the fact that he considers us free beings in a world diminishes the role of biology as a determinant of behavior. According to these theorists, we possess inherent needs and are subject to certain environmental influences, but these factors alone do not determine entirely what we do. As theorists and therapists, they are more concerned with how we perceive and evaluate our internal needs and the external events we encounter in our environments (see "Psychological and/or Reality Environment").

Social determinants play a particularly significant role in the theory of Adler, for whom social interest is an intrinsic characteristic of human nature and, as such, a measure of mental health. Ellis tells us that biological and cultural determinants coexist as a dimension of the complex, unified system that is human personality and describes us as biosocial beings. Bandura and Skinner recognize the importance of biology but largely ignore it in practice in favor of certain principles of learning. To Skinner, we are reactive biological beings who respond solely to external reinforcement principles. Bandura agrees that nearly all behavior is learned but, unlike Skinner, asserts that learning occurs as a result of a continuous and reciprocal triadic interaction between personal, behavioral, and environmental determinants.

It would seem, then, that of the nine theorists reviewed here, most agreed that it is naive to consider only heredity or only environment as the primary determinant of behavior. The ideal fusion of this issue, it appears, is the study of different hereditary factors in interaction with different environmental stimuli. A graphic overview of the theorists' stances on this issue is illustrated in Figure 11–1.

CONSCIOUS AND/OR UNCONSCIOUS DETERMINANTS

Both Freud and Skinner take extreme positions on this issue. For Freud, the unconscious is by far the deepest and most significant stratum of the three levels of consciousness. Moreover, he proclaims that our unconscious is comprised of basic psychobiological motives that create most of our major problems. Skinner, in contrast, finds the unconscious little more than speculation, a presumption impossible to validate scientifically; he, therefore, sees neither need nor reason to ascribe any human behavior to the unconscious.

Adler, Ellis, Glasser, May, Perls, and Rogers believe that human behavior is purposive, and collectively they view the unconscious as something we are unable or unwilling to formulate clearly or that we either do not understand or withhold from understanding. Both Rogers and Perls refer to an innate bodily wisdom that, for the healthy, may offer intuitive—hence, unconscious—directives. In both instances this unconscious wisdom is part of

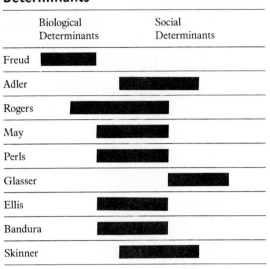

FIGURE 11.1 **Biological versus Social Determinants**

	Biological Determinants	Social Determinants
Freud	██	
Adler		██
Rogers	██	
May	██	
Perls	██	
Glasser		██
Ellis	██	
Bandura	██	
Skinner	██	

the organismic tendency toward being (Perls) or becoming (Rogers). May's concept of the unconscious is the repression of potentialities for knowing and experiencing; he, as many whose theories are teleological, rejects any hypothesis of the unconscious as an internal state or entity.

Nearly all here-now therapists, which includes Rogers, May, Perls, Glasser, and Ellis, work toward awareness of present cognitions, feelings, experiences, and actions. For these theorists, unconscious motivations, while sometimes evident in abnormal behavior, play a relatively minor role in the lives of normal, healthy persons. Indeed, awareness in and of the present is central to the theory of Gestalt therapy, and Perls created rules for therapy that help clients to develop the means to attain greater awareness that can then be employed to work through impasses, make interpretations, and resolve unfinished business from the past. Awareness and ownership of present feelings and behavior are criteria employed by Rogers to assess therapeutic progress. A graphic view of the theorists' positions on this issue appears in Figure 11–2.

CONDITIONING AND/OR FREEDOM TO CHOOSE

Freud and Skinner are strict determinists. Neither holds a place in his theory for concepts such as free will, choice, self-determinism, or self-actualization.

FIGURE 11.2   Unconscious versus Conscious Determinants

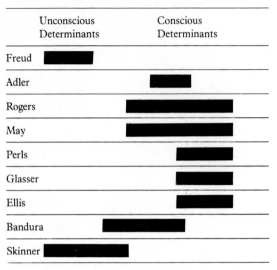

	Unconscious Determinants	Conscious Determinants
Freud	■	
Adler		■
Rogers		■
May		■
Perls		■
Glasser		■
Ellis		■
Bandura		■
Skinner	■	

Freedom is an illusion. Cognitions, emotions, and behaviors are but links in a chain of causally related phenomena, determined largely by unconscious instinctual forces (Freud) or antecedent events (Skinner). Thus, while we may appear to ourselves and others as active, choosing beings, our behavior is the result of internal drives (Freud) or external reinforcements (Skinner).

Adler subordinates causal determinants of behavior to a creative self that enables us to choose the opinions and attitudes we hold toward our heredity and environment, thus transcending their influences. Rogers writes of an experiential freedom, an integral part of our inherent actualizing tendency that permits us to think independently, live authentically, and determine our values and directions. May's stance on this issue is clear: we are literally condemned to freedom and responsibility; living and choosing are synonymous. Still, May is quick to remind us that this does not imply that there are no limits or restrictions, because he asserts that we must accept the ground of our existence, including the limits of body, intelligence, social controls, illness, and death. Perls views us as capable, autonomous, responsible beings as long as we are aware and knowing in the present. According to Perls we choose what we accept and reject, what we think and feel, what we trust and value, what we demand and respect, what we are aware of and attend to, and what we deny and avoid. Ellis also maintains that we possess the potential for a wide range of existential freedom, and with hard work and long practice, we can choose to develop rational sensitivity that, at least to a limited degree, permits us to transcend our biological and experiential antecedents.

Bandura's position on this issue is one of reciprocal determinism. While we are definitely influenced by the antecedents and consequences of our behavior, we mediate these influences and consequences through our cognitive processes. Thus, although we cannot be considered cause independent of our behavior and environment, we also cannot be considered simple reactions to environmental influence. The positions of the nine theorists on the issue are represented graphically in Figure 11–3.

EARLY AND/OR CONTINUOUS DEVELOPMENT

Practically every therapeutic approach acknowledges the importance of the formative years on human development. However, of the nine theorists presented in this book, Freud and Skinner place the greatest emphasis on the continuity of development. Their theories clearly imply that events that occur in the present are systematically related to events that took place in the past because we learned patterns of behavior in the past that determine our present reactions to environmental stimuli. Further, they assert that development is a lawful and consistent process.

In contrast, Ellis, Glasser, Perls, and to some extent, Rogers, explicitly stress lack of continuity—hence, the lack of predictability—in development. These theorists emphasize the relative independence of functioning adults

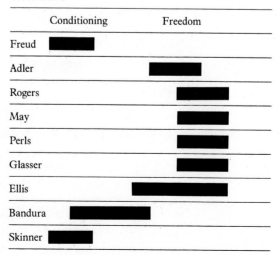

FIGURE 11.3 Conditioning versus Freedom

from the events of infancy or childhood. Adler, Ellis, May, Perls, and Rogers endow us with the existential freedom to choose our attitudes toward any event of the past—thus, the power to transcend the dysfuctional influences of that event in the present. Glasser gives us the capacity to change our behavior that, in turn, changes past feelings and attitudes.

In brief, while we are not immune to early childhood experiences, neither are we immutably shaped by them. The majority of these theorists believes that it is possible in theory to consider both the effects of early experiences and the immediacy of the present in attempts to explain present human behavior (see Figure 11–4).

PSYCHOLOGICAL AND/OR REALITY ENVIRONMENTS

This issue creates a dilemma for all theorists of counseling and psychotherapy: How can we possibly know the absolute nature of reality? Our personal realities are unique and private constructions. While the theorists agree that survival depends on our ability to recognize and adapt to a physical and cultural reality, some, whether in theory or practice, avoid a reality environment as a determinant of behavior. We have only our perceptions of reality to guide us, and our perceptions are limited by imperfect senses and are influenced by individual experiential histories and current expectations.

FIGURE 11.4   Early Development versus Continuous Development

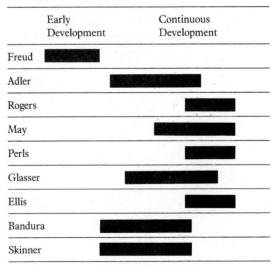

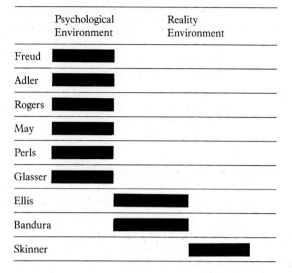

FIGURE 11.5 Psychological Environment versus Reality Environment

	Psychological Environment	Reality Environment
Freud	■■■■	
Adler	■■■■	
Rogers	■■■■	
May	■■■■	
Perls	■■■■	
Glasser	■■■■	
Ellis		■■■■
Bandura		■■■■
Skinner		■■■■

Rogers tells us that we perceive and attend to what is congruent with our self-concepts. Bandura argues that our current understanding and expectations about ourselves, our behavior, and the world determine our perceptions. Glasser claims that our perceptions are detemined by the controlling stations of our minds. May believes our perceptions are influenced by our individual streams of consciousness and personal value systems. Similarly, Ellis insists that we filter our perceptions of reality through our personal belief systems. Perls maintains we attend to the figure. And Freud and Skinner assert that our past experiences shape our current perceptions. While none is a pure phenomenologist in the sense that perception is the sole deteminant of behavior, all are to some degree phenomenological. They vary in the emphasis they give the psychological environment, from Rogers and May, for whom phenomenology is a central concept, to Skinner, who, at least in practice, ignores this issue entirely by concentrating on the principles of operant reinforcement (see Figure 11–5).

UNIQUENESS AND/OR COMMONALITY

A phenomenon recognized by most theorists of counseling and psychotherapy is that, while we hold much in common with others of our species, we all sense and experience our uniqueness; further, just as we are aware that we are duplicates of no other, we are equally certain that we are not the same persons we were in the past. Given this recognized phenomenon of a sensed unique-ness, the issue is not so much a question of uniqueness versus commonality but a question of emphasis. Adler, Glasser, May, Perls, and Rogers grant uniqueness central emphasis in their theories. Ellis proposes unconditional self-acceptance; he views self-rating and self-evaluating as irrational and dys-functional. Skinner explicitly denies the crucial significance of this issue, strongly asserting that what most theorists consider the self is nothing more than a repertoire of acquired behaviors and, as with all acquired behaviors, subject to the principle of learning (see Figure 11–6).

IMPORTANCE OF ROLE OF SELF-CONCEPT

Self-concept, whether viewed as an association of psychological processes or an accumulation of attitudes and feelings, occupies a conspicuous or central role in many theories of counseling and psychotherapy. For May, Perls, and Rogers, the concept of self emerges from an awareness of being or becoming; in their theories, self is both process and entity and gives our behavior unity and stability. For Glasser, the concept of self is identified with either success or failure. In Adler's theory the creative self enables us to rise above the in-fluences of our biology and environment. We creatively use the influences of our biology and environment to construct our unique styles of life. Bandura prefers the term, *self-efficacy*, but as with person-centered therapy, a major

FIGURE 11.6 Commonality versus Uniqueness

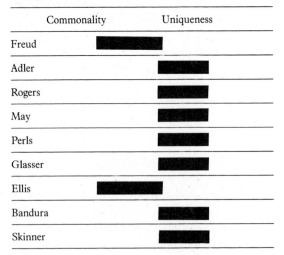

	Commonality	Uniqueness
Freud	██████████	
Adler		██████
Rogers		██████
May		██████
Perls		██████
Glasser		██████
Ellis	██████████	
Bandura		██████
Skinner		██████

goal of social learning therapy is strengthening the client's belief in his or her self-efficacy.

While Ellis recognizes the influence of self-concept on behavior, he strongly asserts that self-rating (in the sense of rating one's essence or personhood) is irrational; we are, after all, only—but totally—human. Skinner's conception of learning and behavior focuses almost entirely on reinforcement; thus, with self defined as simply a repertoire of learned behaviors, the self or self-concept plays a minor role in his theory.

NUMBER AND WEIGHT ASSIGNED TO MOTIVATIONAL CONCEPTS

Adler, Rogers, Perls, and Glasser explain motivation with a single, global construct. For Adler, it is a striving toward superiority, perfection, and completion. Rogers calls his motivational concept the actualizing tendency of the organism, the need to become fully functioning. Perls's theory focuses on the organism's need to strive for wholeness, an integration of thinking, feeling, and behaving. And Glasser refers to a need for success identity.

Skinner, consistent with his experimental approach, ignores any internal, unconscious drives or needs; however, he, too, subscribes to an abbreviated set of motivational concepts based on operant reinforcement principles. Freud's complex theory of psychoanalysis is at the other end of the continuum. Literally thousands of instinctual urges and drives press for fulfillment by creating an intolerable tension in the id.

EXPLANATION OF LEARNING

Concern with the learning process in the theories of counseling and psychotherapy varies considerably. At one end of the continuum there are the detailed explanations of Bandura and Skinner, and at the opposite end is May, who offers only a general treatment of the learning process. Freud, Perls, and Rogers are satisfied to view learning in terms of global principles that govern all behavior. For Freud, learning occurs through the establishment of cathexes. Still, as Hall and Lindzey (1978) point out, "although there may be some neglect of the learning process, there is an abundance of interest in the products of learning" (p. 684).

IMPORTANCE OF GROUP MEMBERSHIP

While none of the theorists fails to recognize the importance of the primary group on early development, only Freud views the formative years in the family as critical. Deficiencies that occur during early stages of development are likely to cause difficulty during adult years. For Freud, the child is the father of the man—hence, the child's early relationships with members of the family group are crucial. Adler also stresses the importance of family relationships on early development. The mother, especially, is responsible for the child's development of social interest, the primary measure of mental health in Adler's theory. In addition, Adler asserts that during this highly significant period of the child's life, unconscious life goals and unique styles of life are developed.

Rogers, May, Perls, Glasser, and Bandura ascribe responsibility to the primary group for meeting the innate needs of the developing child. For Rogers, a most significant need is the need for positive regard; for Perls, it is the need for personal contact and interaction required for meeting physiological and psychological needs; for May, the sense of identity and consciousness; for Glasser, the need for identity; and for Bandura, the need for modeling necessary for most early learning and the actualization of potential.

Group membership continues in importance as we move from the formative years into adulthood, and Rogers views the encounter group as an opportunity to provide growth experiences, particularly for those who experience difficulty adjusting to change, clarifying values, overcoming feelings of depersonalization or alienation, establishing interpersonal relationships, or developing self-reliance.

While Skinner is convinced that it is the individual who acts, he is equally certain that the reinforcement of group contingencies easily outweighs the total consequences that can be generated by its individual members acting alone. So, although Skinner attributes less influence to groups as determinants of behavior, he recognizes that we can enhance the probability and increase the strength of reinforcement by joining a group.

Bandura has demonstrated that we move toward those groups whose members we perceive share our interests and values. Further, he asserts we give and receive mutual reinforcement to preexisting bents through our group affiliations. For Bandura, then, groups partly determine the potentialities we cultivate and actualize.

IMPORTANCE OF REWARD

Theorists vary considerably on the stance they take on this issue. Skinner assigns reward (or reinforcement) the greatest significance; indeed, principles of operant reinforcement are the basis of his theory. According to Skinner, all learning is attributable to the contingencies of reinforcement.

Both Ellis and Bandura view reward as an important ingredient of learning and an integral part of therapy. Unlike Skinner, however, they grant us the uniquely human capacity for anticipatory thought and give us the capacity to shape conditions for our own purposes.

For Rogers, May, and Perls, external rewards are suspect. These theorists are concerned primarily with internal reward—that inner sense of satisfaction or gratification that comes with all experiences that facilitate the innate actualizing tendency. Similarly, Glasser defines those experiences that fulfill our identity needs as inherently rewarding. Internal reward is implicit in Freud's concept of the pleasure principle, as well as in the reciprocal relationships in the three major systems of the psyche. Gratification of id's instinctual needs is innately rewarding.

GOALS OF THERAPY

A comparison of nine theorists' resolutions of the eleven basic issues reveals nine distinct and widely divergent views of human nature. Given that the goals of therapy are rooted in the therorists' resolutions of these issues, it is not surprising that their goals for helping clients are equally diverse.

Freud, who believes the unconscious is responsible for most of our problems, would attempt to make the unconscious conscious: "where id is, there shall ego be." His goal, then, is to bring repressed material into consciousness. His major tool is interpretation, and his raw materials are free associations, dreams, and transference neuroses. His utlimate goal is reorganization.

Adler also makes use of interpretation, but his goal is a comprehensive understanding of his clients' life-styles, and to this end he gathers data on earliest memories, dynamics of the family constellation, childhood disorders, day and night dreams, exogenous factors, and basic mistakes. In addition, he offers encouragement and support as his clients consider available options or alternatives.

For Rogers, who is convinced that a facilitative relationship is both necessary and sufficient, therapeutic goals are directly related to the therapists' attitudes and focus entirely on the quality of the therapeutic relationship. May, also concerned with the encounter of two beings in the world, works toward a full awareness of existence and presence while simultaneously confronting guilt and anxiety.

Perls strives for awareness, his ultimate goal being the clients' discovery that they do not and never really did need a therapist. He frustrates his clients into an awareness that they possess the inner strength and personal resources to cope with the challenges of living. Further, by moving his clients through the polarities of the impasse and concentrating on the what and how of present behavior, Perls helps his clients realize that they can accept the risk of transcending rather than adapting to their problems.

Glasser's goal is to assist his clients' development of success identities. He accomplishes this through warm, personal involvement and realistically planned, responsible behavior. He is not hesitant to use his relationship with his client to motivate the client toward commitment and responsible action.

Ellis's ultimate goal is reorganization through cognitive awareness and philosophical restructuring. Thus, he teaches his clients the advantages and methods of rational sensitivity.

Primarily through modeling, Bandura assists his clients to learn desired or required behaviors and to extinguish maladaptive behaviors that lead to grief, difficulty, or negative consequences. Specific goals are determined by the client and agreed to by the therapist.

Skinner is interested in the scientific prediction and control of behavior. His goal, after careful problem assessment and formulation, is to help his clients change their behavior through contingency management.

THERAPEUTIC RELATIONSHIP

While all nine theorists recognize the potential influence of the therapist-client relationship on the process of therapy, they differ considerably on the therapeutic role of the relationship and on the emphasis they give it in theory and practice. According to Rogers, the intensely personal and subjective person-to-person relationship is the heart of the therapeutic process. He not only deems the therapeutic relationship necessary but also defines it sufficient when the therapist is perceived by the client as a person who is genuine, accepting, empathic, and caring. For Rogers, the therapeutic relationship is both means and end, both content and process of therapy.

May describes the therapeutic relationship as a full, selfless, sensitive presence that communicates a deep caring for the client's welfare and a continued faith in the client's potentialities. He looks at therapy as an encounter of two beings in the world together.

Perls agrees that the ideal therapeutic relationship is an I-Thou encounter. However, in the safety of the therapeutic relationship, he uses the encounter to frustrate his clients into working through unfinished business, remnants from the past that interfere with present functioning.

Glasser speaks of a warm, personal involvement without entanglement or the promotion of dependence. He believes therapists must genuinely present themselves as persons concerned with their clients' needs, plans, aspirations, and successes. With the single exception of clients' excuses, therapists must be accepting and understanding at all times.

Ellis believes that the therapist-client relationship contributes to a sound working alliance when the therapist communicates high credibility, professional competence, mutual respect, and a genuine interest in and commitment to helping the client change. Unlike Rogers, however, Ellis is convinced that while a sound client-therapist relationship is desirable, it is not always necessary and seldom ever sufficient. Should clients change an irrational belief to a rational one because they felt they needed the therapist's approval, the therapist would undoubtedly tell them that, while changing the belief was rational, the reason for making that change was not.

Bandura is interested in a therapeutic relationship that will enhance the value of the therapist as a model. He strives, therefore, to communicate warmth, concern, empathy, authenticity, authority, prestige, self-confidence, and self-assurance.

Skinner believes the ideal therapeutic relationship is one in which the therapist has expressed a spontaneous demonstration of accurate listening, acceptance, understanding, and respect. Since all behaviorists are active participants in the therapeutic process, they do wish to be perceived by the client as professionals who are knowledgeable, confident, and highly skilled.

FINAL COMMENTARY

While nine may seem a small sample in light of the many theories currently practiced (Parloff, 1976, for instance, reports 130 different approaches), they are sufficiently representative to demonstrate that, as a group, theories of counseling and psychotherapy are diverse. Even with a sample this small, differences, inconsistencies, and contradictions are evident, both within and across theoretical orientations. A sample of nine also appears to be sufficiently representative to support the need for some kind of rapprochement and consensus or, at the very least, the desirability for identification of commonalities—those therapeutic assumptions that appear to cross theoretical boundaries and contribute to successful therapy.

While rapprochement may seem desirable by some in the field (Goldfried, 1982; Lazarus, 1977; Patterson, 1980; Prochaska, 1979), numerous obstacles prevent consensus of any kind. Patterson (1980) contends that the theorists present the greatest obstacles. For theorists attempting to convince others of the efficacy of their approach, there are few, if any, advantages in highlighting similarities with other theories. Indeed, theorists strive to be unique; they focus on their differences. When they do acknowledge similarities, they attribute the effectiveness of their theories to their own unique concepts, goals, strategies, and techniques. Considerable significance is attached to the ownership of ideas. Again, Patterson (1980) points out that pitting one's ideas against all others is a well-established practice in this discipline. Strupp (in Goldfried, 1982) asserts that entrenched theories propagate a strong faith in their advocates while rapprochement calls "for dispassionate observation of the phenomena, critical analysis, and ingenuity" (p. viii).

Is rapprochement possible? Is it desirable? What is your view? Your answers will come, no doubt, as you begin to formulate and construct your theory of counseling and psychotherapy.

REFERENCES AND SUGGESTED READINGS

Burks, H.M., Jr., & Stefflre, B. 1979. *Theories of counseling,* 3rd ed. New York: McGraw-Hill.

Hall, C.S., & Lindzey, G. 1978. *Theories of personality,* 3rd ed. New York: John Wiley & Sons.

Goldfried, M.R. 1982. *Converging themes in psychotherapy: Trends in psychodynamic, humanistic, and behavioral practice.* New York: Springer.

Lazarus, A.A. 1971. *Behavior therapy and beyond.* New York: McGraw-Hill.

Lazarus, A.A. 1977. Has behavior therapy outlived its usefulness? *American Psychologist* 32: 550–554.

Parloff, M.B. February 1976. Shopping for the right therapy. *Saturday Review,* pp. 14–16.

Patterson, C.H. 1980. *Theories of counseling and psychotherapy,* 3rd ed. New York: Harper & Row.

Prochaska, J.O. 1979. *Systems of psychotherapy: a transtheoretical analysis.* Homewood, Ill.: Dorsey Press.

12

Developing a Personal Theory of Counseling

A THEORY OF COUNSELING and psychotherapy must be more than conjecture, inference, or assumption. It must be more than an assemblage of principles, hypotheses, and postulates. It must be more than a mixed assortment of cause-effect relationships. It must be more than a set of methods, strategies, or techniques. And while a theory must be personally relevant for the therapist employing it, it certainly must be more than a personal perspective or implicit ideology.

A theory of counseling and psychotherapy must be an attempt to organize and integrate all that is known about the human condition in an effort to answer the basic issues of human behavior. Moreover, a theory of counseling and psychotherapy must be presented in a meaningful, internally consistent framework that promotes descriptions, explanations, and expectations. Further, it must be accessible to systematic study so it can be questioned and tested—the greatest test being whether or not it will bear the trial of experience. It must be both functional and operational. Finally, a theory of counseling and psychotherapy must be a process that continues for the life of the therapist embracing it. Its consequences must continue to fit the realities of therapy; otherwise, it must be revised or discarded.

ALTERNATIVES

For student-counselors in search of a personal therapeutic stance, there appear to be three alternatives: (1) rejecting all theory and theorizing, (2) identifying with an existing theory, and (3) adopting an eclectic position to construct a theory of their own.

Rejecting All Theory and Theorizing

After exposure to a variety of conflicting theories and learning that even the most fundamental therapeutic principles and constructs are largely relative to a particular point of view when examined closely, it is natural for many counselor-candidates to experience some degree of theory aversion. It is also natural, during their aversive experience, for these students to entertain the notion of declaring a pox on all theorists' houses. Some, in fact, do just that, claiming that they will withhold allegiance until a scientifically validated theory has been established. The more thoughtful and foresighted students, however, quickly realize that little comfort is gained from retreating to a state of "know-nothingness." They recognize, too, that theirs is a profession of human concerns that cannot wait for *the* theory of counseling and psychotherapy to be discovered. Their clients are often in need of immediate intervention, attention, and assistance. These students also realize that, while there is a trend toward theoretical convergence, it is highly improbable that a single theory will ever be created that can account for all complex human behavior. Further, they can see that a rejection of the theory of the human condition is ultimately a rejection of self. Counselors and therapists must hold some credible, critical account for human behavior if they are to understand themselves and their clients. No theory means no organization, no guidelines to give direction, and no base for explanations and predictions. At best, the false comfort of no theory is fleeting.

Identifying with an Existing Theory

If in their reading student-counselors discover a theorist whose resolutions of the eleven basic issues match their own, one with whom they can identify fully, they are indeed fortunate. Much, although certainly not all, of their work has been done for them. Another has provided them with a personally relevant, integrated set of assumptions, principles, and related strategies that have proven functional over time. Finding their theory does not end their search, however. While there is knowledge to be gained from pushing a single theory to its limits, there are also cautions to be observed and dangers to be avoided.

Theory remains only theory regardless of how persuasive the theorist or how large the number of loyal followers it attracts. By definition, theory is not fact; not even those theories alleged to be scientific are fact. While every theory presented in this book contains elements of truth and demonstrates a high degree of explanatory value, there is danger in prematurely accepting any theory as dogma. Even the most comprehensive and tested theories cannot offer certainties beyond the possibility of revision. Theories are to be questioned, revised, and when a better theory is formulated, discarded.

Theories should never be confused with the realities they describe; they are only partial vistas of reality. Experientially and conceptually our concepts of reality are composed of fragments; our vision is limited. Those who do choose an existing theory nearly always modify it to fit their unique personalities and experiences. The ultimate judge of any theory is the counselor or therapist who uses it. There will, in time, be differences, shifts in emphasis perhaps, that, however minute, will express and enrich the theorist's view of the human condition. Everyone theorizes, and in this sense at least, everyone is eclectic.

Adopting an Eclectic Approach

While some student-counselors discover a theory they can accept totally, many do not. When they reach this point in their preparation, student-counselors typically report that they find something in nearly every theory with which they can identify. The implication of this statement is clear; they have also found in every theory concepts and assumptions that run counter to their personalities and ideologies. Further, there is the implication that they are seeking direction for the next step in their quest for a personal theory.

Anxious to avoid the confusion their dilemma holds for them, many of these students succumb to the temptation of quick, albeit naive, solutions. Intuitive eclecticism appears the most common solution to this dilemma; these students simply take from the theories with which they are acquainted those principles, constructs, methods, and techniques they consider acceptable. Describing this approach, Phares (1984) writes, they "take a little self-concept, add a bit of supergo and a pinch of reinforcement, mix them together in a bowl of humanism, and let them simmer in a social learning pan" (pp. 621–622). Unfortunately, these intuitive eclectics soon discover that their supposedly acceptable theoretical elements do not mix well. They end with a loose collection of inconsistencies and contradictions that quickly turns sour when applied or when looked to for direction or prediction. Phares, of course, is referring to the novice or intuitive eclectic whose loose, uncritical, and unsystematic theoretical structures result in behavior that is inconsistent and, hence, unpredictable.

Eclecticism has always drawn heavy critical fire from the formalists who are convinced that all counselors and therapists following an eclectic approach sacrifice consistency and integration for expediency. Patterson (1980) describes eclectic counseling during the 1940s as what "individualistic counselors, resistant to theory and consistency, practiced" (p. 570). He reminds us, however, that eclecticism has gained significantly in stature and scholastic respectability since that time (p. 570). Today, greater numbers of writers and therapists are defining the criteria they use to make their choices, and they are developing new concepts of eclecticism and new, increasingly comprehensive, systematic, and integrating foundations for their eclectic approach. While many of the formalists in the field believe it is not time to integrate so many diverse and complex theories, an increasing number in the field now see convergence as a distinct possibility in the future. In the 1970s, the majority of the therapists surveyed described themselves as eclectics.

Convinced that all therapists are eclectic and realizing there are no simple answers to personal theoretical development, Lunde (in Burton, 1974) informs his readers, "It is not a question of whether or not to be eclectic but of whether or not to be consistent and systematic" (p. 385). Student-counselors cannot shelve their responsibility for constructing a personal theory of counseling by turning it into an intellectual game or academic exercise. Their obligation to their clients is far too real for that. Developing an eclectic approach to therapy requires an enterprising juxtaposition and a genuine confrontation of their work with the values, thoughts, and research of others. And, while independence of observation and thought is essential to an eclectic stance, so are understanding, respect, and tolerance for other theorists. Before students in search of a personal theory of counseling and psychotherapy can choose the best, they must become fully aware of all that are available—no small achievement in a discipline overburdened with diverse and contradictory theories. The eclectic approach, then, is no shortcut to theory formulation. Indeed, when properly traveled, it is a most difficult path to follow.

A BASIC-ISSUES APPROACH TO THEORY CONSTRUCTION

While it would be presumptuous to claim that the eleven theoretical issues selected for analyzing the theories in this book are the only or even the most basic issues awaiting resolution by today's theorists and therapists, it can be stated that these eleven issues have survived numerous attempts at resolution over the years and, for this reason, merit the label, *basic*. These issues have demonstrated their capacity to serve as an organizing and integrating framework, not only for the presentation and evaluation of a diverse and contradictory theoretical discipline but also for the construction of a personal theory for those electing to follow a basic-issues approach. The eleven basic issues used in this book are an invitation to become a theorist as well as a therapist, to fuse facts with personal values, to experience a unique theoretical synthesis.

An honest, introspective, basic-issues approach can be an exhilarating stimulus for examining those assumptions inherent in one's beliefs and values. Issue resolution can provide the student-counselor with a base for self-experiencing and self-knowledge, as well as for organizing and integrating that experience and knowledge. Personal theories are, after all, an expression of counselors' concerns with their lives and circumstances and their humanity, as well as with the conditions and humanness of their fellow beings.

With every attempt to resolve one of the eleven basic issues, there are implications for the human condition. In short, whether counselors and therapists believe they are innately good or evil, free or controlled, an evolved primate species or a unique self-actualizing being has consequences for both their clients and themselves. Their therapeutic goals, strategies, methods, and techniques are very much influenced by the way they view their shared human nature and the way they relate to the world. Resolutions of the basic issues emerge from the center of lived experience and remind counselors of their shared involvement in the human condition.

Resolution of the eleven basic issues encourages independence of observation, thought, and action. It helps remove expectations of authoritatively defined right and wrong answers, of imposed truths and values. It reduces the likelihood of surrendering to individuals or groups who zealously advocate the superiority of their particular school or theory. Resolving the basic issues facilitates a growing openness to the true complexity of human behavior and diminishes the temptation to view therapeutic strategies, methods, and techniques as a bag of tricks from which to draw indiscriminately when uncertain of direction. Thinking in terms of the eleven basic issues requires involvement, an openness to self and experience, and a flexibility that precludes the tendency to permit personal theory to harden prematurely into dogma. The basic-issues approach to theory formulation makes counselors and therapists aware of inconsistencies and encourages them to seek additional information. At the same time, this approach facilitates adherence to the principle of internal consistency because resolution of one issue provides conditions for the others.

While a counselor's therapeutic approach should be explicit and consistent, it must also be dynamic. As the data of new experiences are perceived and the resolutions of the basic issues are modified, the shape of the counselor's personal theory should change. The eleven basic issues presented here offer structure for experience, but it is a dynamic rather than myopic structure. Basic issues challenge those who dare to take this approach to questions of substance in the human condition. They are required to rethink the nature of humankind and reality. This approach, then, is a dynamic fusion of personal and objective information.

Resolving basic issues is difficult. Signposts along the basic-issues approach to theory formulation might well read: Simple—Not Easy; Difficult—Not Impossible. The direction is simple: resolve, in as great a depth as possible, each of the eleven basic issues. The act, however, of fact-value integration, while not impossible in issue resolution, can be difficult. Crossing swords with a select group of theorists in the field of counseling and psychotherapy can be exciting, but we are influenced far more by the personal theories we discover in ourselves. There is a place for personal knowledge in the understanding of the human condition, including the knowledge of our individual existence. Self-discovery results in a heightened self-consciousness, an intensity of self-awareness.

Issue resolution, then, is a highly personal matter. It involves a deep exploration of personal values, an exploration that may lead to uncertainty. The real struggle, however, lies in integrating the issues into a consistent, personalized system of counseling and psychotherapy that ultimately expresses the counselor's uniqueness, generates correct predictions, and provides continuing therapeutic relevance.

While counselors and therapists may seek confidence in their theory by stretching it beyond its periphery, they can expect no comfort. There is no comfort in the knowledge that, in their attempt to resolve these eleven basic issues, they are not fumbling with a new dilemma. Knowing many before them sought answers to the questions that now concern them is of little help. Still, counselors and therapists must ultimately judge for themselves what is of value, realizing full well there is no single answer for any of the basic issues. The worth of their theory rests entirely in the consequences of their therapeutic experience. Still, the pursuit seems worth the effort since no serious counselor will long apply a theory he or she does not believe in fully. The basic-issues approach to theory construction facilitates knowledge of personal values, and known values are less likely to be imposed than those permitted to go unexamined and unquestioned.

Finally, a basic-issues approach enhances the establishment of an ethical sensitivity far better than assumptions based solely on personal whim or preference. Once student-counselors have resolved the eleven basic issues, their resolutions can serve as an informed and sound base for examining ethical principles.

Phase I: Overcoming Inertia

I'm not ready for this.
It's just too much.
I don't know where to begin.
I sit here, staring at a blank piece of paper, feeling totally disgusted with myself for not being able to write.

I overhear these and similar expressions as my students first attempt to write their personal theories of counseling. Just the idea of writing a comprehensive and consistent theory, of making their implicit knowledge explicit, can undermine the confidence of even the best students. Feeling overwhelmed and blocked, they are unable to begin writing. Such feelings are fairly typical reactions. Those who do manage to draft an opening sentence or paragraph immediately think of ten reasons why their initial attempt is not good enough. In exasperation, they scrap their work and begin again, and again, and again, feeling as dissatisfied with their third or fifth attempt as with their first. Each renewed effort, preceded by increasing periods of staring into space, is all too often accompanied with the belief, "I'll never be able to do this." Inertia sets in, and if left unattended, it can be replaced with panic as the deadline for the assignment approaches. Fortunately, there are ways to overcome inertia.

The steps outlined here not only facilitate the basic-issues approach to theory construction but also demonstrate to you, particularly if you are feeling overwhelmed, how easy it is to get on with the task of theory writing, abandoning undue concern for the goodness or rightness of your words. The goal inherent to this initial phase is process, not product, and the object is a rough compilation of ingredients rather than draft copy.

Step 1: Write Freely and Spontaneously.   Most students are unaware of how much information they already possess on a given issue. At this step, select the issue about which you know the least. Then, armed with only paper and pencil, write—in first person—everything you know about that issue for 20 minutes. Write, as quickly and as tersely as you can, all your thoughts and feelings on the issue you selected, regardless of how senseless or random they appear to you. Do not be concerned about whether your thoughts are good or true, objective or biased. Intentionally denying the need for research, organization, and planning, you will generate many words without the distraction of either the mechanics or the process of writing. Grammar, spelling, and sentence structure are of no concern at this step. Ignore mistakes. How you write is unimportant; only that you write uncritically and continuously for the entire 20 minutes is important. If you become stuck or blocked, simply write, "I'm stuck; I'm not sure where to go from here" until you become unstuck or until the 20 minutes have elapsed.

Step 2: Work with Raw Writing.   After relaxing a few minutes, read through your raw writing and look for ideas, concepts, assumptions, prejudices, or biases. Then indicate, by marking in the margin or underlining, those words, phrases, sentences, or passages you believe to be particularly relevant and important to the issue you selected to resolve. After identifying information you consider worthwhile, record this information on a 3×5 card, limiting each card to a single idea.

Step 3: Focus on Ideas.   When all ideas have been recorded on the cards, review each card and think about the idea or concept expressed there. Permit your ideas, perceptions, and feelings to interact. If, during this interaction, a new idea or insight occurs, record it on a separate card. Continue this process until new thoughts, ideas, or insights no longer emerge.

Step 4: Focus on the Main Idea.   Again, review your cards. This time, however, look for the main idea or theme: Is there a point of view or unifying thread, or is there simply a list of disembodied statements that lead nowhere? Move your cards around freely, rearrange them in various positions, seek order, relatedness, or sequence. Look for gaps or holes and try to fill them. Your purpose is to discover or create some degree of coherence and organization.

Step 5: Prepare an Outline. Using your cards as your guide, write an outline of your resolution. Make your outline as complete as possible, and write it in sentence form.

Step 6: Write the First Draft of the Resolution. Following the outline you just completed, write your first draft of the resolution. Do not work for finished copy; simply sketch an instant, schematic version of the final work. There will be time later for careful thought and research to revise your writing to the level of sophistication you desire. For the present, however, you have overcome inertia. You have learned that, while beginnning is often the most difficult task, it is not impossible. You may have discovered that you possess more information than you thought. You may have learned that ideas have the potential to generate other ideas and concepts. Most important, you have discovered that writing your personal theory need not be agonizing. At the very least, you are no longer staring at blank pages and feeling overwhelmed. You now have a technique and the structure necessary to tackle the remaining ten issues.

While certainly no magic formula, this course of action offers significant advantages as you employ the basic-issues approach for the first time. Free writing on the basic issues is more than a method for swiftly putting words on paper. It is a means of self-expression, a matter of self-exploration and self-discovery. Further, it brings an immediacy to the process of personal theory formulation. You are working with present attitudes, values, and beliefs. Although it is a structured process, the direction you take within that structure is elective. You are not forced to conform to any set of preexisting values, constructs, or techniques. However, while free writing offers you a great deal of latitude, it is not coercively nondirective. While you must often grope through personal dilemma alone, sharing your progress with classmates provides both comforting and rewarding experiences.

Step 7: Use Existing Theories. Once you have drafted a resolution of an issue, compare your response to the responses of the theorists in this book by following the issue across chapters (a separate Table of Contents is provided for this purpose). Look for valid and testable ideas. With which theorist (s) do you agree most? With whom do you disagree most? While reading the resolutions of these theorists, do new ideas or insights emerge? How can you add greater depth and comprehensiveness to your resolution? Are there points in your resolution that you need to clarify, expand, emphasize, or elaborate to improve your positon? If so, do this now.

THE JOURNAL AS PROCESS—Once you become involved in writing your theory, you may discover that new ideas and insights can occur anytime. Carry a journal with you. A journal, divided into eleven sections (one for each of the basic issues), can be a place to store ideas. It provides a place to record and explore both past and present experiences that seem especially relevant to the resolution of particular issues. Some of my students use their journals as an instrument of focus for honing their attention on especially difficult issues. Others use their journals as a technique to crystallize their thinking. Still others report that they keep their journals within easy reach while they are reading, since this is the time most of their ideas and insights occur to them. Whether highly structured or simply permitted to evolve, the journal process proves successful in the development of personal theory; my students swear by it.

QUESTIONS AS PROCESS—When stuck on an especially difficult issue seek questions (see Chapter 1). Consider the many questions each basic issue asks as you attempt to resolve it. While it is impossible to arrive at in-depth answers for every question posed by a basic issue, you can often gather bits and pieces of information sufficient to form some personal insight into your resolution of the issue. Here, as with the ideas that emerge from the free-writing exercise, your questions—and their subsequent answers—become the raw data for outline development and the writing of your initial draft.

Step 8: Check the First Draft. Before moving on to the second and third stages of theory construction (the formulation of goals and techniques), read through your resolutions carefully. Try to judge them with as much detachment as possible. Look for comprehensiveness. Are your resolutions of the issues in as great a depth as you can take them, or have you offered only superficial responses? Look for clarity: Have you stated your positions clearly and well, or are your statements so ambiguous that they are meaningless? Look for evidence that supports your position: Have you given specific examples, cited related research, or considered specific experiences that appear to demonstrate your assumptions, or have you been reticent to explore the most painful and rewarding experiences of your life? Look for congruity of ideas and behaviors: Have you been consistent, or are there obvious conflicts in your resolutions? Look for order and organization: Can you arrange your resolutions of the eleven basic issues in hierarchical order? It is important to determine the impact each issue has had on your life and to arrange the issues in the order of their significance. If you are unable to separate the issues in an order of significance, you may want to place the issues in the order in which you and your prospective clients will deal with them.

Step 9: Revise Your Resolutions. This is the time to turn loose the critic in you: cut the garbage, discard the repetitious, reword the awkward and the unclear, fill the gaps, organize the material by providing headings and subheadings, and check spelling, grammar, and punctuation. Read your paper aloud, listen to the flow, and work on those words and passages that cause you to pause or stumble. Have others read your paper and listen carefully and objectively to their feedback. Mark those words, sentences, paragraphs, and sections they found difficult to understand, and return to these later for revision. Do not be reluctant to cut and paste. Beginning may be the most difficult task, but careful editing and rewriting determine the quality and value of your paper, reflecting the degree of professionalism in your stance.

The basic-issues approach to theory construction is completed in three stages, each determined and dependent on the one immediately preceding it. Moreover, each phase serves as a test for the preceding phase. Resolving the basic issues, then, is but the first, albeit most important, of the three phases since it serves as the foundation on which the others must rest. Phase II (counselor/therapist goals) and Phase III (counselor/therapist behaviors) emerge directly from the issue resolutions.

Phase II: Write the Goals of Counseling

At this stage, select one issue resolution, preferably the one that appears at the top of your hierarchy. Read it carefully and thoughtfully with one question in mind: Believing the way I do about this issue, what would I want to accomplish as a counselor/therapist? Record your answers as they occur to you. Do not concern yourself with wording, just get your ideas on paper. When you have completed the issue, read through your goals, repeating the process until no other goals occur to you. Follow the same procedure with each of the ten remaining issues. You may soon find that you have an extensive list of directives.

Before proceeding to the third stage, review each counselor/therapist goal on your list. Is each of your goals stated explicitly in behavioral terms, or are they vague and unclear? "To establish rapport with my client" is far too general to be a meaningful therapeutic goal. Analyze what you mean by "rapport"; break it down into specific behavioral variables that describe the therapeutic relationship you believe will contribute most to the outcome (in this instance, the establishment of rapport) you desire. You may wish, for example, to communicate—verbally and nonverbally—empathy, positive regard, and genuineness (like Rogers); acceptance, patience, and competence (like Ellis); or warmth, concern, authority, and prestige (like Bandura). The specific variables you select will emerge from the facilitative relationships you describe in your resolutions of the basic issues, particularly the issues of early and/or continuous development, explanation of learning, conditioning and/or freedom to choose, importance of group membership, importance of role of self-concept, and importance of reward. When you have completed your review, write your first draft. Again, you need not be concerned at this stage with final copy.

Phase III: Write the Techniques of Counseling

In this phase of your writing, select one goal, preferably the one that appears at the top of your hierarchy. Think about it, and as you do, ask yourself this question: Having established this as a goal, what specific counselor behaviors must I demonstrate to achieve it? Again, record your answers as they occur to you without concern for grammar, spelling, punctuation, and sentence structure. For example, if the communication of empathic understanding is my goal, I will face my client, maintain a relaxed, direct eye contact, and lean slightly forward. I will listen intently, attempting to immerse myself in my client's inner, subjective world. I will concentrate on the direct and indirect affective messages. I will respond to appropriate verbal and nonverbal cues, reflecting whenever possible the feelings and personal meanings I believe my client is presently experiencing and trying to communicate.

Repeat this procedure for every goal you have listed. You may even want to consider all the behaviors you want to adopt from the moment you greet your client to the termination of the therapy session. All behaviors should, of course, be clearly implied in and congruent with your resolutions.

Critical Revision

Once again, release your internal critic. Test each statement for clarity. Review your goals and techniques for relevance—relevance for your future clients as well as for yourself. Consider how active your participation must be to accomplish your objectives. Determine the criteria for assessing attainment, and describe specific client behaviors to confirm progress. For example: I might consider my attempt to communicate accurate, empathic understanding successful when my client abandons defensiveness and shares more openly his or her inner, subjective experiences. Check carefully to be certain there is sufficient openness and flexibility in your approach to accommodate new empirical and experiential evidence. Finally, ask yourself the question: Is my personal theory a reflection of my highest level of judgment and scholarship at this point in my personal and professional development?

EPILOGUE

Before you close this book, I want to congratulate all of you who accepted the challenge of following a basic-issues approach to formulate your personal theory of counseling and psychotherapy. I hope your struggle with these issues was stimulating. Moreover, I hope your resolutions of these issues contained a few surprises for you. I hope, too, that you understand yourself a little better as a result. More important, I hope your self-understanding will promote understanding and acceptance of others. Finally, I hope you feel that you have taken a step or two toward professionalism.

Now that you have forged a personal theory of counseling and psychotherapy from the basic issues, I would very much appreciate learning about your experiences with this approach. What were your reactions as you struggled with the issues? What were your feelings when you finished? What could your instructor have done to assist you? Have you any suggsestions for improving this approach to theory formulation? I welcome any ideas or recommendations you might have that would help others in their development of a personal approach to counseling and psychotherapy. I wish you well as you take your next step toward professionalism and apply your theory to the reality of the counseling situation.

REFERENCES AND SUGGESTED READINGS

Burton, A., ed. 1974. *Operational theories of personality.* New York: Brunner/Mazel.

Phares, E.J. 1984. *Introduction to personality.* Columbus, Ohio: Charles E. Merrill.

Patterson, C.H. 1980. *Theories of counseling and psychotherapy*, 3rd ed. New York: Harper & Row.

Index